PUBLIC SPEAKING
THE EVOLVING ART

Enhanced Edition

STEPHANIE J. COOPMAN
San José State University

JAMES LULL
San José State University (Emeritus)

WADSWORTH
CENGAGE Learning

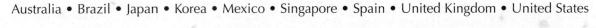
Australia • Brazil • Japan • Korea • Mexico • Singapore • Spain • United Kingdom • United States

WADSWORTH
CENGAGE Learning™

Public Speaking: The Evolving Art,
Enhanced Edition
Stephanie J. Coopman, James Lull

Publisher: Lyn Uhl

Executive Editor: Monica Eckman

Senior Development Editor: Greer Lleuad

Assistant Editor: Rebekah Matthews

Editorial Assistant: Colin Solan

Media Editorr: Jessica Badiner

Marketing Manager: Bryant Chrzan

Marketing Assistant: Darlene Macanan

Marketing Communications Manager:
Christine Dobberpuhl

Senior Content Project Manager: Michael
Lepera

Art Director: Linda Helcher

Print Buyer: Sue Carroll

Senior Text Permissions Editor: Bob Kauser

Photo Permissions Editor: John Hill

Compositor/Production Service: Lachina
Publishing Services

Text Designer: Marsha Cohen/Parallelogram
Graphics

Photo Researcher: Jan Seidel

Copy Editor: Carolyn Smith

Cover Illustration: ©Margaret Lee/izi Art

For product information and technology assistance, contact us at
Cengage Learning Academic Resource Center, 1-800-354-9706

For permission to use material from this text or product,
submit all requests online at **www.cengage.com/permissions**.
Further permissions questions can be e-mailed to
permissionrequest@cengage.com.

Library of Congress Control Number: 2008922693

ISBN-13: 978-0-495-79852-1

ISBN-10: 0-495-79852-5

Wadsworth
20 Channel Center Street
Boston, MA 02210
USA

Cengage Learning is a leading provider of customized learning solutions with office locations around the globe, including Singapore, the United Kingdom, Australia, Mexico, Brazil, and Japan. Locate your local office at: **international.cengage.com/region**

Cengage Learning products are represented in Canada by Nelson Education, Ltd.

For your course and learning solutions, visit **www.cengage.com**.

Purchase any of our products at your local college store or at our preferred online store **www.ichapters.com**.

CREDITS

We have made every effort to trace the ownership of all copyrighted material and to secure permission from copyright holders. In the event of any question arising as to the use of any material, we will be pleased to make the necessary corrections in future printings. Thanks are due to the following authors, publishers, and agents for permission to use the material indicated.

Chapter 9. 227: From Jacqueline Novogratz, TEDTalks: March 19, 2007, ted.com/tedtalks.

Printed in the United States of America
3 4 5 6 7 13 12 11 10

BRIEF CONTENTS

DETAILED CONTENTS

8 Organizing and Outlining Your Speech / 192

9 Beginning and Ending Your Speech / 226

III PRESENTING YOURSELF AND YOUR IDEAS

10 Using Language Effectively / 246

11 Integrating Presentation Media / 276

12 Delivering Your Speech / 296

IV SPEAKING SITUATIONS

BONUS CHAPTERS

See page xviii, Custom Chapters, for information about these bonus chapters.

Group Speaking

Mediated Public Speaking

Enhanced Edition with Workbook

▽ WATCH it SPEECH BUDDY VIDEO LINKS AND ▽ USE it ACTIVITY LINKS

CHAPTER	WATCH IT SPEECH BUDDY VIDEO LINK	USE IT ACTIVITY LINK
1 The Evolving Art of Public Speaking	▶ Meeting the Speech Buddies	▶ What Are Your Public Speaking Goals
2 Building Your Confidence	▶ Using Strategies for Managing Speech Anxiety ▶ Taking a Closer Look at Your Public Speaking Anxiety	▶ Anxiety Management Trainee ▶ What, Me Worry?
3 Ethical Speaking and Listening	▶ Avoiding Plagiarism ▶ Promoting Dialog in Q&A	▶ But Is It Plagiarism? ▶ You Have the Floor
4 Developing Your Purpose and Topic	▶ Brainstorming for and Evaluating Topics	▶ Search and Find Missions
5 Adapting to Your Audience	▶ Analyzing and Using Audience Data	▶ According to Our Data
6 Researching Your Topic	▶ Managing the Research Process	▶ The Research Detective
7 Supporting Your Ideas	▶ Selecting the Best Supporting Materials ▶ Evaluating Media Credibility	▶ Use Your Support System ▶ Press Pass
8 Organizing and Outlining Your Speech	▶ Reviewing Patterns of Organization ▶ Linking Effectively: Transitions	▶ Everything in Its Place ▶ Polite to Point
9 Beginning and Ending Your Speech	▶ Beginning Effectively: Introductions ▶ Ending Effectively: Conclusions	▶ Here We Go ▶ It's a Wrap
10 Using Language Effectively	▶ Engaging Your Audience with Language ▶ Making Language Choices	▶ You're Engaged! ▶ Wrong Word, Right Word
11 Integrating Presentation Media	▶ Using Digital Slides ▶ Integrating Presentation Media	▶ PowerPoint Makeover ▶ Exhibit A
12 Delivering Your Speech	▶ Reviewing Vocal Delivery ▶ Reviewing Physical Delivery ▶ Practicing Your Speech	▶ Speak Up ▶ Stand Tall ▶ Take It from the Top
13 Informative Speaking	▶ Speaking to Inform	▶ Pleased to Inform You
14 Persuasive Speaking	▶ Speaking to Persuade	▶ Persuasion Equation
15 Understanding Argument	▶ Identifying the Elements of Argument	▶ Convince Me
16 Special Occasion and Group Speaking	▶ Evaluating Group Presentations	▶ As a Group

NOTE TO INSTRUCTORS

Although the foundations of effective public speaking have endured since classical times, the internet and other new media have influenced every aspect of public speaking—from the initial stages of topic selection and research to the final stages of practicing and delivering a speech. Consider these current trends:

- Communicators have unprecedented access to information.
- Digitized content is exceptionally easy to appropriate, making the ethics of public speaking increasingly complex.
- Communication technologies—including cell phones, e-mail, instant messaging, video-sharing websites like You-Tube, and social networks like Facebook™—make connecting with others, both locally and globally, faster and easier than ever.
- Digital technologies such as podcasting, webcasting, and presentation software give speakers numerous options for delivering speeches.
- The pervasiveness of the media has made communicators more visually oriented and attuned to pop culture.
- Globalism and increased cultural awareness require that communicators consistently demonstrate a high degree of multicultural and intercultural knowledge.
- Audiences have different expectations, often preferring a friendly, conversational delivery style, presentation media, and messages targeted to their interests.

Taking an applied approach, *Public Speaking: The Evolving Art: Enhanced Edition* and its unique suite of companion resources address the ways in which digital technology, social transitions, and cultural shifts have affected students and the communication discipline. This text offers a unique combination of time-honored, classic public speaking instruction and specific guidelines for effective public communication in today's evolving world.

This new ENHANCED EDITION of the text includes access to a ground-breaking and exciting new technology program called Speech Studio. This new video upload and grading tool was created as a response to instructors and students needing a way to share video, upload speeches, peer-review, rate and grade speeches, and create portfolios. This is the first video performance and assessment program built into a text; in-text prompts for students to visit Speech Studio are included at the beginning and end of each chapter.

If you and your students are fully immersed in digital culture, you'll feel right at home with the package's relevance to your course objectives, and your students will appreciate materials that present useful information in formats they're comfortable using. Conversely, if you and your students only dip into digital culture as needed, you'll find the text to be a reliable guide that understands and respects your selectivity. Regardless of where on the digital-immersion spectrum your students fall, *Public Speaking: The Evolving Art: Enhanced Edition* is committed to enriching their learning experience, helping them maximize their efficiency and effectiveness, and greatly enhancing the quality and impact of their public communication.

DISTINCTIVE FEATURES OF *PUBLIC SPEAKING: THE EVOLVING ART: ENHANCED EDITION*

In addition to comprehensive coverage, *Public Speaking: The Evolving Art: Enhanced Edition* offers several carefully developed features that set it apart from other introductory public speaking texts and help ensure both your and your students' satisfaction.

Flexibility

This text's table of contents appears fairly traditional at first glance. That's not an accident, as the book covers all the topics instructors and students need in an introductory public speaking course, presented in a logical and familiar order. However, each chapter is freestanding so that instructors may use the chapters in whatever order best suits their needs. The text's Enhanced eBook, custom publishing solutions, and iChapters purchasing options for students offer additional flexibility and online tools available only with *Public Speaking: The Evolving Art: Enhanced Edition*. (See pages xiv and xvi for descriptions of the eBook and iChapters.)

A Proven Learning Sequence

Without compromising its flexibility, *Public Speaking: The Evolving Art: Enhanced Edition* provides a sound pedagogical approach in sync with how today's students learn: ▼ **READ it**, ▼ **WATCH it**, ▼ **USE it**, ▼ **REVIEW it**. Each chapter's material, both in the book and online, engages students in a sequence that starts with reading the text, moves to watching unique integrated videos, segues to companion interactive activities that ask students to apply chapter concepts first to hypothetical scenarios and then to their own speech projects, and culminates with an unparalleled array of study and self-assessment resources. Chapter materials are presented within this framework on the first page of every chapter and consistently reinforced throughout. In addition, as a play on the way today's students prefer to learn, the book's shape and design are meant to resemble a computer screen, complete with menus (chapter openers) and hyperlinks (key terms).

Unique Tools Developed to Appeal to Today's Students

Public Speaking: The Evolving Art: Enhanced Edition features a number of tools designed to complement the learning styles and preferences of today's students.

▼ **READ it**

- **The Evolving Art boxes**. Appearing in each chapter, these boxes focus on specific ways in which public speaking has changed over time, highlighting speakers' and listeners' expanding options and increased responsibilities as well as related issues and resources.
- **Speaking Of . . . boxes**. These boxes also appear in each chapter and present brief discussions of topics relevant but not central to the focus of the chapters. The Speaking Of . . . topics can be used for in-class discussion or journal assignments; accompanying discussion questions are provided in the Instructor's Resource Manual (described on page xvii).

▼ **WATCH it**

- **Speech Buddy video links**. Available online around the clock to guide students through the public speaking process, we developed these peer mentor videos to help keep today's students engaged and motivated. The Speech Buddies are a diverse group of four personable undergraduates who have successfully completed the beginning public speaking course: Janine, Anthony, Erin, and Evan. These students appear in brief, easily accessed and close-captioned videos, usually two to three per chapter, to reinforce key concepts covered in the book, model strategies, and introduce video clips from their own and others' speeches. The Speech Buddies bring the text's instruction and examples to life. Featured in WATCH It Speech Buddy Video Link boxes within each chapter, these videos address the following topics and much more:

▶ Using Strategies for Managing Speech Anxiety

▶ Selecting the Best Supporting Materials

▶ Avoiding Plagiarism

▶ Linking Effectively: Transitions

▶ Integrating Presentation Media

▶ Reviewing Physical Delivery

▽ USE it

- **Activity links**. Each Speech Buddy video concludes with a prompt to an interactive activity, which makes assigning the videos easy. Featured in the USE It Activity Link boxes in the text, the activities may be completed in or outside class, and many of them can be adapted for use as group activities. Here's a sampling:

  ▶ The Research Detective (using research strategies)

  ▶ Everything in Its Place (identifying organizational patterns in speeches)

  ▶ PowerPoint Makeover (evaluating digital slides)

  ▶ Take It from the Top (practicing your speech)

  ▶ Persuasion Equation (analyzing a persuasive speech)

  ▶ You Have the Floor (developing questions to ask speakers)

▽ REVIEW it

- **Study and self-assessment resources.** Each chapter concludes with a summary and a Directory of Study and Review Resources, a map of companion resources avail-

able on the online Resource Center such as self-assessment quizzes, the student workbook, Speech Builder Express, InfoTrac College Edition, Audio Study Tools, and an icon prompting students to visit Speech Studio. Also featured are a list of key terms and Critical Challenges: Questions for Reflection and Discussion.

- **Speeches for Analysis appendix.** To get students started analyzing speeches, this appendix presents two public speeches: a transcript of Barack Obama's 2006 speech at the groundbreaking ceremony for the Dr. Martin Luther King Jr. National Memorial and an outline of a student speech, "Turn Off Your TV" by Lisa Taylor. Each speech is accompanied by a brief overview of the speech's context and questions for discussion. The appendix also features a comprehensive list of informative, persuasive, special occasion, and group speeches that students can access through the book's Interactive Video Activities on the Resource Center. These speeches include full informative and persuasive speeches delivered by the Speech Buddies and other students and professionals. (See page xv for a full description of the Interactive Video Activities.)

Public Speaking: The Evolving Art: Enhanced Edition is **also available as an Enhanced eBook**. This version of the book is a web-based, multimedia text in which students are able to read the book's content, launch embedded Speech Buddy videos and videos of speeches by students and public figures, link out to websites, complete interactive activities and homework, and submit self-quizzes. Offering ease of use and maximum flexibility and interactivity for students and other users who truly want to create their own learning experience, the Enhanced eBook for *Public Speaking: The Evolving Art: Enhanced Edition* also includes advanced book tools such as an audio glossary, hypertext index, and bookmarking, streamlined note-taking and note-storing, easy highlighting, and faster searching. The note-taking feature allows students to make annotations right on the electronic page. Students get access to the Enhanced eBook with the printed text, or they can just purchase access to the Enhanced eBook stand-alone.

Because public speaking instruction aims to prepare people to willingly and effectively express themselves in any communication context, *Public Speaking: The Evolving Art: Enhanced Edition* was developed to help students gain the practical public speaking skills they need to further shape our society, not just live in it. This text and its companion resources offer today's students a timely means of improving the communication skills essential to productively evolve in their own personal, work, social, and civic worlds.

COMPANION RESOURCES FOR STUDENTS AND INSTRUCTORS

Accompanying this book is an integrated suite of companion resources to support both you and your students. Many of the student resources are available free of charge when you order them or order access to them bundled with the text. Students whose instructors do not order these resources as a package with the text may purchase them or purchase access to them at **www.academic.cengage.com** and **iChapters.com**.

Student Resources

Students have the option of utilizing a rich array of resources to enhance and extend their learning while using *Public Speaking: The Evolving Art: Enhanced Edition*.

- **Speech Studio**. Practice and present with Speech Studio! With Speech Studio, you can upload video files of practice speeches or final performances, comment on your peer's speeches, and review your grades and instructor feedback.
- **Resource Center**. This useful site offers a variety of rich learning assets designed to enhance the student experience. Organized by chapter and also by type, these assets include self-assessments, web activities, chapter outlines, review questions, and Audio Study Tools. The Resource Center also features course resources such as

the Enhanced eBook, Speech Builder Express 3.0, Interactive Video Activities, and more.

- **Enhanced eBook**. You'll find a full description of this resource that looks like the book but functions like a website on page xiv.
- **Book Companion Website**. The website (**http://www.cengage.com/communication/coopman/publicspeakingenhanced1e**) features study aids such as chapter outlines, flash cards and other resources for mastering glossary terms, and chapter quizzes that help students check their understanding of key concepts.
- **Interactive Video Activities.** Presented within Wadsworth Cengage Learning's unique interactive user interface, the speech videos help students gain experience evaluating and critiquing introductory, informative, persuasive, and special occasion speeches so that they can more effectively provide feedback to their peers and improve their own speeches and delivery. This highly praised resource includes the following features:

  ▶ Transcripts and closed-captioning for all speech videos.

  ▶ Complete-sentence outlines, keyword outlines, and note cards for full-length student speech videos so students can see the connection between creating an effective speech outline and delivering a speech.

  ▶ A "scroll" function that students may choose to turn on or off for full-length speech videos. When the scroll feature is on, synchronized highlighting tracks each speaker's progress through an outline or transcript of the speech as the video of the speaker's delivery plays alongside.

  ▶ A "notes" function that lets students insert written comments while watching the video. At a student's command, the program pauses, enters a time-stamp that indicates where the video was paused, and offers students the ability to write their own critiques of the video or choose from a set of pre-written rubrics that teach students how to effectively evaluate speeches.

▶ Assignable analysis questions with responses written by the text's authors, available when students answer the questions themselves and submit them to their instructor.

- **Audio Study Tools.** This text's Audio Study Tools provides a fun and easy way for students to download audio files and review chapter content whenever and wherever. Students can purchase the Audio Study Tool for *Public Speaking: The Evolving Art: Enhanced Edition* through iChapters (see below) and download files to their computers, iPods, or other MP3 players. In addition, an audio version of the complete text is available for students on CD-ROM on demand. Contact your local sales representative for ordering information.

- **Student Workbook.** This comprehensive workbook provides tools students can use to review, practice, and develop their communication and public speaking skills, such as chapter goals, chapter outlines, key terms, activities, and self-tests.

- **Speech Builder Express 3.0™.** This online program coaches students through the entire process of preparing speeches and provides the additional support of built-in video speech models, a tutor feature for concept review, and direct links to InfoTrac College Edition, an online dictionary and thesaurus, and leading professional organizations' online documentation style guidelines and sample models.

- **InfoTrac College Edition with InfoMarks™.** This online library provides access to more than 18 million reliable, full-length articles from over 5,000 academic and popular periodicals.

- **iChapters.com.** This online store provides students with exactly what they've been asking for: choice, convenience, and savings. A 2005 research study by the National Association of College Stores indicates that as many as 60 percent of students do not purchase all required course material; however, those who do are more likely to succeed. This research also tells us that students want the ability to purchase "a la carte" course material in the format that suits them best. Accordingly, iChapters.com is the only online store that offers eBooks at up to 50 percent off, eChapters for as low as $1.99 each, and new textbooks at up to 25 percent off, plus up to 25 percent off print and digital supplements that can help improve student performance.

- ***A Guide to the Basic Course for ESL Students.*** Written specifically for communicators whose first language is not English, this guide features FAQs, helpful URLs, and strategies for managing communication anxiety.

Instructor Resources

Instructors who adopt this book may request the following resources to support their teaching.

- **Speech Studio.** Assign and assess with Speech Studio, an online video upload and grading program that improves the learning comprehension of your public speaking students. With Speech Studio, students can upload video files of practice speeches or final performances, comment on their peer's speeches, and review their grades and instructor feedback. Instructors create courses and assignments, comment on and grade student speeches with a library of comments and grading rubrics, and allow peer review. Grades flow into a gradebook that allows instructors to easily manage their course from within Speech Studio. Instructors can also export the grades to use in learning management systems. Speech Studio's flexibility lends itself to use in traditional, hybrid, and online courses. It allows instructors to: save valuable in-class time by conducting practice sessions and peer review work virtually; combine the ease of a course management tool with a convenient way to capture, grade, and review videos of live, in-class performances; and simulate an in-class experience for online courses.

- **Instructor's Resource Manual**. This useful manual presents its own PREPARE It, TEACH It, ASSESS It, ADAPT It framework to parallel the student text's READ It, WATCH It, USE It, REVIEW It pedagogy. This manual offers guidelines for setting up your course, sample syllabi, chapter-by-chapter outlines of content, suggested topics for lectures and discussion, and a wealth of exercises and assignments for both individuals and groups. It also includes a test bank with questions of diverse types and varying levels of difficulty. The test bank is also available in electronic, highly customizable format within ExamView® on the PowerLecture CD-ROM (see below).

- **Instructor Resource Center.** The password-protected Instructor Resource Center allows you to see all the assets your students see, helps you determine what you can assign and encourage your students to use, and includes electronic access to the Instructor's Resource Manual, downloadable versions of the book's Microsoft PowerPoint® presentations, a link to the Opposing Viewpoints Resource Center, and more. In addition, a complete audio download of the text is available for instructors on CD-ROM on demand. Contact your local sales representative to receive a copy. Visit the Instructor Resource Center by accessing **academic.cengage.com/ login** or by contacting your local sales representative.

- **PowerLecture.** This CD-ROM contains an electronic version of the Instructor's Resource Manual, ExamView computerized testing, and ready-to-use Microsoft PowerPoint presentations. The PowerPoint slides contain text, images, and cued videos of the Speech Buddy and sample speech videos, and they can be used as is or customized to suit your course needs. This all-in-one lecture tool makes it easy for you to assemble, edit, publish, and present custom lectures for your course.

- **Turn-It-In®.** This proven online plagiarism-prevention software promotes fairness in the classroom by helping students learn to correctly cite sources and allowing instructors to check for originality before reading and grading papers and speeches.

- **Wadsworth Communication Video and DVD Library.** Wadsworth's video and DVD series for Speech Communication includes Communication Scenarios for Critique and Analysis, Student Speeches for Critique and Analysis, and ABC News DVDs for Human Communication, Public Speaking, Interpersonal Communication, and Mass Communication.

- *The Teaching Assistant's Guide to the Basic Course.* Written by Katherine G. Hendrix of the University of Memphis, this resource was prepared specifically for new instructors. Based on leading communication teacher training programs, this guide discusses some of the general issues that accompany a teaching role and offers specific strategies for managing the first week of classes, leading productive discussions, managing sensitive topics in the classroom, and grading students' written and oral work.

- *Guide to Teaching Public Speaking Online.* Written by Todd Brand of Meridian Community College, this helpful online guide provides instructors who teach public speaking online with tips for establishing "classroom" norms with students, utilizing course management software and other eResources, managing logistics such as delivering and submitting speeches and making up work, discussing how peer feedback is different online, strategies for assessment, and tools such as sample syllabi, and critique and evaluation forms tailored to the online course. Available on the Instructors Resource Center.

- *The Art and Strategy of Service-Learning Presentations, Second Edition.* Written by Rick Isaacson and Jeff Saperstein of San Francisco State University, this handbook provides guidelines for connecting service-learning work with classroom concepts and advice for working effectively with agencies and organizations.

- **TLC Technology Training and Support**. Get trained, get connected, and get the support you need for seamless integration of technology resources into your course with Technology Learning Connected (TLC). This unparalleled technology service and training program provides robust online resources, peer-to-peer instruction, personalized training, and a customizable program you can count on. Visit **http://academic.cengage.com/tlc** to sign up for online seminars, first days of class services, technical support, or personalized, face-to-face training. Our online or onsite trainings are frequently led by one of our Lead Teachers, faculty members who are experts in using Wadsworth Cengage Learning technology and can provide best practices and teaching tips.

- **Custom Chapters**. Customize your chapter coverage with two bonus chapters, Group Speaking and Mediated Public Speaking. You can access these chapters online within the Instructor Resource Center, or you can order print versions of the student text that include the extra chapter of your choice. *Public Speaking: The Evolving Art: Enhanced Edition* with workbook is also available.

Contact your local sales representative for ordering details.

These resources are available to qualified adopters, and ordering options for student supplements are flexible. Please consult your local Wadsworth Cengage Learning sales representative for more information, to evaluate examination copies of any of these instructor or student resources, or to request product demonstrations.

ACKNOWLEDGMENTS

This project was truly a team effort, and we greatly appreciate all the work others have contributed to *Public Speaking: The Evolving Art: Enhanced Edition*. Our Wadsworth Cengage Learning team included Lyn Uhl, publisher; Monica Eckman, executive editor; Greer Lleuad, senior development editor; Erin Mitchell, marketing manager; Rebekah Matthews, assistant editor; Colin Solan, editorial assistant; Jessica Badiner, media editor; John Hill and Bob Kauser, permissions acquisitions managers; Jan Seidel, photo researcher; Michael Lepera, senior content project manager; Carolyn Smith, copyeditor; Bonnie Briggle, project manager at Lachina Publishing Services; and Linda

Helcher, art director. Cengage Learning gratefully acknowledges contributors to Speech Studio, including Lynne Blaszak, product manager; Nancy Ludlow, online developer; and Cara Buckley of Emerson College, content developer. System Architect Joe Magly and Lead Interactive Designer Jeff Paradiso went above and beyond to guide this project to excellent completion.

Many people helped develop the ancillary materials that accompany this text: Kathy Werking, University of Louisville, wrote the Instructors' Resource Manual. Cameron Basquiat, College of Southern Nevada, wrote substantial additions to the test bank. Lisa Boragine, Cape Community College, wrote the Speech Studio Instructors' Manual. Matt McGarrity, University of Washington, created the student workbook. Kristen Hoerl, Auburn University, wrote the quizzes for the companion website. Lisa Heller Boragine, Cape Cod Community College, created the Audio Study Tools. Amber Finn, Texas Christian University, created the PowerLecture PowerPoint slides. Kim Cowden, North Dakota State University, and Mike Sloat, Roaring Mouse Productions, directed and produced the Speech Buddy videos. Nita George, San José State University, created the USE It activities and prepared the Interactive Video Activities. And Angela Grupas, St. Louis Community College, and Rita Dienst helped prepare the Interactive Video Activities.

The following instructors provided invaluable feedback, creativity, and classroom experience in developing Speech Studio: Lisa Heller Boragine, Cape Cod Community College; Angela Grupas, St. Louis Community College-Meramec; Daria Heinemann, Keiser University; Valerie Jensen, Central Arizona College; Tom Jewell, Bergen Community College; Delois Medhin, Milwaukee Area Technical College; Teresa Moore-Cornelius, Brevard Community College; Sandy Pensoneau-Conway, Wayne State University; and Julie Weishar at Parkland College.

Many instructors also participated in focus groups during the creation of Speech Studio, and we would like to thank them for their feedback, including: Suzanne Berg, Le Cordon Bleu College of Culinary Arts; David L. Bodary, Sinclair Community College; Erin Bryant, Arizona State University; Michael

Cesarano, Queensborough Community College; Anita Chirco, Keuka College; Carl Christman, Riverside Community College; Shani Clark, Darton College; Oscar Cuan, Valencia Community College; Pat Cuchens, University of Houston-Clear Lake; Mary Albert Darling, Spring Arbor University; Nick De Bonis, Georgia Southern University; Aaron Dimock, University of Nebraska-Kearney; Deidre Holmes DuBois, Valencia Community College; Belle A. Edson, Arizona State University; Vickie Shamp Ellis, Oklahoma Baptist University; Alycia Ehlert, Darton College; Jennifer Ehrhardt, Pensacola Junior College; Amber Epps, The Art Institute of Pittsburgh; Michael A. Fairley, Richmond Community College; Cheryl Ann Farrell, Kauai Community College; James Floss, Humboldt State University; Karyn Friesen, Lone Star College-Montgomery; Valerie Manno Giroux, University of Miami; Jacqueline Glenny, Northwestern College; Neva Gronert, Arapahoe Community College; Cheri Hampton-Farmer, The University of Findlay; Amanda Harsin, Hanover College; Jinaki Hasan, Winston-Salem State University; Thomas Healy, Salem State College; Alan D. Heisel, University of Missouri-St. Louis; Leigh Heisel, University of Missouri-St. Louis; Patricia Hemming, Lac Courte Oreilles Community College; Nancy K. Hoke, Sullivan University System; Kesha Hondo, Santa Ana College; Peggy Hooyenga, Owens Community College; Karen Huck, Central Oregon Community College; Akbar Javidi, University of Nebraska at Kearney; Brooke Kendall, Lane Community College; Stephen Klien, Augustana College; Brian Kline, Gainesville State College; Tim Kowalik, Northwestern College; Joyce Laggan, Cuyahoga Community College-West; Sandra Lakey, Pennsylvania College of Technology; Tina Lim, San Jose State University; Rick Lindner, Georgia Perimeter College; Carly Long, Northern Arizona University; Ulrich Luenemann, California State University-Sacramento; John Maize, Pennsylvania College of Technology; Jennifer Marmo, Arizona State University; Mischelle L. McIntosh, Cedarville University; Josh Misner, North Idaho College; Sally Moore, Linn Benton Community College; M. Nadler, Miami University; Daryle Nagano, Los Angeles Harbor College; Brian O'Donnell, Cuyamaca College; Karen Otto, Florida Community College at Jacksonville; Miri Pardo, St. John Fisher College; Doug Parry, University of Alaska-Anchorage; Sandra L. Pensoneau-Conway, Wayne State University; Matthew Petrunia, Fashion Institute of Technology, SUNY; Evelyn Plummer, Seton Hall University; Jeff Pomeroy, Southwest Texas Junior College; Adam D. Roth, University of Rhode Island; Alena Amato Ruggerio, Southern Oregon University; Anna J. Small Roseboro, Calvin College; Robabeh Shirandasht, University of Nebraska-Kearney; Cynthia Smith, Indiana University; Jason Stone, Oklahoma State University-Oklahoma City; David Tatum, Ranken Technical College; Jason Teven, California State University-Fullerton; Kristan Tucker, Bowling Green State University; Jeffrey Tyus, Youngstown State University; Amy Way, Arizona State University; Jon Williams, Niagara County Community College; and Hwei-Jen Yang, Clarion University of Pennsylvania.

We also wish to thank all the reviewers, focus group participants, class-testers, and advisors who contributed to this project: George Barnett, State University of New York, Buffalo; Tim Behme, University of Minnesota, Twin Cities; Marcia Berry, Azusa Pacific University; David Bodary, Sinclair Community College; LeAnn Brazeal, Kansas State University; Ellen Bremen, Highline Community College; Cynthia Brown El, Macomb Community College; Michael Bruner, Humboldt State University; Merry Buchanan, University of Central Oklahoma; Nancy Burroughs, California State University, Stanislaus; Lelani Carver, University of Kansas; Jennifer Cochrane, Indiana University—Purdue University Indianapolis; Christy C. Coker, University of North Carolina, Charlotte; Karen Cornetto, University of Connecticut; Diana Crossman, El Camino College; Patricia A. Cutspec, East Tennessee State University; Allison DeStefano, Waubonsee Community College; Danielle Endres, University of Utah; Steven Epstein, Suffolk County Community College; James Floyd, Central Missouri State University; John Fincher, Citrus College; Andie Fultz, Portland State University; Joseph Ganakos, Lee College; Kathleen Golden, Edinboro University of Pennsylvania; Ruth Goldfarb, Nassau

Community College; Angela Grupas, St. Louis Community College; Trudy Hanson, West Texas A&M; Dayle Hardy-Short, Northern Arizona University; Carla Harrell, Old Dominion University; Brian Heisterkamp, California State University, San Bernardino; Kelly Herold, Winona State University; Carrie Higgins, Purdue University, North Central; Jennifer Hill, University of Utah; Kristen Hoerl, Auburn University; Angela Holland, Community College of Southern University; Dini Homsey, University of Central Oklahoma; Kesha Hondo, Santa Ana College; Alexis Reisig-Hopkins, Butler County Community College; John Howe, Community College of Philadelphia; Ronald Howell, Illinois Central College; Heather Howley, Cazenovia College; Christopher Hull, Georgetown University; Karla Hunter, Dakota Wesleyan University; Frank Irizarry, University of Florida; John Jackson, University of Colorado, Boulder; Timothy James, Community College of Southern Nevada; Elena Jarvis, Daytona Beach Community College; Cynthia Jones, Westminster College; Jim Katt, University of Central Florida; Sheree Keith, Macon State University; Kirstin Kiledal, Hillsdale Community College; Susan Kilgard, Anne Arundel Community College; Richard Kirkham, Fullerton College; Staci Kuntzman, University of North Carolina, Charlotte; Betty Jane Lawrence, Bradley University; Anthony Lenzo, Purdue University, Calumet; Sherry Lewis, University of Texas, El Paso; Rick Lindner, Georgia Perimeter College; Leslie Henderson, McLennan Community College; Vicki Marie, San Joaquin Delta College; Charla Markham, University of Texas, Arlington; Joe (Jose) Martinez, El Paso Community College; Deborah Meltsner, Old Dominion University; Sherry Messina, Red Rocks Community College; Kendra Mitchum, Rowan Cabbarrus Community College; Dante Morelli, Suffolk County Community College; Melanie Morgan, Purdue University; Holly Payne, Western Kentucky University; Scott Paynton, Humboldt State University; Mindy Peck, Florida Metropolitan University; Sandy Pensoneau-Conway, Wayne State University; Brian Pilling, Westminster College; Rachel M. Pokora, Nebraska Wesleyan University; Shelly Presnell, Shasta College; Bill Price, Georgia Perimeter Community College; Thomas Reinert, University of Wisconsin, La Crosse; Rebecca Roberts, University of Wyoming; Hannah Rockwell, Loyola University Chicago; Douglas Rosentrater, Bucks County Community College; Alena Amato Ruggerio, Southern Oregon University; Kristi Schaller, University of Georgia; Heather Seipke, University of Michigan, Flint; Theresa Shaton, Kutztown University; Bill Sheffield, Clark State College; Alisa Shubb, American River College; Helene Shugart, University of Utah; Amy Slagell, Iowa State University; Christine Smith, George Mason University; James Spurrier, Vincennes University; Robert Sullivan, Ithaca College; Sally Tannenbaum, California State University, Fresno; Katherine Taylor, University of Louisville; Satoshi Toyosaki, University of Wisconsin, LaCrosse; Frank Trimble, University of North Carolina, Wilmington; Scott Turcott, Indiana Wesleyan University; Jeffery Tyus, Sinclair Community College; Joseph Valenzano, University of Nevada, Las Vegas; Tasha Van Horn, Citrus College; Emily Vu, Santiago Canyon College; David Walker, Middle Tennessee State University; Beckie Welty, Santiago Community College; Kim Wilcox, Penn Valley Community College; Dan Wildeson, St. Cloud State University; David Williams, Texas Tech University; Melinda Womack, Santiago Canyon College; and Kathryn Wylie, John Jay College—C.U.N.Y.

NOTE TO STUDENTS

Welcome to *Public Speaking: The Evolving Art: Enhanced Edition*!

The basics of public speaking haven't changed much since classical times, but how you go about preparing a good speech and learning about public speaking have changed a great deal. This book and the resources that go with it bridge traditions and innovations in public speaking and learning in ways designed just for you.

Each chapter and the companion resource materials for this text follow a consistent learning sequence that makes the book enjoyable and easy to use. You'll start by reading the text: **▼ READ it**. Then you'll watch peer mentor and sample speech videos: **▼ WATCH it**. After that, you'll use interactive activities that apply chapter concepts and help you develop your own speeches: **▼ USE it**. Finally, you'll use an array of study and self-assessment resources to reinforce what you've learned: **▼ REVIEW it**.

Most of the companion resources are free when your instructor orders them, but they're also available for sale to you at **academic.cengage.com** and **iChapters.com**. For more information, refer to the inside back cover of this book.

With this edition, you can also practice and present with Speech Studio. With Speech Studio, you can upload video files of practice speeches or final performances, comment on your peer's speeches, and review your grades and instructor feedback.

Successfully completing a public speaking course will help you develop communication skills you'll use throughout your life in a wide range of settings and for a variety of purposes. We look forward to helping you develop those skills.

Stephanie J. Coopman, San José State University
James Lull, San José State University

1 The EVOLVING ART of PUBLIC SPEAKING

READ it

WATCH it

USE it

REVIEW it

You may not realize it, but you use public speaking skills every day, although probably not always in the formal way most people associate with speaking in public. You answer questions in class, participate in meetings at work, tell classmates about a concert you attended, or persuade friends to go to a restaurant you like. Keep these experiences in mind as you take this public speaking course, because they form the foundation for broadening and improving your public speaking skills.

Why do I want to do that? you may ask.

Here's why: Students are often required to give presentations in college classes. And effective public speaking skills are an advantage on the job. Public speaking abilities can also help you contribute to your community and gain greater self-confidence. In short, taking a public speaking course will help you develop communication skills that you will use throughout life in a wide range of settings and for a variety of purposes.

Public Speaking Is an Evolving Art

> **READ it** The information-driven world you live in offers many new opportunities for **public speaking,** providing speakers with an array of options for preparing and delivering speeches. Unlike speakers twenty years ago, or even most speakers just ten years ago, you can search the internet and online databases when researching a speech topic. When you deliver your speech, you have the option of using multimedia presentation software such as PowerPoint and Keynote to enhance your message. In some situations, you may even deliver your speech via video conference or webcast.

A situation in which an individual speaks to a group of people, assuming responsibility for speaking for a defined length of time.

Access to so much information and so many options brings additional responsibilities. For example, speakers must use only the most reliable sources to support their speeches, and clearly document those sources. The ease of copying digital files can get speakers into trouble when they don't keep track of their sources.

Audiences also have more options and responsibilities today. As society becomes less formal, audiences respond more favorably to speakers who take a personal and conversational approach, use stories in their presentation, and include visual materials.[1] In addition, audience members may not be in the same physical location as a speaker or may access a video of a speech online weeks or even years after it was delivered. Similarly, with the help of voice-recognition software, audience members may listen to a speech in a language they don't know as it is simultaneously translated into a language they understand. And just as speakers today have easy access to information, so do audience members. They may even go online and use a database to check a fact or detail while listening to a presentation, or they may text-message a friend to confirm the accuracy of a speaker's statements. This ease of access to information means that speakers must research their topics more carefully than ever.

With so much information and so many communication technologies readily available, you might even wonder why anyone has to give presentations any more or why someone might choose to attend a public lecture. Even in the information age, public speaking remains a basic form of human communication. Why? Because public communication fulfills fundamental human needs and serves practical, communal, and social purposes.

But as societies change—economically, demographically, technologically, culturally—so do speakers and audiences. As a result, how humans are taught and learn to be effective speakers and listeners, and the details of what audiences consider an effective presentation, also change. Instruction must fit the current time, speakers, and audiences. That's why this text is more than just a textbook—it's a multimedia package of learning resources.

The Digital Divide

Are you familiar with the concept of the digital divide? This divide accounts for the fact that not everyone accesses the internet regularly, particularly in less developed countries. Even in the United States, more than 20 percent of adults have never used e-mail or gone online. The digital divide acknowledges other differences, too, such as those based on age, race, education level, and internet connection speed.[2] Although the digital divide is narrowing, speakers can't assume that everyone in their audiences is fully versed in online technology.

Over the past 2,500 years, much has changed for public speakers and their audiences: who has the opportunity, or authority, to speak; what makes an audience consider a speaker reliable, or credible; sources of information a speaker may access; the different ways a speaker may deliver a speech; and an audience's expectations. In all these areas, opportunities, options, and expectations have multiplied, contributing to an increasingly complex—and sometimes overwhelming—context for public speaking. **Table 1.1** on pages 6 and 7 presents some of the ways in which public speaking has evolved in Western societies from classical times to today's global, digital information age. Notice the extent of this evolution regarding a speaker's sources of information and delivery options.

Comparing the classical era with the information age highlights the many communication options speakers and listeners have today. As in ancient Greece, you get information from conversations, speeches, and written correspondence, yet now you also get information from DVDs, satellite radio, cable television, and of course internet sources. And the Greeks had only one way to deliver a speech—in person. Today, many speeches are still given face-to-face, yet you might also give a speech during a videoconference, or your speech might be recorded for podcasting later. With each age, the fundamentals of public speaking have remained essentially the same, but the particulars of it, such as how a speaker researches a topic, have changed. This text and its accompanying print and electronic materials provide a guide to both the basics of public speaking and what public speakers today need to know.

Public Speaking Is a Life Skill

When you think about public speaking, you probably focus most on the act of delivering a speech. However, a public speaking course gives you a chance to develop

TABLE 1.1 ▶ Evolving Aspects of Public Speaking

	CLASSICAL ERA (GREECE, 500–100 BCE)	MIDDLE AGES (EUROPE, 1000–1500 CE)	INDUSTRIAL AGE (INDUSTRIAL REVOLUTION, MID-1700S–EARLY 1900S CE)	INFORMATION/DIGITAL AGE (INFORMATION REVOLUTION, 1960–PRESENT)
WHO MAY SPEAK (RACE, CLASS, GENDER, AGE)	• Well-educated men	• Well-educated men • Less educated but activist men	• Well-educated men • Well-educated women • Less or uneducated but activist men • Less educated but activist women	• Well-educated men • Well-educated women • Less or uneducated but activist men • Less educated but activist women • Uneducated women • Teenagers and young adults • Children
WHAT MAKES A SPEAKER CREDIBLE	• Character, logic, emotion	• Character, logic, emotion	• Character, logic, emotion • Information literacy • Media literacy • Cultural literacy	• Character, logic, emotion • Information literacy • Media literacy • Cultural literacy • Computer literacy • Global literacy
SPEAKER'S SOURCES OF INFORMATION	• Conversations • Handwritten books (scrolls, tablets, etc.) • Speeches • Correspondence	• Conversations • Handwritten books (scrolls, tablets, etc.) • Speeches • Correspondence • Almanacs • Pamphlets	• Conversations • Handwritten books (scrolls, tablets, etc.) • Speeches • Correspondence • Almanacs • Pamphlets • Newspapers • Magazines • Analog radio • Sound recordings • Telephone • Telegraph • Morse code • Movies • Newsreels • Photographs	• Conversations • Handwritten books (scrolls, tablets, etc.) • Speeches • Correspondence • Almanacs • Pamphlets • Newspapers • Magazines • Analog radio • Sound recordings • Telephone • Telegraph • Morse code • Movies • Newsreels • Photographs • Microfiche

SPEAKER'S SOURCES OF INFORMATION			• Microfiche	• Super 8 movie cameras • Broadcast television • Satellite radio • Cable television • Satellite television • Facsimiles • Photocopies • Audiotapes • Videotapes • CD-ROMs • DVDs • Mobile media (PDAs, cell phones, MP3 players, digital cameras, digital video cameras) • Internet (websites, e-mail, ftp sites, databases, search engines, wikis, blogs, podcasts, RSS feeds, TV, movies, newspapers, magazines, speeches, music, radio, social networks, listservs, chat rooms, news alerts, webcasts, webcams, PDFs)
SPEAKER'S ETHICAL CHALLENGES	• Lying • Distortion • Manipulation • Plagiarism	• Lying • Distortion • Manipulation • Plagiarism (print sources)	• Lying • Distortion • Manipulation • Plagiarism (print sources) • Plagiarism (non-print sources)	• Lying • Distortion • Manipulation • Plagiarism (print sources) • Plagiarism (non-print sources) • Plagiarism (digitized sources)
SPEAKER'S DELIVERY OPTIONS	• In person	• In person	• In person • Mass media	• In person • Mass media • Mediated/electronic (synchronous) • Mediated/electronic (asynchronous)
AUDIENCE'S EXPECTATIONS	• Eloquence • Drama	• Eloquence • Drama	• Eloquence • Authority	• Informal eloquence • Narrative • Multimedia-enhanced delivery • Availability of audio and/or video recording of a speech

many other communication skills, such as managing communication anxiety, listening effectively, adapting to an audience and building your credibility, finding and using information, organizing ideas, and presenting ideas and information.

DEVELOPING TRANSFERABLE SKILLS

Transferable skills, such as finding information and organizing ideas, can be transferred from one context or occasion to another. So when you learn to manage anxiety in your public speaking class, you'll be able to apply that skill in other settings, such as a job interview. The skills you learn in your public speaking class will help you in other communication situations as well.

Being More Confident and Managing Speech Anxiety

Nearly everyone gets nervous when speaking in public. Good speakers have learned to cope with that anxiety. Successfully completing a public speaking course will provide you with an important source of confidence that will help you manage speech anxiety.[3]

The process of *habituation*—fearing a situation less as it becomes more familiar, or *habit*-like—helps you manage your speech anxiety over time, just as doing almost anything repeatedly makes you more comfortable doing it. For example, you probably experienced some nervousness the first time you attended a college class. After a few class meetings, though, you likely became more comfortable because you had a better idea of what to expect. Repetition alone isn't enough, however; you also need positive experiences. You didn't become more comfortable taking college courses only because you attended a certain number of class sessions. Your comfort level increased because you started to get to know your classmates, you made a comment that your instructor praised, or you successfully completed the first assignment. In other words, you were encouraged to come back and feel more comfortable.

A public speaking course can provide a process of habituation grounded in positive events. You'll get positive feedback about your speeches, and you'll get constructive suggestions about what you might change so that you give a more effective speech next time. Both kinds of feedback give you direction and remind you that you have the support of your instructor and classmates. The increased confidence and decreased anxiety you experience as your public speaking class progresses will transfer to speaking situations outside of class. When speaking opportunities arise, such as giving your input at a neighborhood meeting or talking to high school students about the importance of graduating, you'll feel enthusiastic about them. Chapter 2 covers specific strategies for increasing your confidence and managing the common psychological and physiological effects of public speaking anxiety.

Being a Better Listener

Poor listening skills can cause all sorts of problems—missing a key point during a staff meeting, misunderstanding a physician's advice, giving an inappropriate response to a friend's question. A public speaking course will sharpen your listening skills.[4]

As you build your communication skills, one goal is learning how to listen reciprocally, meaning that all participants in a communication scenario listen to one another with open minds and their full attention. Skilled communicators listen openly even when they disagree with someone. Chapter 3 presents specific strategies that will help you become a more effective listener and better at compensating for others' poor listening skills in any communication context.

Adapting to Different Audiences and Building Your Credibility

Gathering and analyzing information about an audience helps you identify audience members' interests and concerns, what they know about your topic, and how they might respond to what you say. Whether you're telling coworkers about a new software program, running for election to the student government, or entertaining friends with tales from your travels, knowing your audience is essential to getting your message across. Chapter 5 explains the best methods for researching and analyzing audiences.

Another, related skill is building credibility. Speaker credibility refers to how much an audience views the speaker as competent, friendly, trustworthy, and dynamic. How you establish and maintain your credibility as a speaker varies from audience to audience and topic to topic. As a result, knowing how to communicate your credibility will help you get your ideas across to others no matter what the context. Suppose, for instance, that you'd like to get your college to provide more funding for student organizations on campus. Your message will be much more persuasive if the school's administrators view you as a credible spokesperson. Chapter 5 provides more detail on the four components of credibility and how they apply to speaking in public.

Finding and Using Reliable Information

Knowing how to locate information, evaluate its reliability and applicability for your purpose, and use it ethically and effectively can serve you well in all aspects of your life. Finding and assessing information at work is an obvious example. But research skills are essential for your home life as well. A recent study found that 80 percent of internet users in the United States search for health information online, yet very few check the sources of that information.[5] So millions of Americans rely on health information that may or may not be valid, reliable, and accurate. Learning how to systematically find, analyze, and evaluate information in your public speaking class will help you avoid poor and discredited information. Chapter 6 covers the process of research in depth.

Organizing Ideas and Information Effectively

Listeners expect and need clear organization, which speakers can provide by using common patterns of organization such as chronological (how something develops over time), spatial (physical relationships between things), cause-and-effect (how one thing results in another), and problem-solution (identifying a problem and discussing how to solve it). To further help audiences follow what they're saying, public speakers use purposeful transitions to link points together. Organizing your ideas also involves outlining your speech. An outline keeps you on track and gives you a basic plan for researching, constructing, and delivering what you want to say about your topic.

Public speaking students develop ways to better organize their ideas both in and outside the classroom.[6] Whether you're giving directions to your home or explaining how to use a new piece of equipment, a general outline, pattern of organization, and navigation signals make it easier to understand what you're saying. Organizing your points before you speak can give your ideas greater impact. Chapter 8 covers how to organize and outline your ideas.

Presenting Ideas and Information Effectively

Effective communication requires *mindfulness*, in which you consciously focus on a situation and maintain awareness of what you say and how others respond.[7] Mindfulness is especially important in public speaking situations, and being mindful in your public speaking course will help you be more mindful in your other interactions.

A related skill set is planning, preparing, and using presentation media effectively. Integrating PowerPoint, Keynote, or other digital slide software has become a requirement for most business presentations. You might not use digital slides to tell your friends about your trip to Africa, but you might put together an online slide show to go with the podcast you recorded while traveling. Chapter 11 gives you tips and strategies for using presentation media.

Public speaking skills are *life skills*. That is, you'll use what you learn in your public speaking class in all aspects of your life. **Table 1.2** summarizes the transferable skills learned in a public speaking course, how they're developed, and how they benefit you in everyday life.

TABLE 1.2 ► Transferable Life Skills Gained in a Public Speaking Course

TRANSFERABLE SKILL	HOW PUBLIC SPEAKING HELPS YOU DEVELOP THE SKILL	EXAMPLES OF HOW THE SKILL MIGHT BENEFIT YOU IN EVERYDAY LIFE
Being more confident and managing communication anxiety	• Habituation • Using proven strategies	Feeling more comfortable talking with people in unfamiliar social situations
Being a better listener	• Understanding listening • Listening reciprocally	Understanding better what a friend has to say, and the friend understanding you better
Adapting to different audiences and building your credibility	• Knowing how to research and analyze audiences • Increasing competence and dynamism	Being able to confront a friend or coworker about a difficult issue without damaging the relationship
Finding and evaluating information	• Recognizing appropriate and reliable sources • Assessing the accuracy and validity of information	Researching a company you think you would like to work for
Organizing ideas	• Understanding patterns of organization • Understanding how people process information	Explaining to a classmate the advantages and disadvantages of wireless computer networking
Presenting ideas effectively	• Communicating mindfully • Knowing how to plan and prepare effective presentation materials	Consciously integrating effective presentation resources into a speech about college life at your high school

SPEAKING EFFECTIVELY IN COMMON PUBLIC COMMUNICATION CONTEXTS

Even in today's era of text messaging, instant messaging, chatting, blogging, and the like, you often engage in public communication in a wide range of contexts. This section discusses four of those contexts: the college classroom, the workplace, your community, and social events.

In Classes

You've probably done classroom speaking, such as answering an instructor's question, giving a report, or explaining an idea. As a result, you likely recognize that students have many unplanned and informal speaking opportunities, including telling stories, having impromptu conversations, and collaborating on assignments.

Communication across the curriculum (CXC) has become commonplace on most campuses.[8] Rather than requiring oral presentations only in communication courses, CXC involves speaking assignments in all sorts of classes, from biology to dance. If you haven't already, you'll get plenty of opportunities to develop your public speaking skills in your other classes.

In the Workplace

As the basis of our economy continues to shift from manufacturing to information, the ability to communicate well becomes even more essential to professional success.[9] Employers in all types of organizations and industries rank effective oral and written communication skills as the most important skill set for college graduates to have when they enter the workforce (**Figure 1.1**). Organizations need people who effectively interact with coworkers, supervisors, and the public, and research shows that students who successfully complete a class in public speaking improve their communication skills in the workplace.[10]

You may think, "I'll never do any public speaking in my job." It's true, you might be able to avoid public speaking situations at work, but it's likely that in avoiding them you'll miss opportunities to advance your career. Even in professions such as accounting—usually not associated with public speaking—excellent oral communication skills are essential for building business contacts and getting promoted.[11] Some companies even hire speech coaches

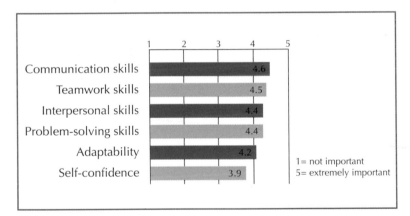

▲ FIGURE 1.1

Communication-related Skills Employers Rated Most Important *Source: Results of the National Association of Colleges and Employers Survey*

to help employees improve their speaking abilities before considering them for promotion.[12] However, it's better to arrive at interviews with those skills already developed.

In Communities

Citizens who are willing to speak in their communities make up the very foundation of a democracy.[13] When you use your public speaking skills to discuss issues with others in your community, you contribute to a more informed society and feel a greater sense of belonging. In short, you participate in democracy at its most basic level.[14] The skills you develop in your public speaking class can help you contribute more to the various communities to which you belong.

AP Photo/Scott Erskine

▲ Mike Sessions, 18 years old when he was elected mayor of Hillsdale, Michigan, used his public speaking skills to win over voters and unseat the incumbent mayor.

Consider the example of Mike Sessions, the high school student who won the Hillsdale, Michigan, mayoral campaign in 2005. Just days after turning 18 and registering to vote, Mike filed his intention to run for mayor as a write-in candidate in his south-central Michigan town. Each day after school, Mike went from door to door, telling people who he was and why he was running for mayor. The young candidate spoke at the Kiwanis Club, a record shop, and the local firehouse. In the end, his determination paid off: He won the election, defeating incumbent Don Ingles by two votes.[15]

At Social Events

Many social events, such as graduations, wedding receptions, retirement banquets, and family reunions, call for public speaking. Casual get-togethers like birthday celebrations, going-away parties, neighborhood barbeques, and dinners with friends often become more meaningful when attendees mark the moment with a few brief comments to the group. Such occasions serve important cultural functions by transmitting values and strengthening the social fabric.

When you celebrate graduating from your college or university, for example, you may be called on to say a few words, even if the event is an informal gathering. Successfully completing a class in public speaking will help you prepare a speech your audience will remember, and that truly expresses the meaning of the occasion for you. Social events offer fairly regular opportunities to further develop and maintain your public speaking skills throughout your life.

Foundations of Public Speaking

The earliest humans used rudimentary speech to convey their thoughts and experiences to others, forming the initial foundation for public communication. Just as they do now, speeches in this primal time allowed people to convey their experiences and inner thoughts to others.[16] You may live in a time defined by globalization, mass media, information technology, and popular culture, but the need to express your thoughts and feelings will always play a prominent role in your life.

Beginning with the Sophists (500–300 BCE), the ancient Greeks demonstrated an early concern with the study of public communication in the Western tradition. The Sophists were teachers who typically traveled from place to place giving lectures to students, seeking to teach them how to communicate well in a democratic society. Whereas the Sophists focused on excellent delivery as the hallmark of an eloquent speaker, the philosopher Socrates (c. 470–399 BCE) and his student Plato (428–348 BCE) identified good reasoning as the basis of effective public speaking.[17]

ARISTOTLE'S *RHETORIC*

Aristotle (384–322 BCE), a student of Plato, took a systematic approach to studying **rhetoric**, as public speaking was called at the time.[18] In Aristotle's major work, *Rhetoric,* he emphasized the importance of adapting speeches to the specific situation and audience—a foundation of public communication that holds true today and is often referred to as **audience-centered communication.** Adapting to audiences and building your credibility are part of an audience-centered approach. If, for example, you're attempting to convince your classmates to get more involved in their community, you might stress the benefits of listing volunteer work on a résumé. In discussing the same topic with parents of young children, you could shift your focus to how their activities might help make the community a place where their kids can thrive.

Another enduring foundation of public speaking is what Aristotle called proofs, or the various types of support a speaker uses for a specific audience and occasion. Aristotle identified three types of proofs, or appeals: *logos, pathos*, and *ethos*. Logos refers to rational appeals based on logic, facts, and analysis. Traditional examples of logos

Aristotle's term for public speaking.

Adapting a speech to a specific situation and audience.

include the use of scientific evidence and the arguments prosecutors and defense attorneys use in courts of law as they attempt to establish the facts of a case. But presenting a report at work or recounting your friend's accomplishments when you nominate her for a leadership position often also involve logos. Pathos occurs when speakers appeal to the audience's emotions, as with the poignant photos often used to convince us to contribute to charitable organizations. Appeals based on ethos rest on the speaker's credibility or character. When you speak at a neighborhood meeting or offer your comments in class, the audience evaluates your trustworthiness and believability—key components of good character and credibility.

A fourth type of appeal, *mythos*, focuses on the values and beliefs embedded in cultural narratives or stories.[19] Contemporary scholars introduced this concept, observing that stories represent important cultural values that may appeal to an audience. Chapter 15 covers all four types of appeals and provides detailed guidance about how to use them to support a speech's message.

▲ The ancient Greek philosopher Aristotle's writing about oratory still influences the teaching of public speaking today.

CICERO AND THE FIVE ARTS

The Roman statesman Cicero (106–43 BCE) categorized the elements of public communication into five "arts of public speaking," or canons of rhetoric, that are still applicable today.[20] Cicero argued that these five arts—invention, arrangement, style, memory, and delivery—constitute the groundwork for learning about public speaking. The five arts provide guidelines for speaking effectively in public.

1. **Invention** focuses on discovering what you have or want to say. As the first art, invention occurs when you find an idea, line of thought, or argument you might use in a speech. Choosing a topic (Chapter 4) and developing good arguments (Chapter 15) are both part of invention.

   Discovering what you want to say in a speech, such as choosing a topic and developing good arguments.

2. **Arrangement**, the second art, refers to how you organize your ideas. This art accounts for the basic parts of a speech (introduction, body, conclusion) as well as the order in which points are presented (Chapter 8). Good organization helps maintain the audience's attention and keeps them focused on the ideas the speaker presents.[21] For example, sometimes a speaker tells the end of a story first because the audience will then be curious about how the ending came about. At other times, the speaker tells a story in the order in which events happened because the end will be a surprise.

   The way the ideas in a speech are organized.

3. The third art, **style**, involves the language you use to bring a speech's content to life (Chapter 10). Consider the differences between saying, "My trip last summer

   The language or words used in a speech.

The Arts of Public Speaking across Cultures

The five arts of public speaking come from the Western cultural tradition, but other cultures emphasize these same core principles of public speaking as well. Buddhist preaching in Japan, for example, follows similar principles. Established guidelines specify what subjects preachers can discuss (invention), the way in which ideas are organized (arrangement), the type of language used (style), what information requires memorization (memory), and how the voice and body should be used when preaching (delivery). Many of these guidelines are highly detailed, such as those for using a specific organizational pattern for a sermon: recite a verse from a religious text, explain the verse's central theme, tell a relevant fictional story, tell a true story, and make concluding comments. Although not all Buddhist preachers rely on this way of organizing their sermons, many still use this traditional organizational pattern.[23]

Using the ability to recall information to give an effective speech.

The presentation of a speech to an audience.

A story used in a speech or other form of communication.

was fun" and, "My adventures last summer included a strenuous but thrilling trek through the Rocky Mountains." Both statements reflect the same idea, but the second one grabs the audience's attention—they want to know more about the "thrilling trek."

4. **Memory,** the fourth art, refers to using your memory to give an effective speech. Memory goes beyond simple memorization and highlights the importance of practicing public speaking skills (Chapter 12).[22] That is, when you present a speech, you rely on everything you've learned about public speaking, your topic, the audience, and the occasion.

5. As the fifth art, **delivery** occurs when a speech goes public—when it is presented to an audience. Delivery involves how you use your voice, gestures, and body movement when giving a speech. Chapter 12 covers how to achieve the natural, conversational delivery style today's audiences expect and prefer.

STORYTELLING

Humans' early attempts at public communication likely took the form of storytelling, with speakers relating their activities with a sense of drama and adventure. Listening to and telling stories requires narrative thinking, relying on **narratives,** or stories, to connect the self with the world, envision what could be, apply logic to identify patterns and causal connections, and structure events in a logical order.[24] Because storytelling is so basic to human communication and human existence, today's audiences often welcome a story or an anecdote, a very brief narrative.

Although life today differs in numerous ways from life in earlier times, much of what humans have learned about public communication in even the distant past still holds true. Just as the importance of interacting with friends and family and telling stories has remained the same throughout human existence, so have the foundations of public communication retained their relevance.

Public Speaking and Human Communication Today

Public speaking shares some characteristics with other communication contexts, but also differs in several important ways. Understanding these similarities and differences will help you develop your public speaking skills as well as identify how those skills apply in other contexts.

CONTEXTS FOR HUMAN COMMUNICATION

Communication scholars traditionally use the following categories to identify contexts for human communication:

- *Interpersonal communication* occurs between two or more people interacting with each other as unique individuals. You develop your relationships with friends, family, and coworkers through interpersonal communication.
- In *small-group communication*, three or more people interact to accomplish a task or reach a shared objective. Local theater groups, committees, and project teams are examples of small groups.
- *Organizational communication* takes place within and between organizations for the purpose of accomplishing common goals, such as creating products and offering services. Organizations often provide the setting for speeches, as when a department manager gives a presentation to senior executives.
- *Mass communication* originates with a media organization such as NBC, *People* magazine, XM Satellite Radio, or AOL (America Online) and is transmitted to large, fairly anonymous, and often diverse audiences.
- *Public communication* occurs when an individual speaks to a group of people, assuming primary responsibility for speaking for a limited amount of time.

TRADITIONAL MODELS OF HUMAN COMMUNICATION

Models of human communication provide a visual representation of the elements of the communication process. Early models portrayed human communication as moving in a single direction, from a sender to a receiver. Communication scholars refer to this description as the transmission or linear model of communication (**Figure 1.2**).

The interactional model expands on the transmission model by adding two key elements: channel and feedback. In this model, *messages* pass from a sender or source through a channel to a receiver or receivers. The *channel* refers to the mode of communication, such as in person or by telephone, text message, or webcam. Receivers respond to sources with *feedback,* so communication becomes two-way (**Figure 1.3**). Like the transmission model, the interactional model provides a simplistic view of communication, with messages and feedback going back and forth between sender and receiver.

First introduced over forty years ago, the transactional model elaborated on the earlier two models by viewing communicators as simultaneously senders and receivers. This shift in thinking about communication highlights the active role of listening.

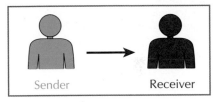

▲ **FIGURE 1.2**
The Transmission Model of Communication *Source: Adapted from Laswell (1948).*

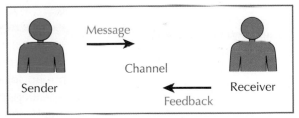

▲ **FIGURE 1.3**
The Interactional Model of Communication *Sources: Schramm (1955); Berlo (1970).*

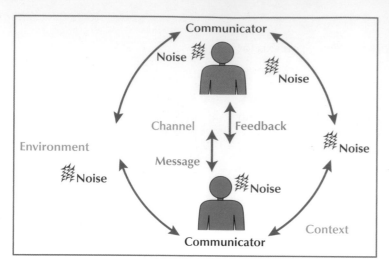

▲ FIGURE 1.4
The Transactional Model of
Communication *Source: Adapted from
Barnlund (1970).*

The ability to access and share
information in multiple forms from
multiple locations in ways that
transcend time and space.

The person who assumes the primary responsibility for conveying
a message in a public communication context.

In addition, the model adds three important elements: noise,
context, and environment. *Noise* refers to any interference
that prevents messages from being understood. The *context* is
the setting for the interaction, such as a conference room or
grocery checkout line. The *environment* includes all the outside forces that might affect communication, such as current
events or even the weather (**Figure 1.4**).

A NEW MODEL OF COMMUNICATION FOR TODAY'S PUBLIC SPEAKERS

Although the transactional model provides a useful start for
understanding the public speaking process, it was developed
long before the internet and any sort of digital communication. Any current model of communication must account for a
pervasive communication environment, in which information
can be accessed and shared in multiple forms from multiple locations in ways that transcend time and space.[25] Today you can e-mail photos to your friends using a cell phone,
download music files to your MP3 player, watch videos on your laptop, and chat with
coworkers using a webcam. Location-specific media such as wired or land-line phones,
television, and desktop computers still play an important role in our lives, as do mobile
analog media such as newspapers, books, and analog radio. But mobile digital media
provide the foundation of today's information-rich world. With mobile digital media such
as cell phones and personal digital assistants (PDAs), you can communicate any time
with anyone for any reason from nearly any place around the globe. In addition, digital
cameras and audio recorders allow you to record your experiences wherever you might
be. The internet forms the heart of the pervasive communication environment, linking
various media and people together.

Integrating the notion of a pervasive communication environment with the transactional model of communication presents a more precise view of the evolving art of
public speaking. **Figure 1.5** shows how the eight elements of communication—sender
(speaker), message, channel, receiver (audience), noise, feedback, context, and environment—work together for public speakers in today's digital communication world.

The **speaker** is the individual person—you, a classmate, friend, family member,
neighbor, or coworker—who assumes a central role as initiator or participant in a speech.
In public speaking situations, the speaker is the person who has the primary responsibility

for talking. Yet audience members also fulfill the speaker role when they ask questions or make comments after a speech.

The **message** includes both the words the speaker uses—verbal communication—and how the speaker presents those words—nonverbal communication. When you interpret what someone else says, you pay attention to what they say and how they say it. In public speaking, you listen to the speaker's main points and ideas, and observe how the speaker moves, incorporates gestures, makes eye contact, and uses her or his voice. Notice that Cicero's five arts of public speaking make up the sum total of the message: the speaker's ideas (invention), how the points are organized (arrangement), the specific words the speaker chooses (style), evidence that the speaker knows the topic (memory), and the actual speech presentation (delivery).

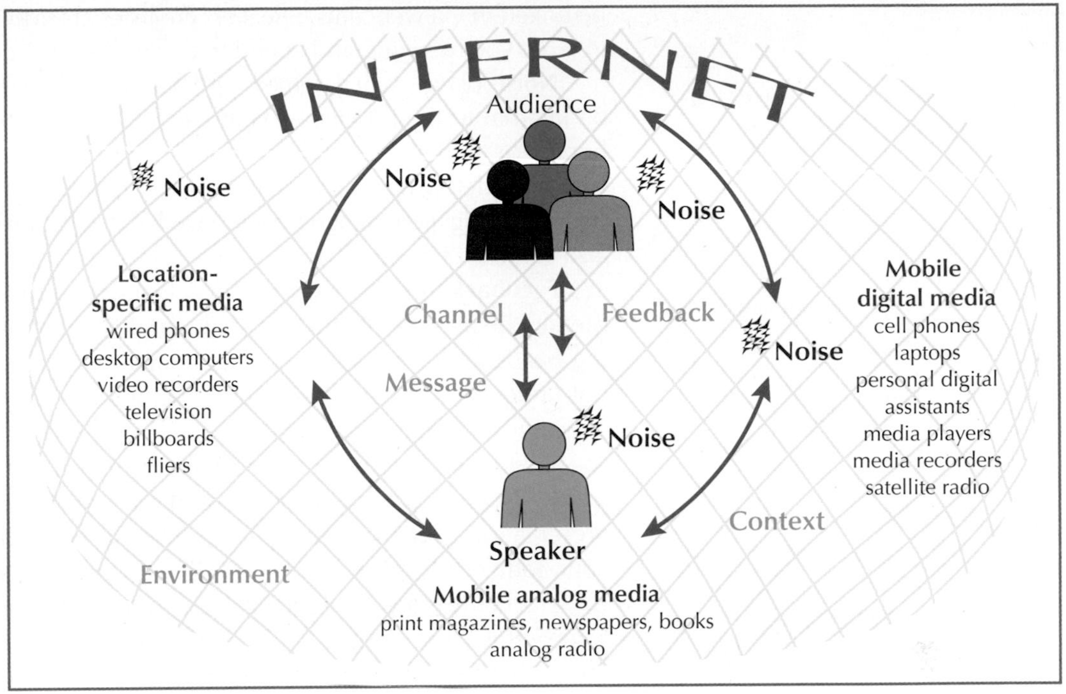

▲ FIGURE 1.5
A New Model of Public Speaking *Source: Coopman (2006).*

The words and nonverbal cues a speaker uses to convey ideas, feelings, and thoughts.

Channel refers to the mode or medium of communication—in-person, print, or electronic. Public speaking often involves multiple channels. In addition to speaking to an audience, a speaker may use overhead transparencies to display a graph, play a clip from a relevant musical piece, and make available a paper handout with additional information. Many more communication channels are available today than in the past. Speakers make presentations in person but may also give a speech via webcam or videoconferencing and often make their digital slides available to the audience. In the business world digital slides make up a key component of many speeches. Audience members may respond using multiple channels as well, such as text messaging a speaker or e-mailing a question.

A mode or medium of communication.

The **audience** refers to the intended recipients of the speaker's message. Today your audience may extend far beyond the people you speak with in person. A speech may be digitally recorded for online distribution at a later time, or some audience members may

The intended recipients of a speaker's message.

be linked in via webcams. Speakers are listeners, too. When you give a speech, you listen to what you're saying and attend to the audience's responses.

Anything that interferes with the understanding of a message.	

Noise occurs when something interferes with understanding a message. Noise may be internal to the listener, as with daydreaming or thinking about something else. Being hungry or tired causes noise as well. External noise includes sounds that prevent listeners from completely hearing what the speaker has to say, such as other people talking or a cell phone ringing. Poor lighting, blurry overhead transparencies, and cluttered digital slides are also sources of noise. Chapter 3 discusses ways to reduce noise and distractions.

Audience members' responses to a speech.	

Feedback from listeners provides speakers with a sense of how the audience is interpreting the message. Nods and smiles indicate that listeners agree and understand. Shaking heads and frowns suggest that audience members may disagree, feel confused, or not understand the speaker's point. Getting feedback from listeners lets you know how effective you are as a speaker and areas in which you might improve. In your public speaking class, you may gather feedback informally by observing your audience as you speak, listening to their questions, and asking them after class what they thought of your presentation. Your instructor might provide more formal ways of collecting feedback from your audience, such as written or oral peer evaluations.

The situation within which a speech is given.	

The **context** for public speaking includes the circumstances or situation within which a speech occurs. Context includes the physical setting for a speech—auditorium, classroom, conference room, the steps of city hall, a museum gallery. The actual space in which the speaker talks influences the message and how the audience responds. A classroom or conference room is generally less formal than a large auditorium filled with hundreds of people. Trying to keep listeners' attention poses different challenges outside city hall than inside a quiet museum gallery. The occasion for the speech also contributes to the context. Audience members have different expectations for a speech commemorating a historic event than for a speech supporting a candidate for political office.

The external surroundings that influence a public speaking event.	

The **environment** refers to all the external surroundings that influence a public speaking event. For example, events occurring at or near the time when a speech is given may play a key role in listeners' reactions. Audience members consider the speaker's message within the context of what's happening in their world. A speech on the importance of saving money for retirement might not seem relevant when a local business just laid off thousands of employees.

Key Issues for Today's Public Speaker

Because communicators can interact with others and access information at nearly any time and in any place, speakers and audiences enjoy new opportunities and challenges. Ethics, critical thinking, cultural awareness, and using presentation software are all issues today's public speaker should be aware of—in every public speaking context.

ETHICS

Ethics merges the Greek word for "character," *ethos*, and the Latin word for "morality," *mores*, and refers to rules or standards within a culture about what is right and wrong.[26] Regardless of the era, ethics are central to public speaking. Computers and digital technology, however, have added layers of ethical issues that speakers and audiences didn't face in the past. For example, with the availability of information in digital form, plagiarism has become easier. *Plagiarism* occurs when you take someone else's idea or work and present it as your own. Chapter 3 provides a more in-depth discussion of ethics, and Chapter 6 covers the specifics of plagiarism in the context of research as well as a detailed guide to evaluating sources.

CRITICAL THINKING

With access to so much information in digital formats, public speakers and their audiences must be especially vigilant and consistently use their critical thinking skills. As discussed in Chapter 6, speakers must ask critical questions when evaluating what speakers say, such as "Where did this information come from?" and "Is this evidence from a credible source?" Information literacy involves the ability to access, select, evaluate, and use information effectively.[27] Knowing how to sort through less useful information to get the information you really need is a skill you'll apply every day throughout your life. Whether you're searching for information about your speech topic or trying to identify the best car for your transportation needs and budget, information literacy skills are a must.

CULTURAL AWARENESS

Effective listeners and speakers display sensitivity to others' cultural perspectives. Whether speaking to a relatively homogeneous or a very diverse audience, successful speakers always keep in mind ways of looking at the world that don't match their own views. Today more than ever, for speakers to do well, they must demonstrate they are aware and respectful of other cultures. Chapters 5 and 10 address the specifics of cultural awareness for public speakers.

USING PRESENTATION SOFTWARE

What's considered good delivery has changed considerably since Aristotle's time. The sophisticated presentation software available today has conditioned audiences to anticipate a certain level of flair in most public speaking situations. Audiences expect creativity, such as integrating relevant video and audio clips into digital slides or showing an image that will provoke discussion. However, overreliance on presentation software, especially digital slides, detracts from your message.[28] Chapter 11 provides concrete guidelines for using presentation software and other presentation media effectively.

A Brief Guide to Successful Public Speaking

No recipe exists that promises an excellent speech every time. And even the best planning doesn't always lead to the results you anticipated. Still, approaching public speaking in a systematic way greatly increases your likelihood of success. Presenting a speech involves six basic stages (**Figure 1.6**):

1. Determining your purpose and topic (Chapter 4)
2. Adapting to your audience (Chapter 5)
3. Researching your topic (Chapter 6)
4. Organizing your ideas (Chapter 8)
5. Practicing your speech (Chapter 12)
6. Presenting your speech (Chapter 12)

These stages blend together—they're integrated parts of a whole, rather than discrete units. For example, as you're analyzing your audience (stage 2), you revise your topic focus (stage 1). What you find out about your audience (stage 2) will influence how you research your topic (stage 3). When practicing your speech (stage 5), you may decide that the flow of your ideas won't work with your audience (stage 2), so you go back and make some modifications in the organization of your ideas (stage 4).

Although public speaking may seem to be all about presenting, most of a successful speaker's work takes place behind the scenes, well before the speaking event. Let's go through each activity in the speechmaking process.

DETERMINING YOUR PURPOSE AND TOPIC

To begin, you need to decide on your overall goal, or the general purpose of your speech. First speeches in a public speaking class usually aim to inform or enhance listeners' knowledge of a topic. For example, in introducing a classmate, you'd want your audience to learn a few key bits of information about the person. Some first speeches seek to entertain listeners by sharing anecdotes and using humor, such as telling your audience a humorous story about your summer vacation. Speeches to persuade focus on changing people's behaviors, values, or attitudes. For example, trying to convince audience members to exercise regularly involves persuasion.

After you've identified the speech's general purpose, you need to choose your topic. Sometimes your instructor will assign a topic for your first speech, such as introducing yourself to the class. In other cases, your assignment may be more broadly defined, such as informing the audience about an important campus issue. Whatever topic you choose, aim to pick something of interest to you and your audience.

ADAPTING TO YOUR AUDIENCE

In choosing your topic, keep your audience in mind so your speech will interest them. More in-depth research allows you to design your speech for your audience. Demographic characteristics, such as ethnic background, age, sex, education, and income, provide initial clues for understanding your audience. Let's look at a simple example. Imagine you're speaking to two groups about the need for affordable housing in your community: housing developers and a tenants' rights organization. Even without doing extensive research, you can imagine that the two groups have different interests and positions on the topic.

Adapting to your audience means that you apply the information you've gathered about them in designing your speech. Target your message to *this* particular audience in *this* particular time and place. Use audience-centered communication that engages your listeners and helps you achieve your goal for the speech. You want your audience to feel as if you're speaking directly to them.

RESEARCHING YOUR TOPIC

You have many sources of information for your speech topics—books, magazines, newspapers, government publications, institutional websites, and interviews with individuals. But begin with yourself and what you already know about the topic.

Once you've identified your own knowledge base, seek out other sources of information. Often a trip to the library and a brief conference with the reference librarian helps tremendously in locating the information you need. All campus libraries include extensive electronic databases that provide gateways to academic journals, newspapers, legal opinions, trade publications, and numerous other sources.

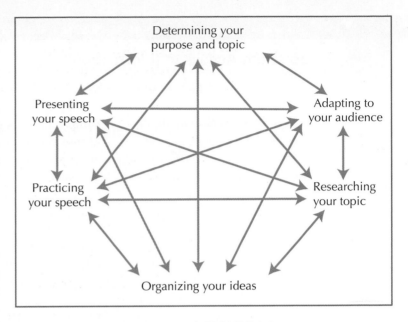

▲ **FIGURE 1.6**
The Process of Giving a Speech

Too Much Access to Information?

With the advent of the internet, options and opportunities for accessing information multiplied exponentially. For speakers, the internet has made it easier to find a wealth of information about any number of topics from a variety of sources. Government, university, nonprofit organization, news media, and other institutional websites offer valuable resources for the public speaker. Electronic databases available through your campus library's website give you access to newspapers, magazines, academic journals, and other digital material. Researching a speech topic has never been easier—or more challenging.

The explosion of information available online means people often suffer from information overload, or having so much information that they're overwhelmed and unable to sort through it all. Successful speakers research topics strategically to find the most valuable information and sift out what's irrelevant. Chapter 6 explores this topic in greater depth.

You've probably already searched the internet for information about a wide range of topics. However, finding what you need for a speech is another matter. Locating relevant information online requires determining the right key terms associated with your topic. For example, if you're introducing a classmate who enjoys surfing, you may want to find out more about this activity. Typing in "surfing" on Google produces over 50 million webpages, ranging from internet surfing, to the surfing lawyer, to mind surfing—not exactly relevant to your speech. However, adding key terms to "surfing," such as "sport," "ocean," and "surfboard," refines your search.

ORGANIZING YOUR IDEAS

Organizing your ideas involves identifying the main points you want to cover in your speech and putting them in a logical order: introduction, body, and conclusion.

Gaining your audience's attention in the introduction encourages listeners to focus on your ideas. Startling statistics, engaging quotes, rhetorical questions, brief anecdotes, and vivid visual materials that are relevant to your topic provide useful strategies for getting your audience focused on your topic. You'll also preview your main points in the introduction, as with "The two campus services I'll cover today are the university credit union and the computer recycling program." Once you've done that, you've set the stage for the body of your speech, which includes all your main points organized in some logical way. For example, if you were describing a stadium, you might begin with the outside, then take the audience through the gates, then into the first level, and on through the arena using a spatial organizational pattern. However you organize your ideas, the pattern must be clear to your audience. Chapter 8 covers this topic more fully.

Outlining your speech shows how you've arranged your ideas. With an outline, you develop a numbered list of your main points and all the points supporting them. Successful public speaking requires creating and using three different kinds of outlines for different stages in the development of your speech: working, complete-sentence, and presentation. **Table 1.3** provides an overview of each type of outline, including what it's used for (function), what it includes (key features), and in which chapter of this text you'll find it covered.

Probably the most neglected part of a speech, a fluent conclusion helps ensure you'll achieve the purpose of your speech. In ending your speech, you'll summarize the main points and let your audience know you're finished. So you might say something like, "Let's review what I've covered today . . ." or "To summarize, the most important aspects

TABLE 1.3 ▶ Types of Outlines

TYPE OF OUTLINE	FUNCTIONS	KEY FEATURES	CHAPTER
Working	Assists initial topic development; guides research	Includes main points and possible sub-points; revised during research process	4: Developing Your Purpose and Topic
Complete-sentence	Clearly identifies all pieces of information for the speech; puts ideas in order; forms basis for developing the presentation outline	Uses complete sentences; lists all sections of speech and all references; revised during preparation process	8: Organizing and Outlining Your Speech
Presentation	Assists in practicing and giving your speech	Uses keywords; revised as you practice your speech; often transferred to note cards for use during practice and the final presentation	12: Delivering Your Speech

of . . ." Then end with a memorable statement, such as, "Now you've met Bailey—political science major, entrepreneur, and future mayor of this city." Chapter 9 provides more information on beginning and ending a speech effectively.

PRACTICING YOUR SPEECH

In practicing your speech, first go through your complete-sentence outline, talking out loud, listening for how your ideas flow and fit together. Second, give your speech aloud again, checking that you're within the time limit. Based on how well you meet the time limit and how your ideas work together, edit and revise for clarity and ease of understanding.

Third, transfer key words from your complete-sentence outline to note cards. Include only those words that trigger your memory. What you write on your note cards will become your presentation outline—the outline you'll use when you give your speech to the audience. Now, stand up and say your speech, just as you would if your audience were there. Hold your note cards in one hand and incorporate presentation media such as digital slides or posters as you speak. Because you're using your notes as a reminder, you'll need to glance at them only briefly and infrequently.

Strive to give an excellent version of your speech rather than a perfect speech. As you're practicing, your speech will be a little different each time. That's okay. You're aiming for a conversational presentation that you adapt to your audience as you're speaking.

PRESENTING YOUR SPEECH

When you present your speech, manage your voice and your body, your presentation media, your audience, and your time. To manage yourself, dress for the occasion, matching what you wear to the setting, audience, and topic. Glance at your note cards to remind you of what you planned to say, while maintaining good eye contact with your audience. Speak loudly so your audience can easily hear you. Move with purpose and spontaneity, using gestures that appear natural and comfortable.

For your first speech, you probably won't have slides, videos, or other presentation media. However, if you're introducing yourself and one of your passions is jazz music, a 10-second clip of a favorite song would increase your audience's attention. To manage your presentation media, arrive early on the day of your speech and check the equipment you're going to use. Remember that sometimes technology fails—be prepared for that.

Analyzing your audience members provides you with the foundation for managing them as you present your speech. What you know about your listeners gives you some clues about their possible reactions to your speech. Making eye contact allows you to get a sense of how they're responding to what you say.

Monitor your time so you can pace yourself. Adjust your speech if you find you're going to exceed or fall short of the time limit. Effective public speaking means having the flexibility to manage your time to meet situational demands.

Now that you've learned about the basics of giving your first speech, it's time to meet the Speech Buddies. They will be your guides as you work through this book, providing advice and tips for giving better speeches.

Introducing the Speech Buddies

The Speech Buddies are a crew of college students who are available all day, every day in online videos to serve as peer mentors while you're using this text and its various learning materials. These students—Janine, Anthony, Erin, and Evan—all completed a public speaking course like the one you're taking now. Intended to be an essential part of your experience while using this text, the Speech Buddies guide you through the

▼ WATCH it SPEECH BUDDY VIDEO LINK

Meeting the Speech Buddies

◄◄ ▐▐ ►►

In this video, Janine, Anthony, Erin, and Evan briefly introduce themselves and talk about an aspect of the role public speaking plays in their lives. As you watch the video, think about how you've used public speaking skills in the past and how you'll be able to apply what you learn in this course in the future.

▼ USE it ACTIVITY LINK

What Are Your Public Speaking Goals?

After watching the video, click on the interactive activity link to put the chapter to use. This activity includes a series of prompts that will help you identify your immediate and long-term public speaking goals.

process of preparing and delivering effective speeches by telling you about their own public speaking experiences and introducing video clips that present examples from their speeches and those of others. The Speech Buddies also direct you to the interactive activities that accompany each video and give you a chance to use the principles covered, first by applying them in hypothetical scenarios and then to your own speech.

SUMMARY

As an evolving art, public speaking has changed from the classical era to today's information age in six key areas: who may speak, what makes a speaker credible, where speakers find information, what ethical challenges speakers face, how speakers deliver their speeches, and the audience's expectations. Tracing public speaking across the centuries illustrates how public speaking has evolved from a time when only well-educated men could speak, and only to a live audience, to an era in which nearly all members of society have the opportunity to speak and can choose among multiple delivery options.

In the public speaking class you're taking now, you'll acquire many transferable skills. Learning how to successfully present a speech increases self-confidence, improves listening skills, teaches audience adaptation and credibility strategies, expands your ability to locate and evaluate information, and provides techniques for better organizing and presenting your ideas.

Your public speaking class won't be the first time you give a speech—nor will it be the last. Many instructors across a wide variety of disciplines require student participation in discussions, debates, and presentations. Oral communication skills are essential to doing well in the workplace. Engaging in public talk at the community level keeps you informed and more connected with others. Speaking at social events contributes to important societal and cultural rituals.

Although new communication technologies have transformed how people communicate, four core ideas provide the foundation for public speaking in any age. First, public speaking requires audience-centered communication in which speakers focus on listeners' needs, knowledge, and interests. Second, public speakers must choose excellent supporting materials that fit the audience, topic, and occasion. Third, public speaking incorporates five arts, or divisions: invention, arrangement, style, memory, and delivery. These categories provide guidance in learning about public speaking and developing a speech. Fourth, public speaking encourages narrative thinking, allowing communicators to use their imaginations, recognize patterns, structure past events, and identify their relationships with each other and with the world.

Models of human communication have evolved from the transmission model that views communication as one-way, to more sophisticated models that incorporate today's complex communication environment. Public speaking has eight elements: speaker, message, channel, audience, noise, feedback, context, and environment. The speaker is the person who has the primary responsibility for presenting information. The speaker's message includes both verbal and nonverbal communication. Public speaking typically involves multiple channels of communication, such as integrating presentation media while speaking in person. The intended recipients of the speaker's message are the audience. Noise can interfere with the audience's ability to understand the message. The audience provides feedback in the form of nonverbal responses, questions and comments, and other communication with the speaker. The context for public speaking includes the physical setting and the occasion.

Key issues for today's public speaker center on ethics, cultural awareness, and using presentation software. Increased access to information puts greater ethical responsibilities on speakers to carefully research their speeches and scrupulously document their sources. Speakers must remain especially vigilant against plagiarism. Speaking today also requires applying critical thinking skills to reflect on and evaluate information. In addition, because they have so many opportunities to learn about others' perspectives, speakers must speak with cultural sensitivity. Finally, although presentation software provides an important mechanism for developing visually rich presentations, poor use of digital slides detracts from the speaker's message.

The speechmaking process involves six basic stages. First, determine your speech's topic and purpose. Second, analyze your audience so you can adapt your speech to them. Third, thoroughly research your topic. Fourth, organize your ideas in a way that fits your topic, purpose, and audience. Fifth, rehearse your speech aloud, preferably in front of an audience. Sixth, manage your voice and body, presentation media, audience, and time when you present your speech.

Even in today's information- and technology-driven age, excellent public speaking skills remain central to excelling personally and professionally, and for participating in a democratic society. Your public speaking class provides an important opportunity to learn the fundamentals of speaking in public. So get ready to speak up and make your voice heard.

Guide to Your Online Resources

Your Online Resources for *Public Speaking: The Evolving Art* give you access to the Speech Buddy video and activity featured in this chapter, additional sample speech videos, Speech Builder Express, InfoTrac College Edition, and study aids such as glossary flashcards, review quizzes, and the Critical Challenge questions for this chapter, which you can respond to via e-mail if your instructor so requests. In addition, your Online

Resources feature live WebLinks relevant to this chapter, including the Pew Internet & American Life Project, which reports on the impact of the internet on families, communities, work and home, daily life, education, health care, and civic and political life in the United States. Links are regularly maintained, and new ones are added periodically.

▼ REVIEW it DIRECTORY OF STUDY AND REVIEW RESOURCES

In the Book

Summary
Key Terms
Critical Challenges

More Study Resources

Speech Studio
Quizzes
WebLinks

Student Workbook

1.1: Introductory Speech
(Introduce Each Other)
1.2: Introductory Speech (Story)
1.3: Rating a Speaker in Terms
of All Five Canons
1.4: Adapt a Message to Different Audiences
1.5: Describe a Speech in Terms
of the Communication
Model

Speech Buddy Videos

Video Links

 Meeting the Speech
Buddies

Activity Links

 What Are Your Public
Speaking Goals?

▶ Sample Speech Videos

Adam, self-introduction
speech

Anna, "Study Abroad,"
impromptu speech

Uriel and Kelly, "El Equipo
Perfecto," self-introduction
speech

Speech Builder Express

Outline
Introduction
Conclusion

InfoTrac

Recommended search terms
Public speaking skills
Public speaking in the workplace
Public speaking at social events
Public speaking in the
community
Public speaking and storytelling
Confident public speaking
Managing speech anxiety
Ethical public speaking
Human communication models
Digital divide

Audio Study Tools

"Study Abroad," impromptu
speech by Anna

Critical thinking questions

Learning objectives

Chapter summary

Key Terms

arrangement 15

audience 19

audience-centered
   communication 14

channel 19

context 20

delivery 16

environment 20

feedback 20

invention 15

memory 16

message 19

narrative 16

noise 20

pervasive communication
   environment 18

public speaking 4

rhetoric 14

speaker 18

style 15

Critical Challenges

Questions for Reflection and Discussion

1. How important is storytelling when you get together with family and friends? Reflect on some of the stories your family or friends tell. What do those stories tell you about the connections between the family members or friends and their world? Can you identify a logical sequence the stories tend to follow? How do the stories spark your imagination?

2. The next time you seek information online—any kind of information—carefully consider the believability of the information. Ask yourself: Who posted this information? Why did they post it? What response do they want from me? Use your critical thinking skills to work on your information literacy skills.

3. Consider the other students in your public speaking class. How can you be culturally sensitive to your classmates' perspectives? What information can you provide your classmates so they can be more sensitive to your cultural background?

4. The information age brings with it special challenges for managing your communication environment, especially shutting out sources of noise. What are some strategies you can use as an audience member to combat noise that interferes with the speaker's message? As a speaker, what can you do to help your audience shut out noise?

5. How mindful are you in your communication with others? How much attention do you pay to the way you present your ideas? What can you do to become more mindful in all your interactions with others?

2 BUILDING YOUR CONFIDENCE

Andersen Ross/Getty Images

Stage fright. Speech phobia.

Communication apprehension. Speech anxiety. Whatever they're called, the feelings of uneasiness, panic, and even dread associated with public speaking are real and common. The vast majority of Americans find public speaking more frightening than natural disasters, cancer, and other life-threatening situations—even death.[1] Speech anxiety cuts across gender, ethnic background, age, and for students, even grade point average.[2]

Speakers experience a wide range of sensations and behaviors that spring from the internal causes of nervousness. They may include quavering voice, shaky hands, change in body temperature, itchy skin, dry mouth, mind going blank, increased heart rate, shortness of breath, increased rate of speech, trembling legs, sweaty palms, or cold hands and feet.[3] These symptoms can occur at any time—before, during, and after your speech.

Luckily, you can remove many of the causes of speech anxiety, reduce its symptoms, and use your nervous energy in positive ways. You've already taken the first step—research shows that completing a class in public speaking helps reduce speech anxiety.[4] In this chapter, you'll learn about why you get nervous in public speaking situations, how you can manage that anxiety, and ways to build your confidence. You'll always feel somewhat nervous when speaking in public.[5] That's natural and normal. The trick is to manage your anxiety so that your nervous energy helps, rather than hinders, your speech.

What Is Speech Anxiety?

READ it In the simplest terms, speech anxiety refers to fear of speaking in front of an audience. Speech anxiety begins with uncertainty.[6] For most people, speaking in public is not an everyday situation. You communicate with others every day, but probably not in a situation as formal and structured as a speech. The change in context from your regular, everyday interactions with others to an unfamiliar, public interaction naturally makes you nervous. To get an idea of your speech anxiety level, complete the Personal Report of Public Speaking Anxiety (PRPSA)[7] in **Figure 2.1**.

Fear of speaking in front of an audience.

▼ FIGURE 2.1

Personal Report of Public Speaking Anxiety (PRPSA)

Directions: Below are thirty-four statements that people sometimes make about themselves. Please indicate whether or not you believe each statement applies to you by marking whether you:

strongly disagree = 1   disagree = 2   are neutral = 3   agree = 4   strongly agree = 5

_____ 1. While preparing for giving a speech, I feel tense and nervous.

_____ 2. I feel tense when I see the words *speech* and *public speech* on a course outline when studying.

_____ 3. My thoughts become confused and jumbled when I am giving a speech.

_____ 4. Right after giving a speech, I feel that I have had a pleasant experience.

_____ 5. I get anxious when I think about a speech coming up.

_____ 6. I have no fear of giving a speech.

_____ 7. Although I am nervous just before starting a speech, I soon settle down after starting and feel calm and comfortable.

_____ 8. I look forward to giving a speech.

_____ 9. When the instructor announces a speaking assignment in class, I can feel myself getting tense.

_____ 10. My hands tremble when I am giving a speech.

_____ 11. I feel relaxed while giving a speech.

_____ 12. I enjoy preparing for a speech.

_____ 13. I am in constant fear of forgetting what I prepared to say.

_____ 14. I get anxious if someone asks me something about my topic that I don't know.

_____ 15. I face the prospect of giving a speech with confidence.

_____ 16. I feel that I am in complete possession of myself while giving a speech.

_____ 17. My mind is clear when giving a speech.

_____ 18. I do not dread giving a speech.

_____ 19. I perspire just before starting a speech.

_____ 20. My heart beats very fast just as I start a speech.

_____ 21. I experience considerable anxiety while sitting in the room just before my speech starts.

_____ 22. Certain parts of my body feel very tense and rigid while I am giving a speech.

_____ 23. Realizing that only a little time remains in a speech makes me very tense and anxious.

_____ 24. While giving a speech, I know I can control my feelings of tension and stress.

_____ 25. I breathe faster just before starting a speech.

_____ 26. I feel comfortable and relaxed in the hour or so just before giving a speech.

_____ 27. I do more poorly on speeches because I am anxious.

_____ 28. I feel anxious when the teacher announces the date of a speaking assignment.

_____ 29. When I make a mistake while giving a speech, I find it hard to concentrate on the parts that follow.

_____ 30. During an important speech, I experience a feeling of helplessness building up inside me.

_____ 31. I have trouble falling asleep the night before a speech.

_____ 32. My heart beats very fast while I present a speech.

_____ 33. I feel anxious while waiting to give my speech.

_____ 34. While giving a speech, I get so nervous that I forget facts I really know.

Scoring: To determine your score on the PRPSA, complete the following steps:

Step 1 Add the scores for items 1, 2, 3, 5, 9, 10, 13, 14, 19, 20, 21, 22, 23, 25, 27, 28, 29, 30, 31, 32, 33, and 34.

Step 2 Add the scores for items 4, 6, 7, 8, 11, 12, 15, 16, 17, 18, 24, and 26.

Step 3 Complete the following formula: 72 – total from step 2 + total from step 1 = your score on the PRPSA.

Your score should be between 34 and 170. If your score is below 34 or above 170, you have made a mistake in computing the score. Scores above 131 indicate high speech anxiety. Scores below 98 indicate low speech anxiety. Scores between 98 and 131 indicate moderate speech anxiety. Research on speech anxiety shows that the average score is 115.

Source: McCroskey, J. C. (1970)

Sources of Speech Anxiety

Speech anxiety stems from seven different sources of uncertainty: the speaker's role, your speaking abilities, your ideas, the audience's response, the setting, the technology used, and how others will evaluate you. Those sources are summarized in **Table 2.1**.

UNCERTAINTY ABOUT YOUR ROLE AS A SPEAKER

Like most people, you're probably much more familiar with listening than with speaking in public. In the speaker role, you may wonder, Will they understand me? How should I use notes? What does the audience expect? Those uncertainties can begin long before you present a speech—even in the early stages of preparation you might feel your heart rate go up as you think about your speech.[8] The less certain you are about your role as speaker, the more nervous you will feel about presenting a speech.

UNCERTAINTY ABOUT YOUR SPEAKING ABILITIES

A second uncertainty associated with public speaking concerns your speaking abilities. You may wonder, What am I able to do as a speaker? You likely haven't had many oppor-

TABLE 2.1 ▶ Uncertainties and Questions about Public Speaking

UNCERTAINTY ABOUT . . .	QUESTION SPEAKERS ASK THEMSELVES
the speaker's role	What should I do?
my speaking abilities	What am I able to do?
my ideas	How well do I know my topic?
the audience's response	How will others react?
the setting	How familiar/unfamiliar is the space?
the technology	Will the technology work?
how others will evaluate me	What impression will I make?

tunities to test your skills as a communicator in formal, structured situations. You may lack confidence in your abilities as a public speaker; you may not be sure you have the skills you need to speak effectively. If English is not your first language, you may also feel uncertain of your ability to make your message clear. The less confidence you have in your speaking skills, the more apprehension you will feel about public speaking.[9]

UNCERTAINTY ABOUT YOUR IDEAS

In everyday conversations you don't expect people to thoroughly research every topic they talk about. In contrast, your public speaking audience expects you to be an authority on your subject. Nobody wants to appear foolish, and certainly not in front of a group of peers. You may ask yourself, How well do I know my topic? The less sure you are about your knowledge of your topic, the more nervous you will feel about giving the speech.

UNCERTAINTY ABOUT THE AUDIENCE'S RESPONSE

When you have a pretty good idea about what will happen in a given situation, you feel fairly comfortable. In public speaking, you don't know exactly how audience members will respond to your message.[11] You might ask yourself, Will they understand my point? Will they respect me and my ideas? Will they agree or disagree with me? Will they find my speech interesting, or think it's boring? When you present a speech, you risk having your ideas rejected. The less you believe you can predict the audience's response to your speech, the more anxious you will feel.

UNCERTAINTY ABOUT THE SETTING

As a student, you're used to the instructor standing in the front of the room. As a speaker, you're the one up there in front. The room seems very different from this vantage point—and even more intimidating when you face an auditorium filled with 500 people. While you may be accustomed to public settings as an audience member, you're probably less used to such settings as a speaker.[12] The more unfamiliar the setting, the more nervous you may feel about your speech.

UNCERTAINTY ABOUT TECHNOLOGY

You instant message and chat with friends from your home computer. If you lose your internet connection, you may be annoyed and frustrated, but not embarrassed. In contrast, when the laptop you're using for your speech freezes, you panic and your anxiety level soars. When thinking about giving a speech, you'll probably ask, Will the technology work?

Lack of familiarity with technical equipment and concerns about it working increase a speaker's nervousness.

UNCERTAINTY ABOUT EVALUATION

Fear of negative evaluation plays a major role in students' anxiety about public speaking and contributes to physical symptoms such as elevated heart rate and queasiness. Even after you learn how your instructor grades speeches, you may feel nervous about how your classmates will respond. In other public speaking situations, such as giving an oral report at work or nominating someone at a meeting, speakers are also concerned about how others view them.[13] Research shows, however, that the **spotlight effect** leads a speaker to *think* people observe her or him much more carefully than they actually do.[14] Many of the little things you may do when speaking—stumbling over a word, briefly losing your train of thought, skipping to the wrong digital slide—are far more noticeable to you than to the audience. Of course, listeners will evaluate your presentation, but the spotlight probably isn't nearly as bright as you might think.

A phenomenon that leads us to think other people observe us much more carefully than they actually do.

Strategies for Building Your Confidence

The remainder of this chapter travels through the whole itinerary of the public speaking experience—from the weeks before the speech to the hours afterward—to identify what you can do at each stage to effectively manage speech anxiety and build your confidence. You'll learn about specific strategies for managing your speech anxiety as public speaking becomes a more familiar and comfortable activity.

MAINTAINING A POSITIVE ATTITUDE

Research shows that taking a positive attitude truly helps lessen your anxiety about speaking in front of others, while negative thoughts increase anxiety.[15]

Think of speech anxiety as intelligent fear, a natural response that can serve a positive purpose. With intelligent fear, you use the responses associated with fear, such as heightened emotions, increased sensitivity to your surroundings, and greater attention to sensory information, to give a better presentation.[16] Taking a positive attitude toward public speaking also can become a self-fulfilling prophecy in which you define the situation as positive one, leading you to act in ways that move you toward a positive outcome. If you have a positive attitude toward public speaking, you:

- Look forward to sharing information with your audience.
- View public speaking as an opportunity to influence others ethically.

- Welcome the chance to entertain others with humor and stories.
- Listen eagerly to what others have to say in their speeches and during discussion.

Feeling more positive about public speaking takes time; it won't happen overnight. Developing a positive attitude toward public speaking provides a first step toward managing your speech anxiety.

VISUALIZATION, RELABELING, AND RELAXATION

Visualization, relabeling, and relaxation are three methods you can use to view public speaking in a more positive way and improve your effectiveness when you speak.

Visualization

When you apply visualization to public speaking, you think through the sequence of events that will make up the speech in a positive, detailed, concrete, step-by-step way. Visualize the place, the audience, and yourself successfully presenting your speech. Focus on what will go right, not what will go wrong.[17] Use all your senses to really *feel* what will happen. Visualize yourself:

> Imagining a successful communication event by thinking through a sequence of events in a positive, concrete, step-by-step way.

- Gathering your notes, standing up, and walking to the front of the room.
- Facing the audience, making eye contact, smiling, and beginning the speech.
- Observing audience members nodding, jotting down a few notes, and listening intently.
- Presenting each main point.
- Incorporating effective presentation resources.
- Giving the conclusion and listening to audience members clapping.
- Answering questions readily.
- Thanking the audience, walking back to your seat, and sitting down.
- Congratulating yourself on giving an effective speech.

Psychologists, teachers, athletes, actors, and many others emphasize the importance of controlling your feelings when facing the challenge of a public presentation. You may already have visualized success in challenging situations. When you visualize your speech going well, you will reduce your anxiety and build your confidence.[18]

Relabeling

Relabeling involves assigning positive words or phrases to the physical reactions and feelings associated with speech anxiety. You stop using negative words and phrases like *fearful* and *apprehensive*, and instead use positive words like *thrilled* and *delighted*. When your voice quavers a bit and your hands shake, attribute those sensations to your body

> Assigning more positive words or phrases to the physical reactions and feelings associated with speech anxiety.

and mind gathering the energy they need to prepare for and present the speech. Say to yourself, "I'm really excited about giving this speech!" rather than, "I'm so nervous about this speech." Skeptical? Try it! Your anxiety won't magically disappear, but relabeling puts your response to public speaking in a positive light and can increase your ability to manage your anxiety.

Relaxation Techniques

Relaxation techniques help reduce the physical symptoms of stress, such as increased heart rate and tense muscles. Developing good breathing habits provides the foundation for relaxing. Three exercises increase breathing efficiency, reduce nervousness, and help you relax.[19]

The first exercise, *diaphragmatic breathing*, relies upon smooth, even breathing using your diaphragm. Sit or stand with your feet flat on the floor, shoulder width apart. With your hands just below your rib cage, breathe in with an exaggerated yawn while pushing your abdomen out. Exhale slowly and gently, letting your abdomen relax inward.

The second exercise, *meditation breathing*, helps your body relax. Begin by breathing with your diaphragm, but this time focus on every aspect of the breathing process and how it feels. Clear your mind of all thoughts and concentrate on the rhythm of your breathing: in breath, out breath, in breath, out breath.

The last exercise, *tension-release breathing*, combines diaphragmatic breathing with relaxing specific parts of your body. Begin by finding a comfortable position and breathing naturally. While you're breathing, identify tense muscle areas. Then inhale fully, using your diaphragm. As you slowly exhale, relax one tense muscle area. Continue this pro-

SPEAKING OF...

Can-do Language

How you label things shapes your experiences with them. Do you view difficult times as *challenges* or as *problems*? Do you focus on *opportunities* or on *barriers*? When you think of public speaking as a chore, you're probably not going to get very excited about your next speech. In contrast, if you think of public speaking as talking about your ideas and getting feedback from an audience, you're more likely to anticipate your next speech with enthusiasm. That enthusiasm can motivate you to thoroughly plan and prepare for your presentation.

TABLE 2.2 ▶ Visualization, Relabeling, and Relaxation

STRATEGY	BRIEF DEFINITION	EXAMPLE
Visualization	Imagining successful presentation	Envision audience's positive response to speech introduction.
Relabeling	Assigning positive words to anxious feelings	Use "lively" or "energetic" instead of "nervous."
Relaxation techniques	Reducing physical symptoms of stress	Engage in meditation breathing by focusing on how it feels to breathe.

cess until you feel completely relaxed. This exercise can be done systematically by starting at your head and progressing to your toes, or vice versa.[20]

Managing speech anxiety begins with developing a positive attitude toward public speaking. Visualizing a successful presentation, relabeling anxious feelings, and using relaxation techniques are three proven ways to increase your positive feelings and reduce your anxiety. **Table 2.2** summarizes these strategies.

Building Your Confidence before the Day of Your Speech

▼ You need more than a positive attitude to increase your confidence. Effectively completing all the planning and preparation steps in the speechmaking process will help you gain confidence in your speaking abilities and reduce your nervousness. Use the following strategies to manage anxiety as you develop your speeches.

START PLANNING AND PREPARING YOUR SPEECH EARLY

Getting an early start on speech preparation reduces speech anxiety. Schedule plenty of time to work on your speech—and stick with that schedule. Students who procrastinate invariably experience higher levels of speech anxiety than those who get an early start.[21]

Using Strategies for Managing Speech Anxiety

◀◀ ❚❚ ▶▶

In this video, Janine reviews and demonstrates the steps used in visualization, relabeling, and relaxing. You may want to watch the segment twice, first to find out how each strategy works, and then to take notes to use when you try the techniques yourself.

Anxiety Management Trainee

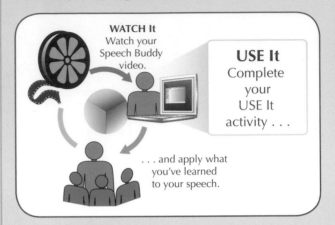

WATCH It
Watch your Speech Buddy video.

USE It
Complete your USE It activity . . .

. . . and apply what you've learned to your speech.

This activity guides you through visualizing, relabeling, and relaxing. After you've tried out each strategy, you're asked to identify which ones worked best for you.

CHOOSE A TOPIC YOU CARE ABOUT

If you're highly interested in your topic, you'll focus more on it and less on yourself.[22] Chapter 4 goes into greater detail about how to choose a topic. For now, consider some topics you might want to discuss with an audience. How passionate do you feel about these topics? Are you willing to speak out about them, even with people you may not know very well? Will you get *really* nervous talking about them in front of your audience? Some nervousness is okay, but if you think speaking on a particular topic will make your anxiety unmanageable, avoid that topic. Choose topics you find compelling, you believe others should know about, and you feel comfortable speaking about.

BECOME KNOWLEDGEABLE ABOUT YOUR TOPIC

Thoroughly researching your topic, discussed in depth in Chapter 6, will greatly increase your confidence and success as a public speaker.[23] What you present in your speech

Managing Time for Speech Preparation

Scheduling and managing time has never been easier, thanks to computer technology. The technology doesn't save you any time per se, but it can help you watch the calendar and the clock. Electronic reminders on your cell phone or e-calendar can encourage you to keep on schedule so that you actually *use* the time you block out to work on your speech. Use the calendar function on your cell phone, PDA, or computer to plot a timeline for creating your speech, and arrange for the program to send you reminders when milestones, such as completing your research, are approaching.

comprises only a small portion of what you know about the topic. If you *don't* do your research, you *will* be nervous about your speech.

LEARN ALL YOU CAN ABOUT YOUR AUDIENCE

Research your audience to reduce your uncertainty about who they are, what they know about your topic, how they feel about it, and how they are likely to respond (Chapter 5). Becoming familiar with your audience makes it easier to design your speech for them and increases the likelihood they will respond positively to it.[24]

PRACTICE YOUR SPEECH

Rehearse your speech until you feel comfortable talking about your topic (Chapter 11). If possible, practice in a location similar to the one where you'll give your speech—classroom, conference room, auditorium—to reduce your uncertainty about the setting. Practicing in front of others provides you with observers who can give you feedback and reduce your anxiety. And research shows that practicing your speech before an audience—especially four or more people—not only reduces your anxiety but also results in a higher evaluation of your presentation.[25] As you practice, you'll discover what body movements are appropriate for you and your speech. You'll also identify how best to use your notes and integrate presentation media.

Some people don't experience a high degree of anxiety when anticipating a public speaking situation. Although low anxiety may seem like an advantage, it can result in little motivation to plan and practice a speech. Failing to rehearse a speech, however, will have a negative impact on the presentation and likely result in increased anxiety during the speech.[26] Even the best speakers practice.

Fear that others will react negatively if one appears inept at using technological aids.

In addition, practicing with the technology you'll use reduces your **technophobia**—the fear of others reacting negatively when you appear technologically inept. If you haven't practiced with the technology, you'll feel unprepared, which is guaranteed to increase your anxiety and negatively impact your delivery.[27]

KNOW YOUR INTRODUCTION AND CONCLUSION WELL

Successfully presenting the introduction of your speech will boost your confidence, help calm your nerves, and reduce worrisome thoughts that increase anxiety.[28] Knowing that you'll finish with a smart, smooth, and memorable conclusion will increase your positive attitude and lessen your nervousness throughout your speech. One useful strategy for knowing your introduction and conclusion well is to write them out word for word. Then read them aloud a few times, listening to how they sound and making any necessary changes. Once you're satisfied with your introduction and conclusion, commit them to memory as best you can. Although generally you don't want to memorize your entire speech, memorizing your introduction and conclusion will help you present them more fluently and lessen your anxiety.

Careful planning and preparation reduce some of the uncertainties public speakers face. Implementing these long-term strategies increases your confidence and helps you generate positive feelings. The next section explains more short-term strategies for managing speech anxiety.

Building Your Confidence on the Day of Your Speech

If you've adopted a positive attitude toward public speaking and have planned, prepared, and practiced your speech, you should feel confident about your presentation. But still—your hands are shaking, your stomach is queasy, and your mouth is dry. How can you get rid of these last-minute jitters? The strategies in this section will help you manage your anxiety on the day of your speech.

BEFORE PRESENTING YOUR SPEECH

On the day of your speech, appearing confident keeps your positive energy alive. The following techniques provide ways to boost your confidence the day you give your speech.

- *Dress for the occasion.* Although great clothes can't make up for a poorly prepared speech, if you're dressed appropriately for the setting you'll feel more comfortable and your nervousness will lessen. Not sure what to wear? Think of how a speaker would dress to gain *your* respect. Choose clothes that convey a professional appearance and fit the occasion.

- *Keep all your notes and materials organized.* Put all the materials for your speech in a single location where you'll remember to bring them with you. When you arrive, arrange your things so you can calmly and confidently walk to the front of the room when it's your turn to speak.

- *Arrive early.* Give yourself plenty of time to get to your speaking location. If you come rushing in at the last minute, or even late, you'll increase your stress level.

▲ Dressing for the speaking occasion will give you confidence and lower your speech anxiety.

- *Take calming breaths.* Taking a few calming breaths before your speech will help you relax. Recall what you learned earlier in the chapter about diaphragmatic and meditation breathing. Exhale completely and then push out the last bit of air. Pause for a second or two, then gently inhale. Pause again, then exhale, this time as you would naturally. Follow this pattern for a minute or so, thinking only about how you're breathing. You should feel calmer as your body gets the oxygen it needs and you clear your mind and focus on what you're going to say.

- *Warm up your voice.* Get ready to speak by using your voice, either talking aloud in a private spot without others around or with other people at the speaking event. You'll warm up your voice, and chatting with others will help you relax.[29]

- *Make sure all technical aspects of your speech are ready to go.* If you are using a laptop computer and LCD projector that aren't yours, for example, be absolutely sure the equipment will be in the room. After you arrive, check that the system is set up and functioning properly. If you are using an overhead projector, make sure it works and provides a clear image on the screen. By taking care of these details, you will reduce technological uncertainty (Chapter 10).

- *Concentrate on the other speakers.* It's tempting to practice your speech one last time while you're waiting to speak, reviewing your notes while others are presenting. This increases speech anxiety because it requires you to focus on yourself. Instead, actively listen to what others are saying and you'll feel calmer.

You might even gather some information you can weave into your speech—and better adapt your message to your audience (Chapter 5). Writing down speakers' main points and participating in the question-and-answer sessions after their speeches will help focus your attention on what others have to say.

Keeping your speech anxiety in check during the hours and minutes of the day on which you present requires continued planning.

DURING YOUR SPEECH

Even with the most thorough preparation, you'll probably experience some anxiety as you give your speech. You can use the following strategies to manage anxiety during your presentation.

- *Display your positive attitude.* You've chosen a topic in which you're interested, done your research, analyzed your audience, organized your ideas, and practiced your speech. You're dressed for the occasion, and you arrived early at the location of your speech. You're an expert on your topic, and you're happy to have the opportunity to tell your audience about it. So when it's your turn to get up and speak, put into motion the positive scenario you previously visualized:

    Calmly walk to the front of the room.

    Face your audience and look at all your listeners.

    Take a deep breath and smile.

    Clearly, confidently, and enthusiastically begin your speech.

- *Expect to experience some speech anxiety.* You'll likely feel nervous at some point—it's normal! Most speakers become nervous before they speak, with anxiety generally decreasing after presenting the introduction,[30] but your anxiety may fluctuate throughout your speech. With more experience, you'll have a better idea of when you'll feel anxious. Remember, you're managing your speech anxiety, not getting rid of it.

- *Turn your anxiety into productive energy.* Relabel speech anxiety as a positive source of body energy. Put that nervousness to work in appropriate gestures, body movement, facial expressions, and tone of voice. For example, use the little energy jolt you feel when facing an audience to increase your voice volume and gesture expressively to highlight key points in your speech.

- *Avoid overanalyzing your anxiety.* As you present your speech you may wonder why you're experiencing some speech anxiety and be tempted to analyze it right then. But thinking about your speech anxiety distracts you from what you want to say and makes you more nervous. Acknowledge your anxiety, yet don't dwell on it. Later you can reflect on your presentation and how you felt.

- *Never comment on your speech anxiety*. Most people experience the illusion of transparency, believing their internal states, such as speech anxiety, are easily observable by others. Studies show that speakers consistently rate themselves as more nervous than audience members do.[31] However, if you don't say you're nervous, the audience won't know you are. But if you point it out, listeners will search for signs of nervousness, distracting them from what you're saying. Also, you'll sense their scrutiny and feel even more anxious. Instead, remain positive. If you feel and act confident, you'll be perceived that way.

  > The tendency of individuals to believe that how they feel is much more apparent to others than is really the case.

- *Focus on your audience, not on yourself*. Analyzing your audience (Chapter 5) helps you concentrate on their needs and interests rather than on yourself. Then you'll put your efforts toward effectively presenting your message, reducing your self-consciousness and nervousness. Viewing audience members as friends rather than opponents also diminishes anxiety.[32]

- *Pay attention to audience feedback*. When you display your positive attitude, your audience will return that energy with nods, smiles, and eye contact. This doesn't mean that every audience member will agree with your message, but they will find your confidence agreeable. This audience feedback reduces uncertainty about your role as a public speaker and lessens your anxiety.

- *Make no apologies or excuses*. If you misstate a point, get out of order on your major or minor points, or mispronounce a word, simply make the correction and go on. For example, if you realize you've missed a major point, finish the point you're discussing, then say something like, "To put this in context . . ." and go back to the point you accidentally skipped. Avoid excuses such as, "My computer crashed last night, so I don't have my digital slides." Excuses hurt your credibility, and your audience may respond negatively, heightening your own nervousness.

Nearly all speakers experience some speech anxiety during their presentations. Use that anxiety or energy to your advantage for a more focused and dynamic speech.

AFTER YOU'VE PRESENTED YOUR SPEECH

You might still feel some anxiety after you've finished your speech—that's perfectly normal. Here are some ways to manage that anxiety.

- *Listen carefully to audience members' questions*. Give yourself time to formulate your responses. Ask for clarification if you're not sure you understand a question.

Taking a Closer Look at Your Public Speaking Anxiety

◀◀ ❚❚ ▶▶

Anthony and Janine appear in this video. First they describe their dominant fears or sources of public speaking anxiety, and then they briefly discuss how they manage those fears.

What, Me Worry?

This activity gives you a chance to identify your own fears associated with public speaking and develop a plan for managing your speech anxiety.

For example, you might say, "I'm not exactly sure what you mean by that. Would you elaborate on your question?" Attending to audience members' questions with full concentration will keep the focus on your audience and help you manage anxiety. Many speakers find that their feelings of nervousness decrease considerably during the question-and-answer period after the formal speech.

- *Recognize that speech anxiety can occur even after you finish your speech.* Some speakers say that reflecting back on their speeches makes them more nervous than actually giving their speeches. When this happens, think about your overall presentation. Review what you did well and what you could improve next time, but don't blame yourself for any feelings of nervousness that you experience after your speech.

- *Reinforce your positive attitude.* Congratulate yourself on completing your speech. Reflect on all the work you put into your presentation.
- *Identify useful strategies for managing speech anxiety.* Recall the times during your speech when you felt most comfortable. What strategies worked well in managing your nervousness?
- *Develop a plan for managing anxiety to use in future public speaking situations.* You've learned about ways to manage speech anxiety, but you need to adjust those strategies to fit your personality and speaking style. List ways to manage anxiety that you'll apply in future speeches. Then consider additional strategies that will increase your confidence and decrease your nervousness.

For most speakers, speech anxiety tapers off at the end of the speech. But some speakers still experience some anxiety after the formal speech is completed.

Nearly everyone experiences speech anxiety, and you probably will, too. Speech anxiety won't go away, but you've learned about many ways to manage it. **Table 2.3** summarizes strategies for increasing confidence before, during, and after your speech.

TABLE 2.3 ▶ Strategies for Building Your Confidence

TIME LEADING UP TO SPEECH DAY	SPEECH DAY, BEFORE YOU SPEAK	SPEECH DAY, WHILE YOU'RE SPEAKING	SPEECH DAY, AFTER YOU SPEAK
• Maintain a positive attitude • Start speech preparation early • Choose a topic you care about • Become an expert in your topic • Thoroughly analyze the audience • Practice thoroughly and effectively • Know your introduction and conclusion • Use visualization • Use relabeling • Use relaxation techniques	• Dress appropriately • Keep all speech materials organized • Arrive early • Take calming breaths • Warm up your voice • Check on technical equipment • Listen to other speakers; don't mentally rehearse • Use visualization • Use relabeling • Use relaxation techniques	• Display your positive attitude • Expect to feel some anxiety • Turn anxiety into productive energy • Avoid overanalyzing your anxiety • Do not comment on your anxiety to your audience • Focus on the audience, not yourself • Attend to audience feedback • Make no apologies and give no excuses	• Listen to audience members' questions • Know that anxiety may occur • Reinforce your positive attitude • Identify effective anxiety management strategies • Develop plans for managing future speech anxiety

SUMMARY

You'll never be completely free of your fear of public speaking—and that's good. Why? Because those feelings motivate you to prepare for your speech. When you think about the day you're scheduled to speak, you should feel a little jolt and think, "I need to finish my research," "I need to learn more about my audience," or "I need to practice my speech again." Without nervousness to motivate you, you might not prepare thoroughly for your speech, and will likely do poorly as a result.

The key component of managing speech anxiety is developing a positive attitude toward public speaking. Visualization, relabeling, and relaxation techniques help you develop that attitude, increase your confidence as a speaker, and decrease your nervousness. Still, you need more than the right mental framework to manage your fear of public speaking. Thorough planning, preparation, and practice give you the confidence that you are truly ready for your presentation. All speakers must learn to live with feelings of nervousness. In this chapter, you've learned about many concrete strategies to cope with these feelings. As you develop ways to manage your speech anxiety, you'll become more confident as a speaker. Rather than overwhelming you, the nervousness you feel can help you present a dynamic, engaging, and audience-centered speech.

Guide to Your Online Resources

Your Online Resources for *Public Speaking: The Evolving Art* give you access to the Speech Buddy video and activity featured in this chapter, additional sample speech videos, Speech Builder Express, InfoTrac College Edition, and study aids such as glossary flashcards, review quizzes, and the Critical Challenge questions for this chapter, which you can respond to via e-mail if your instructor so requests. In addition, your Online Resources feature live WebLinks relevant to this chapter, including sites on sources of speech anxiety and additional relaxation techniques. Links are regularly maintained, and new ones are added periodically.

Key Terms

illusion of transparency 47	speech anxiety 34	technophobia 44
relabeling 39	spotlight effect 38	visualization 39

In the Book

Summary
Key Terms
Critical Challenges

More Study Resources

Speech Studio
Quizzes
WebLinks

Student Workbook

2.1: Identifying Confident
     Behaviors
2.2: Identifying Nervous
     Behaviors
2.3: Visualizing Success
2.4: In for Five, Hold for Five,
     Out for Five
2.5: Unique New York

Speech Buddy Videos

 Video Links

Using Strategies for Managing
Speech Anxiety

Taking a Closer Look at Your
Public Speaking Anxiety

Activity Links

Anxiety Management Trainee

What, Me Worry?

▶ **Sample Speech Videos**

Jessica, self-introduction
speech

Loren, "Wear a Ribbon,"
impromptu speech

 **Speech Builder
Express**

Outline
Introduction
Conclusion

 InfoTrac

Recommended search terms
Confident speech delivery
Anxiety and speech delivery
Managing speech anxiety
Visualization techniques
Relabeling techniques
Relaxation techniques

Audio Study Tools

Self-introduction speech by
Jessica

Critical thinking questions

Learning objectives

Chapter summary

Critical Challenges

Questions for Reflection and Discussion

1. One uncertainty speakers face in public speaking is how the audience will respond to their ideas. Reflect on situations in which you think an audience will reject your ideas. How might fear of rejection lead you to avoid possible speech topics? What might be some positive aspects of such avoidance? What might be the drawbacks of avoiding possible speech topics?

2. The spotlight effect suggests that speakers overestimate how much others notice their actions. Consider recent public speaking situations in which you've been an audience member, such as a classroom lecture or a presentation at work. Describe the speaker's attire and mannerisms, gestures, voice, main ideas, and other speech content. How observant were you? What are the implications of the spotlight effect? Are audience members not observant enough? Or are speakers too worried about themselves and how they appear to others?

3. One long-term strategy for building confidence is developing a positive attitude toward public speaking through visualization, relabeling, and relaxation techniques. Are there any negative aspects of developing a positive attitude? That is, can speakers be too positive? What issues might speakers need to be careful of in visualizing a successful presentation? Could relabeling prevent a speaker from accurately identifying important concerns? Can a speaker be too relaxed?

3 ETHICAL SPEAKING and LISTENING

SPEECH BUILDER EXPRESS

SPEECH Studio

© Ronald Karpilo/Alamy

Ethical communication refers to the moral aspects of speaking and listening, such as being truthful, fair, and respectful. Ethics are central to human communication. In a few important ways, digital technology has increased the ethical responsibilities communicators must accept when they interact with others.[1] For instance, you now have access to a wealth of information online. How do speakers apply ethical standards to determine what information to use and what to avoid? You can also easily integrate audio and video files into presentations. What ethical guidelines should speakers apply when using these media? Colin Powell, for instance, used digital imagery in presenting his case to the United Nations for invading Iraq. Later, some of those images, such as satellite photos, turned out not to be what he claimed they were.[2] Although the U.N. did not pass a resolution supporting the war, the U.S. Congress found the message persuasive and voted to authorize the president to send troops to Iraq.

Audience members also have digital technology at their disposal that raises

ethical communication
The moral aspects of our interactions with others, including truthfulness, fairness, responsibility, integrity, and respect.

ethical dilemmas. Should listeners record a speech without the speaker's knowledge? When two reporters taped a Supreme Court justice's speech to students in Mississippi without permission, a U.S. marshal forced them to erase the recordings.[3] As a public figure, what the justice has to say is newsworthy, yet the reporters failed to notify the justice of their intent to record the speech. Ethical issues such as these present challenges for both public speakers and their audiences.

Ethical Responsibilities in the Classroom

READ it According to the National Communication Association (NCA), "ethical communication enhances human worth and dignity by fostering truthfulness, fairness, responsibility, personal integrity, and respect for self and other."[4] This short statement offers clear guidance for speakers. For example, ethical speakers present accurate information, consider all sides of an issue, carefully research their topics, and demonstrate respect for themselves and their audiences.

The psychological and emotional tone that develops as communicators interact with one another.

The statement also applies to audience members. Our listening skills form an important basis for a productive **communication climate**—the psychological and emotional tone that develops as people interact with others.[5] Ethical listeners come to a speaking event prepared to use active listening skills and provide meaningful feedback. Working together, ethical speakers and listeners promote a supportive communication climate in which everyone feels free to express ideas in a respectful manner. In contrast, a defensive communication climate develops when listeners and speakers behave disrespectfully and inhibit the free expression of ideas.

As a speaker and listener in your public speaking class, you can help create an ethical community of communicators in which each person assumes personal and shared responsibility. A public speaking class requires each student to assume a high degree of personal responsibility because so much of the work is undertaken outside of class. To excel in this class, you must make a firm commitment to developing your public speaking skills. A strong and enjoyable sense of community develops as speakers and listeners share the responsibility of working together to produce a supportive communication climate.

Building Community Online

Online communication can help you build community in your public speaking class. Social networking sites such as Facebook and MySpace allow you to develop webpages for others in your class to view. Your classmates get to know more about you, and you get to know more about them. This information makes it easier to analyze your audience and helps build a sense of community. In addition, you can use e-mail and chat to form online study groups and interact with others in class. With internet communication, developing a supportive classroom community isn't limited to the few hours a week you may meet in person.

Principles of Ethical Communication

Many professional organizations have adopted codes of ethics. For example, the National Speakers Association requires members to sign an ethics statement before they join. The Academy of Management established ethical principles to guide members in their teaching, research, management practices, and professional interactions. Similarly, the Association for Educational Communications and Technology adopted a code of ethics centered on commitment to the individual, society, and the profession.[6] **Table 3.1** on pages 58 and 59 provides abbreviated versions of these organizations' codes of ethics.

The National Communication Association outlines a set of principles for ethical communicators that are especially relevant to public speaking (**Figure 3.1** on page 60)[7]. The following section discusses each of these principles.

TRUTHFULNESS, ACCURACY, HONESTY, AND REASON

Communication is the fundamental social behavior that links one human being to another. Just as you want to be respected, so do others. You create this respect through truthful, accurate, honest, and logical interaction with others. Truthfulness includes crediting sources of information. A high school principal in New York recently lost his job when it was revealed he had given a commencement address using someone else's speech, reciting it word for word and not mentioning the true author. And an Oregon radio station canceled a local chef's cooking show when station managers found out he used information from other sources without acknowledgment.[8]

Ethical audience members listen completely to the speaker's message and provide constructive feedback. During the question-and-answer session that often follows a speech, for instance, make relevant comments that demonstrate that you listened carefully to the speaker's ideas.

TABLE 3.1 ▶ Codes of Ethics for Three Professional Organizations

NATIONAL SPEAKERS ASSOCIATION (NSA) CODE OF PROFESSIONAL ETHICS	ACADEMY OF MANAGEMENT (AOM) GENERAL ETHICAL PRINCIPLES	ASSOCIATION FOR EDUCATIONAL COMMUNICATIONS AND TECHNOLOGY (AECT) CODE OF ETHICS
ARTICLE 1 The NSA member shall accurately represent qualifications and experience in both oral and written communications. ARTICLE 2 The NSA member shall act, operate his/her business, and speak on a high professional level so as to neither offend nor bring discredit to the speaking profession. ARTICLE 3 The NSA member shall exert diligence to understand the client's organization, approaches and goals in advance of the presentation. ARTICLE 4 The NSA member shall avoid using materials, titles and thematic creations originated by others, either orally or in writing, unless approved by the originator. ARTICLE 5 The NSA member shall treat other speakers with professional courtesy, dignity and respect.	1. RESPONSIBILITY AOM members establish relationships of trust with those with whom they work (students, colleagues, administrators, clients). They are aware of their professional and scientific responsibilities to society and to the specific communities in which they work. AOM members uphold professional standards of conduct, clarify their professional roles and obligations, accept appropriate responsibility for their behavior, and seek to manage conflicts of interest that could lead to exploitation or harm. 2. INTEGRITY AOM members seek to promote accuracy, honesty, and truthfulness in the science, teaching, and practice of their profession. In these activities AOM members do not steal, cheat, or engage in fraud, subterfuge, or intentional misrepresentation of fact. They strive to keep their promises, to avoid unwise or unclear commitments, and to reach for excellence in teaching, scholarship, and practice. They treat students, colleagues, research subjects, and clients with respect, dignity, fairness, and caring.	SECTION 1. COMMITMENT TO THE INDIVIDUAL In fulfilling obligations to the individual, the members: 1. Shall encourage independent action in an individual's pursuit of learning and shall provide open access to knowledge regardless of delivery medium or varying points of view of the knowledge. 2. Shall protect the individual rights of access to materials of varying points of view. 3. Shall guarantee to each individual the opportunity to participate in any appropriate program. SECTION 2. COMMITMENT TO SOCIETY In fulfilling obligations to society, the member: 1. Shall honestly represent the institution or organization with which that person is affiliated, and shall take adequate precautions to distinguish between personal and institutional or organizational views. 2. Shall represent accurately and truthfully the facts concerning educational matters in direct and indirect public expressions. 3. Shall not use institutional or Associational privileges for private gain.

FREEDOM OF EXPRESSION, DIVERSITY OF PERSPECTIVE, AND TOLERANCE OF DISSENT

Ethical communication means respecting the U.S. Constitution, especially the First Amendment:

> Congress shall make no law respecting an establishment of religion, or prohibiting the free exercise thereof; or abridging the freedom of speech, or of the press; or the right of the people peaceably to assemble, and to petition the Government for a redress of grievances.

This amendment embodies the basic principle that freedom, diversity, and tolerance for differing viewpoints are essential to democracy. For public speaking, this principle gives you the freedom to speak your mind about controversial topics. But with that freedom comes the responsibility to research your topics so that the speeches you give reflect

▼ FIGURE 3.1

National Communication Association Ethical Principles

1. We advocate truthfulness, accuracy, honesty, and reason as essential to the integrity of communication.

2. We endorse freedom of expression, diversity of perspective, and tolerance of dissent to achieve the informed and responsible decision making fundamental to a civil society.

3. We strive to understand and respect other communicators before evaluating and responding to their messages.

4. We promote access to communication resources and opportunities as necessary to fulfill human potential and contribute to the well-being of families, communities, and society.

5. We promote communication climates of caring and mutual understanding that respect the unique needs and characteristics of individual communicators.

6. We condemn communication that degrades individuals and humanity through distortion, intimidation, coercion, and violence, and through the expression of intolerance and hatred.

7. We are committed to the courageous expression of personal convictions in pursuit of fairness and justice.

8. We advocate sharing information, opinions, and feelings when facing significant choices while also respecting privacy and confidentiality.

9. We accept responsibility for the short- and long-term consequences for our own communication and expect the same of others.

Source: National Communication Association, 1999.

an informed perspective. You may have strong views about contentious subjects such as cloning, the death penalty, and immigration. Informed and responsible public speaking requires that you learn about these topics so that you can articulate your position in meaningful ways.

Respecting others' perspectives is one hallmark of the effective listener, which is discussed in greater detail later in this chapter.[9] For example, instead of avoiding speakers whose positions differ from yours, this ethical principle suggests that you attend those presentations and listen with an open mind in order to better understand viewpoints that differ from your own.

UNDERSTANDING AND RESPECT FOR OTHER COMMUNICATORS

You show respect for a speaker's ideas by demonstrating your interest—maintaining eye contact, taking notes, and giving relevant feedback. As the speaker is talking, consider the main points presented in light of what you already know about the topic. Also fully understand the speaker's message before responding. For example, if you disagree with a speaker's position on gun control, you might want to first check for clarification, saying something like, "If I understand you correctly, you support our current laws on gun ownership and want no changes in those laws. Is that a fair interpretation?"

Similarly, as a speaker, listen carefully and respectfully to questions. Try to gather more information from listeners if they object to your ideas. You might say, "In my research, I found strong support for changing our current gun laws. But I know not everyone agrees with that position, including some experts. So I'd like to hear more about your thinking on the issue." In addition, listen to questions without interruption before responding.

▲ Speaking out about contentious topics is one of the hallmarks of a democratic society, but be informed when you speak out and listen carefully to all viewpoints.

ACCESS TO COMMUNICATION RESOURCES AND OPPORTUNITIES

Without the resources needed to communicate, individuals lose the opportunity to participate in their immediate and larger communities. As a speaker, adhering to this ethical principle means using all the resources available as you progress through the speechmaking process. The ethical speaker also participates in public discussions and encourages others to join in. The ethical listener thoughtfully considers and responds to what others say, increasing all participants' access to information in the process.

Hate Speech versus Free Speech

Professor Gerald Uelmen, dean of Santa Clara University's Law School and a fellow of the Markkula Center for Applied Ethics, presents arguments both for and against campus hate speech codes. In arguing for such codes, he notes the harm done to individual students and the campus climate when colleges and universities allow hate speech. He also notes that restricting hate speech encourages logical debates, rather than relying on denigration and oppression. In arguing against such codes, Professor Uelmen observes that they run counter to the First Amendment's guarantee of free speech. In addition, students may avoid speaking out and expressing their opinions, fearful of violating the hate speech code. To learn more about this issue, read Professor Uelmen's comments on the Center's website, scu.edu/ethics.

Words that attack groups such as racial, ethnic, religious, and sexual minorities.

PROVIDING A COMMUNICATION CLIMATE OF CARING AND MUTUAL UNDERSTANDING

Creating a supportive communication climate gives everyone an equal opportunity to communicate and encourages the open exchange of ideas. As an ethical speaker, you'll deliver speeches that address the needs of specific audience members. For example, you'd deliver a very different speech on emergency preparedness to third-graders than you would to college students. As an ethical listener, give each speaker your undivided attention—turn off your cell phone, avoid irrelevant comments and distracting movements, and focus on the speaker's message.

AVOIDING AND CONDEMNING DEGRADING COMMUNICATION

Words *do* hurt people.[10] **Hate speech**—words that attack groups such as racial, ethnic, religious, and sexual minorities—is hurtful and degrading. That's why many colleges and universities have adopted policies against hate speech. And research shows that those policies work. Although college students report high levels of tolerance for diverse viewpoints, the same is *not* true for hate speech.[11] Avoid using hate language in your speeches, and challenge others who use it.

COURAGEOUS EXPRESSION OF PERSONAL CONVICTIONS

It's difficult to speak out against perceived injustices in society, but often that's how social progress is made. In the twentieth century, because a few people were willing to speak out in support of voting reforms, women and African Americans—who before that time had been excluded from political life—gained the right to vote. That's the kind of situation in which freedom of expression counts most. In choosing your speech topics, embrace ethical issues that demand your audience's attention.

Henry Louis Gates, Jr., chair of the African and African American Studies Department at Harvard University, provides a good example of courageous expression of personal convictions. In a speech at the Commonwealth Club, he made the following statement:

> The other reason our people are still impoverished . . . is because we need a revolution in attitude and behavior within the African-American community itself. No white racist makes you get pregnant when you're 16 years old. We do not have time for this form of behavior anymore. It is killing our people. No white racist makes you drop out of school. No white racist makes you not do your homework. No white racist makes you equate academic or intellectual success

with being white. If George Wallace and Bull Connor and Orval Faubus had sat down, in their wildest drunken bourbon fantasies in 1960, and said, "How can we continue to control them niggras?"—as they would have said—one of them would have said, "You know, we could persuade them to have babies in their teens, do crack cocaine, run drugs, and equate education not with being Thurgood Marshall, Martin Luther King, but with being white. Then we'll have them." Ladies and gentlemen, that's what's happened to our people. We have lost the blackest aspect of the black tradition.[12]

Those are tough words. But Professor Gates chose to speak out about his ideas for regaining what he called "the black tradition," even if those ideas might be controversial for his audience. Choosing to speak about and listen to topics such as disability rights, racial profiling, and child labor shows a genuine commitment to fighting injustice.

SHARING INFORMATION, OPINIONS, AND FEELINGS

Ethical communication requires gathering as much information as possible, but *never* at the expense of others' right to privacy and confidentiality. Suppose you e-mail an expert on your topic. Is it all right to use the person's reply without asking for permission? Although legally most e-mail is considered public communication, people generally think of e-mail exchanges between individuals as private communication. In this case, ask the person's permission before including the information in your speech, and then tell your audience the source. Clearly, public online communication, such as listservs, chats, newsgroups, and other discussion forums, typically aren't considered private. Still, it's best to check with the group before using any information they provide.

GUARDING AGAINST THE THREAT OF UNETHICAL COMMUNICATION

Imagine a world where ethics and morality didn't influence life. Would you choose to live in that world? Let's consider a hypothetical example. Assume that a student speaker described the health benefits of a variety of herbal medicines sold in natural foods stores. The speaker didn't take enough time to research the topic, relying on a single pamphlet for information. Several audience members decided to try the medications and later reported that they were expensive and did not help them at all. A few even became ill. This may seem like an extreme example, but you might be surprised by the degree to which audience members take you seriously and act on information you give them.

ACCEPTING RESPONSIBILITY FOR THE CONSEQUENCES OF OUR COMMUNICATION

This principle is particularly relevant today, when a speech presented to a small audience may eventually be transmitted far beyond the immediate context and live forever in electronic archives. For example, when he was speaking with newspaper publishers at a convention in San Francisco, California, Governor Arnold Schwarzenegger suggested closing the U.S. border with Mexico. His comments caused a public outcry. He quickly apologized, saying he meant "secure" the border, not close it. By taking responsibility for what he had said, Governor Schwarzenegger corrected the harm his words might have caused. Everyone says things they didn't mean to say. When you do make mistakes, recognize your error and repair the damage.

As these principles suggest, ethical speakers respect and encourage diverse opinions, do not tolerate communication that degrades and harms others, balance sharing information with respect for privacy, and listen closely before evaluating and critiquing. These principles apply to all your communication interactions, not just in your role as a public speaker or audience member.

Recognizing and Avoiding Plagiarism

Presenting someone else's ideas and work, such as speeches, papers, and images, as your own.

Reports of plagiarism and other forms of academic dishonesty are rising on college campuses around the world.[13] **Plagiarism** refers to taking someone else's ideas and work, including speeches, papers, and images, and presenting them as your own, whether intentionally or unintentionally. A recent survey found that over one-third of college students reported copying information directly from an internet source without providing a reference.[14] That's one form of plagiarism, but you don't have to copy something word for word to plagiarize. Using other people's ideas without crediting them is plagiarism, too.

COPYRIGHT LAWS AND FAIR USE

A type of intellectual property law that protects an author's original work (such as a play, book, song, or movie) from being used by others.

Presenting others' work as your own not only violates basic ethical principles but is illegal. Article I, Section 8, of the United States Constitution provides the basis for **copyright** or intellectual property laws:

> The Congress shall have power . . . to promote the progress of science and useful arts, by securing for limited times to authors and inventors the exclusive right to their respective writings and discoveries.

Copyright laws, including the Digital Millennium Copyright Act of 1998, protect original published and unpublished works that authors develop from others using those works. **Fair use,** however, allows you to use *limited* portions of an author's work *if* you credit the source of the information. Citing your sources also allows your audience to learn more about your topic and check your evidence. If you're presenting information you believe your audience might view unfavorably, citing your sources lets them know that the ideas did not originate with you.[15] Finally, citing your sources tells the audience you've done your research on the topic.

> Using someone else's original work in a way that does not infringe on the owner's rights, generally for educational purposes, literary criticism, and news reporting.

CITING SOURCES IN YOUR SPEECH

Effective public speakers provide **oral citations,** or brief references to their sources, during their speeches. The following examples demonstrate how to set up an oral citation and punctuate it:

> Brief reference to a source during a speech.

> According to the Disability Rights and Independent Living Movement website, "People with disabilities throughout history have been defined as objects of shame, fear, pity, or ridicule."

> Here's another holiday present—computer viruses. A recent article in the *Detroit Free Press* noted that as spammers flood inboxes with junk mail, viruses and worms follow along. And instant messages have become a favorite virus target as links to infected files are designed to look like they come from your friends.

Janice L. Krieger, a communication consultant, found in her research that "shared mindfulness"—individuals actively processing information together—produced highly effective decisions in crisis situations. Her article in the *Journal of Business Communication* focused on how aviation students' communication contributed to or detracted from mindfulness when they faced an emergency in the cockpit.

In each of these cases, the speaker orally tells the audience who authored or published a particular piece of information. Chapter 6 provides additional guidelines for integrating oral citations into your speeches, along with instructions on how to include written citations in your speech outline.

Copyright laws also cover visual and audio materials such as films, songs, and photographs. When you integrate these materials into your speeches, cite your sources just as you do with more traditional forms of information. For example, if you include a brief clip from a movie, tell your audience the film's title. Similarly, name an artist's song either before or after playing the short segment. With images, simply include the source on your digital slide or overhead transparency, as **Figure 3.2** shows.

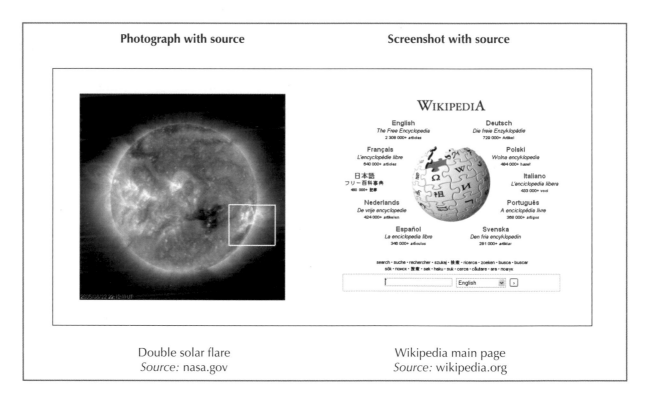

► FIGURE 3.2
Sample Images with Sources

Photograph with source — Double solar flare
Source: nasa.gov

Screenshot with source — Wikipedia main page
Source: wikipedia.org

Recognizing the importance of avoiding plagiarism is part of being an ethical speaker. Keeping careful records of the information you gather for your speech is the first step in avoiding plagiarism. You'll use the notes you take during your research to accurately attribute what you say to the appropriate source. In addition, orally citing your sources lets the audience know you've done your research, and that in turn enhances your credibility.

Ethics and Cultural Diversity

Applying the ethics of communication requires you to respect cultural differences.[16] **Culture** refers to shared values, beliefs, and activities.[17] Cultural commonalities and differences are constructed, reinforced, and revealed through communication. People become socialized into their own cultures directly through communication with their family, friends, and neighbors, for instance, but also indirectly through the media

> Values, beliefs, and activities shared by a group.

WATCH it SPEECH BUDDY VIDEO LINK

Avoiding Plagiarism

◀◀ ❙❙ ▶▶

In this video, Erin shows examples of how to correctly cite sources in a speech as well as examples of when not citing sources results in plagiarism. You may want to take notes for reference later.

USE it ACTIVITY LINK

But Is It Plagiarism?

This activity asks you to evaluate excerpts from sample speeches to determine whether sources have been acknowledged properly.

and other social institutions. So culture is about what people share as a group and what makes their group different from other groups.[18] **Cultural diversity** refers to differences in cultural backgrounds and practices around the globe.

Cultural norms are rules for how members of a culture should behave. Some norms are explicit or stated, such as military codes of conduct. Most norms, however, are implicit or unstated, such as how to act when attending a guest lecture on campus. No one tells you how to behave at a lecture. Instead, you learn by observing what other people do in this and similar situations. Because norms are rules rather than laws, communicators may negotiate changes or modifications in norms. For example, your classmates and instructor might discuss the best way to structure the question-and-answer session after a speech rather than adhere to the same structure all the time. In addition, norms generally change over time in response to changes in the environment. For example, when mobile phones were first introduced, communicators didn't have any norms to govern when people made or received calls. Now, especially in public places, there are explicit norms about mobile phone use. Most instructors enforce the rule that mobile phones and similar communication devices must be turned off during class.

What is appropriate in one culture may not be appropriate in another. When you're speaking publicly, your audience likely will include a range of cultural differences based on age, gender, ethnicity, disabilities, religion, sexual orientation, and socioeconomic level. Effectively analyzing your audience will help you adapt to your audience's cultural norms.

AVOIDING ETHNOCENTRISM

Ethnocentrism is the belief that our view of the world is better than anyone else's. Of course, individuals seldom consciously think, "My perspective is the best." Ethnocentrism appears when communicators think, "How can *those people* believe in *that*?" or, "People over/under 40 just don't know what's really going on in the world." When you start thinking that anything different from your point of view is inherently wrong, strange, or bad, you're experiencing ethnocentrism.

Ethnocentrism influences how individuals evaluate other communicators' competence and credibility.[19] That is, the more ethnocentric people are, the more likely they are to think individuals who appear different from them are less trustworthy and capable. Ethnocentric listeners, for instance, may respond negatively to a speaker who doesn't share their cultural background. It's okay to disagree with others' perspectives. The problem occurs when you think our way of doing things is always better.

Ethnocentrism can also prevent people from speaking out about difficult issues, especially those associated with race, class, and gender.[20] When communicators think ethnocentrically, they avoid questioning societal and cultural practices that promote discrimi-

Differences in cultural backgrounds and practices around the globe.

Prescriptions for how people should interact and what messages should mean in a particular setting.

The belief that one's own worldview, based on one's own cultural background, is correct and best.

nation against people based on their ethnic background, religious beliefs, socioeconomic status, sexual orientation, disability, sex, and other demographic categories. Confronting ethnocentrism means confronting accepted ways of doing things that disadvantage particular groups of people. Thus, in recounting his experiences as a civil rights attorney, lawyer Johnnie Cochran told his audience about how he came to question and then challenge an accepted way of doing things in law enforcement:

> In Los Angeles, we had this infamous choke hold, applied by the Los Angeles Police Department officers very often to women, children, whomever. It was a surprise maneuver, to take somebody down, where the officer felt this person might give them some trouble: a shoulder smash, the officer's behind you, you're choked out, in submission. The problem with the application of this hold in Los Angeles in 1979 and 1980 was that 17 young men died as a result of this choke hold. Fifteen were black and two were brown, and so it was being applied to these young people, perhaps the disenfranchised of society, and I had a lot of concern about that.

> About 1981, I got the James Thomas Mincey case. He was choked out; he didn't die right away, his mother observed it, she was one of my star witnesses and we ended up winning that case. But more important than winning, we used that case to obtain a moratorium on the choke hold in Los Angeles. The chief of police then was Darryl Gates. They were trying to understand why it was that all these black kids were dying and Darryl Gates's famous quote was, "Well, you know, with 'normal' people. . ." As though African Americans weren't.[21]

In his speech, Cochran revealed the serious consequences that can result from ethnocentrism and the difficulty of challenging long-held beliefs. He also noted the offensiveness of the police chief's ethnocentric comment suggesting that African Americans are not normal.

Stepping out of your own cultural beliefs and values can prove challenging because your cultural worldview is so much a part of your sense of self. All individuals come to accept their perspectives as simply the way things are and should be. But when people believe their way of thinking is superior to other ways, they're practicing ethnocentrism and violating the principles of ethical communication.

AVOIDING SEXISM

Exhibiting cultural sensitivity also means recognizing the role of gender in public speaking. While *sex* refers to the biological category a person's body fits into (female, male, or intersex), *gender* refers to socially established roles defining what is perceived as masculine and feminine in a given culture.

At many different times throughout history, public speaking was considered an activity unbecoming to women. In ancient Greece, girls attended school and learned a wide range of subjects, but not public speaking.[22] Women were prohibited from speaking out in public venues. The early history of the United States reflects a similar bias. The first reported speech by a woman occurred in Indiana in 1828. Twenty years later, with the start of the woman suffrage movement, more and more women took to the podium to speak out for women's voting rights to audiences who shouted, heckled, threw rotten vegetables, and spit on them.[23]

Today you expect to hear both women and men giving speeches. Still, because of gender roles, audience members often have different expectations for male and female speakers. As a result, audiences tend to evaluate a speaker's credibility based partly on gender. For example, audiences focus closely on the trustworthiness of a female speaker's sources but are more concerned with how a male speaker organizes his ideas, maintains eye contact, and uses his voice. Even when speakers exhibit similar behaviors, men often are viewed as more persuasive than women.[24]

Sensitivity to gender requires that speakers make conscious language choices. Use gender-neutral or nonsexist language such as *humanity*, *fire fighter*, and *flight attendant* rather than gendered language such as *mankind*, *fireman*, and *stewardess*. In addition, frame topics to appeal to all listeners. If you give a speech on the importance of team sports for girls, for instance, make your topic relevant and interesting to everyone in your audience. You might do this by pointing out what girls learn when they play team sports and how those lessons help them function better in society—a benefit for everyone.

Listening and Public Speaking

To find out how people use their local libraries, members of the board of the Americans for Libraries Council embarked on a nationwide "listening tour." Maine's Governor's Office on Health Policy and Finance launched a listening tour to find out citizens' perspectives on a state health care plan. In St. Petersburg, Florida, school superintendent Clayton Wilcox held four listening tours to gather parents' ideas for greater community involvement in the public schools. Hillary Rodham Clinton began her first U.S. Senate bid with a listening tour.[25] All these listening tours highlight the importance of listening in a democratic society.

Especially in a public speaking class, communicators place most of our focus on speaking. Yet without listeners we would not have speakers. On speech days, ethical listeners arrive early, prepare themselves to listen carefully, take notes, and respond appropriately to speakers' ideas and perspectives. Making a commitment to listen is a vital part of ethical communication, but it's just the beginning.

CHARACTERISTICS OF LISTENING

Hearing is the physical process of receiving sounds. **Listening** involves much more: not only receiving or hearing but also selecting, assigning meaning to, responding to, and recalling sensory stimuli.[26] How do you become an excellent listener? In developing your listening skills, it helps to understand the basic characteristics of good listening (see **Table 3.2**).

The physical response to sounds.

Involves hearing, interpreting, responding to, and recalling verbal and nonverbal messages.

Listening Is Creative

Listening is creative in that you apply your imagination, past experiences, and knowledge to what others say. You take speakers' words, tone of voice, and body movements and use these to create for yourself the meaning of their messages. For example, when others talk about their childhood adventures, you might associate what the speakers say with your own experiences while growing up.

Listening Is a Dynamic Process

As a dynamic process, listening is an ongoing, ever-changing collaboration between speaker and listener.[27] Do you feel both tired and inspired after listening to your classmates' speeches? You should! The activity of listening requires your complete concentration and attention—your energy. But there's a nice reward: The information you gather from your classmates' speeches will stimulate new ideas and thoughts.

Listening Is Intentional

Listening depends on your intention to focus on the speaker as you strive to comprehend the meaning of the person's message. As a listener, dedicate yourself to listening carefully to each speaker. As a speaker, listen to your audience's responses and questions.

TABLE 3.2 ▶ Characteristics of Listening

LISTENING IS:	LISTENING INVOLVES:
• creative • intentional • a dynamic process	• all the senses • interpretation • response • being selective

Listening Is Selective

In listening, you selectively receive and attend to aural and other sensory stimuli. At times, you make a conscious decision to listen (or not listen) to what others are saying. At other times, you are not aware of the choices you make. **Information overload** occurs when you receive too much information and are unable to interpret it in a meaningful way.[28] Selective listening helps you identify and interpret what is important and what is not from all the information you receive every day.

Occurs when individuals receive too much information and are unable to interpret it in a meaningful way.

Listening Involves All the Senses

When you listen, you concentrate on what others say and how they say it.[29] Physical settings, gestures, movements, vocal qualities, eye contact, and facial expressions all contribute to your interpretations of others' messages. So when you listen to a speech, you notice all these aspects of the situation. Then you use that information as you interpret the speaker's message.

Listening Involves Interpretation

When you listen to others, you *interpret,* or assign meaning to, their messages based on your own experiences and knowledge. However, the interpretive element of listening is not a completely individualistic process because your culture and society provide shared frameworks for interpreting messages.[30]

Listening Involves Response

Appropriate verbal and nonverbal responses let speakers know you're paying attention and reflect your effectiveness as a listener. Smiling, making eye contact, nodding in agreement, and other nonverbal cues show that you're listening.[31] You might also ask questions at the end of a speech.

TYPES OF LISTENING

There are different reasons for listening and different ways of listening.

- In *empathic* listening, you want to know the feelings and emotions the speaker is conveying. When a speaker is giving a eulogy, for instance, you listen with compassion and understanding to the emotional components of the message.
- In *appreciative* listening, you listen for enjoyment, as when listening to a stand-up comedy routine or an after-dinner speech.
- When you listen for *content,* you gather information, focusing on the speaker's main ideas, as when an instructor lectures.

- Finally, *critical* listening requires that you evaluate the speaker's credibility, ideas, and supporting evidence.

Most public speaking situations call for critical listening. For example, when listening to a persuasive speech, you might try to identify the feelings that motivated the speaker to choose her or his topic. You might also laugh at a humorous story and smile as you recall a similar situation. You might want to take a few notes on the main ideas presented. Once you've listened with empathy, with appreciation, and for content, you're ready to evaluate the speech.

IMPROVING LISTENING EFFECTIVENESS

Research shows that immediately after a lecture listeners recall only about 50 percent of what the speaker said.[32] Setting goals, blocking out distractions, managing listening anxiety, suspending judgment, focusing on the speaker's main points, taking meaningful notes, and using all your senses are strategies that will help you improve your listening skills.

Set Goals

Different public speaking situations call for different types of listening. Setting goals that correspond with the situation improves your listening skills. For example, after-dinner speeches are generally meant to entertain, so the listener's goal might be to simply enjoy the presentation. When a speaker toasts a newly married couple at a wedding reception, listeners would likely focus on the feelings associated with the occasion. However, in most classroom speaking situations the listener's ultimate goal is to critique speeches. As an audience member in your public speaking class, listen for the speaker's emotions (empathic listening), enjoy the speaker's sense of humor (appreciative listening), and identify the speaker's main ideas (content listening), keeping in mind your final goal of evaluating the speaker's message.

Block Distractions

The human brain processes information about three times faster than speakers can talk.[33] That leaves listeners time to get distracted by internal and external noise. As discussed in Chapter 1, noise occurs when something interferes with your understanding of messages. **Internal noise** includes thoughts, emotions, and physical sensations. Thinking about the movie you watched last night or noticing hunger pangs caused by skipping breakfast can prevent you from turning your full attention to the speaker. **External noise** includes conditions in your environment that interfere with listening. Outside noise, cramped

> Thoughts, emotions, and physical sensations that interfere with listening.

> Conditions in the environment that interfere with listening.

© David Young-Wolff/PhotoEdit

▲ How effective is this speaker's solution for helping listeners block distractions in this speaking situation? In what other ways could he help the audience better listen to his message?

Anxiety produced by the fear of misunderstanding, not fully comprehending, or not being mentally prepared for information you may hear.

seating, and an uncomfortable room temperature challenge your active listening skills. By blocking distractions, however, audience members can concentrate on what speakers are saying.

Manage Listening Anxiety

Just as speakers experience anxiety when giving a speech, listeners sometimes become anxious. **Listening anxiety** stems from the fear of misunderstanding, not fully comprehending, incorrectly recalling, or being unprepared mentally for information you may hear. Students often experience anxiety when listening to a lengthy lecture that they know they'll be tested on.[34] The physical symptoms are similar to those of speech anxiety. Manage listening anxiety by focusing on the speaker, clearing your mind of extraneous thoughts, and maintaining a positive attitude.

Suspend Judgment

Suspending judgment is related to an ethical principle of communication: "Strive to understand and respect other communicators before evaluating and responding to their messages."[35] Ethical listeners first listen for content and empathy and then evaluate the speaker's message. Controversial topics such as sex education in public schools, capital punishment, welfare policies, and nuclear power can trigger immediate emotional responses. Recognize those responses and then listen carefully to the speaker's ideas, even if they don't correspond with your own.

Focus on the Speaker's Main Points

Focusing on the speaker's main points is particularly important in content and critical listening. To evaluate what the speaker has said, you first need to understand the main ideas being presented. Speakers often call attention to their main points by stating them in the introduction and reviewing them in the conclusion.

Take Effective Notes

Taking effective notes when listening to a speech helps you recall what the speaker said and prepare good questions.[36] Your notes need not be extensive—a few key words will do. Here's a system that promotes effective listening: Divide a piece of paper into three columns. Label the first column "Important Points," the second column "My Response," and the third column "My Questions." As you listen to the speaker, write down your notes in the appropriate column.

Use All Your Senses

To improve your listening, use all your senses, paying attention to how speakers talk as well as what they are saying. While you listen to the speaker's main points, observe nonverbal cues such as gestures and tone of voice. Your senses will give you clues to the speaker's feelings about the topic.

Listening and Dialogue

▼ Communicators often think of public speaking as a one-way communication process, or **monologue**, in which speakers talk to listeners. Yet in reality ethical public speaking requires **dialogue**, in which speakers and listeners communicate *with* each other. Dialogue focuses primarily on content, taking a collaborative approach in which you invite speakers to express their ideas. Listeners are concerned more with arguments, reasoning, evidence, and claims than with criticizing delivery. Dialogue suggests an ethic of care in which listeners are concerned with truly understanding the speaker.[37]

How important is dialogue? Just ask the company rated highest in a recent survey of employee satisfaction, WL Gore & Associates. The company's success stemmed from creating effective dialogue between subordinates and supervisors. In all of the top ten companies, bosses sought out employee feedback, then acted on employees' concerns. At companies where bosses talked a lot and listened little, employees reported greater levels of stress and a strong desire to find a new job.[38] Wouldn't you rather work in a place where people engage in dialogues rather than monologues?

Creating true dialogue requires a passion for comprehending the speaker and performing well as a listener.[39] One way to create effective dialogue is to ask good questions. Ethical listeners ask questions that help the speaker clarify or elaborate on the main ideas presented. Even when you disagree with a speaker, focus your questions on gaining more information, not on presenting your point of view. Each question should take just a few seconds to ask. Good questions are:

- *Open-ended*—Begin questions with *How, Why, What, Where*. For example, ask, "How do you think your proposal will affect local residents?" rather than, "Will your proposal affect local residents?"

Occurs when speakers and audience members aren't actively engaged in the public speaking process and neither party listens to the other.

Occurs when speakers are sensitive to audience needs and listen to audience members' responses, and listeners pay careful attention to speakers' messages so they can respond appropriately and effectively.

▼ **WATCH it** SPEECH BUDDY VIDEO LINK

Promoting Dialogue in Q&A

◄◄ ▌▌ ►►

In this video, Janine provides tips on participating ethically in a dialogue between speaker and audience.

▼ **USE it** ACTIVITY LINK

You Have the Floor

In this activity, you'll develop questions for clips from speeches and suggest comments that audience members might make.

- *Direct*—Just ask the question, avoiding a long-drawn-out preface. For example, ask, "What do you think will be the impact of these changes over the next ten years?"
- *On topic*—Stick with the topic. If you think there's a weakness in the speaker's argument, ask about it, but be sure it relates to the speaker's message. For example, ask, "You discussed a few drawbacks associated with this new assessment program in K-12 schools. What have teachers and administrators done to address these issues?" Compare this with, "I know this isn't really related to what you talked about, but I was wondering what you think about the amount of homework teachers assign in their classes."
- *Genuine requests for information*—Ethical listening fosters a supportive communication climate. Conversely, using derogatory language and intentionally distorting the speaker's message produce a defensive communication climate.[40]

As an active listener, ask questions that encourage speakers to provide more information. Compare these questions:

1. "You mentioned some statistics on college students' use of file sharing. What are the sources of those statistics?"

2. "I'm sure you're wrong about those statistics you mentioned on college students and file sharing. What sources are you using? I want to look them up."

- In the first question, the listener respectfully asks for the information, giving the speaker a chance to state the sources more precisely. In the second question, the listener attacks the speaker, who will in turn feel compelled to respond defensively. Dialogue evaporates, and a battle ensues over who is "right" and who is "wrong."

With good questions, listeners continue the dialogue the speaker began. Effective listeners avoid monopolizing the question-and-answer session. Listening attentively during speeches and asking good questions that promote the free exchange of ideas are the hallmarks of an ethical listener.

SUMMARY

Ethical communication provides a foundation for effective public speaking and listening. Ethical speakers present accurate and balanced information, carefully researching their topics, using reliable sources, and adhering to copyright laws. Plagiarism is a particularly pressing ethical problem. By recording the sources for your information, referring to those sources in your speech, and listing each source in a written bibliography, you'll avoid plagiarism. Thoroughly preparing for your presentation, using language appropriate to your audience, and giving your speech in a manner that demonstrates respect for the audience help create a productive communication climate.

Audience members also have ethical responsibilities. Ethical listeners give speakers undivided attention, respect diverse perspectives, and listen to the entire speech before making a final judgment. In addition, both ethical speakers and listeners demonstrate genuine sensitivity to cultural differences.

Effective listening helps speakers and listeners connect comfortably with each other. Lack of commitment, jumping to conclusions, becoming distracted, poor note-taking, and asking inappropriate questions detract from the public speaking experience. When listeners become fully engaged, they create a meaningful dialogue between speaker and audience.

In the Book

Summary
Key Terms
Critical Challenges

More Study Resources

Speech Studio
Quizzes
WebLinks

Student Workbook

3.1: Quality Questions
3.2: Slant
3.3: Using Outlining to Take Notes
3.4: Identify and Adapt to Norms
3.5: Source Citation

Speech Buddy Videos

 Video Links

Avoiding Plagiarism
Promoting Dialogue in Q&A

Activity Links

But Is It Plagiarism?
You Have the Floor

▶ Sample Speech Videos

Chuck, "Anatomy of a Hate Crime," personal significance speech

Cara, "Creationism versus the Big Bang Theory," invitational speech

 Speech Builder Express

Outline
Supporting materials

 InfoTrac

Recommended search terms

Ethics and public speaking
Ethical communication
Communication climates
Plagiarism
Fair use and public speaking
Citing sources and speeches
Cultural diversity and communication
Listening and public speaking
Improving listening
Effective listening
Critical listening

Audio Study Tools

"Anatomy of a Hate Crime" by Chuck

Critical thinking questions

Learning objectives

Chapter summary

Guide to Your Online Resources

Your Online Resources for *Public Speaking: The Evolving Art* give you access to the Speech Buddy videos and activities featured in this chapter, additional sample speech videos, Speech Builder Express, InfoTrac College Edition, and study aids such as glossary flashcards, review quizzes, and the Critical Challenge questions for this chapter, which you can respond to via e-mail if your instructor so requests. In addition, your Online Resources feature live WebLinks relevant to this chapter, including links to sites about avoiding plagiarism and sites for the Intercultural Communication Institute, the Ethics Resource Center, and the International Listening Association. Links are regularly maintained, and new ones are added periodically.

Key Terms

communication climate 56

copyright 64

cultural diversity 68

cultural norms 68

culture 67

dialogue 75

ethical communication 55

ethnocentrism 68

external noise 73

fair use 65

hate speech 62

hearing 71

information overload 72

internal noise 73

listening 71

listening anxiety 74

monologue 75

oral citations 65

plagiarism 64

Critical Challenges

Questions for Reflection and Discussion

1. Should speakers in college classrooms be able to choose any topic they wish? Or should some topics be off limits? How do you balance free expression, pursuing justice, and promoting a caring communication climate? Think about the public speaking class you're in right now. What topics, if any, do you think students should not be allowed to speak about? Why do you think this way?

2. Review the Speaking Of . . . box titled "Hate Speech versus Free Speech" on page 62. Should there be laws against hate speech? What are the implications for not allowing certain kinds of speech? Does free speech mean you can say anything you want to anyone?

3. Recall a recent experience in which you were a critical listener. How well did you listen with empathy and appreciation? How well did you listen for content? How did you evaluate what the speaker said? What did you learn from listening critically?

4 DEVELOPING YOUR PURPOSE and TOPIC

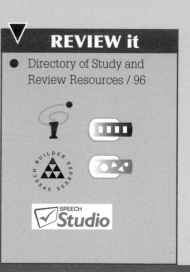

© Mary Kate Denny/PhotoEdit

When you talk with other people, you usually have a goal, or purpose, in mind.[1]

You may be trying to make them understand an idea you have or appreciate an experience you've had. Perhaps you're trying to influence their opinion about a subject or motivate them to do something. Maybe you're just trying to get a laugh. Having a well-defined purpose is especially important in public speaking. Identifying a clear purpose is essential from the very beginning of your speech preparation. You have to know what is expected of you, what you plan to do in response, and what you can expect to accomplish as a result. Four key steps make up the early part of speech preparation:

- First, you determine your general purpose.
- Second, you evaluate and select your speech topic.
- Third, you combine your general purpose and topic to identify your specific purpose.
- Fourth, you phrase the thesis of your speech as you develop your topic.

Determining Your General Purpose

▼ **READ it** The **general purpose** of your speech refers to your overall goal, and answers the question, "What do I want my speech to do?" The general purpose of your speech typically corresponds with one of the most common types of speeches: informative, persuasive, and entertaining.

SPEAKING TO INFORM

When you give a speech to inform, your goal is to describe, explain, or demonstrate something. Informative speeches serve to increase listeners' knowledge about a **topic**, or the main subject, idea, or theme of your speech. When the general purpose is to inform, your objective is to help the audience understand and recall information about a topic. In the professional world, informative presentations include employee orientations and project reports. Within communities, they include project proposals and policy updates.

SPEAKING TO PERSUADE

When you speak to persuade, you attempt to reinforce, modify, or change audience members' beliefs, attitudes, opinions, values, and behaviors. Your objective is to prompt the audience to alter their thinking and possibly take action. You might equate persuasion with advertising and politics. Yet when a student nominates a friend for president of a fraternity, a minister gives a sermon, a community member advocates disaster preparedness, or a university president presents a five-year vision to the faculty, these are persuasive speeches too.

SPEAKING TO ENTERTAIN

In an entertaining speech, the speaker seeks to captivate the audience and have them enjoy the speech. Special occasions often provide the context for such speeches. After-dinner speakers, for instance, charm and humor the audience. Entertaining speeches typically include jokes and stories.

KEEPING YOUR GENERAL PURPOSE IN MIND

For any particular speech, you'll concentrate on a single general purpose: to inform, persuade, or entertain. As you develop your speech, always keep your general purpose in mind. Although you might include humor in an informative speech, your ultimate goal is to inform, not to entertain. Similarly, you might offer explanations in a persuasive speech, but your primary objective is to persuade, not to inform. And you might give your opinions in an entertaining speech, yet in the end you want to entertain, not to persuade, your audience. If you try to both entertain and persuade, for example, you won't do either one very well.[2] Think about humorous television commercials in which you can recall the joke but not the product advertised. Focusing on one general purpose helps you achieve your overall goal for the speech.

Giving speeches of these types and for these purposes extends the communication skills you already have because you inform, persuade, and entertain people all the time. And they inform, persuade, and entertain you. Once you know your speech's general purpose, your next step involves coming up with possible speech topics.

Brainstorming for Possible Topics

A public speaking event gives you an opportunity to speak to an audience, but what will you speak about? Carefully selecting your topic sets you on the road to delivering an effective speech. So where do you begin? By **brainstorming**—a free-form way of generating ideas without evaluating them. Brainstorming happens in many ways. As you go about your daily routines, topic ideas may pop into your head, so be ready to record them. A newspaper article, webpage image, radio talk show, or television program may trigger ideas for your speech. Trying out something new may also help you think of alternative topics.[3] Take a new route to a friend's apartment, listen to some new music, spend some time in a new coffee house.

> The free-form generation of ideas in which individuals think of and record ideas without evaluating them.

At some point, you'll want to set aside a specific time to generate ideas or expand on the ones you generated previously. Choose a place where you feel relaxed, yet still alert and attentive. The main point of brainstorming is to write down all the topics you might want to talk about without evaluating them. Simply record whatever comes to mind. And be creative. At this stage you don't want to censor yourself.[4] The rules of brainstorming are few but important (**Figure 4.1**).

Asking yourself key questions can help you focus the brainstorming process. The questions should be broad enough to encourage creativity, but not so broad that you stray far from your original goal. Here are some examples:[5]

- What do I talk or text message about with my friends?
- What are my interests and hobbies?
- What unique experiences have I had?
- What am I passionate about and what will I argue about?

If this strategy doesn't get ideas flowing, check the headlines from a major news source or web portal, or use search engines' pages that list issues, such as dmoz.org.

▼ **FIGURE 4.1**

Rules for Brainstorming
- Generate as many ideas as possible.
- Write down every idea— whatever comes to mind.
- Avoid evaluating your ideas.
- Be as creative and imaginative as possible.

Subjects discussed in blogs and podcasts can also provide topics for brainstorming. When you find an article or post that interests you, write down the topic, as well as any others you associate with it.

A photo or other image may also give you an idea for a speech topic. Certain images are widely distributed and recognized. For example, people worldwide see images from the Iraq war shortly after they become available, just as they saw images of Hurricane Katrina and the Indian Ocean tsunami. These images suggest a range of topics, such as volunteer relief efforts, disparities between rich and poor people in affected areas, causes of natural disasters, use of technology to prepare and issue warnings—the list goes on.

When brainstorming for possible speech topics, think not only in terms of ideas or words that come to mind but also in terms of images that have impressed you. YouTube videos and personal postings on social networking sites like Facebook may provide topic ideas. Start brainstorming for topic ideas well before you're scheduled to present your speech. Research shows that brainstorming works best when done over several sessions.[6] Trying to brainstorm under the pressure of having to give your speech in a few days will not help you think of your best ideas, make the best choice, or do justice to the topic you choose.

▼ High impact images of significant events can help you brainstorm for a range of possible speech topics.

Evaluating and Selecting Topic Ideas

▼ Before finally selecting a topic, think about your own interests and knowledge, the availability of resources, and the time and setting for your speech. Evaluating possible topics based on key considerations such as the following can speed up your topic selection process:

- Consider your own interests.
- Consider the audience.

- Consider resource availability.
- Consider the time limit, time of day, and current events.
- Consider the setting and event.

CONSIDER YOUR OWN INTERESTS

In evaluating your topics, first consider your own interests and what you know. Ask yourself these questions:

- How interested am I in this topic?
- What do I know about this topic?
- How comfortable will I be talking about this topic?

If your answer to the first question is, "not very interested," cross that topic off your list. Your audience will immediately know if you're not enthusiastic about it. A topic you feel passionate about will energize you and produce a more dynamic and interesting speech. However, having little knowledge of a topic may also motivate you or give you a chance to learn more about it. But before choosing a topic you don't know much about, be sure you have enough time and resources to research it fully. Finally, consider how comfortable you are talking about a topic. If it's something you don't like discussing with your friends, you probably won't want to give a speech about it.

CONSIDER THE AUDIENCE

Although you'll do more research on your audience after you've chosen your topic, at this point you need to do some preliminary research to get a general idea of audience members' knowledge and interests. Ask yourself these four questions about your audience when evaluating the topics on your list:

1. How relevant is this topic for my audience?

2. Why do audience members need to know about this topic?

3. Will I be able to interest my audience in this topic?

4. How much does my audience already know about my topic?

As you evaluate topics, always put yourself in the audience's place. Choose speech topics that resonate with audience members. Some topics may not seem directly relevant to audience members; you may need to provide that link. However, if the topic probably won't pique listeners' interest and you can't think of any reasons why they should know about the topic, cross it off your list. In addition, balance relevance and interest with knowledge level. If a topic is relevant and of interest but audience members already know quite a bit about it, you have to either take an unusual approach to the topic or remove it from your list.

CONSIDER RESOURCE AVAILABILITY

As you narrow down your list of possible speech topics, conduct a preliminary check of possible topic resources. Audience members listen for evidence from a variety of sources and can quickly discern if the informational base of your speech is too thin. So when choosing a topic, be sure you can locate and access relevant and valid resources.

CONSIDER TIME

Consider your potential topics in terms of your time limit, the time of day, and current events.

Time Limit

Successful public speakers stay within their time limits. Examine your list of topics. Can you cover each topic within the allotted time? You may need to narrow or broaden particular speech topics, depending on the time frame.

Time of Day

Are you presenting your speech in the early morning? Late afternoon? Evening? *When* you present your speech influences your choice of topics. Giving a speech encouraging the use of public transportation could work well during peak commute periods. You might strike a responsive chord when advocating healthy eating habits if you were to speak on that topic around lunch time. Try to associate your topic with the temporal rhythm of the day and the biological and behavioral conditions that fit those time periods.

· · · · · · · · · · **THE EVOLVING ART**

Using Your Campus Library to Find Resources

You have ten possible speech topics; you don't want to do a thorough search on each one to determine whether enough information is available. How can you make this initial resource check more efficient? Skip Google and Yahoo! and go right to the main page of your campus library's website. There you'll find links to databases for newspapers, journals, magazines, government publications, and other sources, as well as the library's catalog. A quick search will give you a general idea of how much information is available for each topic. In addition, nearly all college libraries include an e-mail, chat, or telephone help desk. A meeting in person with a librarian to discuss resources for possible speech topics can also prove helpful.

Current Events

Timely or current speeches enhance your credibility and help you relate your topic to your audience. In choosing a topic, consider how it fits with events in the news and what people are talking about. Select topics that connect current events with the audience's emotions and avoid connections that might reflect poorly on your topic. An upbeat talk about the health of the national economy wouldn't work very well on a day when high unemployment figures are released, but it could work very well if unemployment is decreasing.

▲ Where you're speaking—a large auditorium, a small conference room, or something in between—will influence your choice of a topic.

CONSIDER THE SETTING AND SPEAKING EVENT

The place where you'll present your speech figures in selecting an appropriate topic as well. Are you speaking in a large auditorium, a conference room, or a classroom? Are you speaking to 1000, 100, or 10 people? What might be appropriate for a small classroom context may not prove effective in a large auditorium. In the classroom, the setting is more personal; in an auditorium, there's a greater distance between the speaker and the audience.

Place also refers to the event—the content of the speech should be consistent with the event. For example, if you're presenting an after-dinner speech, you don't want to talk about a serious topic such as skin cancer. When giving a commencement speech, focus on the positive aspects of the students' education and prospective careers rather than envisioning a future of gloom and doom. In addition, consider the event as a whole. Are you the only speaker, or are others presenting as well? Identify who might be speaking before or after you and consider how your topic complements theirs.

Identifying Your Specific Purpose

The **specific purpose** is what you want to achieve in your speech. In writing your specific purpose, you merge your general purpose, topic, and audience to identify the particular objective you want to accomplish. For example, if the general purpose is to inform and your topic is your campus's student government, your specific purpose might be, "To inform my audience about the two branches of our campus's student government, executive and legislative." This statement integrates your general purpose, to inform, with your topic, student government, and what you want your audience to know, the two branches of student government.

A concise statement articulating what the speaker will achieve in giving a speech.

The specific purpose is a clear, concise statement about your topic that focuses on a single purpose and incorporates the response you want from the audience. For a speech to inform, your specific purpose will begin with something like the following:

- To inform my audience about . . .
- To teach my audience . . .
- To make my audience aware of . . .
- To demonstrate to my audience how to . . .

Each statement begins by placing the audience at the center of attention and refers, directly or indirectly, to the general purpose—in this case, to inform. Then you add in the topic, as with:

- To inform my audience about how face recognition systems work.
- To teach my audience strategies for time management.
- To make my audience aware of the services offered at the campus career center.
- To demonstrate to my audience how to take a perfect photograph.

Identifying a specific purpose helps you conceptualize your speech from the audience's point of view. It centers your attention on what you want your audience to know and why they should listen to you. Thinking this way keeps you clearly focused on the reason you're speaking in the first place—to inform the audience.

Speeches to persuade often aim to produce a mental or emotional response or to prompt audience members to take a specific action, such as "exercise daily," "donate blood," or "support legislation." A statement of specific purpose for a persuasive speech might begin with:

- To persuade my audience to . . .
- To convince my audience that. . .
- To deepen the empathy my audience feels. . .
- To motivate my audience to. . .

When merged with a topic, these examples become:

- To persuade my audience to support a campus-wide smoking ban.
- To convince my audience that genetically modified foods are safe.
- To deepen my audience's empathy for people living in poverty.
- To motivate my audience to vote.

In speeches to entertain, the specific purpose includes engaging and amusing the audience. Your statement of specific purpose would begin like this:

- To entertain my audience with . . .
- To amuse my audience with. . .

- To delight my audience with. . .
- To inspire my audience with . . .

When merged with a topic, these examples become:

- To entertain my audience with humorous aspects of working in an office cubicle.
- To amuse my audience with the zaniness of family summer vacations.
- To delight my audience with unusual inventions of the past.
- To inspire my audience with offbeat ways to simplify their lives.

Considering the response you want from your audience keeps them uppermost in your mind. Writing down your specific purpose or goal brings together the general purpose, topic, and audience, providing a reference point that will keep you on track.[7] **Table 4.1** provides additional examples of the links among general purpose, topic, and specific purpose.

TABLE 4.1 ▶ Examples of General Purpose, Topic, and Specific Purpose

GENERAL PURPOSE	TOPIC	SPECIFIC PURPOSE
To inform	Women in comics	To inform my audience about the history of women in U.S. newspaper comics
To inform	Wild mushrooms	To teach my audience about the differences between poisonous and edible mushrooms
To inform	Emergency kits	To demonstrate to my audience how to assemble an emergency-preparedness kit
To persuade	Zoos	To persuade my audience that zoos serve important purposes for many animals
To persuade	Bicycle helmets	To convince my audience to wear a bicycle helmet whenever they cycle
To persuade	Poverty	To help my audience feel more empathy for local residents living in poverty
To entertain	Advertisements	To entertain my audience with sample advertisements that will never be shown on television
To entertain	Nutrition	To amuse my audience with the college student's version of the food pyramid
To entertain	Sports	To inspire my audience with true stories of accomplished athletes in little-known sports

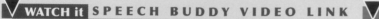

WATCH it SPEECH BUDDY VIDEO LINK

Brainstorming for and Evaluating Topics

In this video, Anthony and Janine demonstrate the process of brainstorming and evaluating topic ideas.

USE it ACTIVITY LINK

Search and Find Missions

In this activity, you have a chance to try brainstorming and evaluating topic ideas.

The specific purpose of your speech guides important decisions in later stages of the speech process, such as researching your topic, deciding on supporting materials, organizing your ideas, making language choices, and integrating presentation resources. As you work on your speech, ask yourself, Will this quote, statistic, audio clip, or other material help me achieve my specific purpose?

Phrasing Your Thesis

Your general purpose points you in the direction your speech must take—informing, persuading, or entertaining. Your specific purpose addresses how you want your speech to affect your audience. Your **thesis** summarizes your plan for achieving the specific purpose. A thesis is presented in a single sentence that captures the central idea or essence of your speech. In that statement you crystallize your speech in a way that embodies your topic and the main ideas you'll address. Ask yourself, "What is the central idea I want my audience to get from my speech?" That's your thesis.[8]

A single declarative sentence that captures the essence or central idea of a speech.

Your thesis incorporates the topic, flows from the specific purpose, and directly addresses how you will elicit the response you want from your audience. In short, it summarizes the content of your speech. Here are some examples:

Topic: Telemedicine

General purpose: To inform

Specific purpose: To educate my audience about the role of telemedicine in health care.

Thesis: Telemedicine uses new communication technologies for consultations between doctors, interactions between patients and doctors, and monitoring patients at remote locations.

Topic: Sustainable Land Development

General purpose: To persuade

Specific purpose: To convince my audience that sustainable land development is an essential part of strengthening the local economy.

Thesis: Sustainable land development addresses the community's immediate needs and positions our city as a desirable location for future businesses by protecting our natural environment.

Topic: Online dating services

General purpose: To entertain

Specific purpose: To amuse my audience with stories about my experience using an online dating service.

Thesis: From setting up my profile to searching through the online personals and finally going on a date, my first experience with an online dating service is one I'll never forget.

Each thesis statement frames the main points for the speech. It also refines the topic and provides guidance for your research.

Sometimes you'll determine the thesis as soon as you've written the specific purpose—you have a clear idea of your topic, what you want to accomplish, and how you'll get there. More commonly, the thesis emerges as you begin developing your topic.[9] As you begin thinking about your topic and conducting preliminary research, you'll identify specific points or ideas that will help you achieve your specific purpose. The next section takes you through the first steps of developing a topic and creating a working outline.

Building Your Working Outline

▼ Once you know your general purpose, have selected a topic, and have determined the specific purpose of your speech, you're ready to begin putting together your working outline. Chapter 1 introduced the **working outline**, which guides you during the initial stages of topic development, helping to keep you focused on your general purpose and clarify your specific purpose. As your working outline evolves, you'll include the speech topic, general purpose, specific purpose, thesis, and key words for the main ideas and subpoints you want to address. Later you'll construct a complete-sentence outline. Then, in the final stages of preparing your speech, you'll create a presentation outline. **Table 4.2** shows where you are in the process of giving a speech based on the type of outline you're creating or using.

An outline that guides you during the initial stages of topic development, helping to keep you focused on your general purpose and clarify your specific purpose.

TABLE 4.2 ▶ Types of Outlines

YOU ARE HERE ▶

TYPE OF OUTLINE	FUNCTIONS	KEY FEATURES	CHAPTER
Working	Assists in initial topic development; guides research	Includes main points and possible subpoints; revised during research process	Chapter 4: Developing Your Purpose and Topic
Complete-sentence	Clearly identifies all the pieces of information for the speech; puts ideas in order; forms the basis for developing the presentation outline	Uses complete sentences; lists all sections of speech and all references; revised during preparation process	Chapter 8: Organizing and Outlining Your Speech
Presentation	Assists in practicing and giving your speech	Uses keywords; revised as you practice your speech; often transferred to note cards for use during practice and the final presentation	Chapter 12: Delivering Your Speech

Imagine that for an informative speech, you decide to tell your classmates about the most important factors students should consider when choosing a major. Every college student has dealt with this problem, so this subject will be familiar to your audience. Your topic is "Choosing a Major," and your specific purpose is, "To make my audience understand how to choose a college major."

BRAINSTORMING FOR TOPIC DEVELOPMENT

The first step in topic development is brainstorming for ideas you may want to include in your speech.[10] Here are some ideas students consider important when trying to choose a major:

- Career goals after college
- The university's reputation in the chosen field
- How long it will take to graduate
- The student's life goals
- Majors the student really would not like
- Areas of strongest skills
- Whether the department is admitting new majors
- Potential earnings in jobs related to the major
- Quality of instructors
- Things the student really likes to do
- Job market for students graduating in the major
- Requirements in the major
- Whether the university offers the major
- Department resources to help students

GROUPING IDEAS TO SELECT MAIN POINTS

Once you have a list of ideas for your topic, distill each one down to a single word or short phrase. This will make it easier to identify links among them. Choose accurate and clear terms that capture your ideas:

- Career goals after college (career goals)
- The university's reputation in the chosen field (reputation)
- How long it will take to graduate (time to graduation)
- The student's life goals (personal goals)
- Majors the student really would not like (what you don't like)

Limit Your Working Outline

Carefully consider each idea you include in your working outline. Including too many points is one of the biggest problems students encounter when learning how to develop a topic. You'll have to make some tough decisions to avoid cluttering your speech with points that may be interesting but don't advance your specific purpose. Learning how to effectively edit your ideas at this stage will save you time and effort as you progress through the speech-making process, and it will greatly improve the flow and impact of your speech.

- Areas of strongest skills (what you're good at)
- Whether the department is admitting new majors (openings)
- Potential earnings in jobs related to the major (money)
- Quality of instructors (instructors)
- Things the student really likes to do (what you like)
- Job market for students graduating in the major (job market)
- Requirements in the major (requirements)
- Whether the university offers the major (curriculum)
- Department resources to help students (student support)

Next, group ideas together into more general categories. You're striving for internal consistency in each group of key words. In terms of your speech, **internal consistency** means the ideas that make up any main heading or subheading have a logical relationship to one another. For the speech on choosing a major, the ideas fall into three major categories (**Table 4.3**): practical considerations (reputation, time to graduation, job market, money, and requirements), academic resources (openings, instructors, curriculum, and student support), and personal considerations (career goals, personal goals, what you enjoy, what you don't like, and what you're good at).

By identifying and grouping ideas into main themes, you reduce a topic to logical categories and can begin to visualize what the skeleton, or main points, of the speech might look like. The thematically arranged categories provide an initial structure for your main ideas and what you might talk about under each one. For example, in the speech on choosing a major, the "practical considerations" category includes reputation, time to graduation, job market, money, and requirements. The themes and corresponding ideas provide the basis for your initial working outline (see **Figure 4.2**), which helps you accomplish the following tasks:

A logical relationship among the ideas that make up any main heading or subheading in a speech.

▼ **FIGURE 4.2**

Initial Working Outline for "Choosing a Major"

Topic: Choosing a Major
General purpose: To inform
Specific purpose: To inform my audience about how to choose a college major

I. Practical considerations
   A. Reputation
   B. Time to graduation
   C. Job market
   D. Money
   E. Requirements

II. Academic resources
   A. Openings
   B. Instructors
   C. Curriculum
   D. Student support

III. Personal orientations
   A. Career goals
   B. Personal goals
   C. What you enjoy
   D. What you don't like
   E. What you're good at

TABLE 4.3 ▶ Idea Groupings for "Choosing a Major"

PRACTICAL CONSIDERATIONS	ACADEMIC RESOURCES	PERSONAL CONSIDERATIONS
• Reputation • Time to graduation • Job market • Money • Requirements	• Openings • Instructors • Curriculum • Student support	• Career goals • Personal goals • What you enjoy • What you don't like • What you're good at

- Analyze your audience based on your topic and main ideas for your speech.
- Research your main themes using keyword searches.
- Create the complete-sentence outline that you will use as you organize the information you've gathered.

WRITING THE THESIS

The initial grouping of ideas for the topic of choosing a major suggests the following thesis: "Three factors influence how to choose a major: practical considerations, academic resources, and personal considerations." This sentence sums up the core of the speech, indicates how you intend to fulfill your specific purpose, and can serve as your preliminary thesis statement. Add it to the information at the beginning of your working outline (**Figure 4.3**). This preliminary thesis may change as you analyze your audience and research your speech, but it's a good place to start.

As you analyze your audience and research your topic, refer back to your working outline to help keep yourself on track. Although you may make important changes in your outline as you develop your speech, in general you want to stay focused on your main points, and a working outline is a reliable tool that will help you do that.

▼ **FIGURE 4.3**

Adding the Thesis to the Working Outline for "Choosing a Major"

Topic: Choosing a Major
General purpose: To inform
Specific purpose: To inform my audience about how to choose a college major.
Thesis: Three factors influence how to choose a major: practical considerations, academic resources, and personal considerations.

SUMMARY

Every speech you present has one overall goal or general purpose: to inform, to persuade, or to entertain. The general purpose determines the nature of your speech.

In brainstorming for topics, list all the topic ideas you can think of without evaluating them. Often brainstorming begins long before you finally write down your topic ideas. But setting aside some time to gather together all your topic ideas will help you consider your options more clearly.

Evaluate possible topics in terms of five areas: yourself, your audience, available resources, time, and setting. Choose a topic that is appropriate for yourself, the audience, and the situation. Also make sure you can find enough information to present a well-researched speech.

Your specific purpose—what you want to achieve—merges your general purpose and topic with the response you seek from your audience. As you work on choosing a topic, you'll frame the specific purpose.

Phrasing the thesis is a crucial step in topic development. Your thesis flows from your specific purpose and indicates how you will achieve the objective of your speech. Written as a single declarative sentence, the thesis captures the essence of your speech by incorporating the main points you plan to address.

Developing your topic starts with brainstorming for ideas associated with that topic. The next step is to identify themes and group them by category. These categories become the main points of your speech and suggest the thesis—the essence of what you'll cover.

Your topic, general purpose, specific purpose, thesis, and main points form the basis of your working outline. The working outline provides a tentative plan for your speech that may change as you learn more about your topic and audience. This early work gives you a solid foundation for analyzing your audience, researching your topic, identifying appropriate supporting materials, and determining the best way to organize your ideas.

▼ REVIEW it DIRECTORY OF STUDY AND REVIEW RESOURCES

In the Book

Summary
Key Terms
Critical Challenges

More Study Resources

Speech Studio
Quizzes
WebLinks

Student Workbook

4.1: Audience Feedback on Topics
4.2: Brainstorming Lists
4.3: Audience-Centered Specific Purpose
4.4: Phrasing Thesis Statements
4.5: Working and Reworking Your Working Outline

Speech Buddy Videos

 Video Links

Brainstorming for and Evaluating Topics

Activity Links

Search and Find Missions

▶ Sample Speech Videos

Tiffany, "Meat-Free and Me," informative speech

Husam, "How to Become a Successful Business Person," informative speech

Speech Builder Express

Goal/purpose
Thesis statement
Outline

 InfoTrac

Recommended search terms
General purpose and speech
Specific purpose and speech
Thesis statement and speech
Brainstorming
Public speaking topics

Audio Study Tools

"How to Become a Successful Business Person" by Husam

Critical thinking questions

Learning objectives

Chapter summary

Guide to Your Online Resources

Your Online Resources for *Public Speaking: The Evolving Art* give you access to the Speech Buddy video and activity featured in this chapter, additional sample speech videos, Speech Builder Express, InfoTrac College Edition, and study aids such as glossary flashcards, review quizzes, and the Critical Challenge questions for this chapter, which you can respond to via e-mail if your instructor so requests. In addition, your Online Resources feature live WebLinks relevant to this chapter, including sites that provide ideas for finding speech topics. Links are regularly maintained, and new ones are added periodically.

Key Terms

brainstorming 83

general purpose 82

internal consistency 94

specific purpose 87

thesis 90

topic 82

working outline 92

Critical Challenges

Questions for Reflection and Discussion

1. Being open to new ideas and perspectives helps us exercise our critical thinking skills. How can you brainstorm for topic ideas with an open mind? What are some ways in which you might broaden your perspective on speech topics? How might you apply the strategy of trying out something new to come up with creative topic ideas?

2. Consider events and issues that are currently in the news. How might these serve as a springboard for topic ideas? How will these current events and issues influence your topic choices?

3. As you develop your topic—generating ideas and grouping them together— consider the assumptions you're making about the topic and your audience. Are there alternative ways of approaching the topic and categorizing ideas? How might you group ideas differently? How might you think about the topic in new ways?

5 ADAPTING to YOUR AUDIENCE

WATCH It
Watch your Speech Buddy video.

USE It
Complete your USE It activity . . .

. . . and apply what you've learned to your speech.

SPEECH Studio

© Jeff Greenberg/PhotoEdit

Successful speakers adapt their messages to appeal to specific audiences. When Microsoft Chairman Bill Gates recently went on his annual fall college tour, he talked about the empowering role of computers at all the schools he visited, but he adjusted his speech for each audience. At the University of Michigan he said, "Microsoft hires about thirty people from the University of Michigan a year, including a lot of our top people. . . So, let me thank you for that, and hope we can keep up that incredibly strong relationship." He began his speech at the University of Waterloo with, "Well, it's great to be here. As you heard from some of your alums, Waterloo has contributed an amazing amount to Microsoft."[1] Even those brief acknowledgments let audience members know that Gates had prepared his speech with them in mind.

Tailoring a speech to fit your audience requires getting to know the people you'll be addressing—their interests, views, and familiarity with your topic. Your knowledge about the audience begins with **audience analysis**. Analyzing your audience won't

audience analysis
Obtaining and evaluating information about an audience in order to anticipate their needs and interests and design a strategy to respond to them.

guarantee a successful speech, of course, but it's a critical step toward a favorable outcome.

Audience analysis and adaptation continues from the first stages of speech preparation through the actual presentation of the speech and beyond.[2] Analyzing your audience means anticipating their needs and interests and designing a strategy to respond to them. As you deliver your speech, audience feedback becomes another key source of information.[3] Are audience members smiling, frowning, making eye contact with you, or looking out the window? Prepare yourself in advance to respond appropriately to listeners' nonverbal cues, adapting your speech based on that feedback. If there is a question-and-answer exchange following the presentation of your speech, listen carefully to what the audience has to say and respond appropriately.

▶ One way Bill Gates adapts to his audience is by mentioning them at the beginning of his speech.

REUTERS/Nicholas Roberts/Landov

What Is an Audience?

READ it The term *audience* originally referred to a group of people who share a common interest and physically gather together, usually in a public or semipublic setting such as a public plaza, theater, or stadium. With the arrival of film, movie theaters became another common gathering place for audiences. Radio, television, and the internet have audiences too, of course, but audiences for these media are physically dispersed. Granted, when radio and television were new, it was common for family and friends to gather around them as a communal audience. Today, however, you are more than likely to be an audience of one. Still, the idea of audience is much the same as it was in Aristotle's time: **Audience** refers to the people the speaker addresses.

The people a speaker addresses.

Appealing to audiences becomes more challenging as new communication technologies allow us to reach a broader range of people. For example, bloggers try to attract readers by encouraging them to link to their blogs. Campus libraries design their websites to serve as public relations tools, reaching out to students, alumni, potential donors, and faculty.[4] Online marketers also attempt to reach specific audiences.[5] For instance, personal profiles associated with Yahoo! Mail and Hotmail accounts allow marketers to tailor their advertisements to those audiences. In each case, the speaker, or sender, tries to learn as much as possible about audience members to design messages that will appeal to their interests, needs, and perspectives.

THE AUDIENCE-SPEAKER CONNECTION

Successful speakers view audience members as partners in public speaking, so speakers and listeners work together to create the speech situation.[6] Speakers succeed only to the degree they effectively connect with their audience. Audiences of all kinds have one basic question in mind: "How does this apply to me and my experiences?" In trying to understand a speaker's message, they seek to make a connection between what the speaker says and themselves. So when you address an audience you must be able to interest them, intrigue them, or otherwise respond to their needs or appear to advance their interests.[7]

Thorough audience analysis is the first step in an **audience-centered** approach to your speech. Analyzing and adapting to the audience is crucial for media producers, writers, theater producers, politicians,[8] and all public speakers, including you.

Describes a speaker who acknowledges the audience by considering and listening to the unique, diverse, and common perspectives of its members before, during, and after the speech.

CLASSROOM AUDIENCES

A college speech class differs from most public speaking situations. As a college student, you have some built-in advantages when you prepare your speeches. You'll share more about yourself than you do in almost any other class. You and your classmates can't avoid getting to know one another. For most students, that's an enjoyable part of the experience. And even though any audience can prove challenging to win over, the students you'll speak to this term will want you to succeed.[9]

This unusual access to your audience means that even before you give your first graded speech, you'll have a basic impression of your audience. By applying the listening skills presented in Chapter 3, you'll learn even more about your audience as the term progresses. But becoming familiar with your audience involves more than gaining basic impressions. Adapting your speech to your audience requires determining in advance as precisely as possible who your audience is and what they know and think about your speech topic.

Adapting to a Diverse Audience

Only if you understand the basic characteristics of your audience and have some idea of their knowledge and feelings about your topic can you tailor your speech to reach them effectively. Politicians and advertisers convince people to vote for them or buy their products by tailoring their messages to their **target audience**—the particular group or subgroup they are trying to reach. For public speakers, the target audience includes the people the speakers most want to inform, persuade, or entertain. You might, for instance, give a speech at a community center on the need for improved pedestrian safety features on busy streets. Although your audience may be mostly neighborhood residents who agree with your position, your target audience is the city council members in attendance who can actually do something about the problem. Similarly, if you wanted to advocate curriculum changes at your college, you'd target your speech at faculty and administrators—the people with the power to make the changes you seek. Marketing is based on the notion that sellers of goods and ideas must know who their target audiences are and how to connect with them. And just as in marketing, public speakers must analyze their target audience in order to determine the best way to present their ideas.

There is never just one audience in a room, even a public speaking classroom.[10] Particularly in today's media-driven world, students—like all audiences—have access to a wide range of information about a variety of topics. Thus, although the students in your public speaking class will have some shared experiences, they'll also differ in many ways. Part of your responsibility as a speaker is to recognize the diversity of backgrounds, knowledge, interests, and opinions among the members of your audience and plan your presentation accordingly.

The particular group or subgroup a speaker most wants to inform, persuade, or entertain.

MEETING THE CHALLENGES OF AUDIENCE DIVERSITY

Based on census data, the U.S. government predicts that by the mid-twenty-first century the population will be even more diverse than it is now.[11] Today America is one of the most diverse countries in the world, with a wide array of people from a variety of cultural, religious, educational, and economic backgrounds. In U.S. colleges, the number of African-American, Latino, Native American, and Asian American students nearly doubled in the late twentieth century, from 15 percent of all college students in the mid-1970s to 29 percent nearly thirty years later.[12] When you present a speech, more than likely you'll face a diverse audience. Trying to adapt your speech to people with a range of backgrounds, experiences, and interests may seem daunting, but that diversity can work to your advantage and result in a successful experience for you and your audience.[13]

Speaking to a diverse audience can have positive outcomes. When you interact with people whose backgrounds differ from your own, you learn how to

- Promote a more supportive communication climate that welcomes differing perspectives on topics and issues.
- Draw from a wider pool of knowledge and information that contributes to a better learning experience for all participants.
- Foster positive intergroup relationships in a cooperative fashion.
- Better articulate your own cultural identity and understand those of others.
- Acknowledge and respect differences while avoiding ethnocentrism.
- Advocate constructive dialogue about contentious topics.

At the same time, diverse audiences pose challenges. For example, most humor relies on cultural context—if members of your audience don't share that context, they likely won't find your attempts at humor very funny. In addition, inadvertently excluding part of your audience through the language you use or information you present hinders your ability to achieve the goal of your speech.

TECHNIQUES FOR SPEAKING TO DIVERSE AUDIENCES

Although speakers have many strategies at their disposal in adapting to diverse audiences, research reveals five particularly effective techniques: identify commonalities, establish credibility, include supporting materials relevant to specific audience groups, use appropriate language, and continuously attend to all segments of your audience. Applying these techniques depends on a careful and thorough analysis of your audience.[14] Together, these techniques acknowledge audience diversity yet promote an inclusive communication climate.

First, search for commonalities among audience members related to your topic. If you're giving an informative speech on home schooling to a group with mixed opinions and knowledge of the topic, you might begin by establishing the importance of a good education in general—something all audience members can agree on.

Second, establish your credibility on the topic through enthusiasm, friendliness, and expertise. Regardless of their knowledge, beliefs, and attitudes, audience members are more likely to listen when you give an engaging presentation, appear warm and outgoing, and demonstrate knowledge of the subject.

Third, include supporting materials that resonate especially with one group yet at the same time leave other audience members with positive or neutral feelings. For example, in an informative speech about women's college basketball, you might mention that women started playing basketball at Smith College in 1892—just one year after the game was invented. Audience members who follow women's basketball likely will find this fact particularly important, while others may simply view it as interesting.

Fourth, use language that appeals to all members of the audience. Choose words audience members find meaningful. This may require defining your terms or avoiding jargon and specialized language that only a few audience members will understand.

Fifth, continuously attend to all segments of your audience. Acknowledge the variety of their experiences throughout your presentation, rather than addressing each group in separate sections of your speech. For example, in a persuasive speech encouraging listeners to become more informed voters, integrate appeals to the full range of audience members, from completely uninformed to highly informed, in all parts of the speech instead of dedicating a specific section to each group.

Implementing these techniques requires knowing your audience as thoroughly as possible. In the next section you'll learn how you can begin to analyze your audience by examining basic audience characteristics.

▼ Even if you are very different from the members of your audience, adapting to them by identifying commonalities, establishing credibility, providing relevant supporting materials, using appropriate language, and continuously attending to them can help you make a connection with them.

John Giustina/Getty Images

Using Demographic Information

In any speaking situation, successful speakers assess the size of the audience and their demographic characteristics. **Demographics** are key characteristics of populations; those characteristics are often used to divide a population into subgroups. Important demographic categories include age, sex or gender identity, race and ethnicity, educational level, income level or social class, sexual orientation, dis/ability, religious affiliation, relationship status, and parenting or guardian responsibilities.

> The ways in which populations can be divided into smaller groups according to key characteristics such as sex, ethnicity, age, and social class.

Effective communicators use demographics to identify their target audiences. Demographics do not paint a complete picture of any individual or group, but knowing the demographics of your audience gives you a good place to start imagining their possible needs and interests and how you might approach your topic.

GATHERING DEMOGRAPHIC DATA

In the classroom setting, student speakers have an advantage over speakers in other settings. For speeches you give in class, some demographic categories—educational level, for instance—will be obvious. You can also note the ratio of women to men and get a good sense of their age range. You may have some idea of their ethnic backgrounds. Some demographic information is less easily revealed, however. For example, you may not know the income level or socioeconomic class of audience members, although you can sometimes make reasonable assumptions by considering the type of school you attend and observing such factors as clothing and language.

Like speakers in educational settings, those in workplace or social settings often know a considerable amount about their audience beforehand. For instance, you would probably have a good sense of the demographic composition of the audience for a speech at work or to members of a club you belong to. Speakers in other settings often don't have personal access to their audience before the speaking event. In such situations, the best source of information is the person or organization that invited you to speak. Ask them for information about the composition of the audience—the size and purpose of the group, their demographic characteristics, what they know about the topic, how they feel about it, what they might expect from the speaker, even how best to reach them with your message. Gathering this information will help you prepare and present your message effectively for that particular group.

Demographic information about an audience can best be obtained through personal observation, systematic inquiry (e.g., using a questionnaire), or consultation with people who are familiar with that audience. But sometimes those options aren't available.

SPEAKING OF...

Demographic Stereotyping

While demographic analysis can provide valuable insights into attitudes that tend to differ according to people's race, age, social class, gender, sexual orientation, and so on, each audience member must nonetheless be treated as an individual who very well may not conform to the stereotype. Speakers should be sensitive to real differences between audience subgroups without making assumptions about any particular audience member. Keeping this principle in mind is especially important during the question-and-answer session following the presentation of your speech.

Demographic information about the American public—for example, the political affiliations of men and women, people of different races, northerners and southerners—can also be found on the websites of national opinion polling organizations like the Pew Research Center, the Gallup Poll, the Zogby Poll, and the National Opinion Research Center at the University of Chicago.

Using Psychographic Information

Psychological data about an audience, such as standpoints, values, beliefs, and attitudes.

In contrast to audience demographics, **psychographics** focuses on psychological data such as standpoints, values, beliefs, and attitudes (**Figure 5.1**). Marketers rely on psychographic data to develop strategies that might motivate consumers to buy a company's products or services. For example, healthy and unhealthy eaters differ not only in their eating behaviors but also in their values associated with food and health. Marketing to these two groups requires different strategies that address each group's psychological orientations. As with marketing, understanding the psychographics of your audience will help you develop your speech so as to meet your overall objective or specific purpose.

The psychological location or place from which an individual views, interprets, and evaluates the world.

▼ **FIGURE 5.1**
Levels of Psychographic Data

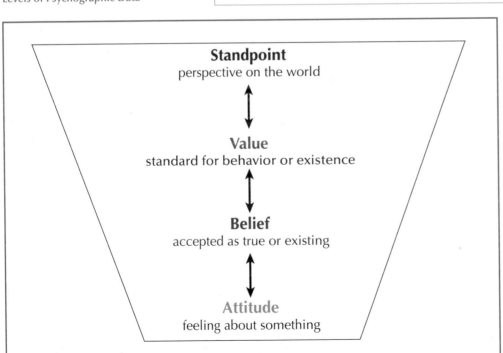

AUDIENCE STANDPOINTS

Standpoint refers to the location or place from which an individual views, interprets, and evaluates the world. Standpoints typically stem from individuals' positions in society based on demographics, such as socioeconomic status, sex, dis/ability, and age. The groups to which an individual belongs—for example, a Catholic Latina college student with a learning disability who comes from a working-class family, or a 40-year-old African-American gay man from an upper-middle-class family—influence his or her view of society.[15] Within any audience, members hold a variety of standpoints, which influence their values, beliefs, attitudes, and behaviors.

Considering standpoints moves audience analysis beyond simply categorizing individuals based on demographics. Standpoints recognize the different ways in which audience members view the world. In the case of a classroom audience, all the members may share the experience of being a college student. But they likely have different standpoints arising from their differing positions in society. For example, first-generation college students likely view higher education differently than do second-, third-, and fourth-generation college students.

In a speech on diversity to middle- and high school students in Granite Falls, Washington, *Seattle Times* publisher Frank Blethen[16] recognized different standpoints in his audience and sought to bridge them in this way:

> The Reverend Dr. Martin Luther King, Jr. Holiday. What is it? What is it not? First, what it is not: It is not a black holiday. It is not a yellow holiday. It is not a brown holiday. It is not a white holiday. It is not a man's holiday. It is not a woman's holiday. It is not a baby boomer holiday. It is not a generation X or Y holiday. It is not a poor person's holiday. It is not a rich person's holiday. It is not a religious holiday. It is not a commercial shopping holiday. It is not a day off.
>
> So, what is it? It is America's celebration. It is each of our individuals' day of celebration. It is a moment of rejoicing for all Americans. It is a moment of reflection for all Americans. It is a moment of renewal on our long diversity journey. It is a moment of challenge for each of us.

As Blethen's speech illustrates, identifying audience standpoints highlights similarities as well as differences among audience members.[17] Members of the same generation may share a common standpoint that transcends religion or class. Conversely, women in a particular society may share a common standpoint regardless of age—a standpoint that differs from that of men in that society.

AUDIENCE VALUES

A **value** serves as a standard of behavior. You've learned your values from the people you interact with, from the mass media, and from your society and culture. You express your values when you judge something as good or bad, excellent or poor, right or wrong, attractive or unattractive. Your standpoint influences your values. For example, research on environmentalism found that women view altruism as a more important value than do men, which in turn leads them to be more concerned about the environment.[18] If you were giving a speech on an environmental issue, knowing that women and men in your audience have differing value priorities would help you adapt your speech to both groups.

An ideal that serves as a standard of behavior.

Companies carefully analyze their audiences' values when developing an advertising campaign. Apple Inc., long known for its innovative advertisements, faced this issue with its Mac versus PC ads. Although the campaign was highly successful in the United States, audiences in Great Britain and Japan didn't find the ads as appealing or funny. The company even developed ads specifically for British and Japanese audiences. Yet after those ads were aired, audiences had even more negative views of the company and sales dropped. Surveys found that what was viewed as hip and trendy in the United States was considered smug and overbearing in Britain. And the Japanese consider directly attacking a competitor—which Apple does—unseemly and obnoxious.[19]

One method for accessing audience values is the VALS (Values and Lifestyles) Survey. Developed by SRI Consulting Business Intelligence, the survey groups people into eight categories based on fundamental values and resources.[20] *Innovators* have extensive resources and value independence, variety, and high-quality products and services. *Thinkers* are typically highly educated, conservative, and well-informed. *Achievers* are goal-oriented and value collaboration, stability, and the image they project. *Experiencers* tend to be young and energetic, valuing self-expression, risk-taking, and anything new. *Believers* focus on family and community, and value tradition and convention. *Strivers* have somewhat limited resources but value getting ahead and fitting in with their social group. *Makers* take a do-it-yourself orientation, valuing self-sufficiency, practical skills, and autonomy. *Survivors* have few resources and often struggle with daily life, so they value safety, security, and stability.

Knowing the values your audience members think are important can help you choose a topic they're interested in, identify relevant supporting materials, and deliver your speech in a way they will find informative, persuasive, or entertaining.

AUDIENCE BELIEFS

Something an individual accepts as true or existing.

Like values, an individual's beliefs flow from his or her standpoint. A **belief** is something a person accepts as true or existing. You seldom question your beliefs, even when someone challenges them or new information seems to contradict them. For example, new research indicates that consuming large quantities of antioxidants can have negative health consequences. Yet if you believe that antioxidants can improve your health, you might interpret the research with skepticism, thereby keeping your belief intact.

AUDIENCE ATTITUDES

How an individual feels about something.

An **attitude** is how a person feels about something. Attitudes indicate approval or disapproval and liking or disliking of a person, place, object, event, or idea. You might like the bus driver, approve of the new student union building, dislike a concert you recently attended, and disapprove of your city's plan for redeveloping the downtown area. Your attitudes are related to your standpoint, values, and beliefs, but these psychographic variables are not always consistent. For example, from the standpoint of a person with a disability, you might value universal access to public transit, believe that public transit is essential to your community, yet dislike your local public transit system. These conflicting psychological factors may stem from a negative experience or from a conflict between two competing beliefs.

GATHERING PSYCHOGRAPHIC DATA

A **behavior** is an observable action by an individual. Psychographic factors—standpoints, values, beliefs, and attitudes—intersect in complex ways to influence behavior. If you believe that homelessness is an important societal issue, for instance, you might volunteer at a local homeless shelter one day a week. Because psychographics underlie behavior, speakers often observe audiences in order to identify their standpoints, values, beliefs, and attitudes.

> An observable action.

In your public speaking class, careful observation will help you gather psychographic data about your audience. What do your classmates talk about before class? What topics do they choose for their speeches? How do they respond to other students' speeches? The

---

●●●●●●●●●● **THE EVOLVING ART**

Byte-Sized Audience Expectations

Audiences today are accustomed to media snacking—consuming a variety of media in bite-sized chunks, skipping from one medium to the next, or paying attention to several media simultaneously.[21] You may text message while flipping through a few blogs and listening to your iPod, chat on your cell phone while watching a video on YouTube and download-

ing the podcast of a class lecture. In a world of 30-second micro videogames, 2-minute versions of rock music classics, and 11-minute online TV episodes, audiences expect rapid information delivery. Does this mean you should develop your speeches as a series of sound bites? No. Audiences may like to snack, but they also want substance.[22] Still,

to keep their attention, you must consider their media-saturated environment and the tendency to move quickly through media choices—channel surfing, hyperlinking, scrolling—to find the information they want. Adapting to your audience involves understanding their expectations about the information you provide and how you deliver it.

more you interact with and observe the other students in your class, the more familiar you'll become with who they are and how they think.

Most of the speeches you'll give, however, will not be in front of students you get to know over the course of many class meetings. In some situations you may have little access to your audience beforehand and will need to make educated guesses about them based on general knowledge about the groups to which they belong (such as students at an urban high school or members of a bowling league). Still, in many instances you'll be familiar with your audience through work or social interactions. In those cases, reflecting on what you know about your audience will give you important insights into their standpoints, values, beliefs, and attitudes. For example, consider the topics they talk about, the ideas they argue about, the emotions they express, and how they behave when they meet someone new. Observing audience members well before you give your presentation will help you adapt your speech to their particular characteristics.

As with demographic data, another way to gather psychographic data about audience members is to have them complete an audience research questionnaire. The next section explains how to develop such a questionnaire.

Developing an Audience Research Questionnaire

A questionnaire used by speakers to assess the knowledge and opinions of audience members; can take the form of an e-mail, web-based, or in-class survey.

Speakers use **audience research questionnaires** to gather information about audience demographics and psychographics. Getting a sense of your audience's standpoints, values, beliefs, and attitudes—especially those related to your topic—will greatly influence the way you research, organize, and present your speech. Developing and distributing your questionnaire well in advance of speech day will help you keep your audience at the forefront throughout the speechmaking process. [23]

An effective audience research questionnaire features two basic types of questions—closed-ended and open-ended.

ASKING CLOSED-ENDED QUESTIONS

A question that limits the possible responses, asking for very specific information.

Closed-ended questions give the respondent a set of possible answers from which to choose. For instance, to gather demographic information you might ask questions such as

- What is your sex?

    _____ Female _____ Male

- To which ethnic group do you belong?
  _____ African American _____ Asian American _____ European American
  _____ Latin/Hispanic American _____ Native American _____ Other

Similarly, you may want to learn basic facts about the audience that will help you develop an effective approach to your speech topic. If you want to persuade your audience to stop watching television, for instance, or to watch it more selectively, you might include closed-ended questions, as with

- On average, how many hours do you watch TV each week?
  _____ 0–9 _____ 10–19 _____ 20–39 _____ 40 or more
- Do you have a television in your bedroom? _____ Yes _____ No
- Why do you usually watch TV?
  _____ because I'm bored _____ to socialize with family or friends _____ to escape
  _____ as a reward _____ to learn things _____ for entertainment _____ other

You can also use the questionnaire to gather psychographic data related to your topic. If you are developing an informative speech about your school's 150th anniversary, for example, you might ask these questions:

- Our school has a long history of excellent education.
  _____ True _____ False
- It's important to me that people in the community have a positive view of our school.
  _____ Agree _____ Disagree
- I would enjoy participating in events to celebrate our school's 150th anniversary.
  _____ Yes _____ No _____ Maybe

You can find out about audience members' beliefs by using another closed-ended question format that ascertains the strength of respondents' views. For example:

- Women make excellent bosses:
  _____ strongly agree _____ agree _____ neither agree nor disagree
  _____ disagree _____ strongly disagree
- Marijuana should be made legal for medical purposes:
  _____ strongly agree _____ agree _____ neither agree nor disagree
  _____ disagree _____ strongly disagree

Responses to these questions will give you an idea of what respondents believe as well as how strongly they believe it. Your classmates probably already have experience with these kinds of questionnaires, so they should be able to give you informed responses.

ASKING OPEN-ENDED QUESTIONS

Closed-ended questions can provide important information about the basic characteristics and beliefs of your audience. But speakers usually want more information. **Open-ended questions** are designed to elicit more in-depth information by asking respondents to answer in their own words. Additional insights can be gained by asking questions such as

- What do you know about the social security system?
- Why do you think people in our community are homeless?
- What changes, if any, would you make in our school's basic course requirements?
- What does the word *freedom* mean to you?

A broad, general question, often specifying only the topic.

COMBINING QUESTION TYPES

Combining closed-ended and open-ended questions can serve to clarify audience positions and elicit additional useful information. Here are some examples:

- Should the academic year for high school be extended to 12 months?
  _____ Yes _____ No
Why did you answer that way? _____
- Have you ever thought about joining a fraternity or sorority?
  _____ Yes _____ No
Why or why not? _____
- Do you think it's a good idea to keep a handgun at home?   _____ Yes _____ No
Why do you think this? _____

Leave enough room after each open-ended item for respondents to give useful answers, and keep your questionnaire short.

DISTRIBUTING YOUR QUESTIONNAIRE

If you have in-person access to your audience, you can distribute paper questionnaires. However, if you don't, you may want to use an online distribution method. The easiest way to administer an audience research questionnaire online is through a free survey-building website. These websites offer much more than ease of use and anonymous responses; often they provide tools for organizing and tabulating survey data. Putting your audience research questionnaire on a survey-building website works well for audiences outside the classroom as well. You'll find links to a few of these websites, as well as various polling sites, on this book's website. Once you've developed your survey, contact your audience with the link and a deadline for completion.

Keep the length of your questionnaire manageable. Five to ten questions usually will give you plenty of data and avoid burdening your audience. If your questionnaire is too long, respondents will tire of answering questions and may not respond as fully as you'd like (or at all). In addition, you'll likely end up with far more data than you need, causing you to waste time sifting through irrelevant information.

QUESTIONNAIRES FOR NON-CLASSROOM AUDIENCES

Your public speaking class presents a special case in which you can gather large amounts of information about your audience. Distributing an audience research questionnaire is more feasible and practical in the classroom than in other public speaking situations. Yet even if you can't use a formal questionnaire, you can still ask audience members questions.

In the best-case scenario, you'll develop a questionnaire that your audience will complete in advance. For example, if you'll be giving a presentation to a local community group, you could ask the group's leader to e-mail members the link to your online survey along with a brief statement explaining the survey's purpose.

But surveying your audience isn't always possible. Sometimes you'll have to make do with asking a few people key questions. If you don't know any members of your audience, you might contact the person who organized the event and ask for the names of some of the audience members. Then e-mail or phone those individuals, asking them questions that will give you a sense of your audience's knowledge level, standpoints, values, beliefs, and attitudes. When you don't have direct access to your audience, pose your questions to people who are familiar with the group you'll be addressing.

▲ Gathering relevant information about your audience as you prepare your speech will help you be audience-centered and credible when you deliver your speech.

Using Audience Research Data in Your Speech

Data gathered from a well-constructed audience research questionnaire can help you in two ways. First, you will learn more about who your audience is, what they know about your topic, and how they feel about it. Second, the questionnaire gives you data and comments you can refer to in the speech itself.

TYPES OF AUDIENCE DATA

Just mentioning questionnaire data in your speech will catch your audience's attention. But how can you use the data to achieve the best possible effect? You will have two basic types of information to work with: summary statistics and direct quotes.

Summary Statistics

Information in the responses to an audience research questionnaire that reflects trends and comparisons.

Summary statistics reflect trends and comparisons. For instance, you may find that 75 percent of the audience believes that access to affordable health insurance should be a right of all Americans. That is a trend statistic that you obtained by asking, "Do you believe health insurance is a right of all Americans?" But because you also asked respondents to identify their sex, you'd be able to make some simple comparisons. For instance, you may have found that women in your audience are more likely than men to support the idea of universal health care by a margin of two to one. Comparisons like these allow you to break down summary statistics into useful subcategories.

Direct Quotes

Comments written in response to an open-ended question in an audience research questionnaire.

Direct quotes are comments written in response to open-ended questions. For example, after asking the closed-ended question "Should the U.S. military draft be reinstated?" you probably would get some passionate responses to the following open-ended question: "Why do you think that way?" In selecting a quote, choose one that is short, well-written, and clearly linked to the point you want to make, such as:

> The draft should not be reinstated because a voluntary military is more motivated, professional, and dedicated.

Also, the quote should accurately reflect the respondent's sentiments and resonate with the audience. In addition, avoid quotes that might embarrass audience members or portray them in a negative way. Even if such quotes support your point, they'll hurt your credibility and make the audience less inclined to listen.

REFERRING TO AUDIENCE DATA IN YOUR SPEECHES

Summary statistics and direct quotes are valuable material you can use to get the audience's attention, support your main points, make transitions from one point to another, and conclude your speech. For example, you could begin a speech promoting public transportation like this:

> Over 90 percent of the people sitting in this room say they support toughening environmental standards against air pollution, yet very few of you say you

carpool or use public transportation. Today I'm going to show you how you can personally follow through on your interest in protecting the environment by making informed and responsible decisions about the forms of transportation you use every day.

Or you could use a quote as your attention getter:

"It's the biggest scam out there!" That's what one of you said about all the weight loss programs advertised on TV. Let's take a closer look at just what those magical weight loss programs are really all about.

Data from your audience research questionnaire also can be used to support your main points. For instance, you might integrate summary statistics into your speech in this way:

According to the questionnaire you filled out last week, more than three-fourths of you say you expect to take at least five years to finish your college degree—exactly the national average. For most students in the United States, the four-year college degree is a thing of the past.

In addition, summary statistics and direct quotes can provide effective transitions from one point to the next. For example:

That may seem impressive, but does it accomplish what someone in the audience calls "the single most important thing we have to do in America today—stop exporting good jobs to foreign countries"? Let's talk about how that might be done.

Statistics and quotes gleaned from the audience research questionnaire can prove effective in speech conclusions as well—a key statistic or compelling quote will stay with the audience long after the speech is over. You can leave the source of your data implicit and try something like this:

Finally, I encourage each of you to do the right thing and what the vast majority of you say must be done. Demand that the university adopt a strong hate speech policy and that administrators do it now!

When using a quote in a conclusion, you might say something like this:

You've heard my appeal for reforming the way presidential debates are conducted in this country. As one of your classmates asked, "How can the most democratic country in the world fail to represent the full range of diverse voices in this vital exercise of democracy—the Presidential debates?" Think about it.

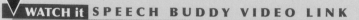
Analyzing and Using Audience Data

◄◄ ❚❚ ►►

In this video, Evan reviews some key points about audience questionnaires and demonstrates how to use questionnaire data in a speech. As you watch the video, consider what you've learned about developing and using audience analysis questionnaires.

According to Our Data

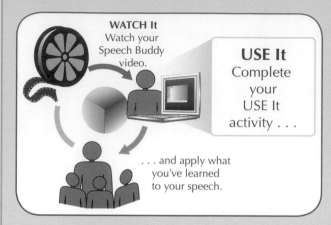

WATCH It
Watch your Speech Buddy video.

USE It
Complete your USE It activity . . .

. . . and apply what you've learned to your speech.

In this activity, you're asked to analyze three sample audiences and make decisions based on available data, and then consider how you might use audience data in your own speech.

▼ Adapting to the Setting

The setting for your speech plays an important role in adapting to the audience. The location of the speech, the occasion, and the time when you give your speech are factors to consider during speech preparation and delivery.

THE LOCATION

The specific location or physical place for your speech—a large auditorium, a small conference room, outside on the steps of your school's student union—influences what you say and how you say it. Identify in advance the advantages and disadvantages of where you'll be speaking. For example, a small conference room can allow for a more informal presentation in which you personalize your speech and easily make eye contact with each audience member. However, that informality may also lead listeners to whisper comments to each other, text message friends, or check e-mail. Even in a casual setting, you'll want to maintain a degree of formality so that audience members will focus on you.

Large auditoriums come with both positive and negative features as well. Such settings often have built-in systems for displaying digital slides, video, and audio. Using these presentation media can prove crucial in maintaining the attention of a large audience. However, listeners are more anonymous—especially if the room is dark and the spotlight is on you—and may be tempted to chat, arrive late, or leave early.

Analyze the room where you will be speaking. You may be accustomed to the setting, but probably from the vantage point of the audience, not of the speaker. Note the room's configuration and the availability of technical equipment. Identify possible sources of noise, such as open windows or doors. Determine whether you'll use a podium, a desk, or nothing at all. Knowing the possibilities and constraints of the location in advance helps you adapt to the setting.

The geographic location of your speech is also a factor to consider. Referring to the place where you're speaking lets the audience know you've thought in advance about the context for your remarks. For example, Time Warner Inc. Chairman and CEO Richard D. Parsons[24] made these references to location during a speech he gave in Chicago:

> This city also has a rich African-American heritage, beginning with Jean Baptiste Point du Sable—a Black man from Haiti—who built Chicago's first permanent settlement in 1779. And your president, Hermene Hartman, publisher of *Savoy* and *N'Digo*, is the latest in a long line of African-American publishers from Chicago who have been role models for many of us who walk in their footsteps today—from Robert Abbott who founded the *Chicago Defender* in 1905 to the late John H. Johnson who founded the Johnson Publishing Company, home of *Ebony* and *Jet,* in 1942.

By integrating information about Chicago's origins and its role in the development of African-American-owned media businesses, Parsons linked his speech to the setting in which it took place.

In some cases, you and your audience may be in different physical locations, as when webcasting or videoconferencing, for example. Gathering information about the possibilities and constraints of these technologies will help you adapt to the setting. Chapter 16 provides more detail about public speaking and new media.

THE OCCASION

The occasion is the reason for the speech. Why have people gathered for this event? Is your audience voluntary or captive? **Voluntary audiences** choose to attend (or not attend) a speaking event, as when you attend a guest lecture on campus because you find the topic interesting or listen to a political candidate's campaign speech at your town hall. **Captive audiences**, in contrast, feel that they *must* attend the speaking event. Mandatory staff meetings at work and required college orientations are examples of occasions when audience attendance is involuntary. The audience for your public speaking class may be considered captive if the course is required. Generally, voluntary audiences are more motivated to listen because they have chosen to attend. Speakers may have to work harder to motivate captive audiences. Knowing in advance the type of audience you will face will help you adapt to the occasion. For example, Cathleen Black, president of Hearst Magazines, explicitly referred to the occasion when she began a speech[25] to a group of magazine publishers:

Individuals who can choose to attend or not attend a speaking event.

Individuals who feel they must attend an event.

Good morning. It's great to be back. The last time I was a speaker at one of these breakfast sessions was 2002. Even though that was a few short years ago, it was a very different world. I talked about our high hopes for *O, the Oprah Magazine*, which went on to make publishing history. I also talked about our high hopes for *Lifetime Magazine*, which didn't. I talked about a lot of aspects of the magazine business. But I mentioned the word Web only twice . . . and then only in passing. I didn't mention social networking, or Google, or blogging, or long-tail marketing, or interactive advertising, or high-speed connections, or tagging, or platforms, or any of the other things that are reshaping the world of publishing. It's not that I wasn't aware of these things. It's just with the ruins of the dot com economy still smoldering . . . it didn't seem like they would be factors any time soon. Obviously, any time soon came a lot sooner than any of us could have predicted.

Black links her previous speech at the same event with her remarks at the current one. By adapting her speech to the occasion, she provides continuity for her listeners.

▼ Consider a speech you might give at this sort of occasion. How do you think you might adapt your speech to your audience in this situation?

Mark Wilson/Getty Images

THE TIME

Adapting to time means taking into account the time of day, the time during the event in which you give your speech, and current events that might impact your speech.

Time of day influences your audience's alertness, interests, and needs. An audience at 7:30 A.M. is very different from the same group at 7:30 P.M., with listeners likely more alert in the morning than in the evening. Speaking close to a mealtime can prove challenging, with audience members distracted by hunger before the meal and drowsy after the meal.

As you prepare your speech, also consider when you'll speak during the occasion. Even if you're the only speaker, your speech will take place within a larger flow of events, such as meetings, workshops, coffee breaks, and the like. As part of adapting to the setting, you acknowledge other events and speakers that occur before and after your speech. In your public speaking class, keeping brief notes on what other speakers have talked about earlier on the day of your speech or earlier in the term will help you integrate your topic with what others have covered. In addition, references to other speakers will personalize the topic for your audience.

Identifying current events and determining their relationship to your topic offers another way of adapting your speech to the setting. Scanning news sources can give you ideas for a current topic of interest to your audience. In addition, integrating current events into your speech helps place your topic within the larger flow of happenings at the local, regional, national, and global levels. For example, referring to a recent increase in unemployment might help audience members understand the importance of thorough preparation for a job search.

Developing Credibility with Your Audience

▼ Regardless of the demographics of your audience, appearing credible to your audience is key to your success. Speaker credibility, or what the Greek philosopher Aristotle called ethos, arises from audience perceptions of a speaker's competence, trustworthiness, dynamism, and sociability. The four dimensions of credibility work together to give the audience an overall impression of the speaker, as shown in **Figure 5.2**. That impression greatly influences whether or not the audience will listen to and believe the speaker.

COMPETENCE

Competence refers to the qualifications a speaker has to talk about a particular topic. Listeners view speakers as more credible when they appear

An audience's perception of a speaker's competence, trustworthiness, dynamism, and sociability.

The qualifications a speaker has to talk about a particular topic.

▼ **FIGURE 5.2**
The Dimensions of Speaker Credibility

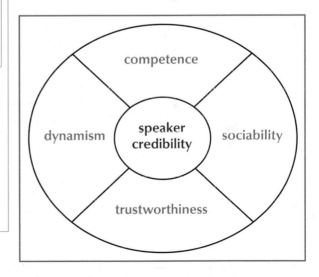

knowledgeable and informed about their topic.[26] This expertise may stem from a speaker's specialized training and experience related to the topic or through careful research. Speakers demonstrate their competence as they present relevant supporting materials. Different audiences will have different expectations about what constitutes effective and appropriate supporting materials.[27] Carefully analyzing your audience will give you insights into what they'll find interesting and convincing.

TRUSTWORTHINESS

An audience's perception of a speaker as honest, ethical, sincere, reliable, sensitive, and empathic.

The second dimension of speaker credibility is **trustworthiness**. Unlike competence, which relates to specific qualifications, information, and authority, trustworthiness is a much more general idea. Audiences regard you as trustworthy when they perceive you to be honest, ethical, sincere, reliable, sensitive, and empathic. Aristotle argued that a trustworthy public speaker must demonstrate **goodwill** by showing she or he has the audience's true needs, wants, and interests at heart.[28]

An audience's perception that a speaker shows she or he has the audience's true needs, wants, and interests at heart.

DYNAMISM

An audience's perception of a speaker's activity level during a presentation.

The third dimension of credibility, **dynamism**, refers to how the audience regards your activity level during your presentation. Dynamic speakers appear lively, strong, confident, and fluent in what they say and how they present their ideas. Audience members listen to, remember, enjoy, and are convinced by speakers who are dynamic.

SOCIABILITY

The degree to which an audience feels a connection to a speaker.

Sociability reflects the degree to which an audience feels a connection to a speaker. Sociable speakers are those the audience regards as friendly, accessible, and responsive.[29] Appearing sociable requires establishing a relationship with the audience—showing how you and the audience share some common ground or similarities. Speaking before a group in California, Queen Noor of Jordan reached out to her audience in this way:

> California has played a seminal role in my journey to the Middle East. It is here that I first became aware of my connection to that remarkable region of the world. When I was growing up, my family lived for a time in Santa Monica. My parents had a bedroom overlooking the ocean, and one day there my mother told me the story of our family. Her ancestors had emigrated here from Sweden, my father's father and uncles had emigrated from the Arab world. I remember sitting there after our conversation, staring out the window at the Pacific Ocean, and feeling connected for the first time to a larger family and a wider world.[30]

Although born and educated in the United States, Queen Noor had not lived there for some time. Referring to an experience in California when she was a child provided a way to connect with her audience. In addition to talking about living in California, Queen Noor used her voice to convey a warm and inviting tone.

SUMMARY

Adapting to your audience requires thorough analysis. Only then can you design a speech that is likely to accomplish your objective. Especially today, audience members represent diverse backgrounds, knowledge levels, and interests. Interacting with diverse groups of people presents many advantages, such as learning how to promote a more supportive communication climate and better articulate your own cultural identity. Demonstrating sensitivity to multiple audiences is a key quality of a successful public speaker. Techniques for speaking to diverse audiences include finding commonalities, establishing credibility, incorporating relevant supporting materials, using language that all audience members understand, and acknowledging all audience members throughout the speech.

When analyzing your audience, you gather two types of information: demographic and psychographic. Demographic information includes age, educational level, socioeconomic status, religious affiliation, ethnic background, disability, and sex. With this information, you can draw some general conclusions about your audience's interests and needs. The perspective of those who invite you to speak is particularly valuable for gathering demographic data, and online sources of demographics and public opinion can also be of benefit.

Psychographic information refers to psychological data about audience members, including their standpoints, values, beliefs, and attitudes. This information provides important insights into what might motivate them. In many cases you will infer audience psychographics based on observable behaviors, such as what they talk about, what they read, and the activities they participate in.

One method for gathering demographic and psychographic data is the audience research questionnaire. Carefully designed closed- and open-ended questions can elicit valuable information about your audience's interests and needs as well as those of various groups within the larger audience.

Information from the audience research questionnaire can be integrated into your speech. Closed-ended questions provide trends and averages, and open-ended questions elicit audience members' feelings, expressed in their own words. Quoting clever or insightful remarks by audience members is a great way to capture their attention, support your main points, make transitions from one point to the next, or create an effective conclusion.

Adapting to your audience also means adapting to the setting in which you give a speech. The location is the physical place where you give your speech, such as an auditorium, a classroom, or the steps of the county courthouse. New communication technologies allow speakers and audiences to participate in events from different geographic locations. The occasion is the purpose of the event. Audiences may attend out of choice, or attendance may be involuntary. The time of the speech, including time of day, speaking order, and current events, also influences the setting for the speech.

Whatever your audience and setting, developing your credibility is crucial to your success as a speaker. Competence, trustworthiness, dynamism, and sociability work together to form a speaker's credibility.

In the Book

Summary
Key Terms
Critical Challenges

More Study Resources

Speech Studio
Quizzes
WebLinks

Student Workbook

5.1: Target Audience Beliefs
5.2: Seeing Your Topic through Your Audience's Eyes
5.3: Design a Questionnaire
5.4: VALS Survey
5.5: Sample Audience Member

Speech Buddy Videos

 Video Links

Analyzing and Using Audience Data

Activity Links

According to Our Data

▶ Sample Speech Videos

Matthew, "Drinking," persuasive speech

Courtney, "Light Pollution," persuasive speech

 Speech Builder Express

Goal/purpose
Thesis statement
Supporting material
Introduction
Conclusion
Works cited
Outline

 InfoTrac

Recommended search terms

Audience and public speaking
Audience analysis
Audience adaptation
Audience centered
Classroom audience
Demographic information
Psychographic information
Personal values
Personal beliefs
Personal attitudes
Survey questions
Online survey services
Research data and public speaking

Audio Study Tools

"Drinking" by Matthew

Critical thinking questions

Learning objectives

Chapter summary

Guide to Your Online Resources

Your Online Resources for *Public Speaking: The Evolving Art* give you access to the Speech Buddy video and activity featured in this chapter, additional sample speech videos, Speech Builder Express, InfoTrac College Edition, and study aids such as glossary flashcards, review quizzes, and the Critical Challenge questions for this chapter, which you can respond to via e-mail if your instructor so requests. In addition, your Online Resources feature live WebLinks relevant to this chapter, including sites regarding opinion polls, such as the Pew Research Center, the Gallup Poll, Zogby Poll, and the National Opinion Research Center at the University of Chicago. Links are regularly maintained, and new ones are added periodically.

Key Terms

attitude 108

audience 101

audience analysis 99

audience-centered 101

audience research questionnaire 110

behavior 109

belief 108

captive audience 118

closed-ended question 110

competence 119

credibility 119

demographics 105

direct quote 114

dynamism 120

goodwill 120

open-ended question 112

psychographics 106

sociability 120

standpoint 106

summary statistics 114

target audience 102

trustworthiness 120

value 107

voluntary audience 118

Begin your search for books related to your topic by checking your campus library's online catalog. Unless you know the title of a book or author, use the keyword function to search for relevant books. When you identify a book you think will be useful, write down its `call number` so you can check it out the next time you're on campus. Or, if it's an e-book, you can review it on screen.

The number assigned to each book or bound publication in a library to identify that book in the library's classification system.

A library's online catalog entry for a book often includes links to related topics. For example, a search for books about global warming produced over 300 titles, including *Creating a Climate for Change: Communicating Climate Change and Facilitating Social Change*, edited by Susanne C. Moser and Lisa Dilling, published by Cambridge University Press in 2007. The subject list included links to related resources in three areas:

- Climatic changes
- Communication in the environmental sciences
- Communication in social action

By clicking on the links to these areas, you could browse other library materials that might be useful for a speech on global warming.

Journals, Magazines, and Newspapers

Published at regular intervals, or periods, periodicals include journals, magazines, and newspapers. Your library provides access to full-text databases of articles from periodicals. Follow the library's instructions for accessing those databases, such as LexisNexis (newspapers, magazines, trade publications, and company information), ProQuest (extensive collection of U.S. and international news sources), and Social Science Full Text (journals in social science and interdisciplinary areas).

Newspapers have the most current print information about your topic. Although you could search the websites of individual newspapers, using a database such as ProQuest allows you to search multiple news sources simultaneously. ProQuest gives you many options for searching, such as selecting specific databases and limiting the date range. Advanced Search allows you to enter multiple words and choose where those words must be present, such as in citations and abstracts. Topic Guide helps you identify additional key words and topics for your search.

Not all periodicals are available online, and some charge a fee for web access, especially for archived materials. Still, you can often identify relevant articles from online indexes such as Academic Search Premier, ProQuest Historical Newspapers, Directory of Open Access Journals, and Global Market Information Database. Then you'll need to make a trip to the library to find articles in paper, microfilm, or microfiche sources.

AP Photo/Moscow-Pullman Daily News, Geoff Crimmins

▲ Although it's tempting to use the internet for all your research, your brick-and-mortar library has much to offer, including special collections and unusual sources that are not always available online.

Government Publications

Cybercrime, endangered species, housing, nursing, solar power, water—these are just a few of the topics addressed in U.S. government publications. The Catalog of United States Government Publications, available free online, indexes documents from the three branches of the U.S. government dating back to July 1976. New publications are added every day. Reports, monographs, handbooks, pamphlets, and audio files are among the types of resources you'll find in government publications. If you were conducting research for a speech on solar power, for instance, a keyword search would yield NASA documents, consumer guides, Senate testimony, and reports from the National Renewable Energy Laboratory related to solar power and other forms of alternative energy.

Reference Works

Maps, atlases, encyclopedias, dictionaries, and various print indexes comprise reference materials you typically may use only in the library. If you were doing research for a speech on water conservation, you might consult maps that will help you (and your audience) pinpoint areas in which people have implemented innovative conservation strategies. *The African-American Almanac* could be a useful resource if you were planning a speech on the achievements of African Americans.

Sometimes it's helpful to precisely define the terms you use in your speeches. Although you can find dictionaries online, more specialized dictionaries are often found only in print. *The Morris Dictionary of Word and Phrase Origins* traces the etymology of words as well as how their use developed over time. Dictionaries not only provide definitions but may cover a wide range of topics, from dance to women artists. For example, *Dow's Dictionary of Railway Quotations* includes excerpts from songs, films, novels, TV broadcasts, and other sources. Visual dictionaries can prove particularly helpful for informative speeches. They include photographs, drawings, diagrams, and illustrations that help readers understand the meanings of words. For example, the *Ultimate Visual Dictionary 2000* defines more than 30,000 terms with detailed color illustrations. *A Visual Dictionary of Chinese Architecture* includes both detailed descriptions and line drawings.

Use your library's online catalog to locate reference materials. Note their locations and call numbers so you can review them when you go to the library.

Nonprint Resources

If you've seen Martin Luther King, Jr.'s "I Have a Dream" speech on film, you understand the potential impact of visual or multimedia resources. Although the words alone move people, seeing and hearing Dr. King deliver this landmark speech influences the audience much more profoundly. His image—gesturing, nodding, scanning the crowd, the deep voice beseeching listeners to fight for freedom—stays with us even if we forget his exact words.

Audio sources available on tape or CDs or for download to your computer or MP3 player may also convey an image or set a tone that a simple verbal description cannot accomplish. For example, an exhibit at the Experience Music Project in Seattle includes interviews with local hip-hop artists. Hearing their stories in their own voices generates an emotional force that visitors can't experience just by reading printed statements.

Today's audiences expect speakers to integrate audio, visual, and multimedia resources into their speeches. Media outlets, public libraries, private and public organizations, YouTube, podcasts, and blogs are all useful sources of nonprint supporting material for your speeches.

USING ORGANIZATIONAL SOURCES

You'll likely encounter instances when you need to contact an organization for information relevant to your speech. Particularly if your topic touches on a local issue, such as how your city addresses traffic problems or the resurgence of the local art community, local organizations often can provide information that is not available from any other source. For example, suppose you're conducting research for a speech on hospice, where terminally ill people and their families receive spiritual, emotional, and medical care. Although you can get information from the National Hospice and Palliative Care Organization's website, you'll also want information about hospice care in your community.

Not every organization has a website, but basic contact information likely is available online. Access this information online using websites such as Yahoo! and Netscape that include a Yellow Pages feature. If the organization you want to contact is not listed in an online directory, use your keywords to search the Yellow Pages in your telephone book. In the case of hospice, the Yellow Pages, whether online or in print, will help you find a local hospice. You can contact the hospice, request pamphlets or other information, and possibly schedule an interview with the director.

ACCESSING INTERNET RESOURCES

Websites, the deep web, blogs, newsgroups, and discussion lists offer additional resources for researching your speeches. More than likely, you've already done a lot of searching for information on the internet. You can probably go online and find the best deals on airline tickets, laptops, and DVD players. But can you find the information you need for a well-researched speech? That's what you'll learn to do in this section.

Websites

Of all the internet resources, you're probably most familiar with websites. However, entering a few keywords into your favorite search engine to find what you need for your speeches won't produce the information you need. Having a research strategy and searching with a purpose are essential. To help you search the web more purposefully, this section explains how to use metasearch engines, search engines, and web directories to find relevant information. Different search tools have different ways of determining which websites are most relevant. Generally, however, **relevance** refers to how closely a webpage's content is related to the keywords used in a search. The better your keywords represent the topic you're researching, the greater the likelihood you'll find relevant information.

> How closely a webpage's content is related to the keywords used in an internet search.

To get you started, **Table 6.2** on pages 138 and 139 presents an overview of internet search tools and their features. Each site is listed here, and you'll find live links to each URL in this chapter on the book's online resources.

> A search tool that does not actually search the web for information, but rather compiles the results from other search engines.

Metasearch engines rely on other search engines to find information on the web. Although metasearch engines like those listed in Table 6.2 may seem like the best strategy for online searching, they provide breadth rather than depth. For example, if you were giving an informative speech on the history of TV, you'd want more general information about the topic. In contrast, a speech focusing on a specific TV genre, such as reality shows, would require more in-depth information. In combining the results of several search engines, metasearch engines reveal the websites and webpages most frequently listed by the different search engines. Metasearch engines' results represent only a small portion of the websites you'd find if you used each search engine individually. The results listed may be the most popular websites each search engine has identified, but they may not be the best or most relevant sources of information.

Metasearch engines can be useful as a starting point—they give you a sampling of websites associated with your topic. Also, some metasearch engines tap into specialized search engines you may not find on your own. For instance, YurNet's specialty search function allows you to search for movie listings, stock listings, weather forecasts, word meanings, eBay items, and real-time webcam views of world cities.

Search engines use sophisticated software programs that hunt through computer documents to locate those associated with particular keywords. Search engines search only files that they've indexed; no search engine has indexed the entire web. And each search engine applies its own methods to scour the web. Thus, different search engines will produce different results, and the same search engine will produce different results on different days. A recent survey of Ask, Google, and Yahoo! found dramatically different results, with only 3 percent of the same links listed on the first page of each search tool.[7] Overall, each search engine produced results that were 85 percent unique to that search engine. So although your natural inclination may be to use just one or two search engines, trying several will give you a more comprehensive search. In addition, 90 percent of search tool users never click past the first page of results.[8] Keep digging; you may find just what you need on page 12 or 20.

> A sophisticated software program that hunts through documents to find those associated with particular keywords.

With the total number of webpages now exceeding 5 billion,[9] finding useful information quickly requires precise searching. Although you may want to initially use metasearch and search engines, web directories like those listed in Table 6.2 can help you refine your search strategies. **Web directories**, also called search indexes, organize webpages hierarchically by categories. For example, Yahoo!'s web directory includes subject areas such as business and economy, health, education, and social science, which are broken down into subcategories. You can browse directories by category or search using keywords.

> An online list that organizes webpages and websites hierarchically by category; also called a search index.

The Deep Web

Traditional metasearch engines and search engines miss billions—that's right, billions—of webpages. Experts estimate that these "missing" webpages account for 80 percent of the

· · · · · · · · · · THE EVOLVING ART

U.S. Government Information Online

The U.S. government is one of the largest collectors of information in the world. Before the internet, these documents were available only in paper form or on CD-ROM. Now, you can simply go to USA.gov or any specific government agency's website to access documents. Looking for information about health issues such as diabetes, cancer, or AIDS? Go to the U.S. Department of Health and Human Services' website (os.dhhs .gov). Want to know more about issues involving new communication technologies? Try visiting the Federal Communications Commission (fcc.gov) or Library of Congress (loc.gov) websites. You can browse all U.S. government sites and perform keyword searches from the U.S. government's web portal.

TABLE 6.2 ▶ Metasearch Engines, Search Engines, Specialized Search Engines, and Web Directories

	WEB ADDRESS	FEATURES
METASEARCH ENGINES		
Clusty	clusty.com	Groups together similar results
CurryGuide	web.curryguide.com	Allows you to set your own preferences and save searches for later review
Dogpile	dogpile.com	Sorts by relevance as well as search engine
Jux2	jux2.com	Allows you to compare the results from major search engines
KartOO	kartoo.com	Visually displays search results in interactive maps
Ixquick	ixquick.com	Lists top ten sites for each search engine in addition to all results
Mamma	mamma.com	Power Search lets you select search sources and preferences
Vivisimo	vivisimo.com	Lists top relevant results as well as clusters by subtopic
ZapMeta	zapmeta.com	Advanced search includes filters by region, domain, and host
SEARCH ENGINES		
AlltheWeb	alltheweb.com	Provides detailed advance search options to limit results
AltaVista	altavista.com	Searches worldwide and in all languages
Ask	ask.com	Offers question-based searching and ideas for related topics
Gigablast	gigablast.com	Includes Giga Bits that offer suggestions for refining your search
Google	google.com	Offers specialized search engines, such as Google Scholar, Video, Wireless, News, U.S. Government
Hotbot	hotbot.com	Allows you to select the search engine you want to use
LookSmart	looksmart.com	Searches more than 5 million articles on a wide range of topics

Lycos	lycos.com	Searches forums, bulletin boards, and newsgroups with discussion search
Wisenut	wisenut.com	Includes WiseGuide and WiseSearch to help you focus your searches
Yahoo!	yahoo.com	Allows you to use tabs to search images, news, local, video, and other specialized content

SPECIALIZED SEARCH ENGINES

Daypop	daypop.com	Searches the "living web"—news sites and blogs updated daily
INFOMINE	infomine.ucr.edu	Librarian-built, searches scholarly resources
MedHunt	hon.ch/MedHunt	Searches medicine-related websites, news, conferences, and images
Scirus	scirus.com	Focuses on science information
SearchEdu	searchedu.com	For education, military, government, dictionary, and encyclopedia sites

WEB DIRECTORIES

InfoGrid	infogrid.com	Covers traditional topic areas plus listings by four grids: info, personal, lifestyle, and kids
JoeAnt.com	joeant.com	Allows you to browse by subject or region of the world
Librarians' Index to the Internet	lii.org	Lists carefully reviewed and selected sites from the experts on accurate information
Open Directory Project	dmoz.org	An international network of volunteers gives this directory a global scope
The Web's Best Directory	webs-best directory.com	Provides links to websites and articles
Yahoo!	dir.yahoo.com	One of the originals, lists new additions to the directory

web. For example, much timely and accurate health information is available only through specialized medical databases.[10] Welcome to the **deep web**, also called the invisible or hidden web, comprised of all the databases and dynamically generated content, such as discussion lists and newsgroup threads, that most regular search engines can't access.

The portion of the World Wide Web composed of specialty databases, such as those housed by the U.S. government, that are not accessible by traditional search engines; also called the invisible or hidden web.

How can you access the deep web? Some specialized metasearch engines, such as BrainBoost and Turbo10, tap into database search engines. Some websites provide directories with links to thousands of databases. **Table 6.3** lists several key access points for the deep web.

Blogs

Blogs, or web logs, are webpages individuals update regularly, often daily, with topical entries. Although early blogs were mostly text, blogs now often include audio and video files.

Short for web log, a webpage that a blog writer, or blogger, updates regularly with topical entries.

TABLE 6.3 ▶ Accessing the Deep Web

NAME	WEB ADDRESS	FEATURES
BrainBoost	brainboost.com	Searches based on question asked
CompletePlanet	completeplanet.com	Allows you to search or browse for thousands of relevant databases
GeniusFind	geniusfind.com	Provides access to thousands of search engines and databases organized by categories
IncyWincy	incywincy.com	Allows you to refine your searches by category
Invisible-web.net	invisible-web.net	Links to a wide range of databases from art to U.S./world history
NewsVoyager	newsvoyager.com	Searches local U.S. newspapers
Search Engine Colossus	searchenginecolossus.com	Provides access to an international directory of search engines
Turbo10	turbo10.com	Connects to more than 3000 search engines

Blogs come in a range of types and purposes. Some blogs focus solely on personal musings, opinions, and activities. Opinions are personal beliefs, evaluations, and sentiments. In contrast, facts are established through careful documentation and verification of events that have occurred.

Corporations have entered the blog world with employee blogs, executive blogs, and customer service blogs. College students use blogs to network with each other. News blogs bring people firsthand accounts of events occurring around the world. For example, blogs proved instrumental in reporting on the December 26, 2004, South Asia tsunami and matching contributors with charities. Blogging also influences the political process, as demonstrated during elections, with bloggers joining the traditional press corps at the Democratic and Republican national conventions. In addition, bloggers have played leading roles in exposing illegal and immoral behavior of U.S. religious and political leaders that led to scandals and resignations.

Like websites, though, blogs can be faked. For example, a teenage blogger's account of her battle with cancer turned out to be a hoax. And even if information in a blog seems accurate, you don't always know the blogger's identity. Some bloggers use an assumed name or fail to reveal their connection to the stories they're blogging about.[11] So you can't always be sure of their motives for writing a blog.

Without the usual gatekeepers watching over bloggers, can you trust any of the information available in the blogosphere? Yes. Millions of people read blogs every day, and those readers often quickly identify and correct false, slanted, and inaccurate information. Regular blog users rate blogs as highly credible and containing in-depth information, though not necessarily fair.[12] As discussed later in the chapter, successful speakers critically examine all information they gather, including what they gather from blogs. **Table 6.4** lists some places to begin a blog search.

> Online text-based forums in which participants discuss particular topics; also called Usenet.

Newsgroups

Newsgroups are online discussion forums that focus on specific topics. Web directories generally

TABLE 6.4 ▶ Accessing Blogs

NAME	WEB ADDRESS	FEATURES
Blogdex	blogdex.net	Identifies the spread of a topic across blogs—the buzz of blogs
Blogdigger	blogdigger.com	Searches for keywords in text, by URL, and by type of media
BlogStreet	blogstreet.com	Lists the Most Influential and Top 100 blogs
PubSub	pubsub.com	Tracks blogs along with press releases and newsgroups in real time
Technorati	technorati.com	Real-time search engine that monitors blogs and links

include a newsgroup category that lists different newsgroups. Learn the Net (learnthenet .com) provides useful information about searching for the newsgroups that fit your interests, subscribing to newsgroups and reading messages, posting your messages, and starting your own newsgroup.

Google Groups gives public speaking students a good place to start searching for newsgroups relevant to particular speech topics. The site hosts newsgroups on a range of topics, and its directory categorizes newsgroups by type and topic. In addition, you can search the newsgroups using keywords. If you were to research a speech on human rights, for example, you could do a search using the keyword "human rights." You would probably find useful information in the "soc.rights.human" newsgroup listed in the results.

Discussion Lists

An e-mail–based distribution list that allows members to e-mail everyone who belongs to the list using just one e-mail address; also called a listserv.

E-mail-based **discussion lists,** also called *listservs,* allow you to e-mail a group of people using just one e-mail address. Generally, individuals join discussion lists because they're interested in a particular topic or activity, such as women-owned businesses, politics, the care of unusual pets, or hiking in the Southwest. Some discussion lists are for members only, while others are open to anyone.

Although you shouldn't expect discussion list members to conduct your research for you, they can provide ideas for sources and topics. Before sending a message, be sure you're familiar with the discussion list's norms and the general rules of interaction. **Table 6.5** provides a list of places where you can find discussion lists.

TABLE 6.5 ▶ **Accessing Discussion Lists**

NAME	WEB ADDRESS	FEATURES
CataList	lsoft.com/lists/listref.html	Allows you to search for lists and view lists by host country or membership size
Coollist	coollist.com	Allows you to start, join, and browse discussion lists by topic area
Tile.net	tile.net/lists	Allows you to browse or search e-mail newsletters and discussion lists
Yahoo! Groups	groups.yahoo.com	Provides many groups to choose from; you must sign up for a Yahoo! ID

Some professional and academic organizations have discussion lists you can sign up for without being a member. For example, if you were researching an issue related to communication, you might want to join the National Communication Association or the American Communication Association's listserv. Members are generally eager to assist students in the research process.

Maximizing Your Search of Internet Resources

▼ This chapter has introduced you to many sources for finding the information you need for your speeches. Effective searching saves you time, aggravation, and frustration. The following guidelines will help you maximize your search efforts.

USE A VARIETY OF KEYWORDS

Search tools produce results based on the keywords you enter. Different libraries, databases, search engines, and web directories use different indexing and keyword systems.[13] Choose your keywords carefully and consider alternatives to your original choice. For example, for "computer literacy" also try "information literacy," "computer knowledge," and "computer learning." Each set of keywords produces different results. Not sure what alternative keywords will help you with your search? Search engines such as Ask and Gigablast will give you suggestions.

USE THE ADVANCED SEARCH OPTION

Many search tools offer an advanced or guided search option that allows you to refine your search by keyword, date, type of media, and other specific parameters. In addition, nearly all search tools include a section on "tips for searching" that explains the best strategies for using that particular search tool.

SEARCH A VARIETY OF SOURCES

Getting multiple perspectives on a topic means going to multiple sources for information. Your library connects you with books, journals, newspapers, magazines, government publications, reference materials, and nonprint resources that will give you a range of viewpoints and perspectives. Organizations, websites, the deep web, blogs, newsgroups, and discussion lists provide additional angles on your topic. You don't need to search every source, but a good sampling increases your expertise on the topic.

A link whose owner has paid a search engine company such as Google to place the link in the results list of a search.

A statement about the legal rights of others to use an original work, such as a song (lyrics and melody), story, poem, photograph, or image.

▼ Government sites such as USA.gov, the web portal for all U.S. government offices and departments, is just one of the many reliable sources you can access on the internet.

USE A VARIETY OF SEARCH TOOLS

Each metasearch engine, search engine, and web directory uses its own search methods. No search tool accesses the entire web, and no database contains all the resources relevant to your topic.

BE WARY OF SPONSORED LINKS

Many metasearch engines, search engines, and web directories support **sponsored links**, listings, or sites. A link is sponsored when its owner pays the search engine or directory for a prominent location or placement on the results page. Sponsored listings in your search results may be at the top of the page, but their ranking is due to the payment of a fee, not relevance. Research has found that less than 40 percent of search engine users understand this difference.[14] A sponsored link *may* be quite relevant to your topic, but you cannot assume it is. Evaluate these websites carefully, as the link is essentially an advertisement. Most search engines, including Google and Yahoo, clearly identify ads and sponsored links at the top and sides of a results page.

SEARCH VISUALLY

As you're searching for information, consider more than text. Nearly all metasearch engines and search engines allow you to search for image, MP3, video, and audio files. Read the **copyright information** carefully before using any files you download. Copyright information is a statement about the legal rights of others to use an original work. Use of website images and similar files in speeches generally is allowed under fair use laws if you credit the author properly.

USE THE HELP BUTTON

Every search tool has a help function. Use it! Help sections explain how to use Boolean operators (and, or, not) or other words (near) and characters (+, –) to refine your search.

http://www.usa.gov

Managing the Research Process

◄◄ ❚❚ ►►

In this video segment, Evan demonstrates some key strategies for researching a speech topic.

The Research Detective

In this activity, you have an opportunity to try out various research strategies and then create a plan for researching your own speech topic.

Conducting Research Interviews

Research interviews can help you obtain valuable information. However, they require thorough preparation, disciplined participation, and follow-up. In this section you'll learn how to meet these requirements and conduct an effective research interview.

Interviews with experts can provide important information. However, particularly in your situation—where your speech and credibility rely on accurate information—the interviews must be carefully planned and implemented. The research interview process consists of six major steps:

1. Determine the interview's purpose.

2. Select interviewees.

Interviewing

Although we usually think of interviews as occurring in person, interviews may be conducted via the telephone, e-mail, chat, text messaging, instant messaging, or videoconferencing. Interviewing is defined by the process of asking and answering questions, not the medium used to interact. If you're using a real-time internet medium such as chat, be sure you're able to capture the interview so you have a record of it. For example, Apple's iChat and AOL's chat allow you to save transcripts of any chat session. Ask your interviewee's permission to save the conversation.

3. Develop questions.

4. Organize the interview.

5. Conduct the interview.

6. Integrate the information.

The sections that follow take a closer look at each of these steps.

DETERMINE THE INTERVIEW'S PURPOSE

Identify your reason for interviewing a particular individual about your speech topic. If you can gather the same information from other sources, there's no need to conduct the interview. In addition, consider how you'll use the expert's information in your speech. If you're not sure how that information will fit in, ask yourself if the interview is really necessary.

Focus on the specific information an expert can offer. Research for a speech on city government, for instance, might greatly benefit from an interview with the mayor to get an insider's view of how local leadership works. That's information you can't obtain in other ways.

SELECT INTERVIEWEE(S)

Choose interviewees with your purpose and what you already know about the topic as your guides. Identify the additional information you need and who may have it. Select interviewees based on their expertise, availability, and willingness to answer your questions. Just because someone has the information you need doesn't mean she or he will reveal it to you.[15] If an interviewee views you as credible, you'll have a better chance of getting the information you want. To enhance your credibility, research the topic and the interviewee, carefully prepare for the interview, use active listening skills, and demonstrate sensitivity to the interviewee's cultural background.

DEVELOP QUESTIONS

The questions you plan to ask form the basis of your **interview guide,** the list of all the questions and possible probes you will ask in the interview, as well as how you'll begin and end the interview. Think of the interview guide as a road map for gathering the information you seek and developing a productive relationship with your interviewee.

A list of all the questions and possible probes an interviewer asks in an interview, as well as notes about how the interviewer will begin and end the interview.

Questions can be categorized in three ways: primary versus secondary, open versus closed, and neutral versus leading.[16] **Primary questions** introduce a new topic or subtopic. They can stand alone, without the need for other statements or questions to provide context. "How did you choose your major?" and "What advice do you have for first-year college students?" are examples of primary questions. **Secondary questions** ask an interviewee to elaborate on a previous response. These follow-up questions may be as simple as "Go on," or more direct, as with, "Please tell me more about your experiences as a tour guide in Southeast Asia." Secondary questions depend on a previous statement or question to make sense.

A question that introduces a new topic or subtopic in an interview.

A question that asks the interviewee to elaborate on a response.

Open-ended questions are broadly worded, often only identifying a topic, such as, "What interesting things did you learn on your trip to Cambodia?" Closed-ended questions seek a specific piece of information. They limit the interviewee's response choices, as in, "On a scale of 1 to 5, with 5 being excellent and 1 being poor, how would you rate the quality of communication in your workplace?"

All the previous examples are **neutral questions** in that they're unbiased and impartial, simply seeking a direct answer. Most of the time, you'll ask neutral questions in research interviews. In contrast, **leading questions** suggest the answer you want. "Wouldn't you agree that soccer is a better sport for children than baseball?" and "Don't you think *24* is the best show on TV?" are examples of leading questions, whereas "Which sport do you think is better for children, soccer or baseball?" and "What do you think of the TV show *24*?" are neutral questions. You've probably heard journalists use leading questions when they're trying to get a particular answer from an uncooperative interviewee. That strategy sometimes works in a press conference, but in a research interview leading questions rarely produce useful information, and the interviewee often feels harassed.

An unbiased and impartial question seeking a forthright answer.

A question that suggests the answer the interviewer seeks.

As you develop your questions, pay close attention to how you've phrased each one. As a general rule, your questions should be neutral and open-ended. For every primary question, you'll need at least one secondary question. You may find that you have a talkative interviewee who needs little prodding, but your interviewee could also be more reticent than you'd anticipated. If you have secondary questions ready, you'll be prepared for either situation. **Table 6.6** summarizes the types of interview questions and when to use them.

ORGANIZE YOUR INTERVIEW GUIDE

After you've developed your questions, you need to put them in order and decide how to begin and end the interview. How you open an interview sets the tone for the entire conversation. Your two main tasks in the opening are to (1) establish rapport and (2) provide orientation. Accomplishing these early on provides a basis for effective communication throughout the interview.[17] If you are interviewing one of your instructors, for instance,

TABLE 6.6 ▶ **When to Use Different Types of Questions**

TYPE OF QUESTION	EXAMPLE	WHEN TO USE
Primary	What college experiences had the greatest impact on your professional career?	Introducing a new topic or subtopic
Secondary	Tell me more about the volunteer work you mentioned earlier.	Eliciting additional information from the interviewee
Open-ended	How did you first become involved in local politics?	The interviewee feels free to talk and is knowledgeable about the topic
Closed-ended	Where were you born?	Seeking a specific piece of information, or the interviewee seems reluctant to talk
Neutral	When do you plan to complete the project?	Always, with rare exceptions
Leading	Wouldn't you say that our campus is a friendly one?	The interviewee is uncooperative

you might talk a bit about a recent class meeting or something else related to the class. If you're interviewing the president of a company, you'll want to keep small talk to a minimum and get to the point of the interview quickly.

A clear orientation lets your interviewee know how you're going to proceed. For the research interview, identify the purpose of the interview, the topics you'll cover, your prior research on the topic, the expected length of the interview, and how the information will be used. For example, the interviewer might say

> I'm researching tax reform for a persuasive speech in my public speaking class. I've read about different ideas the county is considering, but would like your personal views on the topic. As we discussed on the phone, the interview should take about 30 minutes. I'll ask you questions about why you think our county needs tax reform, how you think your proposal will solve current problems, and the predicted effects of your reforms on county residents.

Your prepared questions make up the body, or main portion, of the interview. They should follow a logical sequence. Begin with general questions so you get a sense of the interviewee's breadth of knowledge; then ask more specific questions. Group questions by subtopic. Within each subtopic, ask general questions and then move to more specific ones.

A student who conducted an interview on public transportation organized questions into four groups:

1. How the interviewee got started working in public transportation

2. Promoting public transportation

3. Responding to critics of public transportation

4. The interviewee's predictions regarding future innovations in public transportation

This grouping follows a logical order: asking fairly easy questions about how the interviewee got involved in public transportation, then asking how the interviewee promotes public transportation and responds to critics, and finally inviting the interviewee to speculate about possible innovations in public transportation.

The closing of an interview should leave the interviewee feeling positive and satisfied with the exchange. Ending with, "Well, that was my last question. Thanks!" is abrupt and won't leave either participant feeling comfortable. Generally, the closing progresses through three stages:

1. The *conclusion preview* signals that the interview is drawing to a close. To prepare the interviewee for the interview closing, you might say something like, "My final question is. . ." or "I see we have just a few minutes left . . ."

2. In the *closure statement,* summarize the main points you gleaned from the interview and thank the interviewee for participating. Ask if you may contact the interviewee should you have any questions while preparing your speech.

3. Finally, *post-interview conversation* occurs after the formal interview, once you've turned off your audio recorder or closed your notebook. This informal interaction may include small talk or general discussion of the topic. The interviewee may relax and reveal important information related to your topic. During the post-interview discussion you'll say your final farewells and once again express appreciation for the interviewee's cooperation.

In structuring your questions and determining the opening and closing, you'll complete your interview guide. Flexibility is the hallmark of an effective interviewer. Don't hesitate to stray from your interview guide if the interviewee provides useful, but unexpected, information. **Figure 6.2** presents a sample interview guide.

▶ FIGURE 6.2

Sample Interview Guide

Interviewee: Lauria Quijas, Founder and CEO
Organization: Internet Ideas
Purpose: To gain a better understanding of what is involved in founding a company
Opening:

My name is Barrett Yip, and I am a student at City College taking a class in public speaking. Thank you for taking the time to meet with me. I've browsed through your company's website and I'm so interested to learn more about it.

As I mentioned in my e-mail when we scheduled this interview, I'm researching a speech on the steps involved in starting your own company. This interview should take about 45 minutes. The questions I have cover four main topics: your motivations for starting Internet Ideas, its current status, your view of the company's future, and your advice for anyone wanting to start their own business. As we discussed previously, I will record the interview so I have an accurate record of what you said. What questions do you have before we get started?

1. First I'd like to ask you about the origins of Internet Ideas. What motivated you to start this company?

   1.1. Tell me more about your initial motivation.

   1.2. What else prompted your decision?

2. What made you hesitate to start your own company?

2.1. How did you overcome that hesitation?

2.2. Go on.

3. How did others influence your decision to form Internet Ideas?

3.1. Please give me an example of what people said.

3.2. How did you respond?

4. How did you choose the name *Internet Ideas*?

4.1. What other names did you consider?

4.2. How difficult was it to make the final choice?

5. Let's talk about Internet Ideas as it is today. How do you describe your organization to someone who is entirely unfamiliar with it?

5.1. Why do you say that?

5.2. I see.

6. On the Internet Ideas website the mission statement emphasizes the "open exchange of ideas to revolutionize the internet." How do you go about achieving that mission?

6.1. Is there anything that's kept you from achieving that goal?

6.2. How do you encourage employees to openly exchange ideas?

7. What stories do "old-timers" tell new employees? *[skip this question if time is running short]*

7.1. How does that story fit with your view of the company?

7.2. What do you think of that story?

7.3. A recent article in the local newspaper about Internet Ideas both praised and criticized you and the company. What was your response to the article?

7.4. How did employees respond?

7.5. What effect overall did the article have on the company?

8. Now let's look to the future. In what ways do you think Internet Ideas will be different in five years?

8.1. What about in ten years?

8.2. What other changes do you foresee?

9. Imagine Internet Ideas has made the headlines twenty-five years from now. What would that headline be? *[skip this question if time is running short]*

   9.1. Why do you say that?

10. What would be your role in making that headline happen?

11. As you know, I'd like to start my own company someday. What are the positive aspects of starting your own company?

    11.1. What other pluses have you experienced?

    11.2. Does that apply to any new company?

12. What are the pitfalls in starting your own company?

    12.1. Please give me an example.

    12.2. How can founders avoid that pitfall?

13. What advice do you have for entrepreneurs interested in starting their own company?

    13.1. What other suggestions do you have?

    13.2. Any other bits of wisdom?

14. Finally, is there anything else you think I should know about starting a company?

    14.1. Is there additional information related to the topic I should be sure to include in my speech?

    14.2. What else should I know that I haven't covered?

Closing:

Those are all the questions I have for you. Let me briefly summarize the main points you covered in your responses *[quickly review interviewee's responses here]*.

If I need clarification on something we covered, may I e-mail or phone you? You've given me a lot of firsthand information on starting a company that I'm sure my listeners will be eager to learn about. I know how busy you are, so I really appreciate your answering all my questions. Thank you again for your time.

Once you have prepared your interview guide, practice by reading it aloud several times. Does the opening sound warm and cordial? Have you stated the purpose of the interview and previewed the questions you'll ask? Are the questions clear, neutral, straightforward, moderately open-ended, and relevant to your purpose? Does the closing wrap up the interview and leave the interviewee with positive feelings? You might also conduct mock interviews with family members, friends, or classmates. Play the roles of interviewer and interviewee so you can get a sense of both perspectives.[18]

CONDUCT THE INTERVIEW

You've done all your preparation; now it's time to conduct the interview. Being familiar with your interview guide, recording the interview, choosing an appropriate setting, and monitoring your verbal and nonverbal behaviors will help assure a more productive interview.

Being familiar with your interview guide allows you to use it the way you use note cards in your speeches—to trigger your memory. With the interviewee's permission, record the interview electronically for later review. Also take notes, as equipment sometimes fails. Write down the main points, using key terms that will help you recall what the person said. In addition, record important nonverbal cues, your general impressions, and ideas that occur to you during the interview. For example, if the interviewee seems nervous or uncertain about a response, note that.

Choose an appropriate setting, ideally a quiet, private place free from interruptions, for in-person interviews. For other real-time interviews, such as web chat or telephone interviews, minimize distractions at your location and ask the interviewee to do the same.

Ask one question at a time. Although journalists often ask multiple questions, this strategy seldom succeeds in obtaining the information you want.[19] Interviewees become confused and generally only answer one part of the question asked. For example, instead of asking, "How and why did you begin your own business?" phrase the question as two separate ones. First ask, "What led you to start your own business?" and then, after the interviewee has responded, ask, "How did you go about opening your business?"

Monitor your verbal and nonverbal cues to avoid unintentionally biasing the interviewee's responses. To indicate that you're listening, say "I understand" or "I see." The interviewee should be doing most of the talking, not you. Put all your active listening skills to work. Use eye contact and other nonverbal cues to let the interviewee know you are paying attention.[20]

INTEGRATE THE INFORMATION

Information from experts on your topic can personalize, enliven, and add credibility to each section of your speech. A catchy quote in the introduction can grab your audience's attention as well as establish your credibility. Here's an example:

Speaker: Ever think about the information websites gather as you surf the net? Jamie Anderson, professor of information science here at Southern University for ten years, has. Dr. Anderson told me in a recent interview, "If people knew how much information corporations gathered on each visitor to their websites, they would be shocked and much more careful about their internet use. I do know. That's why I'm dedicated to protecting individuals' online privacy."

The speaker underscores the importance of the topic, making it relevant to her audience by identifying the interviewee as a "professor of information science here at Southern University." She enhances her credibility by pointing out the interviewee's credibility—"for ten years."

Information from an interview can also be a source of personal, recent evidence in the body of your speech. When including quotes or summarized information from research interviews, clearly state your interviewee's full name and title and explain what makes that person an expert on the topic, as the speaker does in the following example:

Speaker: Mae Hawthorne, a local organic farmer for more than fifteen years, predicts three trends in organic farming innovations: incorporating effective farming methods from thousands of years ago, using the internet to link together farmers from around the world, and community-supported agriculture. Others suggest similar trends. For example, ...

Here, the speaker first presented a summary of the interviewee's predictions and then included supporting information from other sources.

Speakers use interview information in the conclusion of a speech in two ways: (1) to provide a sense of closure and (2) to leave listeners in an appropriate state of mind. For example, if you quote an interviewee in your introduction, you could quote the same person in your conclusion, as in the following example:

Speaker: When we go online, we're focused on the information we *get*. But information scientists recognize the dangers in the information we *give* others in our internet travels. Professor Jamie Anderson believes, "The hallmark of the internet is the free exchange of information. However, individuals must know what information they're revealing when they visit websites, and corporations must restrict the personal information they gather."

This quote ties in neatly with the one the speaker used in the introduction, reminding the audience of information presented early in the speech. In addition, a good quote in the conclusion can leave audience members with a lasting, personalized impression of the topic.

When conducting a research interview, be prepared yet flexible, and create a communication climate in which the interviewee feels comfortable. In face-to-face and video chat interviews, balance note-taking with maintaining eye contact. If you record the interview, ask the interviewee's permission first. Don't rely solely on the recording equipment, as it can malfunction. Signal your interest, but avoid leading the interviewee to respond in particular ways. Listen carefully, ask follow-up questions, use your interview guide to keep you on track, and then integrate the information you gather into the introduction, body, and conclusion of your speech.

Evaluating Your Research Materials

As you locate information for your speech, apply three evaluation criteria: reliability, validity, and currency. **Reliability** refers to the consistency and credibility of the information. Information is reliable when it fits with what other experts have concluded and the source is an authority on the topic. An article in *Science* on how carbon monoxide contributes to global warming, for instance, would be reliable because the findings are consistent with those of other researchers and the magazine is well respected in the scientific community.

> The consistency and credibility of information from a particular source.

Validity refers to the soundness of the logic underlying the information. To test the validity of your information, examine the author's conclusions. Are they logical? Does the author provide adequate evidence? For example, when researching a speech about people's shopping preferences, suppose you interview the president of the local chamber of commerce. Your interviewee claims that all downtown parking should be free because having to pay for parking drives away shoppers. However, the only evidence provided to support this assertion is the interviewee's own experience—parking downtown can be expensive, whereas parking at a suburban mall is free. There are at least two reasons not to trust this evidence. First, you don't know that people are avoiding downtown shopping. Second, even if they are, they could be doing so for other reasons, such as the types of stores available and the distance from their homes. In this case, the interviewee's conclusion *might* make sense, but there's no evidence to back it up.

> The soundness of the logic underlying information presented by a source.

Currency refers to the recency of the information. You want information that is as up to date as possible. Even when researching a topic considered ancient history, such as dinosaurs, what is known about the topic changes over time. For example, although the most popular explanation for why dinosaurs became extinct centers on the theory that an asteroid hit the earth at about that time, more recent explanations posit an exploding star or volcanic eruptions as the cause. Checking the date when printed material was

> How recent information is—the more recent, the more current.

Critical Questions for Evaluating Information

- Who is the author?
- Who is the publisher?
- What are the author's purposes?
- What evidence has the author provided to support the conclusions presented?
- Has any information been omitted?
- What are the author's underlying assumptions?
- What inferences or conclusions has the author drawn?
- How current is the information?

▲ FIGURE 6.3

published, a television or radio show was broadcast, or a webpage was revised reveals the currency of your information.

Regardless of its source, critically examine the information you gather. Asking the questions listed here will help you determine the reliability, validity, and currency of information (**Figure 6.3**).

WHO IS THE AUTHOR?

Determine who produced the information and examine the author's credibility. Is the author truly an authority on the topic? For example, Stephen Hawking is well known for his innovative writings in physics. But would you consider him a credible source on accounting or urban planning?

WHO IS THE PUBLISHER?

Is the publisher biased toward a particular view? Would you completely trust information about gun control that appears on the National Rifle Association's website or in a pamphlet?

WHAT ARE THE AUTHOR'S PURPOSES?

Is the author trying to persuade you or sell you something? Or is the author simply trying to help you understand a concept?

WHAT EVIDENCE HAS THE AUTHOR PROVIDED?

Examine the evidence used to support the main points. Does the author use a variety of types of information? How appropriate are those sources? Does the author simply express an opinion without any evidence?

HAS ANY INFORMATION BEEN OMITTED?

As you do your research, you will develop your own base of knowledge about your topic. From what you know, has the author left out any relevant information? Might that information lead to different conclusions?

WHAT ARE THE AUTHOR'S UNDERLYING ASSUMPTIONS?

Examine the assumptions the author makes that are not stated explicitly. Are those assumptions sound? Consider how alternative assumptions might lead to different conclusions. For example, an author might argue that because fluoride helps prevent cavities, the local water supply should be fluoridated. The unstated assumptions are that preventing cavities is a public health issue and the best way to address it is through fluoridated water. In contrast, if you assume individuals are responsible for their dental care, the best way to deliver fluoride is through products such as toothpaste and mouthwash. You start with the same premise—fluoride helps prevent cavities—but make different assumptions that lead to different conclusions.

WHAT INFERENCES OR CONCLUSIONS HAS THE AUTHOR DRAWN?

Are the author's inferences or conclusions valid? In evaluating the information you gather, distinguish between the evidence the author presents and the explanations or conclusions presented. Also identify other inferences or conclusions that could be drawn from on the same information.

HOW CURRENT IS THE INFORMATION?

Does the author refer to statistics or developments that are several years old? Are examples drawn from current events? Does the author's language suggest that the document was written recently or several years ago? For a website or webpage, do many broken links appear on the page? All these clues reveal the information's currency.

Asking these questions will help you identify valid, reliable, and current information for your speech.

Acknowledging Your Sources

▼ Public speakers acknowledge their sources in two ways: orally in the speech and in written form in the bibliography. With **oral citations,** speakers mention, or *cite*, the sources of their information during the speech. Here are some examples that demonstrate both how to set up an oral citation and how to punctuate it:

> **A source of information that a speaker mentions, or cites, during a speech.**

- In a February 2008 blog post, reporter Andrew C. Revin gave examples of "uninventing" suburbia, such as "turning old malls into walkable villages with housing" and creating "car-free, solar-powered" cities.
- Here's something to think about when you're searching for music online. According to a June 2007 article in the *Pittsburgh Post-Gazette*, the phrase "digital music" poses the highest risk of leading searchers to websites containing spyware and viruses.

- Paul E. Madlock, a graduate student at West Virginia University, found in his research that a supervisor's communication competence has a dramatic influence on subordinates' satisfaction with workplace communication. His 2008 article in the *Journal of Business Communication* also reported a direct link between how supervisors communicate and how satisfied subordinates are with their jobs.

In these examples, the speaker tells the audience who authored or published a particular piece of information. If a speaker must also provide a written reference list, these sources would be cited as follows:

Revin, A. C. (2008, February 10). Can we uninvent suburbia? Retrieved February 10, 2008, from dotearth.blogs.nytimes.com.

Shropshire, C. (2007, June 5). Study finds searchers for music, movies, not porn, most dangerous. *Pittsburgh Post-Gazette*. Retrieved June 15, 2007, from post-gazette.com

Madlock, P. E. (2008). The link between leadership style, communicator competence, and employee satisfaction. *Journal of Business Communication, 45*(1), 61–78.

A source's complete citation, including author, date of publication, title, place of publication, and publisher.

Table 6.7 shows how to format written citations, or **bibliographic information**, for a variety of types of information sources. The bibliographic information is a source's complete citation, including author, date of publication, title, place of publication, and publisher. You'll need this information to attribute your sources correctly in your speech and reference list. Most communication researchers use either Modern Language Association (MLA) or American Psychological Association (APA) style to record citations.[21] Ask your instructor which style you should use.

Research Guidelines

Start early, schedule research time, ask questions, keep accurate records—these are just some of the guidelines that will make researching your topic a positive and productive experience. **Table 6.8** summarizes these research guidelines, giving you key points and reminders.

TABLE 6.7 ▶ Documenting Source Information

APA STYLE	
Book	Moran, M. (2008). *Do it wrong quickly: How the web changes the old marketing rules*. Upper Saddle River, NJ: IBM Press.
Essay in book	Esrock, S. L., Hart, J. L., & Leichty, G. (2007). Smoking out the opposition: The rhetoric of reaction and the Kentucky cigarette excise tax campaign. In L. R. Frey & K. M. Carragee (Eds.), *Communication activism: Communication for social change* (Vol. 1, pp. 385–410). Creskill, NJ: Hampton Press.
Journal article	Pais, J. (2008). Random matching in the college admissions problem. *Economic Theory, 35,* 99–116.
Newspaper article	Dean, M. (2008, February 10). Mobile phone, not PC, bridges digital gap. *San Jose Mercury News,* p. 16A.
Webpage	Kaiser Family Foundation. (2008). *Study finds television stations donate an average of 17 seconds an hour to public service advertising*. Retrieved March 10, 2008, from http://www.kff.org/entmedia/entmedia012408pkg.cfm
MLA STYLE	
Book	Denton, Jr., Robert E., and Jim A. Kuypers. *Politics and Communication in America: Campaigns, Media, and Governing in the 21st Century*. Prospect Heights, IL: Waveland Press, 2008.
Essay in book	Fitzgerald, Brian, and Damien O'Brien. "Bloggers and the Law." *Uses of Blogs*. Ed. Axel Bruns and Joanne Jacobs. New York: Peter Lang, 2006. 223–237.
Journal article	Pais, Joana. "Speech Anxiety and Rapid Emotional Reactions to Angry and Happy Facial Expressions." *Scandinavian Journal of Psychology* 48 2007: 321–328.
Newspaper article	Gates, Dominic. "High-tech Business Strategy Dies with Boeing's Flying Web Service." *The Seattle Times* 18 August 2006: A1+.
Webpage	*Earthquakes Claim 709 Lives in 2007*. 3 Jan. 2008. United States Geological Survey. 11 Feb. 2008 <http://www.usgs.gov/newsroom/article.asp?ID=1846>.

TABLE 6.8 ▶ **Research Guidelines**

GUIDELINE	KEY POINTS AND REMINDERS
Start early.	How early to start developing your speech depends on the length of your course (semester, quarter, condensed session), access to the resources you need, and your own approach to research. So get out the calendar, note when your speaking materials and speech are due, and work backward from there. Build in enough time to identify your supporting materials (Chapter 7), organize and outline your ideas (Chapter 8), integrate effective language (Chapter 10), develop relevant presentation media (Chapter 11), and practice (Chapter 12).
Schedule research time.	Block out research time in your daily planner. Think of that time just as you would think of any other appointment, and make a commitment to keep to it.
Ask questions.	Campus librarians and your instructor are key resources in your search for reliable, valid, and current information. When you encounter a sticking point in researching your topic, ask for help. If you wait until speech day, it will be too late.
Keep accurate records.	Carefully record the publication information for each source you find.
Take notes on each source.	When you record a source's bibliographic information, also write down the ideas that seem most relevant to your topic.
Revise as needed.	As you do your research, you may find yourself going off in a direction you hadn't planned on. Review your specific purpose and thesis. Decide whether they need to be revised or your research needs to be refocused.
Know when to move on.	You have a set amount of time to prepare your speech. If you spend too little time on research, your speech will lack substance; if you spend too much time, you'll neglect the other steps in the speechmaking process. When you feel comfortable talking about your topic with others and think you can answer your audience's questions, it's time to move on.
Know when to go back.	Later in the process of developing your speech, you may find gaps in your research or a question you want to answer. Do the additional research necessary to close those gaps and answer that question. Your audience and your confidence depend on your expertise.

Researching your speeches requires three activities: preparing to do your research, gathering information, and evaluating what you've found. Preparing begins with determining what you know and don't know about your topic. Use your own experiences as the basis for developing your research strategy. Preparation also requires identifying multiple perspectives and sources, particularly those that challenge your assumptions.

Its vast variety of sources makes your campus library the logical first stop in gathering information. A short e-mail or in-person exchange with a librarian can save you hours of frustration. Library databases often contain hundreds of full-text databases, so you can download information onto your own computer.

Organizations offer another source for gathering information about your speech topic. A local company or other institution often can provide up-to-date information your audience may find especially relevant.

Other information sources include websites, the deep web, blogs, newsgroups, and discussion lists. Metasearch engines, search engines, and web directories assist you in your quest for information. Specialty search engines provide windows into the deep web, databases that traditional search engines can't reach. By carefully planning and refining your search, you can weed out the junk from the truly useful online resources.

Interviews with experts can yield personal and current information about your topic. Planning and preparation form the basis of a successful interview. Developing a solid interview guide with thoughtfully phrased questions that are logically organized facilitates productive interaction during the interview. Flexibility and a genuine interest in knowing more about your topic will aid you tremendously when you conduct your interview.

As you gather information, evaluate it for reliability, validity, and currency. Ethical speakers present convincing, recent, and well-supported information. In evaluating information, ask critical questions such as, "What are the author's assumptions?" and, "What evidence is presented to support the conclusions drawn?"

Doing sound research means starting early, setting aside specific time to research your topic, asking questions when you run into problems, keeping accurate records, taking accurate notes on each source, revising and refocusing when necessary, knowing when you have enough information, and knowing when to continue your research. Even the most polished delivery can't make up for poor content. So thoroughly, creatively, and carefully research your speech topics.

In the Book

Summary
Key Terms
Critical Challenges

More Study Resources

Speech Studio
Quizzes
WebLinks

Student Workbook

6.1: In-Class Interview
6.2: Myth Search
6.3: Interview Your Teacher
6.4: Evaluating Websites
6.5: How to Start a Hobby In . . .

Speech Buddy Videos

 Video Links

Managing the Research Process

 Activity Links

The Research Detective

▶ Sample Speech Videos

Dory, handed-down story, impromptu speech

Shaura, "Terrestrial Pulmonate Gastropods," persuasive speech

 Speech Builder Express

Goal/purpose
Thesis statement
Supporting material
Introduction
Conclusion
Works cited
Outline

 InfoTrac

Recommended search terms

Multiple perspectives and
  public speaking
Online librarians
Free online library
Evaluating online sources
Citing sources in public
  speaking
Oral citations

Audio Study Tools

Handed-down story speech
  by Dory
Critical thinking questions
Learning objectives
Chapter summary

Guide to Your Online Resources

Your Online Resources for *Public Speaking: The Evolving Art* give you access to the Speech Buddy video and activity featured in this chapter, additional sample speech videos, Speech Builder Express, InfoTrac College Edition, and study aids such as glossary flashcards, review quizzes, and the Critical Challenge questions for this chapter, which you can respond to via e-mail if your instructor so requests. In addition, your Online Resources feature live WebLinks relevant to this chapter, including sites that can assist you in researching information for your speeches, such as the Pew Internet & American Life Project, the Catalog of United States Government Publications, the National Hospice and Palliative Care Organization, Google Groups, the NCA listserv, and the American Communication Association listserv. Links are maintained regularly, and new ones are added periodically.

Key Terms

bibliographic information 158

blog 140

call number 133

copyright information 144

currency 155

deep web 140

discussion lists 142

interview guide 147

keywords 131

leading question 147

metasearch engine 136

neutral question 147

newsgroups 141

oral citation 157

primary question 147

primary source 131

relevance 136

reliability 155

search engine 137

secondary question 147

secondary source 131

sponsored link 144

validity 155

web directory 137

Critical Challenges

Questions for Reflection and Discussion

1. The first step in researching your topic is to determine what you already know. How might what you know get in the way of doing good research? How might you check the reliability, currency, and validity of what you already know about a topic?

2. If something is in a book, journal article, magazine, newspaper or other printed source, is it necessarily accurate? Gatekeepers such as editors can miss both intentional and unintentional errors, as *The New York Times* did in the case of journalist Jayson Blair, who fabricated or plagiarized hundreds of stories. And desktop publishing allows authors to bypass traditional gatekeepers. How can you apply your critical thinking skills to evaluate the accuracy of printed materials?

3. Blogs are criticized for their lack of a gatekeeper such as an editor or publisher. But who's blogging may be just as important. When searching blogs for information about your topic, consider the authors. Are you finding a diversity of perspectives? How might you find a variety of blogs that represent multiple points of view?

4. In using information gathered from interviews, you need to consider what information to include in your speech and what to leave out. For example, how you frame an interviewee's remarks or how you place a quote in your speech can greatly influence how others interpret that information and how they perceive the interviewee. As an ethical speaker, what steps should you take to ensure that you accurately represent what the interviewee said?

7 SUPPORTING YOUR IDEAS

Although you are certainly familiar with Dr. Martin Luther King, Jr.'s instrumental role in the civil rights movement in the United States, you may not realize how his speeches have inspired people in other countries to take action. Shen Tong, one of the students who led the Chinese pro-democracy movement in 1989, spoke at a conference in honor of Dr. King.[1] In the first part of his speech, Shen Tong said:

> To fight without fighting, that is the razor's edge of nonviolence. This is what I believe happened in the American civil rights movement. I am here to learn as well as to inform, so you must teach me. But I know that this definitely happened during the spring of 1989 in Beijing's Tiananmen Square.

He went on to say:

> China has suffered through more than four thousand years of violence and revolution. The Chinese people have suffered oppression and tyranny for over four thousand years. One dynasty after another was established and then violently destroyed.

▼ Shen Tong, a student activist in China and currently president and founder of the Web 2.0 company VFinity, has applied his public speaking skills in many contexts, including guest lectures at universities around the world.

AP Photo/Elise Amendola

Shen Tong then asked the audience to help him understand why some nonviolent protests work and others don't. He said:

> So many nonviolent struggles succeed, like the civil rights movement and Eastern Europe. But the question still remains for the Chinese youth: How? It is time for us to really learn and practice the principle, to learn from the examples of struggles like yours.

Near the end of his speech, Shen Tong related this story:

> And the most moving picture I have in my mind is that of one of my schoolmates: He got a rifle, he held it in his hand and above his head, but the soldiers didn't listen to him. They hold billy club, begin to beat him. But my schoolmate, he kneeled on the ground, still holding the gun above his head till the death.

In his conclusion, Shen Tong argued that achieving democracy in China requires a global commitment:

> All our communities must learn peace from each other. . . . And together, as one movement for human rights and peace worldwide, we will be able to look at the tyrants and oppressors of history and say to them, in Dr. King's words, "We have matched your capacity to inflict suffering with our capacity to endure suffering. We have matched your physical force with soul force. We are free."

As a central participant in the Tiananmen Square demonstrations and a member of the student group that negotiated with the Chinese government during the protests, Shen Tong had a great deal of personal experience he could use in his speech. Yet he also relied on a variety of

supporting materials—narratives, examples, definitions, testimony, facts, and statistics—to bolster his position.

Evidence used to demonstrate the worth of an idea.

Types of Supporting Materials

▼ **READ it** Supporting materials provide the substance of your speeches—the "stuff" that holds together, illustrates, clarifies, and provides evidence for your ideas. When you're researching your topic, you're gathering the supporting materials that you'll use to inform, persuade, and entertain your audience.

Aristotle argued that when speakers present their ideas, they rely on **pathos**, or emotional appeals, and **logos**, or logical appeals.[2] More recent scholars argue that speakers also rely on **mythos**, or appeals to cultural values and beliefs.[3] Shen Tong's story about his schoolmate appeals to emotions such as grief, anger, and sadness. His examples of the civil rights movement and new democracies in Eastern Europe provide a logical reason to support his position. And quoting Dr. Martin Luther King, Jr. appeals to the deeply held belief in freedom that is so prevalent in American and other cultures.

Appeals to emotion.

Appeals to logic.

Appeals to cultural beliefs and values.

Table 7.1 summarizes the types of supporting materials discussed in this chapter.

TABLE 7.1 ▶ Types of Supporting Materials

TYPE	APPEAL	USEFUL FOR	STRENGTHS	WEAKNESSES
Narratives	Emotional, cultural	Engaging audience	Dramatize topic; help audience identify with topic	Single view on topic; distract from focus of speech
Examples	Emotional	Personalizing topic	Make topic concrete; simplify complex concepts	Not able to be generalized; lack representativeness
Definitions	Emotional, logical	Establishing common meaning	Clarify concepts; delineate topic boundaries	Inaccurate or inappropriate; ignore connotations associated with terms
Testimony	Emotional, cultural, logical	Enhancing speaker credibility	Provides specific voices on topic; demonstrates expertise	Biased information (depends on credibility of source)
Facts and statistics	Logical	Demonstrating the scope of a problem	Promote agreement; provide foundation for topic's importance	Overwhelming or difficult to comprehend; subject to manipulation

NARRATIVES

anecdote
A brief narrative.

narrative
A description of events in a dramatic fashion; also called a story.

Sometimes called **anecdotes**, **narratives** describe events in a dramatic way, appealing to our emotions. Well-known cultural, societal, and group narratives appeal to deeply held beliefs and values. The structure of narratives generally includes a beginning, middle, and end. Compelling stories have coherence—audience members can follow the plot. Stories also have a ring of truth—the story seems plausible. Narratives dramatize a topic and help the audience identify with the speaker's ideas, making this form of evidence one of the most persuasive.[4]

Effective storytelling involves some poetic license—a sense of drama, the development of intriguing characters such as heroes and villains, and the use of evocative language. In the lecture she gave upon accepting the Nobel Prize in Literature, author Toni Morrison began with, "Once upon a time there was an old woman. Blind but wise. Or was it an old man? A guru, perhaps. Or a griot soothing restless children." The words "Once upon a time" tell us that this is some sort of story, likely a fable or other traditional narrative. The initial ambiguity about the central character keeps us interested—a woman or a man? A guru or griot? And what is a griot? The audience is intrigued and wants to know more.

When telling a story, you must choose what information to include and what to leave out, where to begin the story and where to end it, and how much of the story's moral or main point you want your audience to figure out for themselves and how much you want to state outright. Too much rambling in telling your story can distract audience members from the main points of your speech. For example, Morrison used the word *griot* in her narrative. Although not all audience members likely knew the word's meaning (a West African storyteller), she didn't stop to define it. Why? Because this would slow down the narrative, and knowing the precise meaning of *griot* wasn't essential to the story. Story-telling requires that you pay special attention to the presentation part of public speaking, using your voice, gestures, facial expressions, and body movement to bring your audience into the narrative. To hear how Morrison used her voice—rhythm, tone, pitch, and timing—as she related her narrative, listen to her lecture on the Nobel Foundation's website (nobelprize.org).

Speakers rely on four types of narratives: their own stories, stories about others, institutional stories, and cultural stories.

Your Own Stories

Shen Tong told a story about his own experiences—an event he had observed. Such firsthand accounts can move audience members in powerful ways. Relating your own narrative personalizes the topic and helps listeners understand why you choose it.

Others' Stories

Stories about others relate events that the speaker didn't directly observe or participate in. During his commencement speech at the University of Pennsylvania, U2 lead singer Bono used this story to illustrate the role Ireland played in the development of American democracy:

> In 1771 your founder, Mr. Franklin, spent three months in Ireland and Scotland to look at the relationship they had with England to see if this could be a model for America, whether America should follow their example and remain a part of the British Empire. Franklin was deeply, deeply distressed by what he saw. In Ireland he saw how England had put a stranglehold on Irish trade, how absentee English landlords exploited Irish tenant farmers and how those farmers, in Franklin's words, "lived in wretched hovels of mud and straw, were clothed in rags and subsisted chiefly on potatoes." Not exactly the American dream. So instead of Ireland becoming a model for America, America became a model for Ireland in our own struggle for independence.[5]

Bono's story connects his audience's history with the history of his own country far more powerfully than if he had simply stated a fact: "You fought the British and won; we're still fighting." And because the story of the American Revolution holds mythic status in the United States, Bono tapped into audience members' strongly held beliefs in freedom and independence. In addition, mentioning Benjamin Franklin, someone with high credibility, enhanced Bono's credibility.

Institutional Stories

Institutional stories center on specific organizations, such as a university, corporation, church, or social club. These stories tell us how individuals should act in the organization and the values it emphasizes. Randy Kelly, former mayor of St. Paul, Minnesota, told this story about a transitional housing program for homeless teens in St. Paul during a state-of-the-city address:

> Laura was 17 when she moved into Rezek House after staying at Safe House. Her mother, an alcoholic and crack cocaine user, had abandoned her family long ago. Her father kicked her out of the house when she refused to turn over her paycheck to him to buy drugs. Laura stayed at Rezek for a year, during which she got back into school and found a better-paying job. . . . Laura has moved on and is doing well.. . . . Let's not fool ourselves. Everyone in this audience is one tragedy, one health crisis, job loss or cruel turn of fortune from being in need ourselves. And so I challenge all of us . . . all of Saint Paul . . . to see ourselves in

SPEAKING OF . . .

Telling Your Story

Think about the topic for your next speech. What got you interested in the topic? How did you decide this would be a good topic for a speech? Why do you feel compelled to bring this topic to the attention of your audience? When you talk with friends, coworkers, and others about this topic, what do you say about it? Considering these questions will reveal your own stories associated with your topic. Using one or two of these personal narratives in your speech can help you relate your topic to your listeners and gain their attention.

those who are most in need. Reach out and build, strengthen and repair the links in this human chain that is our City.[6]

The narrative suggests how St. Paul residents should behave: Work hard, get an education, and contribute to the well-being of others. Laura's success depended both on her willingness to juggle a job and school and on the city's provision of temporary shelter. You don't need to live in St. Paul to understand the moral of the story: Helping others improves life for everyone.

Cultural Stories

You hear and read cultural stories from the time you're very young. You might even think of these stories as myths or fables. Cultural stories best represent mythos as they transmit basic values and ways of behaving. In her Nobel lecture, Toni Morrison[7] began her speech with a tale about communication between people across generations:

> Once upon a time there was an old woman. Blind but wise. Or was it an old man? A guru, perhaps. Or a griot soothing restless children. . . .
>
> In the version I know, the woman is the daughter of slaves, black, American, and lives alone in a small house outside of town. Her reputation for wisdom is without peer and without question. Among her people she is both the law and its transgression. . . .
>
> One day the woman is visited by some young people who seem to be bent on disproving her clairvoyance and showing her up for the fraud they believe she is. Their plan is simple: they enter her house and ask the one question the answer to which rides solely on her difference from them, a difference they regard as a profound disability: her blindness. They stand before her, and one of them says, "Old woman, I hold in my hand a bird. Tell me whether it is living or dead."
>
> She does not answer, and the question is repeated. "Is the bird I am holding living or dead?"
>
> Still she doesn't answer. She is blind and cannot see her visitors, let alone what is in their hands. She does not know their color, gender or homeland. She only knows their motive.
>
> The old woman's silence is so long, the young people have trouble holding their laughter.
>
> Finally she speaks and her voice is soft but stern. "I don't know," she says. "I don't know whether the bird you are holding is dead or alive, but what I do know is that it is in your hands. It is in your hands."

Morrison explained the cultural moral of the story: how individuals exercise power and the moral implications of their actions. She wove the narrative throughout the speech, the bird symbolizing language and the woman symbolizing a writer. Using a cultural narrative, Morrison helped the audience understand something unfamiliar—the experiences of an acclaimed author—with something familiar—a story they'd probably heard before in one form or another.

EXAMPLES

Examples are illustrations or cases that represent a larger group or class of things. Examples make ideas more concrete and personalize the topic, appealing to the audience's emotions. In his speech, Shen Tong stated, "So many nonviolent struggles succeed, like the civil rights movement and Eastern Europe." "Nonviolent struggles" may be somewhat vague in audience members' minds, but most people probably were familiar with the civil rights movement in the United States and the Solidarity movement in Poland.

> An illustration or case that represents a larger group or class of things.

Especially for complex ideas, an example can help audience members get a better grasp of key points and concepts related to the topic. Listening to a speech on the importance of community service, audience members might have a vague notion of what that entails. A few examples, such as volunteering at the local public library and tutoring elementary-school students in math, provide the audience with a clear picture of what community service involves.

Yet examples may give misleading information if they fail to accurately represent the group to which they belong. For example, a 2004 *Science* article reported that a border collie, Rico, correctly associated more than 200 words with their appropriate objects and could learn new words when presented with an unfamiliar object.[8] However, using Rico to represent the learning abilities of all dogs, or even all border collies, would be misleading because few dogs have Rico's ability to recognize language.

The next section discusses three types of examples you might use in your speech: general examples, specific examples, and hypothetical examples.

General Examples

General examples, such as those Shen Tong used, provide little detail; the speaker expects audience members to be familiar with the situation, person, object, or event cited. For instance, if you refer to Yosemite National Park or the Grand Canyon, most people in your audience will probably know about these places—you don't need to explain where they're located or that they're part of the U.S. national parks system.

AP Photo/Paul White

▲ Kofi Annan's work in his role as secretary-general of the United Nations from 1997 to 2006 earned him the Nobel Peace Prize in 2001. His current humanitarian efforts allow him to continue to build on his experiences as a diplomat and public speaker.

Specific Examples

Specific examples give listeners much more detail. In an address to the United Nations General Assembly in 2004, former UN Secretary-General Kofi Annan[9] used these specific examples to support his point that laws are disregarded throughout the world:

> In Iraq, we see civilians massacred in cold blood, while relief workers, journalists and other noncombatants are taken hostage and put to death in the most barbarous fashion. At the same time, we have seen Iraqi prisoners disgracefully abused.
>
> In Darfur, we see whole populations displaced, and their homes destroyed, while rape is used as a deliberate strategy. . . .
>
> In Israel we see civilians, including children, deliberately targeted by Palestinian suicide bombers. And in Palestine we see homes destroyed, lands seized, and needless civilian casualties caused by Israel's excessive use of force.

Because these examples referred to current events, Annan simply could have mentioned each location and listeners would have recognized the issue he raised. Instead, he provided frank and graphic details about each place to underscore his point in a very powerful way.

Hypothetical Examples

In contrast to general and specific examples, which are based on actual events, hypothetical examples stem from conjecture or supposition. That is, with hypothetical examples, speakers ask the audience to imagine something. In a speech on exercise, the speaker might use a hypothetical example such as, "Let's go through a typical day for the average person. Rather than getting out of bed and going immediately to the kitchen, our average person stretches and then warms up by jogging in place for a few minutes. Next, our average person . . . ."

Effective hypothetical examples contain a high degree of plausibility—audience members must believe the situation could actually occur. To make his point about ways to solve current problems such as climate change, Amory Lovins, chair and chief scientist at Rocky Mountain Institute, asked the audience to:

> Imagine a world, a few short generations hence, where spacious, peppy, ultra safe, 120- to 200-mpg cars whisper through revitalized cities and towns, convivial suburbs, and fertile, prosperous countryside, burning no oil and emitting pure drinking water—or nothing; where sprawl is no longer mandated or subsidized, so stronger families eat better food on front porches and more kids

play in thriving neighborhoods; where new buildings and plugged-in parked cars produce enough surplus energy to power the now-efficient old buildings; and where buildings make people healthier, happier, and more productive, creating delight when entered, serenity when occupied, and regret when departed.[10]

Using hypothetical examples of what the future might hold, Lovins encouraged his audience to consider alternative ways of envisioning their lives. Hypothetical examples provide a good way to show audience members what might happen as well as what might not happen. In using hypothetical examples, you're asking your listeners to imagine something, so what you suggest can't be too far-fetched.

DEFINITIONS

Definitions explain or describe what something is. Words have both denotative and connotative meanings. Denotative meanings are the definitions you find in dictionaries—what speakers and writers of a language generally agree a specific word represents. Connotative meanings are the personal associations individuals have with a particular word. Even a simple word like *chair* has multiple denotative meanings—the *Compact Oxford English Dictionary* lists six—and infinite connotative meanings. Speakers use definitions to clarify for audience members how they should interpret a term. In this way, definitions based on a dictionary provide a logical appeal for speakers. Peter K. Bhatia, executive editor of *The Oregonian*, used such a definition in his introduction of Edward Seaton, president of the American Society of Newspaper Editors, at the group's annual meeting:

> The dictionary defines dignity as the quality of being worthy of esteem and/or honor. I've seen Edward in action in many ways this year, living that definition. I saw him standing up before hostile audiences this past summer during debates over ASNE's commitment to diversity. He was ever calm, ever thoughtful, ever listening, and always kept his cool when others around him gave way to emotion.[11]

First, Bhatia defined the word *dignity* for the audience in order to establish a common meaning for the word. Second, he explained how Seaton's actions fit that definition, demonstrating that describing Seaton as dignified was appropriate.

Speakers commonly use two types of definitions: definitions by function and definitions by analogy.

Definition by Function

When speakers define something by its function, they explain what it does or how it works. If you were discussing CDs in a speech on the history of recording audio files, the dictionary definition of the term *CD-ROM* would do little to inform your audience

A statement that describes the essence, precise meaning, or scope of a word or a phrase.

An agreed-upon definition of a word, found in a dictionary.

A unique meaning associated with a word based on a person's own experiences.

members—they already know *what* a CD is. But do they know how it works? Probably not. Marshall Brain explains on the HowStuffWorks website that CDs contain very, very tiny bumps arranged in a spiral pattern that are read by a laser. That's the simple version; the process is more complex than that. But defining a CD by how it works opens up other avenues of discussion, such as why CD burners have become so common and how to purchase the right CD player.[12] Both dictionary and function definitions appeal to audience members' logic by defining words in concrete, agreed-upon ways.

Definition by Analogy

An **analogy** describes something by comparing it to something else it resembles. Speakers often use analogies to help an audience understand something new to them. That is, they use an analogy referring to something familiar to define something unfamiliar to the audience. For example, in emphasizing the importance of learning first-aid techniques, a speaker might say, "It's like studying for an exam—you want to be prepared for any situation that might arise."

Metaphors and **similes** are sometimes grouped with analogies. A metaphor relies on an implicit comparison, while a simile makes an explicit comparison. Shen Tong employed a metaphor in his speech when he stated, "To fight without fighting, that is the razor's edge of nonviolence." He referred to something that was concrete and familiar to audience members—the edge of a razor—to describe something quite abstract: the idea of fighting without engaging in physical conflict. Native American orators use metaphors extensively in their speeches.[13]

As a literary device, metaphors bring an element of poetry to definitions, appealing to audience members' emotions. For example, a dictionary definition of *grief*, such as "intense sorrow, especially caused by someone's death,"[14] doesn't embody the deep feelings of a metaphor like the one used in this speech, presented during a memorial for a member of the Tlingit tribe:

> The river would swell, the river. In the river, in the lake, the rain would fall on the water. When the river had swollen, it would flow under the tree. The earth would crumble along the bank. . . . . When it had broken, down the river it would drift, down the river. . . . From there the wind would blow over it. After the wind would blow over it; it would begin to roll with the waves to a fine sand. When it rolled on the waves to the sand, it would drift ashore. It would be pounded by there by the waves, it would be pounded there. . . . In the morning, sun would begin to shine on it, in the morning. After the sun had been shining on it, it would begin to dry out. My hope is that you become like this from now on, my brothers-in-law, whoever is one.[15]

A type of comparison that describes something by comparing it to something else that it resembles.

metaphor
A figure of speech that makes an implicit comparison between two things.

simile
A figure of speech that makes an explicit comparison between two things, using the word *like* or *as*.

The metaphor of river, earth, wind, and sun moves us and gives us a more comprehensive understanding of what grieving feels like in ways that a dictionary definition cannot.

A figurative analogy compares two things that seem to have little in common yet share some similarity. Figurative analogies often juxtapose objects, processes, or ideas in unique and novel ways, heightening the audience's interest. For example, a speaker explaining how to find a job might compare it to preparing a dinner party for friends— you need to match your skills and interests to your target audience.

Literal analogies don't offer the poetic quality of figurative analogies, but instead appeal to audience members' sense of logic. For literal analogies to work, the things being compared must be sufficiently similar in ways that are relevant to the speaker's point. When they do not share important similarities, the analogy is false. For example, proponents of downtown Detroit's People Mover unsuccessfully tried to popularize this public transportation system by using Seattle's monorail as an analogy. Although the two types of trains share structural similarities, Detroit and Seattle do not. Detroit shares more characteristics with Baltimore and St. Louis, such as an older, somewhat sprawling urban area. Seattle is a younger, more compact city, and people associate the monorail with the 1962 World's Fair, for which the system was built. So while Seattle's monorail enjoys steady ridership, Detroit's People Mover hasn't found the same popularity.[16]

Definitions of all types help audience members understand a topic's scope and increase the likelihood that the speaker and the audience think about the topic in similar ways. Definitions also tell your audience what you *won't* be talking about or how you *won't* use a word. In a speech on stress, for instance, the speaker might talk about the differences between situational stress, which arises in specific contexts, and chronic stress, which never goes away, and then say, "Today I'm going to focus on situational stress."

Although definitions may clarify your topic, they can also cause problems. No matter how clearly you define your terms, audience members always will have connotations associated with those words. For example, Chapter 1 defines the term *style* as the language used in a speech, but you might associate style with fashion or having a flair for doing something. Definitions also may be inappropriate. This often happens when speakers use a standard dictionary definition for a technical term. Chapter 1 defines the term *invention* as Cicero did, to refer to discovering what a speaker wants to say in a speech. But using a dictionary definition of *invention*—creating something new—to describe Cicero's approach would be inadequate because it wouldn't offer the precision needed to apply the term to public speaking.

TESTIMONY

An individual's opinions or experiences about a particular topic.

When speakers use **testimony**, they rely on an individual's opinions or experiences related to a particular topic. Using testimony to support your points works only if listeners believe in the source's credibility. Speakers use testimony from experts, celebrities, and laypeople. For an expert, credibility means extensive knowledge based on research, activities, speeches, and writing about the topic. For a celebrity, audience members must perceive a logical link between the person and the topic. Finally, lay testimony requires that the individual has personal experience with the topic and clearly articulates her or his views.

• • • • • • • • • • **THE EVOLVING ART**

Dictionaries

You're probably familiar with general English-language dictionaries available online, such as the *American Heritage Dictionary of the English Language* (bartleby .com/61), *Cambridge International Dictionaries* (dictionary.cambridge .org), and *Merriam-Webster Dictionary* (m-w.com). Specialized dictionaries provide more technical, precise, and specific meanings for words. How can

you find these dictionaries? You might start with OneLook Dictionary Search (onelook.com). Type in a word and OneLook searches nearly 1,000 dictionaries for definitions. A search for "speech" identifies more than twenty-five definitions in general, art, medicine, and science dictionaries. "Communication" appears in over twenty topic-specific dictionaries as well as twenty-four general

ones. Yahoo! lists dictionaries by subject area, such as financial, law, and music. Google's directory includes dictionaries for symbols, sign languages, and rhyming. Multilingual dictionaries translate words in various languages. Yahoo!, Google, Alta Vista, and other search directories also list dictionaries in languages ranging from Afrikaans to Yiddish.

Expert Testimony

The effectiveness of expert testimony rests on the individual or group's qualifications related to the topic. In quoting well-known civil rights leader Martin Luther King, Jr., Shen Tong used testimony to support his point that meeting oppression with nonviolent resistance works. Audience members consider King's words expert testimony because he was an authority on the topic—his long association with the U.S. civil rights movement gives him credibility.

Celebrity Testimony

The effectiveness of celebrity testimony stems from the person's stature or our overall impression of the person. That is, audiences find the celebrity testimony compelling because of the person's fame or star power, not the person's knowledge about the topic. For example, actor William Macy played a person with cerebral palsy in a film based on a true story. Macy later joined United Cerebral Palsy's (UCP) board of trustees. Listeners consider what he has to say about this disability credible because of his celebrity status, role in the film, and participation in UCP. Actor and *Superman* star Christopher Reeve became a strong advocate for stem cell research after an accident in which he broke two vertebrae in his neck. Both his reputation as an actor and his experience as a person with a disability gave credibility to his views.

Lay Testimony

Lay testimony involves individuals who have experience with a topic but aren't experts or well known. Journalists often use lay testimony when reporting on human-interest stories. For example, in a speech on keeping costs low for college students, the speaker might interview a few students to find out their strategies for saving money.

FACTS AND STATISTICS

Speakers typically rely on facts and statistics when making a logical appeal. Your senses serve as the basis for **facts**, observations you make based on your experiences. **Statistics** are numerical data or information, such as the average price of a home or how many students are enrolled at your university this year.

    For the most part, speakers rely on others when gathering facts and statistics. As Chapter 5 explains, an author's credibility, or **ethos**, influences the degree to which audience members think information is accurate. Source credibility is especially important for facts and statistics. Even the credibility of highly respected sources can be hurt if those sources don't check their facts. During the 2004 presidential race, the CBS television

An observation based on actual experience.

Numerical data or information.

Appeals that are linked to the speaker's credibility.

magazine *60 Minutes* showed viewers memos related to President Bush's service with the National Guard. After questions arose about the documents' authenticity, CBS News revealed that reporters had not reviewed the information thoroughly. Although at the time of the broadcast CBS executives believed the documents were valid, two weeks later they admitted that they'd been tricked and the memos were fake.[17] By using sources that were not credible, CBS News tarnished its own credibility.

You probably think of facts and statistics as objective, yet these supporting materials are still subject to interpretation—and manipulation. For example, if a speaker said, "The number of bicycles stolen on this campus has quadrupled in the past year," listeners would reasonably conclude that bicycle theft was a major problem. However, if only two bicycles had been stolen in the previous year, "quadrupled" would mean eight were stolen in the current year. In contrast, if 50 bikes were stolen the previous year and 200 in the current year, the speaker would have a stronger case for identifying bicycle theft as a serious problem.

Because they appeal to logic, audience members generally find statistics and facts convincing in persuasive situations.[18] But sometimes speakers overwhelm audience members with facts and statistics to such a degree that listeners simply tune out. When selecting facts and statistics as supporting materials for your speeches, always keep your audience in mind. How will they respond? What would you think if you were in the audience?

Facts

When you include facts in a speech, you're not limited to your own observations. You accept others' observations as well. For example, you weren't alive when George Washington became President, but you accept his presidency as a fact based on what others have reported. To support this, you can examine historical documents located in the Library of Congress collections (loc.gov), and read accounts of Washington's inauguration. When Shen Tong stated, "China has suffered through more than four thousand years of violence and revolution," he based his statement of fact on events in history that others had recorded, rather than on his own observations.

Facts generally foster agreement because they often can be verified as true or false. However, audiences do not always interpret facts the same way speakers do. For example, in testimony before Congress urging quick passage of the Specter-Harkin "Pro-Living" Stem Cell Research Bill, actor Michael J. Fox[19] began with two facts:

> The issue of stem cell research is one I know something about, both as a Parkinson's disease patient and as the head of a foundation that is now the largest nonprofit funder of Parkinson's disease research outside of the U.S. government.

Fox began by stating two facts about himself. Based on these facts, the audience could reasonably infer, or draw the conclusion, that stem cell research is something Fox knows about. Later in the speech he provided additional facts related to the bill:

I also know that there's broad support from the American public. Just take a look at the polls, which show a majority of Americans are in favor, including those who consider themselves pro-life. . . . I just heard that sixty-eight religious leaders are supporting this bill. They have come to the same conclusion as a majority of Americans—loosening Federal restrictions through HR 810 is not only pro-life, it is pro-living.

These two facts—polls showing most Americans in favor of fewer restraints on stem cell research and numerous religious leaders supporting the bill—led Fox to infer that the proposed legislation was "pro-living." However, although the majority of Americans seem to embrace federal support for stem cell research, they may not have agreed with the wording of this particular bill. As a speaker, recognizing that your audience may not infer what you do about the facts you present will help you use facts that truly support your ideas.

THE EVOLVING ART

Finding Credible Facts and Stats

The internet provides facts and statistics with just a few mouse clicks. As you know, though, not all sources are created equal—some are more credible than others. USA.gov (usa.gov), the portal for the U.S. government's websites, and FedStats (fedstats.gov), the gateway site for statistics compiled by U.S. government agencies, provide two reliable places to start in your search for facts and statistics about the United States. For international statistics, visit the United Nations' website (un.org). This site hosts a vast array of databases, including FAOSTAT (faostat.fao .org), which covers topics associated with food and agriculture; the International Labor Organization (ilo.org), which focuses especially on child labor issues; and the UNESCO Institute for Statistics (uis.unesco.org), which compares statistics across countries in education, technology, literature, science, and culture. Specific countries and groups of countries also sponsor their own statistics websites, such as EUROSTAT (ec.europa.eu/eurostat), part of the European Union's website; the National Bureau of Statistics of China (stats.gov.cn/english); and Statistics South Africa (statssa .gov.za).

Statistics

Statistics allow speakers to quantify the magnitude of a problem and make comparisons across groups and time periods. For example, a speaker might claim that increased reliance on computers has led to increased incidents of identity theft. How could you find out if this claim is true? By going to the Federal Trade Commission's (FTC) website (ftc .gov), you can view the latest statistics on consumer fraud complaints: In 2005 the FTC reported that 37 percent of the complaints it received involved identity theft. That number becomes important when you learn that the FTC received more than 686,000 consumer fraud complaints—so about 255,000 were related to identity theft. The FTC also compares the percentage of fraud complaints across categories: internet auctions, 12 percent; foreign money offers, 8 percent; shop-at-home/catalog sales, 8 percent; prizes, sweepstakes, and lotteries, 7 percent; and internet services and computer complaints, 5 percent. If you were preparing for a speech on identity theft, these statistics would provide good support for a claim that this problem affects many Americans.

▼ **WATCH it** SPEECH BUDDY VIDEO LINK

Selecting the Best Supporting Materials

◄◄ ❚❚ ►►

Erin discusses different types of supporting materials and introduces examples of supporting materials she used in one of her persuasive speeches.

▼ **USE it** ACTIVITY LINK

Use Your Support System

In this activity, you're asked to watch for and evaluate the different types of supporting materials used in a student speech, and then assess your own speech project to determine how you'll find the appropriate types of supporting materials for it.

In a speech before the U.S. House of Representatives less than two months after the September 11 attacks, Illinois representative William O. Lipinski used statistics to persuade his colleagues that Congress needed to pass legislation addressing airline security:

> Since September 11, the aviation industry has contracted to a very, very significant degree. At Newark, Reagan National, and Houston, flights are down by 35 percent; at Kennedy, 34 percent; Seattle, Boston, LaGuardia, Portland, and San Francisco, they are all down by over 25 percent. The nation's top thirty-one airports are all down a minimum of 18 percent. Since September 11, United Airlines and American Airlines have cut 22 percent of their flights; Northwest, 15 percent; U.S. Airways, 25 percent; Delta, 15 percent; Alaskan Airlines, 26 percent; and Continental, 44 percent.[20]

By using statistics to back up his inference that "people are still not willing to get back into planes to any great degree," the speaker demonstrated that across airports and airlines, there were fewer flights and fewer people flying since the plane hijackings on September 11, 2001.

Supporting Your Speech with Popular Media

▼ The credibility of your supporting materials depends on the credibility of your sources. When using popular media as a source of support for your speech, you must apply the same standards of credibility that you apply to other sources. You can use your awareness and knowledge of **media credibility**, the perceived believability of newspapers, magazines, television, radio, and the internet—to ensure that all of the supporting materials you choose serves your purpose as a speaker.

Audiences are more likely to trust popular media that don't seem to have a blatant bias or project an air of overwhelming self-interest. Keeping factual information separate from opinion and advertising is one way media organizations try to establish and maintain their credibility with their audiences. Still, even the most highly regarded media outlets, such as CNN, CBS, *The New York Times*, and *USA Today*, have been tarnished by recent scandals. As a result, over half the U.S. public does not trust news organizations. Nevertheless, Americans view the news media more favorably than they view political institutions and both major political parties, and they generally agree that the press plays an important watchdog role in American politics.[21]

This section examines the credibility of various media outlets so you can determine which of them might offer the best, most credible support for your speeches.

> Perceptions of believability or trust that audience members hold toward communications media, including TV, the internet, newspapers, radio, and news magazines.

MEDIA CREDIBILITY AND THE INTERNET

In 1995, only 2 percent of Americans went online daily to get their news. Over a decade later, that number had increased to 35 percent—about 50 million people. Nearly one-quarter of all Americans cite the internet as the main source of their daily news. Especially for young people, the internet is fast becoming a favorite source of every kind of information. Nearly 90 percent of teens regularly use the internet, and when they do, over 75 percent go online for news. During the 2006 midterm elections, 31 percent of Americans went online for information about the candidates.[22]

In a sense, depending on the internet for news is unavoidable. Almost three-quarters of Americans are regular internet users,[23] and when they log on every day, they immediately get up-to-the-minute news headlines. In addition, many people sign up for automatic alerts from news sites. One-quarter of all Americans go first to internet sources to find out about the day's news. In the aftermath of Hurricane Katrina, half of all internet users went to mainstream media websites and blogs for news about the disaster.[24]

The internet serves as an essential hub for traditional news sources, and earns high credibility ratings for doing so. For instance, it functions as a conduit for major news organizations in the United States, and operates the same way in many countries and in many languages. It's the place TV networks send you for additional information, for instance, and for updates on their stories twenty-four hours a day. People generally judge a news website as more credible when a familiar newspaper or TV network sponsors the site. CNN.com ranks as one of the most frequently visited of *all* websites.[25] Interestingly, many people view the website of a news source such as *ABC News* or *USA Today* more favorably than they view the television or print versions.[26] As the digital age continues to evolve, making technical distinctions among media less clear, more people will rely on the internet as a trusted source for news.

MEDIA CREDIBILITY AND TELEVISION

Despite the growing popularity of the internet, television remains the most popular news source for Americans. For example, in the days after the September 11, 2001, terrorist attacks, Americans turned first to their televisions to get news of the tragic event, for two main reasons. First, TV is inherently visual. It is tele-*vision*. Even though people know that images can be easily manufactured or altered, they still trust media sources more when they can see for themselves what a news report is about. But TV has another important advantage over other communications media: It is so fully integrated into everyday life that watching the TV news has become a habit for many families and individuals. Even those who've grown up with the internet continue to rely more on TV than on online sources for their news. Audiences trust TV in part simply because they are so used to it.

But not all TV news sources rate equally on credibility. Research shows that CNN and CBS's *60 Minutes* are the most trusted TV news sources overall. Local newscasts are viewed more favorably than cable and commercial network news. Americans generally rank cable TV as more credible for news than the national commercial networks: ABC, NBC, CBS, and Fox.[27]

MEDIA CREDIBILITY, NEWSPAPERS, AND NEWS MAGAZINES

As with television news, the key to newspaper credibility is how local it is—people view their local daily newspaper more favorably than they view cable TV news, network TV news, and major national newspapers. Over 50 percent of Americans read the newspaper daily.

Regular newspaper readers tend to be more interested in news, especially political news, than are those who seldom read a newspaper. Newspapers are viewed as providing more in-depth and wider coverage of issues than television. Readers feel they have more time to analyze the information presented and consider a story's implications. Similarly, because newspaper journalists and editors don't have to work with the severe time constraints of TV newscasts, they have more time and space to develop and present their stories. Some people prefer the interpretive accounts that appear in weekly news magazines like *Time, Newsweek,* and *U.S. News & World Report.* Generally, though, weekly print news magazines receive lower credibility ratings than most metropolitan newspapers.[28]

MEDIA CREDIBILITY AND RADIO

The first electronic mass medium, radio, still maintains an important role in disseminating information, especially through local news stations. Radio also shares with TV the ability to instantly report and update the news. Radio will always have a place as a news medium in America's car-oriented society, with national outlets such as National Public Radio (NPR) ranked higher in credibility than newspapers (but lower than local TV). Still, local radio remains a source of news for about 15 percent of Americans, well below local television (over 65%) and local and national newspapers (28% each), and just ahead of internet news outlets (11%).[30]

Using Media Credibility to Improve Your Speech

▼ Not all audience members consider news media highly credible sources. Still, you shouldn't hesitate to cite news media as sources when appropriate. News media can provide supporting materials that make useful references, examples, and illustrations for your speech. Let's consider the ways you can use the news media effectively in your speeches.

CITING POPULAR MEDIA SOURCES AS REFERENCES

Knowing how people rate the credibility of various media, you can predict to some extent how the audience will evaluate news sources when you mention them in your speech. As you've learned in this chapter, CNN, public television newscasts, respected newspapers, national news magazines, and prime-time TV newsmagazines generate trust more than commercial network TV news. The online outlets of major media organizations enjoy positive ratings, while independent sites are more problematic. With the exception of National Public Radio, radio doesn't rate very high.

Perceptions differ according to who makes up the audience. For a highly educated, sophisticated audience, for example, multiple references to TV news won't help you establish credibility, but references to newspapers might. A study of over 1,600 regular internet users found that respondents in all age groups cited newspapers as the most credible source of information. Younger people reported going to a newspaper website for a local breaking news story, while older people preferred their local television station's website.[31] People also react to the media in terms of their political and ideological biases. Most Republicans and nearly half of Independents think the press is too critical of America, whereas only one-quarter of Democrats hold that view. Conservatives tend to consider the media biased, whereas liberals view the media as fair and trustworthy.[32] And if you feature supporting materials only from sources like *USA Today,* unreliable websites, and magazines such as *People,* you're unlikely to impress any audience.

Up-to-date references from the news media can help you establish the currency of your topic and supporting information. Use news media references in a way that balances well with other sources of information, promotes your specific purpose, and supports your thesis. Use reputable and appropriate sources, then show them off by clearly identifying them during your speech.

USING POPULAR MEDIA SOURCES AS ILLUSTRATIONS AND EXAMPLES

You want to make your speeches as dynamic and stimulating as possible without compromising the integrity of your ideas. Choosing effective media content—video clips, still photos, audio clips, text—to support or exemplify your ideas can greatly enhance your work. Because they appear as special features of your speech, make certain that your media examples have a clear and important purpose that advances your discussion or

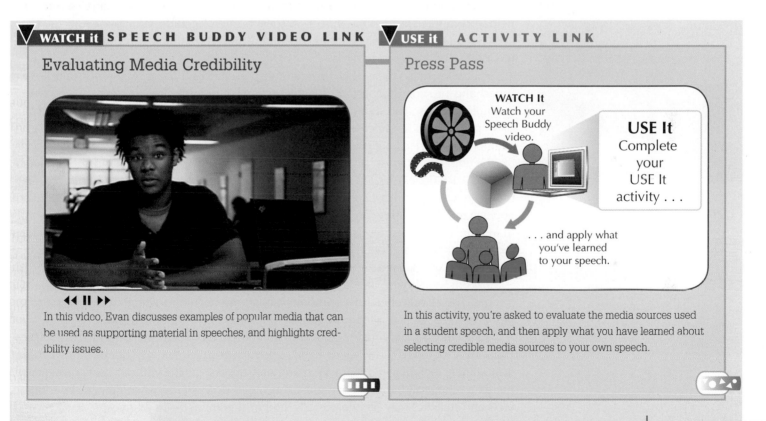

WATCH it SPEECH BUDDY VIDEO LINK

Evaluating Media Credibility

◀◀ ❚❚ ▶▶

In this video, Evan discusses examples of popular media that can be used as supporting material in speeches, and highlights credibility issues.

USE it ACTIVITY LINK

Press Pass

WATCH It
Watch your Speech Buddy video.

USE It
Complete your USE It activity . . .

. . . and apply what you've learned to your speech.

In this activity, you're asked to evaluate the media sources used in a student speech, and then apply what you have learned about selecting credible media sources to your own speech.

argument. And be prepared to defend the credibility of your media references and all the presentation media you use.

In each speech you deliver, use a variety of supporting materials that fit your topic, your audience, the situation, and you, the speaker. Carefully select the sources of your supporting materials, and arrange them well in the structure and flow of your speeches. Your audience will respond to your speeches largely in terms of how well you support your ideas.

SUMMARY

As you research your topic, you'll find information related to your points and ideas. These supporting materials form the substance of your speech. They bring your ideas to life, demonstrate the weight and seriousness of your topic, and help you build credibility. Supporting materials may appeal to your audience's emotions, logic, and cultural beliefs.

There are five basic types of supporting materials. Narratives dramatize a topic and help your audience identify with it. A speech might include your own stories, stories about others, organizational stories, or cultural stories. Telling a good story requires having a sense of timing and drama.

Examples make ideas less abstract and personalize a topic. General examples are broad and provide little detail. Specific examples provide greater detail. Hypothetical examples are based on supposition—the audience imagines the circumstances—and must seem plausible to be effective. Examples help listeners better understand the topic, yet an example can mislead if it doesn't accurately represent the larger class to which it belongs.

Definitions establish a common meaning between the speaker and the audience. Speakers use definitions to clarify concepts and identify the boundaries of a topic. Definitions may explain how something functions or offer analogies for a word or concept. Specialized dictionaries can provide more descriptive and technical meanings for a word than standard dictionaries can. In using definitions as supporting materials, speakers must recognize that the audience likely will associate connotations with words, no matter how those words are defined.

Experts, celebrities, and laypeople may provide testimony or their experiences about a topic. The effectiveness of testimony rests on the degree to which audience members perceive the person as a credible source of information about the topic.

Facts and statistics clearly appeal to an audience's logical thinking processes. These supporting materials show listeners the scope of a problem and can demonstrate a topic's importance. Including too many facts and statistics, especially without using presentation media to show all the numbers and figures, can overwhelm the audience. In addition, facts and statistics may be interpreted—and misinterpreted—in many ways.

In the Book

Summary
Key Terms
Critical Challenges

More Study Resources

Speech Studio
Quizzes
WebLinks

Student Workbook

7.1: Workshop on Supporting Materials
7.2: Source Credibility
7.3: Supporting Material Diversity
7.4: Clarity through Supporting Materials
7.5: Add a Narrative

Speech Buddy Videos

 Video Links

Selecting the Best Supporting Materials
Evaluating Media Credibility

Activity Links

Use Your Support System
Press Pass

▶ Sample Speech Videos

Chris, "Impressionistic Painting," informative speech

Peter, "Drinking and Driving," persuasive speech

Speech Builder Express

Goal/purpose
Thesis statement
Supporting material
Introduction
Conclusion
Works cited
Outline

 InfoTrac

Recommended search terms

Supporting materials and public speaking
Credibility of supporting materials
Narratives and public speaking
Examples and public speaking
Definitions and public speaking
Testimony and public speaking
Facts and statistics and public speaking
Media credibility and public speaking
Using media in speeches

Audio Study Tools

"Impressionistic Painting" by Chris

Critical thinking questions

Learning objectives

Chapter summary

The major communications media—internet, television, newspapers, news magazines, and radio—can also enhance the content and style of your presentations when used judiciously as references, illustrations, and examples. The media inspire different levels of confidence in terms of credibility. For example, local newspapers and television newscasts receive highly favorable ratings from most Americans, yet internet news outlets are increasingly viewed as a first stop for current information.

Guide to Your Online Resources

Your Online Resources for *Public Speaking: The Evolving Art* give you access to the Speech Buddy video and activity featured in this chapter, additional sample speech videos, Speech Builder Express, InfoTrac College Edition, and study aids such as glossary flashcards, review quizzes, and the Critical Challenge questions for this chapter, which you can respond to via e-mail if your instructor requests. In addition, your Online Resources feature live WebLinks relevant to this chapter, including sites that can assist you in finding credible information for your speeches, including the online version of the *American Heritage Dictionary of the English Language* and the website for the United Nations. Links are regularly maintained, and new ones are added periodically.

Key Terms

analogy 176	fact 179	narrative 170
anecdote 170	example 173	pathos 169
connotative meaning 175	logos 169	simile 176
definition 175	media credibility 183	statistics 179
denotative meaning 175	metaphor 176	supporting materials 169
ethos 179	mythos 169	testimony 178

Critical Challenges

Questions for Reflection and Discussion

1. Humans love to tell and listen to stories, so listeners find stories in speeches especially engaging. What are the negative aspects of using narratives in speeches? How can audience members enjoy a story yet listen critically at the same time?

2. Critical listeners closely examine how speakers define words. Definitions can be very powerful in a speech if audience members simply accept the definitions the speaker offers. Reflect on a recent public speaking situation in which you were in the audience. Did you question the speaker's definitions? In what other ways might the terms have been defined? How would those definitions change the nature of the speech and the speaker's conclusions?

3. When you're listening to a speaker, how convincing do you find expert, celebrity, and lay testimony? What makes you skeptical of testimony?

4. Which of the media—radio, television, newspapers, news magazines, internet—do you trust most for news? What are your reasons for trusting or not trusting the different media? If you took a poll of your classmates, what answers do you suppose you'd get? How do you and your classmates judge media credibility?

8 ORGANIZING and OUTLINING YOUR SPEECH

When you organize a speech well, audience members can follow your ideas more easily and better understand what you have to say. In addition, good organization helps you stay on track, keeping your purpose and thesis in mind. With a thoughtful plan for the order in which you want to present your points, you'll feel more confident. Organizing your speech is like planning a trip: Reaching your destination is much less stressful when you know how to get there. In addition, when your speech is well organized, audience members don't need to worry about where you are in your speech, where you've been, or where you're going. Poor organization requires the audience to work hard to put together the pieces of your speech—and probably miss out on some important information along the way. Carefully organizing your speech increases the chances that you'll achieve your specific purpose and that your audience will respond as you'd planned.

The Parts of a Speech

READ it Every speech has four main parts: introduction, body, transitions, and conclusion (**Figure 8.1**). In the first part of the speech, the *introduction,* the speaker must get the audience's attention, indicate the purpose and thesis, establish credibility, and preview the speech's main points. The *body* of a speech includes all the speaker's main points and subordinate points. Speakers use *transitions*, words, phrases, sentences, or paragraphs to move from the introduction to the body, from one point to the next, and from the body to the conclusion. The *conclusion* wraps up the speech, with the speaker reviewing the main points, restating the thesis, and providing closure.

When you present a speech, you proceed from the introduction through the body to the conclusion. But when you put together a speech you typically develop the body and transitions first, the introduction second, and the conclusion last. Figure 8.1 shows the logic underlying this seemingly illogical order. You need to know what you're going to say in the body before you develop the introduction and the conclusion. You may find, however, that as you work on the body of your speech you'll think of something you want to say in the introduction or get an idea for a great way to end your speech. Organizing your speech, like speechmaking in general, doesn't always follow a linear path.

This chapter focuses on developing the body of your speech and connecting your points together, as those are the starting points for most speakers. Chapter 9 discusses how to begin and end your speech.

▶ **FIGURE 8.1**
The Parts of a Speech

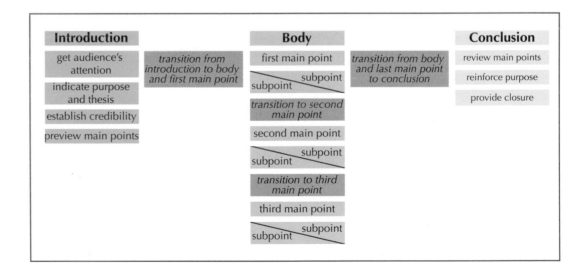

Developing and Researching Your Speech

Organizing the Body of Your Speech

▼

The **body** is where the action of your speech takes place—where you inform, persuade, or entertain your audience. This section identifies and describes the main elements of this part of your speech (**Figure 8.2**).

DEVELOPING YOUR MAIN POINTS

Your working outline provides a useful guide for developing your main points (Chapter 4). The working outline includes your topic, general purpose, specific purpose, thesis, and keywords for the main ideas and subpoints. As you review your working outline, applying the principles of clarity, relevance, and balance will help you identify what points to include and what points to leave out of your speech.

Clarity

Your main points should give your audience a clear idea of what your speech is about and the response you seek. They must also clearly support your specific purpose and be consistent with your thesis. In the following example, notice how the main points elaborate on the ideas expressed in the thesis, providing clarity on the topic of happiness. They also support the specific purpose, allowing the speaker to reach the goal of informing the audience.

Topic: A Scientific Approach to Happiness

General purpose: To inform

Specific purpose: To inform my audience about the science of happiness.

Thesis: According to scientists, the three main components of happiness are involvement with daily activities and other people, contributing in meaningful ways to larger goals, and finding pleasure in everyday life.

Main points:

    I. The first component of happiness is being engaged in activities and interacting with others.

    II. The second component of happiness is feeling like what you do contributes in meaningful ways to some larger goal or objective.

    III. The third component of happiness is simply finding pleasure in the everyday things you do.

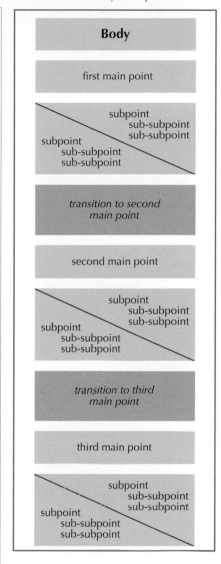

▼ **FIGURE 8.2**
Elements of the Body of a Speech

The middle and main part of a speech; includes main and subordinate points.

Even slightly altering what you want to say about a topic changes the specific purpose and thesis. In turn, the main points must also change to clearly reflect different focus. For example:

Topic: The Myths of Happiness

General purpose: To inform

Specific purpose: To make my audience aware of myths about happiness.

Thesis: Scientists have dispelled three common myths about happiness: Money makes you happy, intelligence makes you happy, and being young makes you happy.

Main points:

    I. "Wealth makes you happy" is one myth scientists have proven false.

    II. "Greater intelligence makes you happier" is a second myth scientists have proven false.

    III. "Youth as the key to happiness" is a third myth scientists have dispelled.

These examples of two approaches to the same topic, happiness, demonstrate the importance of the early steps you take in topic development: clearly refining your topic, phrasing your specific purpose, and writing your thesis statement (Chapter 4).

Relevance

Your main points should be directly relevant to your topic. As you research your topic, you may find interesting information that is only tangentially related to your speech. Although it may be tempting to include those tidbits of data, unless they're directly relevant to your topic they won't help you achieve your specific purpose. You'll always know more about your topic that what you include in your speech—you're the expert—but avoid including information that would detract from your goal. Continually review your specific purpose and thesis, and identify the points that are truly relevant.

Main points must be relevant to one another as well as to the topic. Consider the main points for this informative speech about U.S. science fiction writer Octavia E. Butler:

Topic: The Achievements of Octavia E. Butler

General purpose: To inform

Specific purpose: To increase my audience's awareness of some of Octavia E. Butler's important achievements.

Thesis: Octavia E. Butler's many achievements include winning two Hugo and two Nebula awards, a MacArthur genius grant, and a lifetime achievement award from the PEN American Center.

Main points:

    I. Butler won two Hugo and two Nebula awards for her science fiction stories.

    II. In 1995, Butler became the first, and so far only, science fiction writer to win a "genius grant" from the MacArthur Foundation.

    III. Butler won the PEN American Center Lifetime Achievement Award in writing in 1999.

▲ An informative speech about Octavia E. Butler might focus on the major writing awards she won rather than everything she accomplished in her entire career.

Each main point focuses on an important award that brought Butler recognition. She also achieved success in other ways, such as writing a science fiction movie at age 12 and selling 250,000 copies of her novel *Kindred*. Although these are important accomplishments, they're not directly relevant to a discussion of the awards she won.

Balance

Also consider how balanced your main points are. Each point should be about equal in importance relative both to your topic and to the other points. All your points may not be *completely* equal in importance, but one point shouldn't be much more or much less important than the others. Let's consider an example for an informative speech about an event.

Topic: The Ann Arbor Street Art Fair

General purpose: To inform

Specific purpose: To teach my audience about the many interesting facets of Ann Arbor's annual Street Art Fair.

Thesis: The people, the place, and the art make the annual Ann Arbor Street Art Fair an exciting event to attend.

Main points:

    I. Performers, artists, volunteers, and fair-goers make the Ann Arbor Street Art Fair lively.

In this example, the three aspects of the Ann Arbor Street Art Fair contribute about equally to the event. You'd likely plan to talk about each of them for about the same amount of time.

If not all of the main points you want to discuss are about equal in importance, you can still achieve a rough balance by spending less time on less important points. Consider a speech about the people who come together for the Ann Arbor Street Art Fair:

Topic: The People of the Ann Arbor Street Art Fair

General purpose: To inform

Specific purpose: To inform my audience about the people of Ann Arbor's annual Street Art Fair.

Thesis: The people of the Ann Arbor Street Art Fair include the organizers, volunteers, artists, performers, and fair-goers.

Main points:

I. The organizers work all year planning the event.

II. Volunteers do everything from giving tours of the fair to reuniting lost parents and children.

III. The nearly 200 artists display their creative work.

IV. Performers keep everyone in good cheer.

V. Thousands and thousands of fair-goers from around the world attend the event every year.

You'd probably spend more time talking about the artists and performers because they're the reason people attend the fair. Or you could emphasize the behind-the-scenes work of the organizers and volunteers. Whatever your emphasis, maintain balance by spending a similar amount of time on each point. For example, you could spend two minutes each on the artists and performers, and one minute each on the organizers, volunteers, and fair-goers.

Evaluating the balance of your main points also requires that you identify the appropriate number of points to include in your speech. To help you determine the right number of main points, consider (1) what information you must cover to achieve your specific purpose and (2) how much time you have to present your speech. Say you have five minutes to present the informative speech about the people of the Ann Arbor Street Art Fair. Can you adequately talk about each main point and give sufficient attention to the introduction and conclusion in that amount of time? No. You'd have less than one minute for each main point, giving you little time to provide the audience with any in-depth information. You need either more time or fewer points. If you can't change the amount of time allotted, you must reduce the number of main points. You could, for instance, focus just on the creative people associated with the fair—the artists and the performers. Or you could talk about the unnoticed people—the organizers and the volunteers. Or you could concentrate on the two groups that interact with each other—the artists and the fair-goers.

PATTERNS FOR ORGANIZING YOUR MAIN POINTS

Once you've selected the main points for your speech, organize them in a clear and logical pattern. **Patterns of organization** are structures for ordering the main points of your speech that help audience members understand the relationships among your ideas. Choosing an effective pattern of organization requires careful consideration of your speech topic, general purpose, specific purpose, and thesis.

> A structure for ordering the main points of speech.

Speakers commonly rely on six patterns of organization. An additional pattern used primarily for speeches to persuade, Monroe's motivated sequence, is discussed in Chapter 14. **Table 8.1** provides an overview of the organizational patterns discussed in this chapter.

Chronological

When you use a **chronological pattern** of organization, you arrange your ideas in a time sequence. For example, in a speech on how to build a birdhouse, you'd start with what listeners need to do first, then explain what they need to do second, and so on, covering each step in order of completion.

> A pattern that organizes a speech by how something develops or occurs in a time sequence.

You can also use the chronological pattern to trace the history of a topic. For example, a speech on the history of the internet might focus on major events such as the development of ARPANET—the precursor to the internet—in 1969 and Tim Berners-Lee's idea for the web thirty years later.[1] These events or turning points would provide main points for the speech:

TABLE 8.1 ▶ Patterns of Organization

PATTERN	BRIEF DEFINITION	USEFUL FOR . . .	PROVIDES AUDIENCE WITH . . .	EXAMPLES FROM STUDENT SPEECHES
Chronological	The way in which something develops or occurs in a time sequence	Recounting the history of a subject, a sequence of events, or a step-by-step procedure	A sense of how a topic unfolds over time.	Topic: The Job Search Thesis: Finding a job requires four steps: self-analysis, résumé development, application, and follow-up.
Spatial	The physical or directional relationship between objects or places	Describing an object, a place, or how something is designed	A visual understanding of the relationship between the parts of the topic	Topic: Portland, Oregon—My Hometown Thesis: Portland is divided into four quadrants: northwest, northeast, southeast, and southwest.
Topical	Arranged by sub-topics of equal importance	Explaining the elements that make up a topic	An image of the subpoints within the topic	Topic: Local Public Transportation Can Work for You Thesis: The primary modes of public transit in our area are light rail, trolley, and bus.
Narrative	Dramatic retelling of events as a story or a series of short stories	Encouraging audience involvement and participation	A basis for sharing the speaker's point of view	Topic: Kayaking Adventure Thesis: Kayaking the Menominee River on the Wisconsin-Michigan border was filled with whitewater, white knuckles, and fun.
Cause-and-effect	Shows how an action produces a particular outcome	Demonstrating a causal link between two or more events	A view of the relationships between conditions or events	Topic: Diabetes and Dieting Thesis: Eating too much sugar has caused the recent increase in the number of people with diabetes in the United States.
Problem-solution	Describes a problem and provides possible solutions	Convincing audience members to agree with a particular course of action	A rationale for considering a particular solution to a problem.	Topic: Telecommuting Thesis: Because too many people commute long distances to work, more companies should promote telecommuting.

Topic: History of the Internet

General purpose: To inform

Specific purpose: To teach my audience about important events in the history of the internet.

Thesis: There are four key turning points in the history of the internet: the Advanced Research Projects Agency (ARPANET) connects four major U.S. universities, emoticons are first used, Tim Berners-Lee develops the idea for hypertext, and Napster is launched.

Main points:

I. In 1969 the Advanced Research Projects Agency (ARPANET) connects four major U.S. universities.

II. In 1979 members of a science fiction e-mail list use the first emoticons as a way to express emotions online.

III. In 1989 Tim Berners-Lee develops the idea for hypertext, which becomes the basis for the World Wide Web.

IV. In 1999 Shawn Fanning invents Napster, the peer-to-peer file-sharing program.

Spatial

Speeches that rely on a **spatial pattern** of organization link points together based on their physical relationships, such as their locations. This pattern works particularly well for informative and entertaining speeches about places and objects. For example, when you describe a room you identify the objects in it and their place in terms of each other: "As you walk in the room, the bright orange couch is on the far wall, facing the plasma television and the aquarium." An informative speech on the solar system might discuss each planet in order of increasing distance from the sun: Mercury, Venus, Earth, Mars, Jupiter, Saturn, Uranus, and Neptune. Similarly, a speech to entertain about intriguing places you've visited could start with the location farthest from where you're speaking and progress to the closest one:

> A pattern that organizes a speech by the physical or directional relationship between objects or places.

> *Topic:* Intriguing Places I've Visited
>
> *General purpose:* To entertain
>
> *Specific purpose:* To amuse my audience with the features of some intriguing places I've visited.
>
> *Thesis:* Maine's haunted Hitchborn Inn, Tennessee's Salt and Pepper Shaker Museum, the Mice Graves of Montana's Boot Hill Cemetery, and Seattle's Underground City are four intriguing places I've visited.
>
> *Main points:*
>
> I. Maine's haunted Hitchborn Inn, near Penobscot Bay, may be the greatest distance from us, but sometimes I still feel the ghosts are right here.
>
> II. As we travel west and south, we come to the Salt and Pepper Shaker Museum in Gatlinburg, Tennessee.
>
> III. Heading west and north, we reach Virginia City, Montana, and the graves of three rogue mice buried in Boot Hill Cemetery.
>
> IV. Finally, as we continue west, we reach the intriguing place closest to us, the Underground City of Seattle.

Topical

A pattern that organizes a speech by arranging subtopics of equal importance.

A **topical pattern** of organization divides a topic into subtopics that address its components, elements, or aspects. For example, in a speech on what you learn about people when they play golf, one of our students discussed these three points:

> *Topic:* Learning about People on the Golf Course
>
> *General purpose:* To inform
>
> *Specific purpose:* To inform my audience about what they can learn about people when they're playing golf.
>
> *Thesis:* When people play golf, they reveal how they handle the unexpected, their level of patience, and their concern for others.
>
> *Main points:*
>
> I. Observing people as they play golf gives you insight into how they handle unexpected events.

II. Observing people as they play golf gives you a good indication of how patient they are.

III. Observing people as they play golf lets you know how—or if—they show concern for other people.

These points are clearly relevant to the main topic, what you learn about people by observing them playing golf. However, points also related to golf, such as "Golf is a great game to play" or "You can play golf at any age," would not be appropriate for this speech because they are not subtopics of the topic the speaker is focusing on.

Narrative

With a **narrative pattern** of organization, you structure your main points in story form. Speeches of tribute and introduction often follow a narrative format. Listeners find stories compelling and memorable, which makes the narrative pattern an engaging organizational option.[2]

Many stories follow this sequence: setting the scene, describing an initial conflict, increasing action, escalating conflict, conflict reaching its peak, and arriving at the final outcome.[3] Consider an informative speech on the history of the Fabergé eggs:

A pattern that organizes a speech by a dramatic retelling of events as a story or a series of short stories.

Topic: The History of the Fabergé Eggs

General purpose: To inform

Specific purpose: To inform my audience about the history of Fabergé eggs.

Thesis: The history of Fabergé eggs involves royalty, wealth, theft, legal battles, and a happy ending.

Main points:

I. The first Fabergé egg was produced for Russia's Czar Alexander III in 1885 as an Imperial Easter egg.[4] (*setting the scene*)

II. In 1918 Russia's imperial family was murdered. (*initial conflict*)

III. When their homes were ransacked, eight eggs were lost. (*increasing action*)

IV. Nearly 100 years later a Russian billionaire purchased the missing eggs. (*escalating conflict*)

V. A legal battle ensued. (*peak conflict*)

VI. Finally, just a few years ago, the eight once-missing eggs were returned to Russia. (*final outcome*)

▼ The history of the Fabergé eggs provides intriguing points that work well with a narrative pattern of organization for an informative speech.

AFP/Getty Images

The Nonlinear Narrative

Narrative organizational patterns are less linear than they were in Aristotle's time, when stories were often told in sequence from beginning to middle to end. Audiences today have become accustomed to the nonlinearity of the internet—you can click from one point to another, skipping many points in between. Now narratives often unfold in unpredictable ways, as with the films *Crash, Pulp Fiction,* and *Memento,* which move back and forth in time and between characters. Using narrative to structure your ideas in novel ways can engage the audience—or confuse them. Providing some clues as to how the main points of your narrative fit together will help listeners follow the story and keep them interested in your speech.

Cause-and-Effect

A pattern that organizes a speech by showing how an action produces a particular outcome.

The **cause-and-effect pattern** of organization relies on the idea of one action leading to or bringing about another. When using this pattern you must clearly and carefully link the cause with the effect, providing appropriate and effective supporting materials. Although most often used for persuasive speeches, the cause-and-effect pattern can also be applied to informative speeches. For example, an informative speech on the positive effects of mediation works well with a cause-and-effect pattern of organization.

Topic: Positive Effects of Meditation

General purpose: To inform

Specific purpose: To inform my audience about the positive effects of meditation.

Thesis: By using less oxygen, lowering your heart rate, and altering your brain waves, meditation helps you relax, feel more content, and think more creatively.

Main points:

   I. Meditation causes three changes in your body.

       A. When you meditate, you use less oxygen.

       B. When you meditate, you lower your heart rate.

       C. When you meditate, your theta brain waves—those associated with daydreaming—increase in frequency.

II. These three changes in your body as you meditate have three main effects.

    A. You feel more relaxed.

    B. You feel more content.

    C. You think more creatively.

When you use the cause-and-effect pattern for a persuasive speech, your audience must come to agree with you about what causes a particular circumstance or event. Consider the topic of homelessness in the United States.

Topic: Homelessness in the United States

General purpose: To persuade

Specific purpose: To convince my audience that lack of education and affordable health care cause homelessness.

Thesis: People in the United States become homeless because they lack educational opportunities and do not have access to affordable health care.

Main points:

  I. There are two primary causes of homelessness in the United States.

    A. Serious inequities in the American educational system mean some people have limited educational opportunities.

    B. Many Americans are uninsured and cannot afford regular health care.

  II. These two conditions result in two effects that contribute to homelessness in the United States.

    A. Without a good education, individuals can't get the jobs they need to pay for a place to live.

    B. Without affordable health care, individuals often must choose between getting treatment and paying rent.

If your listeners agree with the initial causes—inequities in the U.S. educational system and lack of affordable health care—they will be more inclined to agree that the effects contribute to homeless. In contrast, if listeners disagree with the causes you cite, or identify different causes, your speech will be less persuasive.

Problem-Solution

When speakers use a **problem-solution pattern** of organization, they're attempting to convince audience members that a specific dilemma or problem requires a particular course of action, or solution. Clearly establishing that a problem exists provides the foundation for persuading the audience that the solution should be implemented. Imagine that the football team at your school perpetually loses money, using more funds than it produces. A persuasive speech that proposes to terminate the football program would be appropriate. If listeners don't think there's a problem, however, they're unlikely to support your solution.

Topic: Ending the Football Program on Our Campus

General purpose: To persuade

Specific purpose: To convince my audience that we should no longer have a football program at our school.

Thesis: The football program at our school drains resources from our campus, so it should be eliminated.

Main points:

    I. The football program at our school loses money each year.

    II. The football program drains money from the school's budget that could be used for other programs.

    III. Our school's football program should be eliminated.

In addition, speakers must demonstrate that the proposed solution will adequately address the issue described and can be reasonably implemented. For example, let's say you identify air pollution as a problem and suggest limiting every household in the United States to one vehicle as a remedy. Audience members, especially in the United States, likely would view your solution as too extreme and difficult to implement. So rather than ask audience members to give up their cars, you could ask them to take a smaller step: giving up driving one day each week. This solution provides a balanced response to the problem and also presents a behavioral change that listeners might consider reasonable.

You've learned about six patterns for organizing your speech: chronological, spatial, topical, narrative, cause-and-effect, and problem-solution. **Table 8.2** demonstrates how the discussion of one topic, voting, changes based on which organizational pattern you apply.

TABLE 8.2 ▶ Applying Patterns of Organization to a Single Topic: Voting

PATTERN	GENERAL PURPOSE	SPECIFIC PURPOSE	THESIS	MAIN POINTS
Chronological	To inform	To teach my audience about key U.S. Constitutional amendments in the history of voting in the United States	Three amendments to the Constitution changed voting in the United States: the 15th, 19th, and 24th Amendments.	I. The 15th Amendment to the U.S. Constitution granted all U.S. citizens the right to vote regardless of race, color, or previous condition of servitude. II. The 19th Amendment gave women the right to vote. III. The 24th Amendment ended the practice of poll taxing, or forcing people to pay a tax to vote.
Spatial	To inform	To help my audience understand the layout of a typical ballot	The layout of a ballot includes four main sections: the election's title and description, the instructions, a list of individuals and items to vote on, and the space to record the vote.	I. The election's title and description are at the top of the ballot. II. How to complete the ballot is explained next. III. Candidates, proposals, propositions, and initiatives are listed in a specified order. IV. Space to record your vote is usually to the right of the item.
Topical	To inform	To make my audience aware of how voting occurs in other democratic countries	The Philippines, South Africa, and Australia provide examples of democratic countries whose voting systems differ from ours.	I. The Philippines' voting system II. South Africa's voting system III. Australia's voting system
Narrative	To entertain	To share with my audience the lighter side of getting out the vote for student elections on a college campus	My adventures in getting out the vote for student government elections on my campus nearly ended my college career but finished on an unexpected note.	I. My campus's student election day was more like doomsday for me. II. Getting out the vote almost got me expelled from school. III. My political science advisor suggested I change my major. IV. The ending of this story surprised even me.

Continued

PATTERN	GENERAL PURPOSE	SPECIFIC PURPOSE	THESIS	MAIN POINTS
Cause-and-effect	To persuade	To persuade my audience that the United States needs standardized federal voting regulations	The lack of consistency in voting rules and procedures across states in our country has led to voting problems on Election Day.	I. Local and state governments are in charge of voting procedures. II. Variation in voting standards has led to ballot counting problems at the national, state, and local levels.
Problem-solution	To persuade	To encourage my audience to consider alternative voting procedures in the United States	Giving people greater flexibility in how they vote will solve the problem of not being able to reach a polling place on Election Day.	I. Many people don't vote because they have difficulty getting to their polling places on Election Day. II. Alternative voting methods, such as mailed ballots, will solve the problem of not being able to get to the polls.

▼ WATCH it SPEECH BUDDY VIDEO LINK

Reviewing Patterns of Organization

◀◀ ❙❙ ▶▶

Anthony helps you review the patterns of organization commonly used to organize the main points of a speech.

▼ USE it ACTIVITY LINK

Everything in Its Place

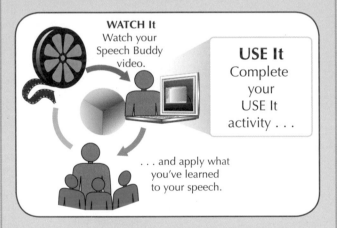

WATCH It
Watch your Speech Buddy video.

USE It
Complete your USE It activity . . .

. . . and apply what you've learned to your speech.

This activity gives you a chance to correct an outline that is organized incorrectly and to identify the pattern of organization used for the outline.

Connecting Your Ideas with Transitions

Effective speaking demands more than researching your topic well and developing a logical way to organize your material. Your speech must also have coherence, an obvious and plausible connection among your ideas. Transitions play an important role in creating coherence: They help direct your audience from one idea or part of your speech to the next.[5] Effective transitions allow you to:

- Move smoothly and clearly from the introduction to the body of the speech.
- Move from one main point to the next main point within the body of the speech.
- Exit from the body of the speech to the conclusion.

Table 8.3 provides examples of transition words and phrases.

Most transitions are short and easy to integrate into your speech, but if you leave them out, your audience becomes confused. Use brief, clear transitions to make it as effortless as possible for listeners to navigate through the content of your speech. This section more closely examines how you can use transitions in three key places: introducing

An obvious and plausible connection among ideas.

A word, phrase, sentence, or paragraph used throughout a speech to mark locations in the organization and clearly link the parts of a speech together.

TABLE 8.3 ▶ Types of Transitions

TYPE OF TRANSITION	WORD OR PHRASE	EXAMPLE
Ordering	*first, second, third; next, then, finally*	First I'll review the history of the missions in California.
Reinforcing	*similarly, also, likewise, in addition, moreover, further*	Also, you could volunteer as a tutor in a local elementary school.
Contrasting	*however, yet, in contrast, whereas, unless, although, even though, instead*	However, your best strategy is to prepare well in advance.
Chronology/time	*when, while, now, before, after, currently, recently, then, during, later, meanwhile*	During this process you must keep a close watch on your time.
Causality	*therefore, so, consequently, since, because, for this reason, with this in mind*	Therefore, learning to manage your money now will help you avoid financial problems in the future.
Summarizing/ concluding	*in summary, let me summarize, finally, let's review, as I've discussed*	Finally, good study habits require evaluating what works and what doesn't.

the first main point, moving from one main point to the next, and finishing the last main point and going on to your conclusion.

INTRODUCING THE FIRST MAIN POINT

After you've given your speech introduction, you're ready to move on to the first main point in the body of your speech. To accomplish this task smoothly, include a brief transition to signpost the direction of your speech. Signposts, which include ordering transitions, such as *first, next,* and *finally,* let audience members know where you are in a speech and where you're going. You might say,

- "Now, let me elaborate on that first point I referred to in the introduction, *(then refer to the first point)* . . . ."
- "As I mentioned, we'll first consider *(first point)* . . . ."
- "To begin, I'll describe *(first point)* . . . ."

After voicing the transition, begin discussing your first main point.

A transition that indicates a key move in the speech, making its organization clear to the audience.

TRANSITIONS BETWEEN MAIN POINTS

When you shift from one main point to the next within the body of the speech, use internal transitions that clearly signpost the direction in which you're going. Here are some examples of what you might say as you move through the body of a speech on human biological cell cloning:

- "Now that I've described what human biological cell cloning is, let's turn to my second main point, the advantages human cloning offers to medical research. . . ."
- "We've learned the basics of human biological cell cloning. Now let's consider what it offers to medical research. . . ."
- "As you can tell, human biological cell cloning is a complex and intriguing subject. Equally intriguing is the potential for medical research, which I want to elaborate on. . . ."

Internal summaries are longer transitions that also help listeners move from one main point to the next. These transitions remind listeners of previously presented information so that they have a solid grasp of those ideas before you move on to the next point. The following example, from an informative speech on the International Spy Museum in Washington, D.C., uses chronological transitions.

A review of main points or subpoints, given before going on to the next point in a speech.

So you'll start your tour of the museum by learning about the basics of espionage and choosing your own cover identity. Fully engaging in this first part of the museum provides the essential framework for enjoying the remainder of your tour. The spy gadgets, weapons, and bugs you'll find in the next exhibit are all the more fascinating when you think about them in terms of your spy identity. Then you'll view those tricks of the trade in action in the third part of the museum, which focuses on the history of spying. Some of the secret spies will surprise you. Now let's turn to more recent history presented in the International Spy Museum.

With eight main exhibits, as well as special exhibits, listeners may well lose track of the information presented earlier. Refreshing their memories about the first three exhibits discussed allows the speaker to move with confidence to the next main point, the fourth exhibit.

In the next example, the speaker uses reinforcing and contrasting transitions in an internal summary during a persuasive speech on the need for greater security in radio frequency identification tags.

Before I move on, let's briefly review the basics of radio frequency identification tags, or RFIDs. These ID tags are becoming commonplace. We use them for our pets—the computer chips we implant that contain information in case our pets get lost. RFIDs are used in the new electronic passports issued by the U.S.

Transitioning with Presentation Media

The presentation media components of your speech, such as digital slides, overhead transparencies, and audio clips, work with your words to provide smooth transitions between points. You may use oral transitions, such as, "As I show in this next slide, . . . ," "In the previous chart I demonstrated how college students typically spend their money today, and in this chart I demonstrate how college students have spent their money in the past," and, "The next music clip will take us to my final point about hip-hop culture. . . ." In these examples you explicitly link what you say with your presentation media. You can also use nonverbal transitions by simply moving to the next slide, transparency, or audio clip as you're stating your transition, as in, "Let's review the main reasons for *(click to main points review slide)* . . . ," "Now that I've explained the first step in the process, let's examine the second step *(show second step transparency)* . . . ," or, "Let's go on to another myth of classical music, that it's boring *(begin audio clip)*. . . ." Transitioning with presentation media can give you a seamless and more dynamic presentation.

government. These tiny chips contain personal information such as your name, birthplace, and date of birth. Additionally, the electronic passports include a digital photograph designed for use with face-recognition software. RFIDs can hold a great deal of information—your medical records, financial history, and other personal data. They're cheap to produce and easy to manufacture. However, as we'll see next, they're also easy to infect with computer viruses.

This internal summary provides an essential link between the explanation of what RFIDs are used for and the potential problems computer viruses could cause.

Internal summaries perform two functions for the speaker: (1) They remind the audience of the key points the speaker has talked about, and (2) they link previous points with the upcoming one. The more you reinforce your ideas by reminding your audience of what you said—without becoming repetitious and long-winded—the greater the likelihood they'll remember your points.

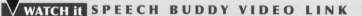

WATCH it SPEECH BUDDY VIDEO LINK

Linking Effectively: Transitions

◀◀ ❚❚ ▶▶

In this video, Erin describes different types of transitions. As you watch the video, keep in mind what you've learned in this chapter about the role and types of transitions, as well as what makes each type effective.

USE it ACTIVITY LINK

Polite to Point

This activity gives you an opportunity to evaluate transitions in sample speeches and suggest ways in which they could be improved.

TRANSITIONS TO THE CONCLUSION

Letting your audience know you're moving from the final main point to the end of your speech prepares them for the conclusion. The transition to the conclusion requires little more than a few words or a phrase. Link the transition from your last main point to the actual content of the conclusion as seamlessly as possible. Consider these examples that use summarizing, or concluding, phrases:

- "In summary, I've covered key points about *(transition and review main points)* . . . ."
- "Let's review the main issues to keep in mind *(transition and review main points)* . . . ."

When you use a transition to signal your audience that the end of your speech is near, they will expect you to finish shortly. For speeches of 10 minutes or less, that generally means no more than a minute for the conclusion. If you indicate you're about to complete your speech yet go on talking for several minutes, the audience will think you've misled them.

Putting Your Ideas Together: The Complete-Sentence Outline

▼ Recall that as you're working on your speeches you'll create three different outlines: (1) the working outline, for initially identifying the main ideas you want to address (Chapter 4); (2) the complete-sentence outline, for elaborating on your points (covered in this chapter); and (3) the presenting outline, for giving your speech (Chapter 12). **Table 8.4** on page 214 reviews these outlines.

THE PURPOSE OF THE COMPLETE-SENTENCE OUTLINE

While your working outline gives you general directions for researching and organizing your speeches and the presentation outline helps you practice and present your speech, the **complete-sentence outline** provides a highly detailed description of your ideas and how they're related to one another.

The complete-sentence outline provides much greater depth than the other two types of outlines. In the complete-sentence outline, also referred to as a *full-sentence* or *preparation outline*, you'll use complete sentences that clearly reflect your thinking and research on your topic.[6] Keep in mind, though, that the complete-sentence outline reflects a plan of your speech, not every word you'll say when you give your presentation.

> A formal outline using full sentences for all points developed after researching the speech and identifying supporting materials; includes a speech's topic, general purpose, specific purpose, thesis, introduction, main points, subpoints, conclusion, transitions, and references.

TABLE 8.4 ▶ Types of Outlines

TYPE OF OUTLINE	FUNCTIONS	KEY FEATURES	CHAPTER
Working	Assists in initial topic development; guides research	Includes main points and possible subpoints; revised during research process	Chapter 4: Developing Your Purpose and Topic
Complete-sentence	Clearly identifies all pieces of information for the speech; puts ideas in order; forms basis for developing the presentation outline	Uses complete sentences; lists all sections of speech and all references; revised during preparation process	Chapter 8: Organizing and Outlining Your Speech
Presentation	Assists in practicing and giving your speech	Uses keywords; revised as you practice your speech; often transferred to note cards for use during practice and the final presentation	Chapter 12: Delivering Your Speech

YOU ARE HERE ▶ (points to Complete-sentence row)

FORMATTING THE COMPLETE-SENTENCE OUTLINE

Using symbols and indentation, outlines provide a visual representation of how you've put your speech together. Outlines show the priority of your ideas, from first to last, and how they're related. Typically, upper-case Roman numerals (I, II, III) indicate the main points of the speech, and these points sit at the left margin of the page. For the first subpoints under a main point, indent one level and use a capital letter (A, B, C). For sub-subpoints, use Arabic numbers (1, 2, 3) and indent another level. For lengthy speeches, you might need to add sub-sub-subpoints, using lower-case letters (a, b, c) and indenting another level, and sub-sub-sub-subpoints, using lowercase Roman numerals (i, ii, iii,) and indenting once again. A period follows each number or letter, as shown in **Figure 8.3**.

Basic Outline Format

I. First main point
   A. First subpoint
      1. First sub-subpoint
      2. Second sub-subpoint
         a. First sub-sub-subpoint
         b. Second sub-sub-subpoint
            i. First sub-sub-sub-subpoint
            ii. Second sub-sub-sub-subpoint

Some basic rules provide the guidance you need for formatting your complete-sentence outline.

Preface the Outline with Identifying Information

Listing your topic, general purpose, specific purpose, and thesis right at the top of your outline keeps you on track as you develop the outline. Clearly label each item, as in this example:

Topic: Taking Good Photographs

General purpose: To inform

Specific purpose: To demonstrate to my audience how to take good photographs.

Thesis: The four guidelines for taking good photographs are to get close, avoid background clutter, go for the action, and check your light source.

State Points and Subpoints in Complete Sentences

Writing out your points and subpoints as complete sentences helps you develop your thoughts more fully. Your working outline, which includes just keywords or phrases, represents the rudiments of your speech—your ideas before you fully developed them. In the complete-sentence outline, you articulate your thoughts more clearly by writing out your points and subpoints in complete sentences. In addition, each main point or subpoint expresses only one idea, so use just one sentence for each point.

Comparing the main points for the working and complete-sentence outlines for the speech on choosing a major, discussed in Chapter 4, demonstrates key differences between the two types of outlines (**Table 8.5**). The complete-sentence outline shows how each point is developed. For example, the sentence "Practical considerations in choosing a major include the department's reputation, the time it will take to graduate, the job market, possible salary, and requirements for the major" suggests five subpoints within that main point. In the working outline, the phrase "practical considerations" doesn't give enough information about how the speaker might elaborate on that point.

List Your Main Points in Order

List main points in the order you'll present them. You'll identify the main points of your speech like this:

I. First main point

II. Second main point

III. Third main point

Maintain Levels of Importance

All items at the same level on the outline should have the same level of importance. That is, all main points must be equally important in relation to your topic, all subpoints must be equally important in relation to a main point, and so on. For example, in a speech on business etiquette, the main points might be:

TABLE 8.5 ▶ Main Points for the Working and Complete-Sentence Outlines

MAIN POINTS IN THE WORKING OUTLINE	MAIN POINTS IN THE COMPLETE-SENTENCE OUTLINE
I. Practical considerations	I. Practical considerations in choosing a major include the department's reputation, the time it will take to graduate, the job market, possible salary, and requirements for the major.
II. Academic resources	II. Academic resources include openings in the program, the department's instructors, curriculum, and support for students.
III. Personal orientations	III. Personal orientations include career goals, personal goals, what you enjoy, what you don't like, and what you're good at.

I. Telephone etiquette is necessary for the four parts of a phone conversation.

II. Face-to-face etiquette is necessary for the three parts of an in-person conversation.

III. Online etiquette is necessary for the three parts of a message exchange.

All three items are of equal importance because they discuss ways to communicate. A fourth main point about "etiquette with the boss" wouldn't fit because it refers to a specific person you might communicate with at work, an idea that is subordinate to the main points about ways in which people communicate.

Subordinate Ideas That Support Your Main Points

The term *subordinate* comes from the Latin *sub*, meaning "under," and *ordinare*, meaning "to order."[7] So subordinate points are those that are "under" your main points, providing evidence and information that support your main ideas. In the speech on business etiquette, the first main point and subpoints might look something like this:

I. Telephone etiquette is necessary for the four parts of a phone conversation.
   A. There are etiquette rules for answering the telephone.
   B. There are etiquette rules for placing a call.
   C. There are etiquette rules for fulfilling your obligations during the phone conversation.
   D. There are etiquette rules for ending a call.

In this example each subpoint provides a piece of information that supports the main idea that etiquette rules apply to different parts of a telephone conversation.

Check the Number of Subpoints

If you can't identify at least two pieces of information to support a point or subpoint, reexamine how you're organizing your ideas, consider conducting additional research, or determine whether the point really requires additional explanation. An informative speech on media literacy might include the following main points and subpoints:

I. Media literacy requires that an individual is an effective consumer and producer of mediated communication.
   A. Media literacy differs from information literacy.
   B. Media literacy differs from digital literacy.

II. Media literacy has three components.
   A. The first component is analyzing mediated communication.
   B. The second component is evaluating mediated communication.
   C. The third component is creating mediated communication.

III. There are three ways to determine whether you're media literate.
   A. Analyze media messages such as television news.
   B. Evaluate media messages such as magazine advertisements.
   C. Create media messages such as webpages.

Notice that each main point has at least two subpoints. For example, if the third main point had been as follows, you'd have to question the strength of the main idea:

III. There's a test for media literacy.
   A. Take the test for media literacy.

Should you just drop it from the speech? Search for more information? Audience members probably would be curious about their media literacy, so stating the main point more clearly and then elaborating on it was the best choice.

Include and Label Your Introduction, Conclusion, and Transitions

Because the preparation outline includes every detail of your speech, incorporate your introduction, conclusion, and transitions into your outline. Some instructors may ask you to write out your introduction and conclusion word for word in paragraph form. Others may ask you to outline those parts of your speech, as shown in the sample complete-sentence outline in **Figure 8.4**. In addition, label your transitions as shown in Figure 8.4. This will help you remember to use them when you give your speech.

Use a Consistent System of Symbols and Indentation

Generally, speakers use the following system of symbols and indentation:

I. First main point
   A. First subpoint
      1. First sub-subpoint
         a. First sub-sub-subpoint
         b. Second sub-sub-subpoint
      2. Second sub-subpoint
   B. Second subpoint

List References for Your Speech

At the end of your outline, list the references for your speech—the sources of all the supporting material you included. In the sample preparation outline in Figure 8.4, the references are listed using the formatting rules of the American Psychological Association. Some instructors require students to use the Modern Language Association reference formatting rules.[8] Check with your instructor to find out how you should format your references. (More examples of how to list references are presented in Chapter 6.)

Sample Complete-Sentence Outline

Title: The Colors of the Filipino Flag

General purpose: To inform

Specific purpose: To inform my audience about the significance of the colors of the Filipino flag.

Thesis: The most significant parts of the Filipino flag are its three major colors: red, blue, and white.

Introduction

I. What's red, blue, white, and brown, has three stars, and has a bright shining sun? *(Pause.)*
   A. Well, it's me wearing this shirt with a Filipino flag.
   B. If you're familiar with what I'm wearing (a shirt called *barong Tagalog*), you can probably infer that I'll be talking about an artifact from the Philippines, my very own culture.

II. In the early stages when I was thinking about this speech, I kept asking myself three questions.
   A. What's something important in my culture?
   B. What do Filipinos value?
   C. What has a lot of meaning and history?

III. I was raised with the motto, "Know history, know self because without history, there's no self."
   A. The Filipino flag helps me know my self—who I am.
   B. This flag tells a lot about Filipino history.
   C. The flag reflects the Filipino culture.

IV. Today I'll talk about the most significant parts of the flag for Filipino history and culture, its three major colors: red, blue, and white.

Transition: To begin, I'll explain the importance of the color red in the flag.

Body

I. Red is the first major color of the Filipino flag.
   A. The color red represents courage or, in the Tagalog language, *ma tapang*.

(continued)

    B.   Courage led the Filipinos toward freedom from Spanish tyranny.

       1.   The Spaniards ruled the Filipinos for more than 300 years.

          a.   The Spaniards were first attracted to the region by its gold and spices.

          b.   King Philip II subsequently decided to expand his empire and took the land.

          c.   Friars (Spanish priests) ruled the Filipinos.

       2.   Courage helped the Filipinos win their freedom from the Spaniards.

          a.   In 1892, Andres Bonifacio formed a secret revolutionary society called Katipunan.

          b.   In 1898, the Filipinos, with the help of the United States, won their freedom from Spain.

Transition: As you can see, red has great meaning for Filipinos. Blue has important meaning as well.

II. Blue is the second major color of the Filipino flag.

    A.   The color blue represents justice or, in the Tagalog language, *justicia*.

    B.   Filipinos consider justice very important in their way of life and in their government.

       1.   Filipinos value justice in their way of life.

       2.   Filipinos value justice in their government.

          a.   The Filipinos stepped into the realm of self-government.

          b.   The commonwealth elected Manuel Luis Quezon as their first president.

Transition: Finally, I'll tell you about the last color in the flag.

III. White is the third major color of the Filipino flag.

    A.   The color white represents equality or, in the Tagalog language, *pan-tay pan-tay*.

    B.   Filipinos consider equality very important in their way of life.

       1.   Ethnic and religious diversity in the Philippines makes equality especially important.

          a.   There is much ethnic diversity, including more than 500,000 Chinese, 60,000 Negritos, and 7,000 Americans and Europeans.

          b.   There are several major religions: Christians, Muslims, and Pagans.

       2.   There is great equality in the household.

a. Unlike men in many Asian countries, Filipino husbands treat their wives as equals.

   b. Filipino wives are usually in charge of the family's money.

Transition: Let's review those questions I was wondering about at the beginning of my speech.

Conclusion

I. There were three questions I wanted to answer.
   A. What's something important in my culture?
   B. What do Filipinos value?
   C. What has a lot of meaning and history?

II. The Filipino flag tells us a lot about the country's culture.
   A. We learned that Filipinos are individuals with great courage, represented as red on the Filipino flag.
   B. We learned that Filipinos are people of justice, represented as blue on the Filipino flag.
   C. And we learned that Filipinos value equality, represented as white on the Filipino flag.

III. Well, with my motto, "Know history, know self because without history, there's no self," I can honestly tell you right now that I do know more about myself and my identity than I ever did before from this very flag, and that as an individual I'm proud to be Filipino.

References

Hemley, R. (2003). *Invented Eden: The elusive, disputed history of the Tasaday*. New York: Farrar, Straus and Giroux.

Kwiatowski, L. (2005). Introduction: Globalization, change, and diversity in the Philippines. *Urban Anthropology and Studies of Cultural Systems and World Economic Development*, 34, 305–316.

Nickles, G. (2002). *Philippines: The culture*. New York: Crabtree.

Pertierra, R. (2006). Culture, social science & the Philippine nation-state. *Asian Journal of Social Science*, 34, 86–102.

Rafael, V. L. (2000). *White love and other events in Filipino history*. Durham: Duke University Press.

Ramos, F. (1995). Will this be the new flag? *Asiaweek, 25*(21), 6–12.

SUMMARY

Organizing your speech effectively helps you provide a clear message for your audience. Every speech includes four key parts: introduction, body, transitions, and conclusion.

The body of the speech comprises most of what you'll present: your main points and supporting materials. The working outline, with a rough sketch of your specific purpose, thesis, and initial ideas for main points, guides you in making the final selection of the main points for your speech. As you select and then develop your main points, apply the principles of clarity, relevance, and balance. Your main points must support your specific purpose and clearly indicate the response you want from your audience. In addition, main points must be relevant both to your topic and to one another, and they must be balanced in terms of their relative importance.

Six patterns of organization are commonly used to organize a speech: chronological, spatial, topical, narrative, cause-and-effect, and problem-solution. The chronological pattern orders points in a time-based sequence. The spatial pattern indicates the physical or directional relationship among objects or places. The topical pattern divides a subject into its components or elements. The narrative pattern entails a dramatic retelling of events as a story or series of stories. The cause-and-effect pattern demonstrates how a particular action produces a particular outcome. Finally, the problem-solution pattern describes a problem and then offers possible solutions to the problem. An effective pattern of organization complements your topic, specific purpose, and audience.

Transitions link together the elements of your speech. Types of transitions include ordering, reinforcing, contrasting, chronology, causality, and summarizing or concluding. Transitions provide signposts for audience members so they know where you are in your speech. Internal summaries are longer transitions that remind listeners of the points covered previously. Key places to use transitions are between the introduction and the first main point, between main points, and between the last main point and the conclusion.

The complete-sentence outline is where you record all the parts of your speech. The most detailed outline you'll produce for your speech, the complete-sentence outline includes your topic, general purpose, specific purpose, thesis, introduction, main points, subpoints, conclusion, transitions, and references. You'll revise and rework this outline as you research your speech and identify appropriate supporting materials. Developing this comprehensive outline clearly identifies each bit of information you want to include in your speech and helps you visualize the order of your ideas.

In the Book

Summary
Key Terms
Critical Challenges

More Study Resources

Speech Studio
Quizzes
WebLinks

Student Workbook

8.1: Subpoint Shuffle
8.2: State It; Explain It; Prove It; Conclude It
8.3: Balance Check
8.4: Organizational Change-Up
8.5: Practice Transitions

Speech Buddy Videos

 Video Links

Reviewing Patterns of Organization
Linking Effectively: Transitions

Activity Links

Everything in Its Place
Polite to Point

▶ **Sample Speech Videos**

Ganiel, "Educational Requirements to Become a Pediatrician," informative speech

Cara, "Left on a Doorstep," self-introduction speech

 Speech Builder Express

Goal/purpose
Thesis statement
Organization
Outline
Supporting material
Transitions
Introduction
Conclusion
Works cited
Completing the speech outline

InfoTrac

Recommended search terms

Organizing a speech
Outlining a speech
Main points of a speech
Subpoints of a speech
Patterns of organization for speeches
Transitions in a speech
Complete-sentence outline
Full-sentence outline
Preparation outline
Formatting a speech outline

Audio Study Tools

"Educational Requirements to Become a Pediatrician" by Ganiel
Critical thinking questions
Learning objectives
Chapter summary

Guide to Your Online Resources

Your Online Resources for *Public Speaking: The Evolving Art* give you access to the Speech Buddy video and activity featured in this chapter, additional sample speech videos, Speech Builder Express, InfoTrac College Edition, and study aids such as glossary flashcards, review quizzes, and the Critical Challenge questions for this chapter, which you can respond to via e-mail if your instructor requests. In addition, your Online Resources feature live WebLinks relevant to this chapter, including sites where you can watch public speeches and evaluate how they are organized, such as C-SPAN.org. Links are regularly maintained, and new ones are added periodically.

Key Terms

body 195

cause-and-effect
   pattern 204

chronological pattern 199

coherence 209

complete-sentence
   outline 213

internal summary 210

narrative pattern 203

pattern of organization 199

problem-solution
   pattern 206

signpost 210

spatial pattern 201

topical pattern 202

transition 209

Critical Challenges

Questions for Reflection and Discussion

1. Although you probably think of narratives as unfolding in a linear fashion, starting with the beginning, then the middle, and finally the end, stories can be told in a variety of ways. Consider a topic you might organize using the narrative pattern of organization. What are the different ways in which you might order the sequence of events? Which order do you think will work best for your audience?

2. The section on organizing the body of your speech includes an example of applying the six different patterns of organization to a single topic. Choose a topic and do the same, identifying the main points you'd cover for each pattern. How does the topic change as you apply each pattern of organization?

3. In everyday conversations, communicators often don't use transitions—they just skip from point to point and topic to topic. But in public speaking, audience mem-

bers rely on speakers to use transitions to show how the different parts of the speech fit together. Choose a speech to view in person or online. How effective are the speaker's transitions? How does the speaker's use of transitions (or the absence of transitions) influence your evaluation of the speech?

4. Outlining helps you visualize all the elements of your speech and determine whether your ideas are organized in the most effective way. Critically examine one of your own outlines. For each section ask yourself, "Is this the best way to say this or present this idea? What are my alternatives?"

9

BEGINNING and ENDING YOUR SPEECH

At a recent Technology, Entertainment, and Design (TED) conference, Jacqueline Novogratz, CEO of the nonprofit Acumen Fund, began her talk[1] about a new approach to helping the poor in developing countries this way:

> I want to start with a story from when I was 12 years old. My Uncle Ed gave me a beautiful blue sweater. . . . It had fuzzy zebras walking across the stomach and Mount Kilimanjaro and Mount Meru right across the chest that were also fuzzy. And I wore it whenever I could, thinking it was the most fabulous thing I owned. Until one day in ninth grade when . . . Matt Musolino, who was undeniably my nemesis in high school, said in a booming voice that we no longer had to go far away on ski trips. We could all ski on Mount Novogratz. I was so humiliated and mortified that I immediately ran home to my mother and chastised her for ever letting me wear the hideous sweater. We drove to the Goodwill and we threw

the sweater away somewhat ceremoniously, my idea being that I would never have to think about this sweater nor see it ever again.

Fast forward eleven years later. I'm a 25-year-old kid working in Kigali, Rwanda, jogging through the steep slopes when I see 10 feet in front of me a little boy, 11 years old, running toward me wearing my sweater. I'm thinking, "No, this is not possible," but so curious I run up to the child . . . grab him by the collar, turn it over, and there is my name written on the collar of this sweater.

I tell that story because it has served and continues to serve as a metaphor to me about the level of connectedness that we all have on this earth. We so often don't realize what our action—and our inaction—does to people we think we will never see and never know. I also tell it because it tells a larger contextual story of what aid is and can be. That this [sweater] traveled into the Goodwill in Virginia and moved its way into the larger industry, which at that point was giving millions of tons of secondhand clothing to Africa and Asia—which was a very good thing providing low-cost clothing. And at the same time, certainly in Rwanda, it destroyed the local retailing industry.

In speaking on a topic with which many audience members likely had little direct experience, Novogratz got their attention with a story they probably could relate to—a painful experience in high school that led to a positive action, contributing clothing to a charity organization. Then the speaker provided an update on the sweater's life: She met a boy in Rwanda who was wearing her sweater. But then what appeared to be a happy ending was not, as Novogratz recounted the damage that clothing contributions did to the Rwandan economy. This brief narrative with its unexpected twist got the audience's attention and prepared them to consider aid to the poor in developing countries in a new way.

In the conclusion to her speech, Novogratz reminded the audience of people's interconnectedness:

> There's enormous opportunity to make poverty history. To do it right, we have to build business models that matter, that are scalable, and that work with Africans, Indians, people all over the developing world who fit in this category to do it themselves. Because at the end of the day it's about engagement, it's about understanding that people really don't want handouts. They want to make their own decisions. They want to solve their own problems. . . . So I urge all of you to think next time as to how to engage with this notion and this opportunity that we all have to make poverty history by really becoming part of the process and moving away from an us-and-them world and realizing that it's about all of us and the kind of world we together want to live in and share.

With her brief closing remarks, the speaker drew a clear link between the speech's beginning and end, neatly tying together the parts of the speech and reinforcing the purpose of her talk.

The beginning and ending of your speech are crucial moments for achieving your objectives. Chapter 8 focused on how to develop the central element of your speech—the body—and how to link together the parts of your speech with transitions. This chapter completes the discussion of the four parts of the speech, elaborating on the introduction and conclusion.

Developing Your Introduction

The beginning of a speech, including an attention getter, a statement of the thesis and purpose, a reference to the speaker's credibility, and a preview of the main points.

READ it In the **introduction** to your speech you gain your audience's attention, explain what you want to accomplish in your speech, establish yourself as an expert on the topic, and tell your audience what you're going to talk about (**Figure 9.1**). The introduction gets your audience ready to listen to the main ideas you'll present in the body of your speech.

Introduction
get audience attention
indicate purpose and thesis
establish credibility
preview main points

▲ **FIGURE 9.1**
Elements of the Introduction

GET YOUR AUDIENCE'S ATTENTION

An audience is more likely to pay attention to and recall what a speaker presents at the beginning of a speech than what is presented in the speech body.

You never get a second chance to make a first impression. The influence of first impressions on later perceptions is known as the **primacy effect**. Audiences tend to recall what the speaker says right at the start of the speech because this is when they're most attentive. In addition, often an audience decides whether or not to even pay attention to a speaker within the first moments of a speech.[2]

The first element of an introduction, designed mainly to create interest in a speech.

The introduction's first element is the **attention getter**, a device used to create interest in your speech. Effective attention getters are relevant to your topic and encourage the audience to listen to you. Popular attention getters include asking a question, describing an especially poignant image, or playing a brief clip from a song. To create an effective attention getter, consider your speech purpose, the amount of time you have to present your introduction, how creative you can be, proven techniques, and presentation media related to your topic.

Consider Your Purpose

The nature of the attention getter depends on the general purpose of your speech, the topic you choose, and the specific purpose you have in mind. Any attention getter should make clear right away that your topic merits your listeners' time and energy. But more than that, an effective attention getter:

- Focuses attention on the importance and relevance of the topic by showing how the topic relates to the audience.
- Entices the audience to want to hear more about the topic by piquing their interest.
- Connects you and your audience by demonstrating your competence in selecting an appropriate attention getter.

- Reduces your nervousness by giving you a well-designed, well-practiced entry to your speech.
- Introduces a theme that joins together the elements of your speech.

In the following example, Oprah Winfrey presented an effective attention getter when she accepted the first Bob Hope Humanitarian Award during the 2002 Emmy Awards:

> Thank you, everybody. Thank you, Tom [Hanks], and Bob and Dolores [Hope], who are home watching I hope, thank you so much, and to everyone who voted for me. There really is nothing more important to me than striving to be a good human being. So, to be here tonight and be acknowledged as the first to receive this honor is beyond expression in words for me. "I am a human being, nothing human is alien to me." Terence said that in 154 B.C. and when I first read it many years ago, I had no idea of the depth of that meaning.[3]

Frank Micelotta/Getty Images

▲ Talk show host and businessperson Oprah Winfrey is well known as an engaging public speaker. She's adept at using attention getters to encourage her audience to listen to her.

Oprah's initial thank you acknowledged some members of her audience, such as Tom Hanks, the Hopes, and those who had voted for her. Then she established a bond with the larger audience—people who were present at the ceremony and watching on TV—and focused attention on the topic by saying, "There really is nothing more important to me than striving to be a good human being." That's something most people can relate to. Winfrey intrigued her audience when she said, "I had no idea of the depth of that meaning." The simple, timeless quote provided a natural transition to the body of her speech.

Creating a theme in the introduction helps join together the parts of your speech. As Winfrey continued her acceptance speech, she emphasized her theme of being human and sharing similar hopes and dreams. You can also use stories to provide a theme for your speech. For example, you might begin your speech with a short human-interest story that you purposefully leave unfinished. Then, as you conclude your speech several minutes later, refer back to the story or characters you introduced in the attention getter. Starting with part of a story and finishing with the rest of it gives your speech coherence. As the audience understands how the elements of your speech tie together, they view you more positively because of your organizational skills.

In the attention-getter for a speech to persuade (Chapter 14), you also want to

- Establish the seriousness of your purpose.
- Dramatize the controversial nature of your topic.
- Initiate the process of persuasion by presenting a strong logical, cultural, or emotional appeal.

Get Your Audience to Tune In, Not Out

Some strategies for getting your audience's attention are more effective than others. You've probably encountered speakers who use these classic lines:

- "Hi, I'm [name]. How are ya doin' today?"
- "Well, uh, yeah, well, my speech is about . . ."
- "I'm a little nervous . . ." Giggle. Pause. Second giggle.
- "Today I'm gonna talk about . . ."
- "Whazzup?"

To avoid these mistakes and encourage your audience to tune in to your speech, get off to a good start by:

- Investing creative energy in developing an effective attention getter.
- Matching the attention getter with the audience, the topic, the situation, and you.
- Creating a separate space at the beginning of the speech especially for the attention getter.
- Practicing the attention getter as a special feature of the speech.

Bill Cosby fulfilled these objectives in the introduction of his "Pound Cake Speech," delivered at the NAACP's gala to commemorate the 50th anniversary of *Brown v. Board of Education*:

> Ladies and gentlemen, these people [the members of the U.S. Supreme Court] . . . opened the doors, they gave us the right, and today . . . in our cities and public schools we have 50 percent drop out. In our own neighborhoods, we have men in prison. No longer is a person embarrassed because they're pregnant without a husband. No longer is a boy considered an embarrassment if he tries to run away from being the father of the unmarried child. Ladies and gentlemen, the lower economic and lower middle economic people are not holding their end in this deal. In the neighborhood that most of us grew up in, parenting is not going on. In the old days, you couldn't hooky school because every drawn shade was an eye. And before your mother got off the bus and to the house, she knew exactly where you had gone, who had gone into the house, and where you got on whatever you had on and where you got it from. Parents don't know that today.[4]

Using facts and examples, Cosby stressed the seriousness of the topic. He referred to his audience's experiences in "the neighborhood that most of us grew up in" to dramatize differences between then and now. Finally, he appealed to the audience's emotions—parents don't know what their kids are up to—and grabbed their attention. Cosby's hard-hitting introduction caught his audience by surprise and made them sit up and take notice.

Consider Your Time

Your attention getter shouldn't last long. It should draw attention to the topic but not cut into the time you need for the body of the speech. Some attention getters last only 15 seconds. Others may take a minute, or even longer in some cases.

Here's how Fran Visco, president of the National Breast Cancer Coalition, began a recent speech at the organization's Advocacy Training Conference:

> This past year, we lost too many women to breast cancer, and we lost too many breast cancer advocates. In addition to the women for whom we have a moment of silence at this conference and to Elva Fletcher, to whom we dedicate this conference, we lost Ann Marcou, one of the founders of Y-Me. And we lost Jan Platner, who died of multiple myeloma but who was on the staff of the National Breast Cancer Coalition, on the board of NBCC and an incredible activist on our behalf. It's been a very difficult year, but it's a reminder of how much more we need to do.[5]

Visco quickly got her audience's attention, personalizing the topic by naming breast cancer advocates who had recently died.

Use Your Creativity

Creating and delivering an effective attention getter presents a special challenge for public speakers. It demands that you use your imagination well. Ask yourself, "How can I attract the audience to my topic in a creative and effective way?" Supreme Court Justice Sandra Day O'Connor demonstrated her creative side in a commencement address at Stanford University. In the introduction to her speech, she poked fun at lawyers and herself:

> A commencement speech is a particularly difficult assignment. The speaker is given no topic and is expected to be able to inspire all the graduates with a stirring speech about nothing at all. I suppose that's why so many lawyers are asked to be commencement speakers; they're in the habit of talking extensively even when they have nothing to say. And in this case President Hennessy asked not only a lawyer but an elderly judge to be the commencement speaker. I was born in Texas. In Texas they say an old judge is like an old shoe—everything is all worn out except the tongue. All in all, it seems we should have no trouble filling our time today.[6]

O'Connor's gentle humor worked well because it was unexpected—most people think of Supreme Court Justices as staid and serious. So O'Connor's tactic charmed her audience and no doubt got the audience's attention.

Try Using Proven Strategies

So far, you've learned about general approaches and ideas for gaining your audience's attention in the speech introduction. You have to decide what you think works best for your audience, your topic, and you. But here are some proven strategies you might want to try.

- *Cite a surprising fact or statistic to call attention to your topic.* Say, for instance, "Do you realize that more than three-fourths of all college graduates don't get jobs in the fields they prepare for?" Or, "According to the Centers for Disease Control, your chances of contracting anthrax are far less likely than your chances of being hit by lightning—twice!" Use this approach with care, however. It's not particularly creative, and unless your fact or statistic really surprises or alarms, it may not provoke much reaction.

- *Tell an emotionally arousing but brief human-interest story.* To begin persuading your audience about the perils of child abuse, for example, you could tell the

MIGUEL RIOPA/AFP/Getty Images

▲ Although she is best known for writing the Harry Potter series, J. K. Rowling's own rags-to-riches story intrigues audiences.

story of a child who becomes ill and eventually dies as a result of health problems caused by parental neglect. You hope to appeal to the audience's sense of basic human rights by pointing out children's vulnerability to abuse. In relating the story, keep it brief and appropriate to the topic, setting, and occasion, as Jacqueline Novogratz did in the example at the beginning of the chapter.

- *Tell a joke to introduce the topic and get the audience interested.* Humor can be a very useful means of stimulating interest. Educators have learned over the years that humor can be an effective way to interest students in the subject matter and to connect with them as people.[7] When we laugh together, we bond with each other. However, that positive experience works well for instructors only if the humor has to do with course material.[8] Similarly, producers of television commercials have learned that humor can attract attention but will be wasted if the audience does not remember the product advertised. Applying this principle to public speaking, be sure to inform or persuade your audience, not just make them laugh. As soon as audience members sense you are telling a joke or delivering a humorous anecdote, they will pay attention to you. People love to laugh and be entertained, so they'll definitely give you a chance to make them react.

- *Use the information you have about your audience.* The audience research you conduct may produce data your audience will find provocative or interesting. For instance, you could begin an informative speech about euthanasia of stray animals by saying, "According to the survey conducted in class, nearly three-fourths of you don't know the meaning of the term *euthanasia*." Using audience data is an effective way to get your audience's attention because people like to hear about themselves. But getting their attention in and of itself isn't enough. The data must be sufficiently intriguing to motivate them to continue listening.

- *Ask a question that you want your audience to answer or consider.* To get an idea of how important a topic is for an audience, you might begin with a question such as, "How many of you couldn't find a parking place on campus this morning?" or, "Have you thought about saving for retirement? If you have, raise your hand." Some speakers ask rhetorical questions—ones that listeners aren't expected to answer—to gain attention. Examples of rhetorical questions are,

"How can we best prepare for the technology of the future?" and, "Do we really know what's in our drinking water?" Rhetorical questions encourage listeners to think about the answer to the question, but they expect the speaker to provide the answer in the speech.

Integrate Presentation Media

Effective public speakers often begin their speeches with presentation media of some kind. Imagine, for instance, that you are giving a speech on traditional Hawaiian dance. Because you know the traditional dances, you begin your speech by briefly demonstrating the classic moves yourself. There's no need to say anything beforehand. Just start the audio clip embedded in your digital slide and start dancing. After a few seconds, you explain what the audience has just seen and state the thesis of your speech.

You can also make comments while showing visual materials to capture the audience's attention and inspire interest. For example, you might display a colorful and richly detailed image of muscle tissue to introduce a speech about MRI (magnetic resonance imaging) technology.

Presentation media can be effective attention getters if they are well designed, technically flawless, well practiced, and clearly relevant to the topic. As with any attention getter, brevity is key. Thirty seconds seems like a brief time, yet in a five-minute speech that's one-tenth of your speaking time. Also consider what *you'll* be doing as audience members listen to or watch the presentation media you've designed for your attention getter. Especially when you're trying to gain your audience's attention at the beginning of your speech, you don't want to find yourself staring off into space while your listeners watch 30 seconds of a film clip. Chapter 11 discusses designing and using presentation media in detail.

INDICATE YOUR PURPOSE AND THESIS

Now that you've gotten your audience's attention, shift smoothly to the next element of your introduction. The best way to do this is to move crisply and directly from the last word of your attention getter to a clear indication of your speech's purpose and thesis.

Recall that the specific purpose succinctly expresses the response you want from your audience ("To help my audience learn the basic steps of jazz dance" or "To teach my audience about how Arabic numerals replaced Roman numerals in mathematics"). When you deliver your speech, you might not state your purpose exactly in those terms. But your audience should know what the purpose of your speech is and what you expect from them. Consider the introduction to a speech by Mary Fisher, a former assistant to

Laughing with You, Not at You

Integrating humor into your speeches serves a variety of positive goals, such as gaining attention and helping the audience feel comfortable with you. Some humor, though, can detract from your speech and hurt your credibility. For example, humor that makes you look incompetent or unintelligent will make audience members wonder why they should listen to you.[9] Offensive jokes instantly turn off the audience. And too much humor gets the audience focusing on the jokes rather than on the points you're trying to make—just like those television commercials with hilarious scenes that viewers recall but then quickly forget the product advertised.

President Gerald Ford. Fisher gave this speech, "A Whisper of AIDS," at the 1992 Republican Convention, at a time when many people believed only "bad" or reckless people could contract AIDS. In her introduction she said

> In the context of an election year, I ask you, here in this great hall, or listening in the quiet of your home, to recognize that the AIDS virus is not a political creature. It does not care whether you are Democrat or Republican; it does not ask whether you are black or white, male or female, gay or straight, young or old. Tonight I represent an AIDS community whose members have been reluctantly drafted from every segment of American society. Though I am white and a mother, I am one with a black infant struggling with tubes in a Philadelphia hospital.[10]

How do you know the purpose of her speech? She doesn't declare outright "My purpose is to make you believe that anyone, including you, can get AIDS." She's more subtle, referring to how people often categorize, and sometimes demonize, others—black/white, female/male, gay/straight, young/old. So she establishes her purpose—her audience knows why she's there and what she wants them to believe. She then states her thesis that AIDS affects "every segment of American society" and that people don't choose to get AIDS.

Indicating the speech's purpose and thesis typically requires just a few sentences. As with the attention getter, you don't want to go on and on. But you do want your audience members to know what you expect from them and the basic idea you're conveying.

ESTABLISH YOUR CREDIBILITY

Now that you have the audience's attention and they understand what they'll get out of your speech, you need to let them know that you're an authority on your topic. Your introduction gives you the first opportunity to show you've thoroughly researched your topic. As with the other parts of the introduction, presenting yourself as a credible speaker takes only a few moments. But those moments play a key role in getting your audience to listen to you. For example, Nigel Atkin, speaking about Aboriginal communities at the University of Victoria in Canada, said in his speech introduction

> I recently worked with the Victoria Foundation to help bridge communication between the foundation, four regional trust advisory committees, and many First Nations, independent Bands, Metis and urban Aboriginal organizations to effect change towards what many Aboriginal leaders call for—the ability in law and capacity to administer services to their own children and families.[11]

Right away the audience knew the speaker had some knowledge of the topic through his own experience. Similarly, if your speech topic is how to save people from drowning and you've worked as a lifeguard, you might say, "In my five years as a lifeguard, I've successfully applied three basic techniques to save someone who's drowning." That brief mention of your experience tells the audience you have some expertise on the topic.

You also let your audience know about your credibility when you refer to the research you've done on your topic. For a speech on staying safe and healthy at work, for instance, you might refer to information you've gathered on the topic, as with, "According to the U.S. Department of Labor, over 4 million people get hurt or become ill at work each year."

PREVIEW YOUR MAIN POINTS

Successful speakers keep audiences focused throughout the speech by describing the speech's structure and repeating main points. Thus, the speaker

- Previews in the introduction what will be said in the body of the speech.

- Presents the main points and subpoints in the body.

- Reviews the main points in the conclusion.

A **preview of main points** concisely tells the audience what the main points of the speech will be, establishing an expectation of what the speech will address. The preview provides the first step in helping the audience follow your main ideas as you move from one main point to the next. Transitions help connect the various elements of the introduction together. For example, you might start an informative speech about herb gardens in this way:

Growing a simple indoor herb garden is easy and enjoyable *(indicate thesis)*. Today, you'll learn how to set up your own garden *(indicate purpose)*. To begin *(transition),* I will explain the basic equipment you'll need that I've found in my many years of herb gardening *(establish credibility)*. Next *(transition)*, I will show you how to plant your indoor herb garden. Finally *(transition)*, I'll give you some tips on keeping your herbs happy and healthy *(preview main points)*.

Similarly, a persuasive speech about meditation could begin like this:

Incorporating meditation into our daily lives reduces stress and can even increase our longevity *(indicate thesis)*. I meditate regularly—and did so this morning as part of my preparation for this speech *(establish credibility)*. As part of a balanced lifestyle, you should take the necessary steps to make meditation part of your daily routine *(indicate purpose)*. There are different types of meditation that will improve the balance in your life that you can easily incorporate into your day-to-day activities *(reinforce thesis)*. To make clear how to start meditating, I will first *(transition)* explain the positive effects meditation can give you. I will then *(transition)* describe several different kinds of meditation. After *(transition)*

CHRIS BERNACCHI/AFP/Getty Images

▲ Audience members view professionals speaking about their industries as highly credible. For example, an airline safety expert talking about an assessment of a crash site is viewed as highly credible because of his direct experience.

The final element of the introduction, in which the main points to be presented in the body of the speech are mentioned.

describing the types, I will explain how you can begin meditating on a daily basis *(preview main points)*.

Even entertaining speeches require a clear preview of main points, as in this example:

Some people claim they learned everything they needed to know in kindergarten, but I learned everything I needed to know my first year of high school *(indicate thesis)*. I think you'll appreciate all the lessons I learned in spite of what my teachers were trying to tell me *(indicate purpose)*. I admit this may sound odd, but I was an unusual teenager, recording my first year of high school like I was writing a documentary *(establish credibility)*. Before I regale you with my many brilliant insights *(transition)*, I will give you some background on my high school. Second, *(transition)* I'll explain the three most important lessons I learned. Finally *(transition)*, I'll tell you how I've applied those lessons recently, even for this class *(preview main points)*.

▼ WATCH it SPEECH BUDDY VIDEO LINK

Beginning Effectively: Introductions

◀◀ ❚❚ ▶▶

Evan presents sample speech introductions and highlights ways of evaluating each. As you watch the video, keep in mind what you've learned about the role of speech introductions, as well as the elements and characteristics of an effective introduction.

▼ USE it ACTIVITY LINK

Here We Go

This activity provides an opportunity to evaluate the introductions of several sample speeches and suggest ways they could be improved.

Developing Your Conclusion

▼ You've presented your main points, and now you're ready to wrap it up. But your speech isn't finished—not quite yet. The flip side of the primacy effect—the critical influence of your speech introduction on the audience's attention and memory—is the recency effect. With the **recency effect** audience members recall what the speaker presents last better than they recall the information contained in the body of the speech.[12] Of course, listeners will remember more than only the beginning and ending of your presentation. However, the primacy and recency effects underscore the key role the introduction and conclusion play in achieving your purpose. The introduction gets your audience ready to listen to your ideas; the conclusion reinforces what you talked about.

In the **conclusion** to your speech you review the main points, reinforce the speech's general and specific purposes, and provide closure so your audience knows your speech is over (**Figure 9.2**). Use the conclusion to continue building rapport with your audience and emphasize your points, but do it efficiently. Audiences perk up when they know your speech is coming to an end.[13] They are ready for you to stop talking, but they are also willing to listen closely to your final remarks. Your words, facial expression, and body movement should all indicate that your presentation has purposefully concluded. By preparing, practicing, and presenting an effective conclusion, you will reinforce your key points, strengthen a call to action or a persuasive argument, and give your audience a lasting impression of your message.

REVIEW YOUR MAIN POINTS

Use the conclusion to remind your audience of the main points presented in the body of your speech. The **review of main points** normally follows a transition word or phrase that indicates you're moving from the body to the conclusion. That is, once you've made the transition from the body of the speech to its conclusion, quickly summarize by restating your speech's main points. When you review your main points, you're helping listeners recall where they've been, but without the specific details. Here are some examples.

In a speech to inform:

In summary *(transition),* today you've learned how to get started windsurfing. I described the history of windsurfing, the equipment you'll need, and where you can try out this fun sport *(review main points).*

Conclusion

review main points

reinforce purpose

provide closure

▲ **FIGURE 9.2**
Elements of the Conclusion

An audience is more likely to remember what a speaker presents at the end of speech than what is presented in the speech body.

The end of a speech, in which the speaker reviews the main points, reinforces the purpose, and provides closure.

The portion of the conclusion of a speech in which the main points presented in the body of the speech are briefly mentioned again.

In a speech to persuade:

Let's review *(transition)* what I covered in my speech. I told you about how you can improve your study habits and get better grades almost immediately. I've described the most common problems students create for themselves, how those mistakes lead to poor results in the classroom, and what to do about it to improve your grades *(review main points)*.

In a speech to entertain:

Now *(transition)* you know my secrets of backpacking in style: Treat your backpacking guide very, very well; bring the proper equipment; and make backup reservations at a nearby resort hotel *(review main points)*.

REINFORCE YOUR PURPOSE

The conclusion gives you a final opportunity to reinforce your specific purpose by highlighting the reason your information is important (for a speech to inform), crystallizing your argument and making a final appeal to the audience (for a speech to persuade), or getting that last laugh (for a speech to entertain).

A sentence or group of sentences included in the conclusion of a speech, designed to make the speaker's thesis unforgettable.

In reinforcing your specific purpose, you provide a **memorable message** to capture the audience's attention in a way that makes the information or persuasive argument you've given impossible to ignore or refute. What you say must be brief, clear, strong, and striking, as in the following examples:

- "We've finally got the evidence that proves what scientists had long suspected: Humans are evolved apes." *(informative speech reporting new DNA evidence)*
- "The three aspects of matching you to the right profession are identifying what you ideally want in a job or profession, what you must have, and what you absolutely don't want." *(informative speech on how to choose a job or profession)*
- "Now's the time to decide: Are you going to give up or shape up?" *(persuasive speech promoting exercise program for college students)*
- "You will be the ones who will have to pay for that new football stadium!" *(persuasive speech against constructing a new stadium)*

PROVIDE CLOSURE

Sometimes speakers find the very end of the speech the most difficult part. You want to exit gracefully and smoothly. You've probably heard speakers say, "That's about it," "Okay,

Imagining the Conclusion

You've probably thought about ways to capture your audience's imagination in the introduction to your speech, but using visual and auditory imagery in the conclusion can make your topic more memorable and reinforce your purpose.[14] Judicious use of presentation media, such as a few video frames, a particularly poignant photograph, or a very short audio clip, can spark your audience's imagination. For instance, in the sample speech conclusion at the beginning of the chapter, Jacqueline Novogratz showed a vivid digital slide of herself talking with a Rwandan man as she told the audience, "Because at the end of the day it's about engagement, it's about understanding that people really don't want handouts. They want to make their own decisions. They want to solve their own problems." The powerful visual image reinforced what she said, making audience members more likely to recall the action she wanted them to take. Presentation software such as Keynote and PowerPoint provides you with useful tools for integrating images, video, and audio into your speech in ways that can have a lasting impact on your audience.

well, that's all I have to say," or "I guess I'm done." The conclusion is the last chance you have to make an impression on your audience, and you want it to be a good one.

There are many strategies for providing closure. You must decide what will work best for your audience, your topic, and you. Here are some specific techniques you might want to try.

- *End with a quotation*. "As author Rita Mae Brown once said, 'The statistics on sanity are that one out of every four Americans is suffering from some form of mental illness. Think of your three best friends. If they're okay, then it's you.'"[15] (*entertaining speech on staying sane in today's world*)

- *Make a dramatic statement*. "And in the ten minutes I've been talking, twenty people in Africa have died of malaria." (*informative speech on the impact of malaria around the world*)

- *Refer to the introduction*. "Now I'll finish the story I started in the introduction. And this story has a happy ending. I found a great summer job that will pay for my two weeks in Mexico over winter break." (*informative speech on how to find a good summer job*)

- *Refer to subsequent events.* "Later, in coordination with the U.S. Department of Justice, AMBER Alert plans were passed in all fifty states." *(informative speech on Americans Missing: Broadcast Emergency Response program)*
- *Reinforce the speaker-audience connection.* "Like many of you, I thought the idea of freedom was a pretty basic thing. But now that I've learned how people in other cultures view freedom and shared that information with you, we all realize that there are many different ways to think of this common word." *(informative speech on defining freedom)*
- *Thank the audience.* "Thank you for considering my proposal to increase the number of elective courses and reduce the number of required courses for all students attending our school." *(persuasive speech on changing graduation requirements)*

▼ **WATCH it** SPEECH BUDDY VIDEO LINK

Ending Effectively: Conclusions

◄◄ ▮▮ ►►

Evan introduces sample speech conclusions and highlights different ways of evaluating each. As you watch the video, keep in mind what you've learned about the role of speech conclusions, as well as the elements and characteristics of an effective conclusion.

▼ **USE it** ACTIVITY LINK

It's a Wrap

This activity provides an opportunity to evaluate the conclusions of several sample speeches and suggest ways they could be improved.

SUMMARY

In the speech introduction you get the audience's attention, indicate your purpose and thesis, establish your credibility, and preview your speech's main points. In creating the attention getter, consider your specific purpose and how much time you have to give the speech. Also, use your creativity and imagination to find a way to make your audience sit up, take notice, and want to listen to your speech. Present your thesis clearly so the audience understands the response you expect. Let the audience know you're an expert on your topic. Conclude the introduction by previewing your main points.

In your conclusion, review your main points, reinforce your specific purpose, and provide closure. Strategies for providing closure including ending with a quotation, making a dramatic statement, referring to the introduction, referring to subsequent events, reinforcing the speaker-audience connection, and thanking the audience. Increase the likelihood you'll achieve your specific purpose by leaving your audience with a lasting and positive impression.

In the Book

Summary
Key Terms
Critical Challenges

More Study Resources

Speech Studio
Quizzes
WebLinks

Student Workbook

9.1: Solid Previews
9.2: Intros and Conclusions
9.3: Notable Quotables
9.4: Imitable Introductions
9.5: LOL

Speech Buddy Videos

 Video Links

Beginning Effectively:
    Introductions
Ending Effectively:
    Conclusions

 Activity Links

Here We Go
It's a Wrap

▶ Sample Speech Videos

Katy, "Why Pi?" informative
speech

Mary Fisher, "A Whisper of
AIDS," persuasive speech

 Speech Builder Express

Introduction
Conclusion

 InfoTrac

Recommended search terms

Speech introduction
Attention getter
Humor in speeches
Establishing credibility in public
    speaking
Speech conclusion

Audio Study Tools

"Why Pi?" by Katy
Critical thinking questions
Learning objectives
Chapter summary

Guide to Your Online Resources

Your Online Resources for *Public Speaking: The Evolving Art* give you access to the Speech Buddy video and activity featured in this chapter, additional sample speech videos, Speech Builder Express, InfoTrac College Edition, and study aids such as glossary flash-cards, review quizzes, and the Critical Challenge questions for this chapter, which you can respond to via e-mail if your instructor requests. In addition, your Online Resources feature live WebLinks relevant to this chapter, including sites where you can watch public speeches and evaluate their introductions and conclusions, such as C-SPAN.org. Links are regularly maintained, and new ones are added periodically.

Key Terms

attention getter 230

conclusion 239

introduction 230

memorable message 240

preview of main points 237

primacy effect 230

recency effect 239

review of main points 239

Critical Challenges

Questions for Reflection and Discussion

1. Getting the audience's attention is a primary function of the introduction to your speech. What must ethical speakers consider when getting the attention of the audience? (You might want to refer to the section on ethical communication principles in Chapter 3.) For example, how might a statistic or fact be *too* startling? How might a story mislead the audience?

2. Speakers often neglect the conclusion of a speech and lose the opportunity to take advantage of the recency effect. What will you do to make sure you develop effective conclusions for your speeches?

10 USING LANGUAGE EFFECTIVELY

As keynote speaker at the 2004 Democratic National Convention in Boston, Barack Obama electrified his audience and launched himself into the national limelight. Without a single digital slide or video clip, Obama brought listeners to their feet and won accolades across the country through, as one newspaper noted, the "power of his words."[1] Language comprises words that invite audience members to listen, stir their emotions, and touch their senses. Near the end of his speech, Obama said

> I'm talking about something more substantial. It's the hope of slaves sitting around a fire singing freedom songs. The hope of immigrants setting out for distant shores. . . . The hope of a skinny kid with a funny name who believes that America has a place for him, too. Hope in the face of difficulty. Hope in the face of uncertainty. The audacity of hope![2]

You could summarize that quote with something like, "Hope is important to achieving our goals." But those words wouldn't adequately describe what Obama was able to achieve. Why not? That's what you'll find out in this chapter.

Language Basics

READ it **Language** refers to the system of words people use when communicating with others. The power of language rests in its ability to create images in the minds of listeners. Those images inform, persuade, and entertain audience members. As a speaker, your words also encourage your audience to think, reason, contemplate, feel, evaluate, and otherwise respond to what you have to say.

How do words work? Words are **symbols** that stand for something else—concrete things such as an object, person, place, or event. Symbols may also represent more abstract ideas, such as freedom, justice, and happiness. Words don't *transfer* information or ideas from your mind to others' minds. Instead, words *trigger* the meanings and thoughts people have in their minds for words. So when Barack Obama said, "It's the hope of slaves sitting around a fire singing freedom songs," his words brought up an image for each person in the audience, but not everyone had the same image. This example underscores the arbitrary, ambiguous, abstract, and active nature of language.

▼ **FIGURE 10.1**
The Arbitrary Relationship among Words, Thoughts, and Objects *Source: Adapted from Ogden & Richards (1923).*

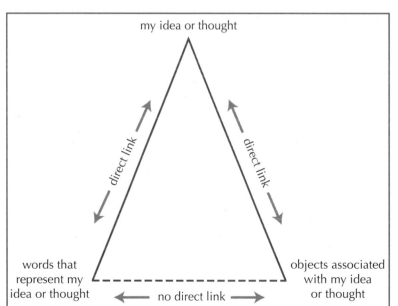

LANGUAGE IS ARBITRARY

Researchers have identified more than 6,800 languages spoken by people around the world.[3] The vast number of languages suggests that the meanings of words are arbitrary. Because there's no direct connection between a word and what it represents, different groups of people have different words that stand for the same things. **Figure 10.1** demonstrates that when you have an idea or thought, there's a direct link between the object that led to your thought and the words you choose to express that thought. But there's no direct link between the object itself and the words you choose.

Consider the word *tree*. In Dutch the word is *boom*. In Greek, it's δεντρο. In Japanese, *tree* is 木. And in Spanish you'd say *árbol*. Each language has a different way of representing what is called "tree" in English. That's why language is considered arbitrary.

Communicators use words to stand for their thoughts and ideas. The link between a word and what it stands for always goes through our minds.[4] As the example in **Figure 10.2** shows, the person views some palm trees, triggering the memory of a vacation in Florida, and then says, "Palm trees remind me of the Florida Keys."

Speakers often forget that a word is not the thing itself. There is no direct link between objects and words. Therefore, the meanings others assign to words—their **interpretations**—may not be what you intend. Former Education Secretary Ron Paige found this out when he referred to the National Education Association (NEA) as a "terrorist organization" in a conversation about education reform with some of the nation's governors.[5] Paige argued that the teachers' union stood in the way of change and misrepresented its members' wishes. But even those who agreed with him noted that the negative feelings associated with the word *terrorist* obscured Paige's main point. After educators and politicians criticized his characterization of the NEA, he apologized for his word choice.

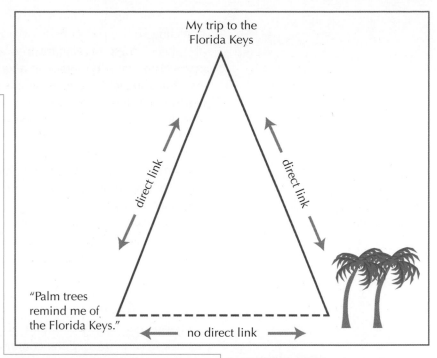

▲ **FIGURE 10.2**
Words, Thoughts, and Objects: An Example *Source: Adapted from Ogden & Richards (1923).*

An individual's internal process of assigning meaning to words.

An agreed-upon definition of a word, found in a dictionary.

A unique meaning for a word based on an individual's own experiences.

LANGUAGE IS AMBIGUOUS

Speakers like to think that if they say "X," others will think "X." But that's not necessarily the case. Language is ambiguous—words have multiple meanings and individuals have their own meanings, or associations, for words and the concepts those words stand for. **Denotative meanings** refer to formal, or literal, meanings—the definitions you find in dictionaries. **Connotative meanings** are the unique meanings you have for words based on your own experiences.

Even words you might think of as straightforward can have multiple meanings, such as the word *car*. The *Compact Oxford English Dictionary* lists two definitions: "a powered road vehicle designed to carry a small number of people" and "a railway carriage or . . . wagon." But that's just the beginning. *Webster's Revised Unabridged Dictionary* lists seven definitions, including "a chariot of war or triumph," "the cage or lift of an elevator," and "a floating perforated box for living fish." Investorwords.com explains that in the financial world *car* means "The amount of a commodity underlying a commodity futures contract." According to *Dorland's Illustrated Medical Dictionary*, CAR refers to the Canadian Association of Radiologists.[6] And those are just the denotative meanings. Think about all the meanings you associate with *car*, such as independence, financial burden, and traveling.

The ambiguity of language impacts all aspects of the speechmaking process. When selecting your topic, consider the words you'll choose to identify it. Would you refer to the speech topic of plagiarism as academic *integrity* or academic *dishonesty*? Would a speech on plans to repurpose a local vacant lot refer to *open space* or to *undeveloped land*? In a speech on the effects of our increasingly global society, would you use the term *anti-globalization* or the term *global justice*? To take just one of these examples, consider the differences between academic dishonesty and academic integrity. *Dishonesty* has negative connotations; listeners will likely think of activities such as cheating on a test or plagiarizing a speech outline. *Integrity* brings up positive associations such as studying for a test and carefully documenting sources for a speech. Making the choice between those two words—*dishonesty* and *integrity*—will influence the **tone** or general mood associated with the speech.

Use of language to set the mood or atmosphere associated with a speaking situation.

How you phrase your topic will guide you in framing the idea, analyzing your audience, conducting your research, and choosing your supporting materials. When you deliver your speech (Chapter 12), the language you've decided on to frame and define your topic will influence how your listeners interpret your message. It's during delivery that the ambiguous nature of language will have its most obvious effects. The way your audience responds to your speech depends in part on the language you choose. Ambiguity isn't necessarily bad, and can even work in your favor. In his speech, for example, Barack Obama stressed the commonalities Americans share:

> Tonight, we gather to affirm the greatness of our nation—not because of the height of our skyscrapers, or the power of our military, or the size of our economy. Our pride is based on a very simple premise, summed up in a declaration made over 200 years ago: "We hold these truths to be self-evident, that all men are created equal. That they are endowed by their Creator with certain inalienable rights. That among these are life, liberty and the pursuit of happiness." That is the true genius of America—a faith in simple dreams, an insistence on small miracles.

Simple dreams, small miracles, life, and *liberty*—these words mean many different things to Americans. Yet they're deeply embedded in American culture, so they call up positive connotations for listeners. Even so, the audience might view these words positively but still not agree on how to define them.

LANGUAGE IS ABSTRACT

You experience your world with all your senses—you smell bread baking, you see a friend smiling, you taste a square of chocolate, you touch the computer keyboard, you hear a coworker laughing. These things exist in the physical world. Although communicators say, hear, write, and read words, what those words represent is abstract. You can place your hand on this page and touch the printed words, but the meanings those words conjure up exist in your mind.

Although all words are abstract, they vary in their level of abstractness. Some words are fairly specific, such as "my friend Kyoung." Others are very abstract, such as "human being." **Figure 10.3** shows how words vary along a continuum from more to less abstract. In the example, "living thing" is the most abstract—the phrase could refer to plants or animals, humans or insects. The words become less abstract as you progress up the levels until you reach a particular living thing, 12-year-old Pink-White, a famous sea otter living in Monterey Bay, California.

U.S. Representative Tammy Baldwin used different levels of abstraction to her advantage in her speech at the Millennium March for Gay and Lesbian Rights in Washington, D.C. At each point in her speech, she contrasted more abstract language with specific examples:

> Never doubt that there is a reason to be hopeful. Never doubt that Congress will pass legislation that expands the definition of hate crimes . . . But we must make it so—by daring to dream of a world in which we are free. So, if you dream of a world in which you can put your partner's picture on your desk, then put his picture on your desk—and you will live in such a world.[7]

By invoking abstract, yet powerful, words, Baldwin provided common ground for the audience to agree with her. Then, using less abstract terms, she told listeners how they could put those abstract ideas into action.

LANGUAGE IS ACTIVE

Like time, language doesn't stand still. As people learn new things about the world and encounter new experiences, they develop new words. Before the internet, words such

▼ **FIGURE 10.3**
Levels of Abstraction in Language

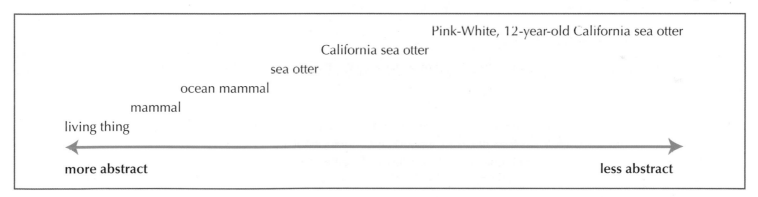

"Mouse, virus, firewall, why can't you computer people come up with your own words, rather than stealing ours?"

as *phishing*, *e-mail*, and *blog* didn't exist. *Merriam-Webster's Dictionary* added 10,000 words to its 11th edition that weren't in the 10th edition, published only five years previously.[8]

Similarly, specific events change the meanings of words. For example, after the 9/11 attacks, *jihad* developed negative connotations. In a Harvard University commencement address, Zayed Muhammed Yasin, a senior graduating with a degree in biomedical engineering, explained the original meaning of *jihad*:

> The word for *struggle* in Arabic, in the language of my faith, is *jihad*. It is a word that has been corrupted and misinterpreted, both by those who do and do not claim to be Muslims, and we saw last fall, to our great national and personal loss, the results of this corruption. Jihad, in its truest and purest form, the form to which all Muslims aspire, is the determination to do right, to do justice even against your own interests. It is an individual struggle for personal moral behavior.[9]

In his speech, Yasin acknowledged the impact of 9/11 on the meaning of *jihad* and sought to replace negative associations with more positive ones.

Communicators continually alter the meanings of words. The advent of the internet brought with it new meanings for *spam, flame,* and *cookie.* You might think of the term web*page* stemming from the pages of a printed book. Yet scrolling through a page on a website is more like unrolling and reading a papyrus document from ancient Egypt.[10]

THE EVOLVING ART

Engaging in Lexpionage

New words enter the English language almost daily. Want to find out more about them? Websites such as Word Spy (wordspy.com), the *MacMillan English Dictionary* (macmillandictionary.com), and World Wide Words (worldwidewords.com) will clue you in on the latest additions. The American Dialect Society (ADS; american dialect.org) identifies the most influential words of the year. For example, ADS members voted *subprime* as the Word of the Year for 2007. Ten years earlier, *millennium bug* was the top choice.

After the December 26, 2004, tsunami that devastated Asia, many businesses reconsidered their use of the word. For example, Toyota changed the name of its Celica Tsunami to Celica Sport Package and a waterpark in Ohio switched the Tsunami pool to Whitecap.

Language is dynamic in another way, too. You've probably heard sayings such as "All talk, no action" and "Actions speak louder than words." Yet language *is* action. You accomplish goals when you use words. For example, in public speaking, speakers inform, persuade, and entertain. Speakers get listeners to think more deeply, laugh out loud, learn something new, change their views, and take action. For example, in the second term of his presidency Bill Clinton addressed the people of the United States on national television concerning his relationship with Monica Lewinsky. As part of his speech, he said

> I did have a relationship with Ms. Lewinsky that was not appropriate. In fact, it was wrong. It constituted a critical lapse in judgment and a personal failure on my part for which I am solely and completely responsible. . . . I know that my public comments and my silence about this matter gave a false impression. I misled people, including my wife. I deeply regret that.[11]

The speech served as an apology for President Clinton's behavior. You take similar actions with words in your everyday conversations. You promise, calm down, cheer up, compliment, accuse, blame, support, criticize, affecting those around you with words.

Language and Culture

Language and culture are inseparable; how you use language reflects your culture, and your culture influences the language you use and how you interpret it. Think about how people in the United States refer to time. You probably say things like, "That's a waste of time," "I like spending time with you," and "Time is money." What does that tell you about American culture? Most Americans view time as a commodity that can be given ("I can give you a few minutes of my time") and taken away ("I won't take much of your time"). You likely think of time as something you "own," referring to "my" time and "your" time. The words people use give strong clues about what's important in a culture and what's not.

Americans generally consider speech and speaking extremely important. The U.S. Constitution guarantees free speech. *Roget's New Millennium Thesaurus* lists nearly seventy synonyms for *speak*—words such as *articulate, blab, hold forth, rap, vocalize,* and *yap.* But what about listening, the other side of speaking? Isn't listening to others' perspectives a central aspect of democracy as well? Of course! Yet it doesn't get the emphasis that

SPEAKING OF...

Kinship and Friendship Language

The next time you're talking, IMing, chatting, or text messaging with friends or family members, pay close attention to the language you're using. Would others know what you were talking about? Families and groups of friends develop their own words related to their shared experiences. Usually communicators don't even realize they've developed these specialized words and meanings until someone outside the group asks what a word or phrase means. Kinship and friendship language brings people together but at the same time it can make others feel left out. You're most likely to use friendship and kinship language on special occasions, such as in a wedding toast or a farewell speech at a going-away party. But such language can also find its way into informative and persuasive speeches. If your listeners aren't part of your language circle, they may have trouble interpreting your words.

speaking gets—*Roget's New Millennium Thesaurus* includes thirty-three synonyms for *listen*, less than half the number for *speak*.[12] Even though communicators listen more than they speak, American culture puts a greater emphasis on speaking than on listening.

Culture tells you what words mean and the associations you should have for them. For example, in the aftermath of Hurricane Katrina, controversy arose over what to call people in New Orleans and other areas who were forced to flee their homes. Were they victims? Survivors? Displaced persons? Refugees? Each word calls up a different image. Generally, *refugee* refers to an individual crossing international borders to avoid political or religious persecution. So the word suggested that the now-homeless people in Louisiana and Mississippi were not U.S. citizens. Yet *displaced person* missed the enormity of the problem. Most media organizations settled on *evacuee* and *flood victim,* although these terms did not fully capture the dire circumstances many people faced.[13] And choosing to use one word over another can lead to different outcomes. For example, people are more likely to buy a "preowned" car than a "used" one—even when it's the exact same car.

In public speaking contexts, culture becomes especially evident when speakers use slang, jargon, idioms, euphemisms, and clichés. **Slang** refers to informal language typically used in an interpersonal setting, such as *whatever, all that,* and *my bad.* Because public speaking is more formal than conversations with your friends, you'll want to avoid using slang in speeches. Slang can give your audience the impression that you're not taking the event seriously or are unprepared. Your friends may think slang is okay, but using slang in a speech will hurt your credibility.

Informal, nonstandard language, often used within a particular group.

Jargon is technical language associated with a specific profession or subject. Since the beginning of the war in Iraq, some military jargon has become more commonplace, such as MRE (meal, ready to eat), IED (improvised explosive device), and SOP (standard operating procedure). Both slang and jargon require an insider's knowledge to understand what the words mean. If you're part of the military culture, for example, you've internalized its jargon as part of your own vocabulary. Similarly, jargon associated with new communication technologies frequently finds its way into everyday conversations. People *IM, blog,* and *chat.* Computer users are concerned about *spam, viruses,* and *worms*, and look for *hotspots* so they can go *wireless.*

Technical language used by members of a profession or associated with a specific topic.

Idioms are expressions whose practical meanings are very different from their literal meanings. Listeners must have a solid command of the language as people use it in everyday conversation to correctly interpret an idiom. Here are some examples of the literal meanings of idioms and their common interpretations:

An expression that means something other than the literal meaning of the words.

- That test was a piece of cake.

    Literal meaning: That test was a confection made of flour, sugar, and eggs.

Idiomatic meaning: That test was easy.

- You'd better hit the books if you're going to pass your classes.

  Literal meaning: You'd better strike your books with your hand or an object if you're going to pass your classes.

  Idiomatic meaning: You'd better study if you're going to pass your classes.

- Would you lend me your ear for a few minutes?

  Literal meaning: Literal meaning: Would you remove your ear and give it to me for a few minutes?

  Idiomatic meaning: Would you listen to me for a few minutes?

If you've grown up speaking English, you might laugh at the literal meanings because you're so accustomed to hearing and using idioms—you don't even think about how you've learned to interpret them.

Speakers use **euphemisms** in place of words that are viewed as more disagreeable or offensive. For example, pornographic movies are called "adult films," and those who star in such movies become "adult actors." Euphemisms can prove useful if you're concerned you might offend your audience. For the most part, though, euphemistic language simply confuses listeners. For example, organizations typically refer to employee layoffs and firings as "downsizing" and "rightsizing," which may sound less harsh, but not to the people who have lost their jobs.

> A word used in place of another word that is viewed as more disagreeable or offensive.

An expression so overused it fails to have any important meaning.

Clichés are trite or obvious expressions—phrases used so often they lack any important meaning. At one point, the remark was original, but overuse has made it dull. Examples of clichés include "the big picture," "thinking outside the box," and "better late than never." Clichés cause problems for speakers in two ways. First, as with slang, jargon, idioms, and euphemisms, listeners must possess the cultural knowledge to interpret clichés. Second, because clichés are overused, listeners may think they've heard the speaker's message before and lose interest in the speech.

If you've grown up in the United States and English is your first language, you probably wouldn't be fazed by someone saying, "Hey dude, whazzup?" "My ISP is down," "We're on the same page," "I fell on my tush ice skating," and "Money doesn't grow on trees." But not all your audience members will have the cultural knowledge necessary to understand slang, jargon, idioms, euphemisms, and clichés. Unless they're an essential part of your speech, minimize your use of these types of language.

Language and Gender

Why examine language and gender in a public speaking class? First, how listeners interpret what speakers say can depend on the listeners' gender.[14] Let's take an example from research on powerful and powerless language. Powerful language conveys the speaker's certainty about the topic. "This proposal will win over our client!" and "Our team effort led to our success" make clear the speaker's confidence. Audience members view speakers who use powerful language as dynamic and competent. Powerless language such as "I guess," "sorta," and "right?" indicates uncertainty and hurts a speaker's credibility.[15] Even in everyday conversations, listeners are less likely to believe someone who sounds uncertain. If you find yourself using powerless language, ask yourself why. Are you unsure of yourself or your information? In that case, it's okay to qualify what you say. Are you using powerless language out of habit? If that's true, then pay careful attention and try to avoid it.

A question added onto the end of declarative statement that lessens the impact of that statement.

A qualifier, such as probably, that makes a statement ambiguous.

Researchers usually categorize **tag questions** as powerless language. Speakers tack on tag questions at the end of a sentence, as in "This proposal will win over our client, *don't you think*?" Men usually interpret "don't you think?" as uncertainty. But women generally view "don't you think?" as an invitation for others to state their opinions. Similarly, **hedges**—words that qualify what the speaker is saying—often function differently for men than for women. Women might interpret "Our team effort *likely* led to our success" as acknowledging that other factors may have contributed to the group's accomplishments. For men, "likely" could indicate a speaker's self-doubt.[16] In addition, listeners evaluate a woman as less competent when she uses tag questions and hedges, whereas such language has little impact on how listeners evaluate men.[17]

Powerful language can lead to similar misunderstandings. Statements such as "This research leaves no doubt that the program will fail" and "Employee morale has never been higher" convey certainty and conviction. But for women such language can also convey arrogance and disdain for other perspectives.

Second, using language that excludes or demeans some audience members will cause many of them to stop listening to you. To be sure you're addressing all members of your audience equally, use **nonsexist language**, or words that are not associated with either sex. Consider the difference between *stewardess* and *flight attendant*. The first word likely conjured up an image of a woman; the second could be a woman or a man. **Table 10.1** provides some examples of nonsexist alternatives to sexist language. Using nonsexist language also refers to the order in which speakers refer to people. Generally listeners think of the first item in a list as the most important and the last as the least important. Do you always say "men and women," "boys and girls," "husband and wife"? To avoid privileging one sex over the other, rotate the order of gendered terms.

Also avoid language that demeans either women or men. For example, referring to a "female doctor" suggests that women aren't typically physicians. Yet in 2005, 25 percent of U.S. physicians were women and women comprised half of the students in medical school.[18] And use gender-neutral pronouns, as in "A student should choose her or his major carefully." Better yet, use the plural and avoid gendered language, such as "Students should choose their majors carefully."

Using nonsexist or gender-neutral language in your speeches also means using similar language for women and men when describing them and their accomplishments. From sports to political campaigns, women and men are often portrayed in very different ways.[19] For example, sportscasters typically describe male athletes in terms of their physical abilities but describe female athletes in terms of their personalities, looks, appearance, and sexual attractiveness.[20] As an athlete, what would you rather hear: "His ability to make the key shots is amazing!" or "She looks fabulous in the team's new uniform!"?

The bias works both ways. When talking about a man in the nursing profession, a speaker might say, "He's so sensitive and caring." But aren't those

> Words that are not associated with either sex.

TABLE 10.1 ▶ Replacing Sexist Language with Nonsexist Language

INSTEAD OF SAYING THIS . . .	SAY THIS . . .
mankind	humankind, humanity
man hours	staff hours, hours
the common man	ordinary people, average person
chairman	chair, chairperson
freshman	first-year student
waitress/waiter	server
male nurse	nurse
lady lawyer	lawyer
career woman	professional

qualities associated with all nurses? In the 2004 presidential election we heard about "soccer moms" and "NASCAR dads." Yet women make up 40 percent of NASCAR fans,[21] and plenty of dads go to their kids' soccer games.

So far, you've learned about the general characteristics and qualities of language. Although written and spoken language share these general traits, they differ in important ways. Since audience members listen to your words rather than reading them, use spoken language in your speeches. The remainder of the chapter focuses more specifically on spoken language.

Spoken versus Written Language

Because spoken and written language differ in important ways, audiences find memorized speeches or speeches read word for word ponderous and difficult to follow. Audiences usually prefer an extemporaneous delivery method (Chapter 12) in which speakers use conversational and engaging language. The specific differences between written and spoken language are explored in this section.

DYNAMIC VERSUS STATIC

In face-to-face public speaking situations, there's limited time for speaking and asking questions. In addition, public speaking occurs "in the moment," as the speaker and the audience come together to create a speaking event. As a result, speaking is dynamic. Unless participants record the event in some way, what they say is fleeting and impermanent. Listeners will recall some of what they hear, but they can't go back and "re-hear" what you've said. Redundancy helps overcome the transient nature of spoken language, and audience members expect some redundancy to help them recall what the speaker said. Speakers therefore preview main points, provide internal summaries, and review key ideas in the conclusion. In contrast, written language is static. Readers can reread a passage of text over and over again, so they don't need the redundancy that listeners need.

IMMEDIATE VERSUS DISTANT

The immediacy of spoken language affects public speaking in several ways. First, listeners receive the message right away, while the speaker is talking, and can provide nearly instantaneous feedback. In contrast, writers receive no immediate feedback from their audiences. Second, public speaking involves all the senses—audience members *hear* how the words are spoken and *see* how the speaker uses nonverbal communication. Gestures, movements, and vocal intonations provide a context for the words speakers use.

Third, immediacy allows speakers to refer to the situation in which the speech is taking place. So speakers can say things such as "I can see you've dressed for the warm weather we're supposed to get later today" and "How many of you have studied for your finals next week?" U.S. Secretary of Labor Elaine L. Chao referred to the speaking situation as she began her talk at the *LATINA Style* 50 Best Practices in Diversity Awards Ceremony:

> Thank you, Barry. It's good to see so many Latinas from the Administration of President George W. Bush . . . . It is great to be back for the fourth year in a row to honor those organizations which are providing the greatest opportunities to Latinas. Today, we celebrate and recognize all those who realize the value that Latinas bring to the workforce.[22]

Chao sprinkled in other references to the speaking event, such as "The first thing I want to do this afternoon . . ." and "Other employers honored today . . . ." When you make references—even brief ones—to the speaking situation, audience members feel as if you're speaking with them personally.

INFORMAL VERSUS FORMAL

When you talk with friends, neighbors, coworkers, and others, your language is rather informal. You might say, "Hey, what's up?" and "How's your day?" You use slang and jargon. Your sentences are short and often incomplete. Ordinarily in these interpersonal situations you're not concerned with choosing the perfect words to express your ideas. In contrast, the language you use when you give a speech is more formal than your everyday conversations, yet still conversational. However, you don't speak as casually in your speeches as you do with your friends, even if your friends are in the audience.

IRREVERSIBLE VERSUS REVISABLE

Once you've said something, it's out there. You can try to take it back, but listeners will still have heard what you said. You can immediately correct what you've said, as with, "Oh, sorry. I meant to say North Dakota, not South Dakota." In addition, you can reframe statements. For example, shortly before the 2005 Academy Awards show, host Chris Rock referred to the event as idiotic and something he'd never watch. He later explained that he intended his remarks to be humorous and not offensive. Question-and-answer sessions also allow us to further clarify and elaborate on what you say in a speech. Shortly after her visit to Darfur, Sudan, Angelina Jolie spoke at the National Press Club in her role as goodwill ambassador for the United Nations High Commissioner for Refugees. After Jolie's formal remarks about the plight of refugee children, journalists asked her for specifics in several areas, such as the National Center for Refugee and Immigrant Children that she recently helped establish. These questions provided a venue for Jolie to elaborate on U.S. and UN plans for addressing the needs of young refugees.[23]

Unlike spoken language, written language allows for nearly infinite revisions—at least until the deadline for submitting a document. For example, this book underwent many, many revisions and multiple drafts as we worked to make the text right for you, our audience.

NARRATIVES VERSUS FACTS

Although you often read stories, storytelling has its roots in oral communication. With its informality and immediacy, spoken language provides an ideal vehicle for telling a dramatic and engaging story. Oral language allows audience participation, sometimes including nonverbal feedback and additional information. The next time you're with friends or family, observe what happens when someone starts telling a story. Others likely will jump in with a bit of dialogue or description. When you're telling a story, it's often a group effort.

Written language more readily handles facts, statistics, and other technical information because readers have time to review numbers and facts. Listeners don't have that luxury. Citing too many facts and statistics during a speech loses their attention—they can't comprehend all the information in one sitting.

RHYTHM VERSUS IMAGE

Spoken language has a rhythm or a flow that helps listeners interpret words. For example, a speaker's vocal pitch goes up with a question and down at the end of a sentence. Speakers pause to give audience members time to contemplate an idea, and speak more loudly when emphasizing a point. Vocal qualities, including pitch, rate, tone, and volume, give additional meaning to a speaker's words.

In contrast, written language is rich in images. Writers and publishers choose specific fonts and layouts for organizing text to increase readability and interest. Arranging text in tables and charts clarifies the writer's ideas. This text, for example, includes tables and figures to visually summarize and highlight key ideas.

Keep the differences between spoken and written language in mind as you read the next section on using audience-centered language in your speeches.

Audience-centered Language

Part of analyzing your audience involves identifying language that's appropriate for them. Language geared toward your audience helps you get your message across in a way that resonates with them. You vary the words you use based on the intended recipients and the situation. For example, you use different language when welcoming newcomers to a student organization than when welcoming friends to a get-together in your home.

Your success as a speaker depends in part on using words that appeal to your audience.[24] This section, summarized in **Table 10.2**, describes ways to develop audience-centered language in your speech: Put your language in context, personalize your language, use inclusive language, use visual language, and spark imagination with your language.

PUT YOUR LANGUAGE IN CONTEXT

The in-the-moment qualities of public speaking work to your advantage. Integrating comments about the physical location, current events, and the speech situation brings spontaneity to your speech and keeps your listeners interested. For a report you're presenting at work, for instance, you might begin with, "The original idea for this project began in this very room, with many of you who are here today sitting around this conference table." Or maybe you're giving a speech of welcome to new students. You could say, "This campus—

TABLE 10.2 ▶ Audience-centered Language

Put your language in context by . . .	• mentioning the location • referring to current events • responding to what happens during the speech
Personalize your language by . . .	• integrating audience analysis information • remarking on what other speakers have said using "we," "us," "you," and "I"
Use inclusive language by . . .	• avoiding language that discriminates and stereotypes
Use visual language by incorporating . . .	• similes • metaphors • parallelism • rhyme • alliteration • antithesis
Spark imagination with your language by using . . .	• imaginative invitations • humor

the people, buildings, and traditions—may seem strange to you now. But by the end of the semester what you see around you today will be familiar and comforting—almost like home." These direct references to the context in which you're speaking help gain and maintain your listeners' attention and let them know you've designed the speech for them.

At a concert in South Africa to raise funds for Nelson Mandela's HIV/AIDS awareness campaign, musician Annie Lennox brought the context into her speech in several ways:

> We have come here tonight to bring your attention to an unacceptable situation. What I have to say is going to alarm you . . . and you need to be alarmed in order to wake up to the fact that the AIDS crisis has reached unprecedented epidemic proportions. Among men, women and children, here and in other parts of Africa, AIDS is effectively causing mass genocide. Let me give you some facts . . . In Africa, more people are wiped out by AIDS every year than in the entire Asian tsunami disaster. There are probably 25,000 people here in the stadium tonight . . . look around and take it in . . . now double that number . . . every day, more than two stadiums like this become infected with HIV. It's horrific . . . think about it. And for every ten that are infected . . . six are women.[25]

Lennox began by referring to the concert's purpose. Comparing the death toll from the tsunami disaster in Asia to AIDS deaths in Africa linked her topic to a current cataclysmic event. Then she asked her listeners to "look around" at the 25,000 people in the stadium and imagine twice that number getting infected with HIV every day. Lennox could have said, "Fifty thousand people contract HIV every day," but visualizing two stadiums filled with concert attendees had a much greater impact.

Putting context in your language also means responding to events that happen during your speech. If many people were to applaud during a speech of tribute, for example, you could say, "I can tell you agree with me" or, "I share your enthusiasm." In your public speaking class, you might acknowledge audience feedback by saying, "I see a lot of heads nodding" or, "Some of you look puzzled."

PERSONALIZE YOUR LANGUAGE

In most public speaking situations, you and your audience share the same physical space. Even with video conferencing, speakers and listeners hear and see each other. As a speaker, this gives you an opportunity to personalize your speech, using language tailored to your audience that promotes dialogue and collaboration.

In your public speaking class you get to know your audience from the speeches they give and from your audience analysis. Integrating information from audience questionnaires can help maintain your audience's attention. You might say something like, "Based on your responses to my questionnaire, about half of you exercise once a week and a quarter of you exercise almost every day" or, "Your responses to my questionnaire helped me narrow down my topic."

You can make your speeches even more personal by referring to specific people in the class. You might even refer to a speech presented earlier in the term, as with "As Sondra mentioned in her speech a few weeks ago . . . ," or to one given shortly before yours, as with "In his speech a few minutes ago, Trent said . . . ." During your speech, you might also comment on a specific audience member's nonverbal communication: "Dana, you look skeptical. Let me tell you more about my idea. . . ."

Audiences expect some informality in spoken language, such as using the pronouns *we, us, you,* and *I* in your speeches. Using these pronouns includes the audience in your speech and encourages them to listen. For example, if you're speaking at a meeting of a student organization, you might say, "We've raised awareness of three important issues on this campus" or, "I'm proud of the work you've accomplished in raising awareness on these three important campus issues."

Words like *we* and *us* let your audience know you share similar experiences, values, beliefs, and attitudes. In her "Consciousness Is Power" speech at the 1995 Asian American Convocation at Brown University, Yuri Kochiyama said

How do we measure Asians? We are not a monolithic entity. We are many different ethnic people. We are Asian immigrants, Asian American, part Asian, Amer-Asian, Asian national, Asian adoptee (mostly Korean), and a Korean category that calls itself "1.5." We are divided by class, religion, culture, language, and political affiliation. But because of racism and discrimination inherent in this society, despite our differences, we are, not just thrust together as Asians, but considered as "outsiders," foreigners, and "not quite Americans."[26]

Kochiyama uses *we* in every sentence. She's telling her audience that she understands their perspective because it's the same as hers.

Audience members also take notice when speakers use *you.* Near the end of her speech, Kochiyama appealed directly to her audience:

For you young Asian American students, or students in general of any background, who are searching, who have the idealism and enthusiasm, and a natural love for all peoples—fight against racism, chauvinism, and imperialism. . . . Your role can be that [of] supporters. You can also support political prisoners—most of whom are Black, Puerto Rican, and American Indian. The world you will help develop will surely be more understanding, harmonious, and just with equal

Just How Personal Is Personal?

Personalizing your language lets the audience know you're speaking with their interests and needs in mind. But how personal should you get? Should you use language that audience members are familiar with but that might prove embarrassing? Should you reveal personal information about yourself that you think might help audience members identify with you but that could be humiliating? The informality associated with spoken language can sometimes lull public speakers into revealing personal information they later regret. Remember that public speaking is just that—public. The language you use with your friends and the stories you tell them may not be appropriate for public speaking.

opportunities; where human dignity and human rights become accessible to all. Leave new footsteps for those following after you.[27]

The word *you* makes Kochiyama's speech more persuasive. Read the same selection below, this time with *students* and *they* replacing *you*:

For young Asian American students, or students in general of any background, who are searching, who have the idealism and enthusiasm, and a natural love for all peoples—fight against racism, chauvinism, and imperialism. . . . A student's role can be that [of] supporters. Students can also support political prisoners— most of whom are Black, Puerto Rican, and American Indian. The world students will help develop will surely be more understanding, harmonious, and just with equal opportunities; where human dignity and human rights become accessible to all. Students should leave new footsteps for those following after them.

The words *students* and *they* create distance between the audience and the topic. In contrast, *you* personalizes the speech and makes listeners feel included. In this example, *you* suggests that audience members can take action and make a difference. Saying *students* and *they* removes the audience from the scene and suggests that someone else— they—will solve the problem.

When you use the pronoun *I*, you let audience members know you're the one who thinks or believes a certain way. "It's important for all college students to take a public speaking class" doesn't have the same meaning—or the same force—as "I think all college students should take a public speaking class." In the first example, the speaker remains distant from the topic; listeners don't know whether she agrees with the statement or not. In the second example, the speaker takes a stand, letting the audience know her position.

USE INCLUSIVE LANGUAGE

Words that don't privilege one group over another.

When you use inclusive language in your speeches, you choose words that don't privilege one group over another. Noninclusive language promotes discrimination and stereotyping, even if the speaker's word choices are unintentional. Language that needlessly emphasizes someone's race, class, gender, age, dis/ability, sexual orientation, and the like is noninclusive.

In the discussion of language and gender earlier in the chapter, sexist and nonsexist language were compared. Sexist language provides a clear example of noninclusive language, but speakers may exclude groups in other ways. Here are some examples:

- Jeannette and her *Latina friend* Maria volunteer at a local food bank.

    Problem: Why identify Maria as Latina? Is it safe to assume that Jeannette is white?

- The *disabled actor* put on a great performance.

  Problem: If the person did not have a disability, would it be okay to say, "The nondisabled actor put on a great performance"? Of course not. What, then, would be the best way to identify the actor being discussed? Something like, "The actor who played the lead role put on a great performance" works fine.

- She's the *senior citizen* on her crew team.

  Problem: Words such as aged, elderly, and senior citizen suggest the person is frail or impaired in some way. If the person's age is significant to the accomplishment, include it, as in, "At 70, she's the oldest active member of her crew team." If age isn't important, don't mention it, as in, "She belongs to a crew team."

- The *primitive people* of Africa relied on oral communication to pass along cultural stories.

  Problem: Primitive implies deficiency or incompetence. Because the reference is to a time period, early is a more accurate word.

▲ Using inclusive language invites all audience members to listen to your speech.

These may seem like small distinctions, but when added up noninclusive language affects everybody—the people it leaves out and the people it singles out.

Using inclusive language doesn't mean talking about people only in generic terms. Sometimes the point you're making requires you to identify people by the various groups to which they belong. When Linda Chavez-Thompson addressed a Hotel Employees and Restaurant Employees convention on immigration reform, she used her own and others' ethnic backgrounds as examples of immigrants in the United States:

> Immigration is the very core of who we are as a movement. Just look at the executive officers of the AFL-CIO. John Sweeney is the son of immigrants from County Antrim, Ireland . . . Rich Trumka is from a family of Polish and Italian miners . . . and I am the daughter of Mexican-American sharecroppers. Immigrants are the history of the union movement . . . but too often in the past, our movement hasn't fully embraced new immigrants.[28]

In this case, identifying each person's ethnic background demonstrated listeners' common bond as immigrants and served as inclusive language. Chavez-Thompson also used inclusive language at other points in her speech, such as "undocumented workers" rather than "illegal aliens" and "workers with disabilities" rather than "disabled workers."

USE VISUAL LANGUAGE

Similes and metaphors are *analogies*—a shorthand way of comparing two dissimilar things. Language devices such as simile, metaphor, parallelism, rhyme, alliteration, and antithesis give your speech force and help your audience visualize your ideas.

Similes suggest that two things share some similar qualities. Similes use *like* and *as* to make a comparison, as in "That story is like an old friend" and "The car rode as smoothly as a tin can on plastic wheels." **Metaphors** equate one thing with another. They often compare something more abstract with something more concrete, such as "Life is a rollercoaster" and "Ideas are wildflowers."

Similes and metaphors make your speech memorable by comparing things that listeners might not think of as ordinarily going together. For example, in his inaugural speech, Thomas J. Schwarz, president of Purchase College, said, "And make it absolutely clear—strengthening these [liberal studies and continuing education] programs is no threat to the arts. *A rising tide does carry all boats.*"[29] Of course, the programs aren't boats and the increased financial support isn't a tide, but the image Schwarz evoked likely stayed in the minds of listeners much longer than if he'd said, "Everyone will benefit."

Similes and metaphors also help audience members understand something unfamiliar by comparing it with something familiar. For example, Vice Admiral Richard H. Carmona, Surgeon General of the United States, said this in a speech presented at a conference on early childhood:

> I'm almost ashamed to say that the medical profession has too often *sent people with disabilities to the back of the bus*. The reality is that for too long we have provided lesser care to developmentally and physically disabled people.[30]

Carmona's reference to "the back of the bus" compared something familiar—the now-illegal practice in the southern United States of forcing African Americans to sit in the back of a public bus—to something that most audience members likely found unfamiliar: the medical treatment of persons with disabilities.

When using **parallelism**, speakers use the same phrase, wording, or clause multiple times to add emphasis. In a speech on domestic violence given in Salt Lake City, Dr. Elaine Weiss used parallelism when telling her own story related to the topic:

> I stayed . . . because I thought it was my fault. . . . I stayed . . . because I believed I could fix it. . . . Finally, and most importantly, I stayed . . . because there was

A language device that compares two things that are generally dissimilar but share some common properties, expressed using *like* or *as*.

A language device that demonstrates the commonalities between two dissimilar things.

Using the same phrase, wording, or clause multiple times to add emphasis.

nowhere to go for support. . . . I stayed, and I stayed, and I stayed . . . and then one day I left.[31]

The last phrase, "and then one day I left," gets its impact from the multiple repetitions of "I stayed . . . because." Through her use of parallelism, Weiss builds up suspense—listeners know she left, but not when—and she holds her audience's attention.

You've likely heard **rhymes** since you were a young child. Rhyming words have similar sounds, usually the last syllable. Advertisers use rhyme to embed their products more clearly in our memories. For example, travel company Thomas Cook uses the slogan "Don't just book it. Thomas Cook it," and Alka Seltzer coined "Plop, plop, fizz, fizz, oh what a relief it is." During O.J. Simpson's 1995 trial for the murder of his ex-wife, Simpson's attorney, Johnnie Cochran, used the phrase "If it doesn't fit, you must acquit" to point out perceived flaws in the district attorney's case. That phrase alone didn't win the jury's not-guilty verdict, but the rhyme helped jurors visualize the defense attorney's contention that the prosecutor's arguments were not supported by the evidence presented.

> Using words with similar sounds, usually at the end of the word, to emphasize a point.

Speakers use **alliteration** when they repeat a sound in a series of words, usually the first consonant. Classic tongue twisters provide examples of alliteration: "She sells sea shells by the sea shore" and "Fat frogs flying past fast." Alliteration can increase audience members' recall, but avoid alliterative phrases or sentences you find difficult to say. In his speech on integrity at Tuskegee University, Samuel P. Jenkins, a vice president of Boeing, described the organization's ethics website in this way: "We established a special portal so *anyone* could reach us *anytime* from *anywhere*, *anonymously* if necessary."[32]

> Repetition of a sound in a series of words, usually the first consonant.

Antithesis refers to the juxtaposition of two apparently contradictory phrases that are organized in a parallel structure. With antithesis, the *meanings* of the phrases are in opposition, but the *arrangement* of the words within the phrases is in alignment. Antithesis gets listeners' attention because the speaker brings together words in an unexpected, yet balanced, way. For example, when NASA astronaut Neil Armstrong became the first person to walk on the moon, he said, "That's one small step for a man, and one giant leap for mankind." Armstrong's use of antithesis underscored how his small action—stepping down onto the moon's surface—represented a tremendous accomplishment for all humankind.

> Juxtaposition of two apparently contradictory phrases that are organized in a parallel structure.

SPARK IMAGINATION WITH YOUR LANGUAGE

Two language techniques can spark your audience's imagination: invitations to imagine and humor. **Invitations to imagine** ask listeners to create a scene or situation in their minds. Visualizing a place or series of events makes the audience feel more involved in your topic.

> Asking listeners to create a scene or situation in their minds.

Use your imagination when developing invitations to imagine. For instance, rather than asking the audience to "close your eyes and imagine" a scene, use a less direct approach. Indirect language invites the audience to participate in a more willing and intimate way. You might want to use phrases like these:

- "The miners were trapped 250 feet below ground and the water was rising. How do you suppose they felt, not knowing if anyone knew they were alive?"

- "Does a weekend of snow skiing at Vail, Colorado, sound like a good idea to you?"

- "What would you have done under the circumstances?"

Some of the best stories are the ones you refer to but don't tell entirely. By reminding your audience of events, circumstances, narratives, or jokes you are confident they already know, you can ignite their imagination without repeating something that is already familiar. University of Chicago professor Martha C. Nussbaum used this strategy in a speech at Georgetown University. She began with, "I want to ask you to pause for a minute, and to think of the ending of a tragic drama, Euripides's *The Trojan Women*," and then told the story in four sentences—just enough to help listeners recall the narrative's key turning points.[33]

Experienced speakers sometimes use jokes to connect with their audiences, especially for particular kinds of public presentations, such as after-dinner speeches. Humorous stories and anecdotes can relax the speaker and create common ground with the audience. Appropriate use of humor can also help the speaker gain the audience's confidence, generate an emotional atmosphere consistent with the purpose of the speech, and provide a pleasant, memorable experience for listeners.

Effectively told humorous stories and asides inherently provoke audiences to imagine and visualize, inviting listeners to actively engage with the speaker's topic. Use short humorous stories to get the audience's attention at the beginning of the speech or to conclude in a dynamic, unforgettable way. For example, Wabash College senior Dustin DeNeal began his commencement speech, "Katabasis and Anabasis: A Four-Year Journey," this way:

I know, I know. You're looking at the title and thinking: "What in the world is this supposed to mean?" Well, to be honest, I'm not completely sure. But out of the countless lessons I'll take away from Wabash, one of the most important is that half the game is looking like you know what you're talking about even if you really don't. Big thanks to campus BS artist Chris Morris for that one. No, seriously.[34]

DeNeal's familiarity with his audience allowed him to gently poke fun at the title of his speech and gain his audience's attention.

Incorporating brief stories, quips, and humorous observations throughout your speech can help illustrate a point in the body of the speech and connect the audience with the topic and speaker. DeNeal included humor at several points in his speech, such as, "We took the road less traveled and committed four years to an all-male institution. What were we thinking?"

Although incorporating jokes and anecdotes into a speech can produce positive results under the right conditions, attempts at humor can detract from the speech if they aren't well planned and practiced. Self-disparaging humor, in which speakers make jokes about their own shortcomings, negatively impacts speaker credibility.[35] Beginning speakers considering the use of humor should keep the following guidelines in mind:

- Make sure the joke or anecdote is appropriate for you, the topic, the audience, and the situation.

- Use humor strategically to attract attention, make a point, illustrate an idea, or conclude in a witty way.

- Don't let the joke or other humorous utterance go on too long.

- Avoid "canned jokes" retrieved online or from joke books.

If you're not comfortable telling jokes or making funny comments, don't include humor in your speech. Some research suggests that women have a more difficult time than men using humor in speeches due to cultural and societal norms.[36] Poor use of humor damages the dialogue you strive to establish with your audience. For example, when accepting an award for leadership, Miami Dolphins player Junior Seau told a derogatory joke about gays. Although he apologized the next day, his remarks offended members of the audience and hurt his credibility.

HYUNGWON KANG/Reuters/Landov

▲ Stephen Colbert, host of Comedy Central's *Colbert Report*, uses humor to draw attention to current political events.

Guidelines for Using Language in Your Speech

▼ The words you choose to convey your message to the audience play a key role in developing your credibility and achieving your purpose. Your language should fit the topic, occasion, and audience. Speaking ethically requires that you use language that is respectful of yourself and your audience. This section explores several specific guidelines

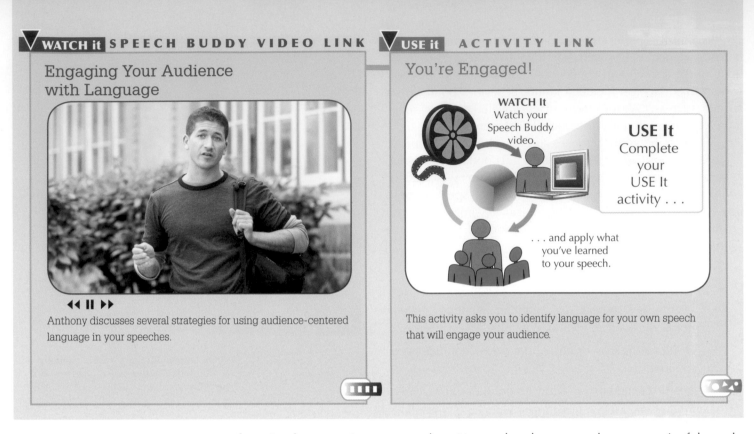

Engaging Your Audience with Language

◀◀ ❚❚ ▶▶

Anthony discusses several strategies for using audience-centered language in your speeches.

You're Engaged!

WATCH It
Watch your Speech Buddy video.

USE It
Complete your USE It activity . . .

. . . and apply what you've learned to your speech.

This activity asks you to identify language for your own speech that will engage your audience.

for using language in your speeches: Use spoken language, choose meaningful words, balance clarity and ambiguity, be concise, avoid offensive and aggressive language, build in redundancy, and don't get too attached to your words.

USE SPOKEN LANGUAGE

Audiences quickly lose interest when speakers read from a manuscript. Choose conversational, engaging, personal, and active language that speaks directly to your audience. Compare "It's important to investigate this topic in depth so students can gain more knowledge of their civil liberties on university campuses" with "I researched this topic so we could learn more about our civil liberties on campus."

CHOOSE MEANINGFUL WORDS

Avoid jargon, idioms, euphemisms, slang, and clichés that listeners won't understand or will find uninteresting. If you must use technical terms, define them clearly. Groups with specialized interests often use jargon or technical language that speakers can weave into their speeches. Still, too much jargon turns off audience members. Even with experts, using a lot of technical language can make listening difficult and tiresome.[37] Thoroughly analyzing your audience will help you strike a balance between precision and comprehension. Use words that are on your audience's level—not above or below it.

BALANCE CLARITY AND AMBIGUITY

Clear language promotes understanding. Compare "Many people believe in this proposal" with "Three hundred and fifty-one individuals signed the proposal." By replacing "many" with an actual number, the speaker provides a concrete indication of the proposal's support. "Many" could mean thousands, tens of thousands, millions, or less than ten. At times, however, ambiguous language can bring people together. Nearly everyone would agree that "We need to give children the best education possible." Such statements motivate audience members to tackle tough projects. If you begin with specific ideas that not everyone supports, listeners will focus on areas of disagreement rather than agreement.

BE CONCISE

Concise language avoids unnecessary words. Compare "We must get the up-to-date version of our computer applications and software packages on a regular basis" (17 words) with "We must regularly update our computer software" (7 words). Which would your listeners rather hear? As you're practicing your speech, listen to the words you use and try out ways to present your points as concisely as possible.

AVOID OFFENSIVE AND AGGRESSIVE LANGUAGE

Connotative meanings often stir deep emotions. People link emotions with words and words with experience. As a speaker, you don't want to use language with negative connotations. You certainly would never use words that denigrate any group. Language that audience members consider aggressive—such as demanding that they take action or questioning their intelligence—puts up a barrier to listening and damages your credibility as a speaker.[38]

BUILD IN REDUNDANCY

Recall the fleeting nature of spoken language. Listeners can't stop, go back, and re-listen to your speech the way they might re-read written material. Build in redundancy through previews, reviews, clear transitions, and internal summaries. A few words, such as "Now let's examine," "As I mentioned earlier," and "Last, I'll talk about," serve to remind your audience of what you've covered and where you're headed.

DON'T GET TOO ATTACHED TO YOUR WORDS

Sometimes speakers get caught up in finding the perfect words for their speeches and forget about the purpose—informing, persuading, or entertaining the audience. As you practice your speech, try out different phrasing and listen to how it sounds. If you focus on choosing the "right" words, you'll lose the flexibility you need to adapt to your audience.

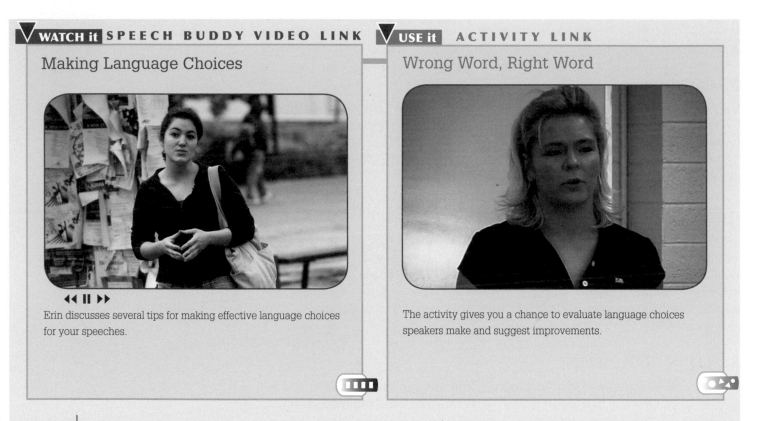

▼ **WATCH it** SPEECH BUDDY VIDEO LINK

Making Language Choices

◄◄ ❙❙ ►►

Erin discusses several tips for making effective language choices for your speeches.

▼ **USE it** ACTIVITY LINK

Wrong Word, Right Word

The activity gives you a chance to evaluate language choices speakers make and suggest improvements.

SUMMARY

Language enlivens your ideas—the words you choose get your audience's attention, help them visualize your main points, and facilitate their ability to remember what you say. Language refers to the system of words you use to communicate with others. It is arbitrary, ambiguous, abstract, and active, characteristics that present speakers with both opportunities and challenges. Because language is arbitrary, audiences may interpret your words in ways you don't intend. Because language is ambiguous, consider both the connotative and denotative meanings of the words you use. Because language is abstract, consider when to discuss ideas and concepts rather than tangible objects and specific actions. Because language is active, the words you use and how you use them change over time.

Language and culture are interdependent. You learn about the meanings of words from your culture, and words help you interpret culture. Slang, jargon, idioms, euphemisms, and clichés highlight the link between language and culture. Because your audiences may not always share your cultural background, it's best to avoid these types of culture-specific words or phrases unless they're essential to the speech. You must also pay attention to gender and language when you give a speech, considering how the gender of your listeners will affect how they interpret your message. In addition, use nonsexist language to avoid alienating some members of your audience.

Spoken language differs from written language in that it is dynamic, immediate, informal, irreversible, based in narrative, and rhythmic, whereas written language is static, distant, formal, revisable, able to describe multiple facts, and rich in imagery. When you give a speech to an audience, use spoken language in an engaging, conversational manner and use audience-centered language. When you take an audience-centered approach, you put your language in context, personalize your language, use inclusive language, use visual language, and spark imagination with your language.

To successfully use language to engage your audience, use spoken language, choose meaningful words, balance clarity and ambiguity, strive for conciseness, avoid offensive or aggressive language, build in redundancy, and don't get too attached to your words.

In the Book

Summary
Key Terms
Critical Challenges

More Study Resources

Speech Studio
Quizzes
WebLinks

Student Workbook

10.1: Written and Spoken Style
10.2: Working Up a Sentence
10.3: Creating Clusters
10.4: Presidential Style
10.5: Dramatism

Speech Buddy Videos

 Video Links

Engaging your Audience
with Language
Making Language Choices

Activity Links

You're Engaged!
Wrong Word, Right Word

▶ Sample Speech Videos

Stacey, "Fallen Soldiers,"
commemorative speech

Brandi, "Feeding the Wildlife:
Don't Do It!" persuasive
speech

Speech Builder Express

Goal/purpose
Thesis statement
Organization
Outline
Supporting material
Transitions
Introduction
Conclusion
Title
Works cited
Completing the speech
outline

 InfoTrac

Recommended search terms
Language and public speaking
Language and culture
Language and gender
Nonsexist language
Spoken versus written language
Inclusive language
Figures of speech
Imagery and language

Audio Study Tools

"Feeding the Wildlife: Don't
Do It!" by Brandi

Critical thinking questions

Learning objectives

Chapter summary

Guide to Your Online Resources

Your Online Resources for *Public Speaking: The Evolving Art* give you access to the Speech Buddy video and activity featured in this chapter, additional sample speech videos, Speech Builder Express, InfoTrac College Edition, and study aids such as glossary flashcards, review quizzes, and the Critical Challenge questions for this chapter, which you can respond to via e-mail if your instructor requests. In addition, your Online Resources feature live WebLinks relevant to this chapter, including sites where you can explore how language is continually evolving, such as macmillandictionary.com and worldwidewords.com. Links are regularly maintained, and new ones are added periodically.

Key Terms

alliteration 267

antithesis 267

cliché 256

connotative meaning 249

denotative meaning 249

euphemism 255

hedge 256

idiom 254

inclusive language 264

interpretation 249

invitation to imagine 267

jargon 254

language 248

metaphor 266

nonsexist language 257

parallelism 266

rhyme 267

simile 266

slang 254

symbol 248

tag question 256

tone 250

Critical Challenges

Questions for Reflection and Discussion

1. Although ambiguity can produce positive results, it can also obscure the speaker's true intentions. Consider your use of ambiguous language. Have you ever used vague language to mislead or deceive others? Or has someone ever misled or deceived you in this way? What was the outcome? How did you feel about what happened? What did you learn from your experience?

2. Similes and metaphors help audience members visualize your ideas. Brainstorm for similes and metaphors that describe your college. How do those analogies help you visualize your campus? How do different similes and metaphors reveal or hide different aspects of your college? What ethical responsibilities do speakers have when choosing similes and metaphors to compare things?

3. Swear words can get your audience's attention and give added impact to what you say. But is it the impact you want? Should you swear in your speech? Recall an instance in which you heard or read about a speaker cursing during a presentation. How did you react? Do you think that's the reaction the speaker intended? Is using such words ever appropriate in public speaking? Why or why not?

11 INTEGRATING PRESENTATION MEDIA

Today's technology offers

an unprecedented array of visual and audio resources that can enhance your speech. **Presentation media** are technical and material resources ranging from presentation software such as Keynote and PowerPoint to flip charts and handouts that speakers use to highlight, clarify, and complement the information they present orally. Knowing how and when to use these resources is especially important for public speakers today because presentation media are often misused. Resources such as PowerPoint can enhance your message, but unimaginative presentation media will bore the audience.

However, when integrated effectively into a speech, even the most low-tech presentation media can greatly enhance the look and feel of your speeches, strengthen your message, and help ensure the speech fulfills its purpose. In this chapter you'll learn about the most popular presentation media used today, the basics of good design, and guidelines for using presentation media effectively.

Why We Use Presentation Media

READ it Audiences appreciate speakers who use technological and symbolic resources creatively. When used appropriately, presentation media can become a core feature of your speeches. Learning how to use presentation media well involves more than simply learning a set of technical procedures. Your use of presentation media must also be properly motivated and well executed to clarify, support, dramatize, exemplify, or complement information you present orally.

You can use presentation media to attract and connect with audience members, spark their imagination, make sure they get the full meaning and impact of what you have to say, and demonstrate your creativity. Used properly, presentation media add something special to your speech by giving the audience additional sensory input about your topic or your argument. However, like everything else in your speech, you must have good reasons for incorporating media into your presentation. You can use presentation media to

- Draw attention to your topic.
- Illustrate an idea that can't be fully described by words alone.
- Stimulate an emotional reaction.
- Clarify a key point.
- Support your argument with a graphical display of facts and figures.
- Help your audience remember your main ideas.

Keep in mind that each type of presentation media has its advantages and its limitations, summarized in **Table 11.1**. The remainder of this chapter explores the most useful applications of the most popular presentation media and considers how you can best employ them in your speeches.

Understanding the Basics of Visual Design

To get the maximum impact from visual presentation media, follow the general guidelines for visual design outlined in **Table 11.2** on page 280. Strive for clarity and concision. For example, too much information on a single digital slide will overwhelm and distract audience members—they'll either dismiss the slide or read it instead of listening to you. Choose your visual materials carefully, using just enough to make your points and call attention to key ideas you want the audience to recall. In addition, use visual materials when images will say more than words. For example, close-up images often have a powerful impact because they're perceived as personal and intimate. To avoid boring your audience, balance variety with coherence by developing a consistent theme

TABLE 11.1 ► Advantages and Limitations of Presentation Media

TYPE	ADVANTAGES	LIMITATIONS
Overhead transparency	Technical simplicity; ease of use	Transparency placement and order; speaker tends to talk to screen
Flip chart and poster	Documents audience feedback and ideas	Lacks a professional look; may be hard for all audience members to see
White board and chalkboard	Records spontaneous thoughts	Writing takes away from speaking time; speaker may appear unprepared, rude
Document camera	Projects images with great detail; can zoom in, capture images, display 3-D renderings	Expensive equipment; complex to use
Video	Evokes emotions in audience; portrays examples	Interferes with speaking pace and audience focus
Handout	Enhances audience recall after speech; reinforces key ideas	Disrupts continuity of presentation; wasteful
Model	Provides specific references; helps audiences visualize materials and concepts	Can be too small or detailed; not suitable for large audiences
Audio media	Sets mood; triggers imagination	Decreases speaking time; distracting
Digital slide	Blends text, images, video, sound	Overused, boring, speech content neglected; speaker tends to talk to screen
Real-time web access	Fresh, current information	Slow connections and download times; available systems can be unreliable

for your visual media while varying the content. Finally, large lettering makes it easier for the audience to see your visual media and grasp your points quickly.

Using Traditional Visual and Audio Media

▼ Traditional visual and audio media used in public speaking include overhead transparencies, flip charts and posters, white boards and chalkboards, document cameras, video, handouts, models, and sound recordings.

TABLE 11.2 ▶ General Guidelines for Visual Design

Keep it simple.	Avoid including too much information in a graphic. The impact should be immediate and clear. By keeping visual material simple, you can also maintain maximum personal contact with your audience.
Emphasize only key ideas.	When you call attention to ideas with a graphic representation, make sure the graphic clearly illustrates your key points or most important supporting data.
Show what you can't say.	The best use of visual media is to reveal material you can't easily describe orally or with text. Photographs, drawings, simple charts, and graphs can all accomplish this objective.
Use close-up photographs and other images.	Select and present photographs, video, and other images that will create real impact. Close-ups can be very effective, especially to evoke emotional responses from your audience.
Keep the number of images you present manageable.	Too many images will tire your audience. Eight or ten images should be the maximum number for most presentations.
Combine variety with coherence.	If you use several images, vary the design enough to make them interesting but keep them aesthetically consistent. For instance, use the same colors or type font, but vary the content. Or mix photographs with graphics that maintain the same style throughout.
Use large lettering.	Use large lettering so the audience can read the text easily. Avoid presenting lengthy blocks of text.

OVERHEAD TRANSPARENCIES

Although most speakers in work-related speaking situations use digital slides and document cameras, overhead transparencies are still often used in classrooms. To use an overhead projector, you must first make transparencies of the material you want to show. **Transparencies** are clear acetate pages displayed by an overhead projector during a speech. By using the presentation, word-processing, or graphics software on your computer, you can create high-quality transparencies in color or black and white. Color is more expensive, but the impact it creates for many applications often makes the extra investment worth it.

A clear, acetate page displayed by means of an overhead projector.

Most classrooms are equipped with an overhead projector for displaying transparencies. If yours is not, arrange to have one delivered to the room on the day of your speech. Check out the location of the overhead projector in the room. Is it mounted on a mobile stand, or will you have to physically place the projector on a table or a stand? Be sure you know this *before* the day of your speech.

To smoothly integrate overhead transparencies into your speech, apply the following guidelines:

- *Display your transparencies only when you talk about them.* Place your first slide on the overhead projector, focus it before you begin your speech, and turn the machine off. When you reach the point in your speech where you want to show the image, turn the projector on. Generally, activate the projector only when you want to project an image. Similarly, if you will spend several minutes on material unrelated to the last image you've shown, turn the machine off. If you intend to show several images, especially in rapid succession, it's okay to keep the machine on between them. When you finish with the final image, turn the projector off for good. If the projector is mounted on a mobile stand, push the stand out of your way to give yourself center stage for the remainder of your speech.

- *Number the sheets in the order in which you'll use them.* Use a small sticker or piece of adhesive paper, about the size of a quarter, for each transparency. Write a number plainly on each dot and place it in the upper right corner of the image. Place each dot consistently in such a way that the dots guide you toward placing the transparency on the projector properly so that the image will appear correctly on the screen. Then make a pile of the transparencies in the order in which you will use them, each with the dot in the same position on the page.

- *Practice with your transparencies before you give your speech.* Take a few minutes before the day of your speech to find out exactly how to position the projector, turn the machine on and off, place your images on the glass properly, and focus the image on the screen. Then practice facing your imaginary audience the way you'll speak to the real audience on the day of your speech.

▲ Although most speakers in the workplace use digital slides in their presentations, it's a good idea to know how to use overhead transparencies. They are easy to prepare and use, and they're still often used in academic settings.

FLIP CHARTS

Sometimes speakers want to document good ideas brought up during an interactive brainstorming session. An excellent medium for accomplishing this is a **flip chart** placed

> A large pad of paper that rests on an easel, allowing a speaker to record text or drawings with markers during a speech.

near the speaker or large sheets of paper propped up on an easel. Even the biggest high-tech companies routinely use flip charts for their in-person brainstorming sessions. The audience stays lively during such interactive meetings, as long as the meeting is attended by a relatively small number of people. In large spaces with large audiences, flip charts won't hold the audience's attention or serve the purpose of facilitating interaction among audience members.

WHITE BOARDS AND CHALKBOARDS

A smooth white board that can be written or drawn on with markers.

Using a **white board** with colored pens, or even a chalkboard with white chalk, can help you achieve the same outcome as a flip chart or an easel. The board, however, should be used *only* when brainstorming with the audience about ideas, never for presenting materials. Although it may be tempting, don't even use it for posting telephone numbers, web addresses, mailing addresses, and the like. Turning your back to the audience while you scribble something on the board can make you look less prepared and professional than you are. You'll be more effective if you project this sort of information in a digital slide during the speech or put it in a handout for distribution after you conclude your speech.

DOCUMENT CAMERAS

A projection device that uses a video camera to capture and display images, including 3-D visual materials.

Document cameras function somewhat like overhead projectors but provide far more sophisticated features. Unlike overhead projectors, which use light and mirrors to display the image on a transparency, document cameras use a video camera to capture and display the image. Document cameras allow you to zoom in on a specific part of an image, capture an image for later use, and show highly detailed images—abilities an overhead projector lacks. As with all presentation media, prepare the images you want to display well in advance and practice using the document camera so you're comfortable with all its features.

VIDEO

To determine whether you should use a video clip in your speech, ask yourself whether it will contribute something truly important to your speech. Showing a video clip can elicit an emotional response from the audience and improve their recall of your speech.[1] But it also changes the mood of the speech and may disturb the relationship between speaker and audience.

With the availability of online video sites such as YouTube, searching for and identifying a relevant video clip has become much easier than it used to be. If you decide to incorporate a video clip into your speech, consider these guidelines:

- *Keep the clip short.* With other visual media, speakers continue talking while showing the images or text. Unless you turn off the audio for the clip, you can't speak while it's playing, so you lose valuable speaking time. In addition, a lengthy video clip takes the audience's attention away from the speaker. Choose a short clip for maximum impact.
- *Treat the video as an integral part of your speech.* Determine how you will transition into and out of the video to provide a seamless experience for your audience.
- *If possible, embed the video within your digital slides.* Presentation software such as PowerPoint and Keynote allows you to embed video in a slide so you can avoid relying on a separate piece of equipment, such as a DVD projector.

Be wary of incorporating a stimulating video clip at the risk of neglecting the most important elements of your speech—the content and the delivery. In addition, keep in mind that relating a film clip to your speech in a way that truly advances your purpose can prove challenging. Audience members may enjoy watching a brief video clip, but it may not inform or persuade them in ways related to your topic.

HANDOUTS

The paper **handout** can be very effective in some instances. For example, you might use a handout to provide a list of website addresses where audience members can make donations to a charity you've described in a persuasive speech. You might give your audience a diagram illustrating how to administer emergency cardiopulmonary resuscitation (CPR) treatment. You could hand out copies of a letter you've written to your state senator promoting tougher child pornography laws, and encourage your listeners to sign and mail them.

> Sheets of paper containing relevant information that are distributed before, during, or after a speech.

Some speakers use a handout in conjunction with other presentation media.[2] For instance, you might use digital slides to provide photographic detail and graphic summaries of the effectiveness of a new cancer-treating drug, then pass out a handout that provides a list of websites where the audience can find additional information about the new treatment.

If you decide to use a handout, think carefully about when you'll distribute it. You have three options: Before you begin the speech, during the speech, or after you conclude. To help you decide which option to use, determine when the audience needs the

Extending the Speech

Experienced speakers use various techniques to extend and enhance the audience's experience beyond the original presentation. For instance, some speakers use a handout that indicates how to contact the speaker or the persons or institutions mentioned in the speech, where to locate relevant web resources, or how to review the digital slides that were presented. Speakers can also collect the e-mail addresses of audience members and send the slides to them after the speech. In some cases, speakers dispense with showing digital slides in their speeches and mail the slides to audience members afterward.

information. Also think about how the physical act of distributing the handout will affect your speech performance. Passing paper around the room is noisy and may disrupt your audience's attention and concentration. In addition, the audience will read the handout and not pay attention to you. All things considered, it's almost always best to distribute handouts *after* you finish your formal remarks.[3]

MODELS

A copy of an object, usually built to scale, that represents the object in detail.

For certain subjects, physical **models** that represent the topic being discussed can add a helpful, sometimes necessary, visual dimension to a speech. Models are especially useful for describing and explaining scientific topics that involve a physical structure. For instance, the molecular structure of an atom can be demonstrated with a model. A small-scale replica of fossil remains can help a speaker describe the physical characteristics of an extinct species. In fact, speeches about medical and biological topics such as the anatomy of the brain or the physiology of hearing would be difficult to present *without* the appropriate model.

Other types of speech topics also lend themselves to the use of models. Community planners and architects often use models to promote their ideas. For example, a model of a proposed new building for the community or campus helps audience members visualize what the structure would look like. An alternative to using a physical model is to use a software program that allows you to project animated three-dimensional models onto a screen. This option eliminates the two greatest disadvantages of using physical models: their small size, which limits the audience's ability to see the model, and the difficulty of trying to handle or show the model during the speech.

SOUND RECORDINGS

Sound, like visual images, can stimulate mental images, triggering the imagination and setting a mood. Sound can provide examples of something that is difficult to explain with words. How might you convince your audience that a proposal for a new freeway through your city is a bad idea? Play a tape of traffic noise—loudly. How might you set the mood for a demonstration of massage therapy? Begin with a few seconds of calming ambient music, played softly. Of course, keep your audience in mind: Avoid music or other sounds that would offend or alienate audience members, such as songs containing profane or sexually explicit language.

Audio technology is usually relatively easy to manage. If the place where you'll be speaking doesn't provide audio equipment, bring your own portable CD or MP3 player and speakers. Better yet, embed the audio file in a digital slide so that you can transition into and out of your audio clip smoothly. Set the volume high enough so everyone can hear the sound clearly, but don't turn it up so loud that it annoys your audience. Some public speakers briefly sing or play an acoustic instrument as part of their speeches. That can be effective too; just don't confuse giving a speech with giving a concert.

Using Computer Technology

▼ Depending on the speaking context, you may want to use a computer to enhance your presentation. The two computer technologies speakers use most commonly are digital slides and real-time web access.

DIGITAL SLIDES: DO'S AND DON'TS

Because of its dominant position, the name PowerPoint has become synonymous with presentation software, but as Mac users know, Apple has presentation software too—Keynote, an easy-to-use program that is rapidly gaining in popularity. **Presentation software** allows computer users to display information in multimedia slide shows.

Without question, presentation software—including Corel Presentations, Lotus Freelance Graphics, and MagicPoint as well as PowerPoint and Keynote—is the most versatile and dynamic multimedia tool for most public speaking purposes. It provides all the advantages of the slide projector, and none of the technical disadvantages. But not every speech or occasion calls for the use of digital slides. Many audiences have tired of overblown PowerPoint-driven speeches. Some classrooms and boardrooms have banned the use of PowerPoint.[4] Still, when used appropriately, presentation software can be very effective.

> Computer software that allows users to display information in multimedia slide shows.

You may already feel comfortable and confident using PowerPoint or Keynote. If you're just getting started, consult the online help and documentation that come with the software. Your school may also provide tutorials for learning how to use presentation software. You can also find free tutorials online. When used in moderation, presentation software can help you produce a more conversational and engaging presentation.[5] But remember: *Presentation software will not give your speech for you*. Nor should it be more prominent than you, the speaker.[6] You give a "speech," not a "PowerPoint presentation," and you and your message must remain the primary focal points.

To use digital slides effectively, follow these guidelines:

- *Carefully develop your speech and then consider how you'll support your oral materials with digital slides*. Avoid taking the reverse approach, overpreparing your digital slides and underpreparing the rest of your presentation. The success of your speech depends primarily on the quality of what you've got to say.[7]

- *Use digital slides sparingly*. Audiences tire of too much visual information and will tune you out if they feel visually overwhelmed.[8] When used inappropriately, digital slides take the emotion and personality out of the speech and diminish the vital connection between speaker and audience.[9] Use digital slides in a way that keeps your audience connected to you and your topic.

- *Balance creativity with clarity and predictability with spontaneity*. Avoid depending on the standard templates, clip art, and animation techniques that presentation software programs provide. Because PowerPoint is so widely used today, everyone immediately recognizes those predictable visual forms. Research has found that although audiences generally prefer digital slides to overhead transparencies, the software's animations and sound effects are viewed negatively.[10] Keep your slides clear and easy for the audience to understand.

The next section provides more specific strategies for designing slides and managing the computer hardware for presenting them.

DIGITAL SLIDE DESIGN TIPS

With presentation software, you have more elements to consider than with other visual media. For example, you can make visual transitions from one slide to the next and select special effects that animate your graphical material. These features represent real advantages over other presentation media, but only when you use them strategically and sparingly.

The general guidelines for visual design presented in Table 11.2 outline most of what you need to know about designing digital slides. If you use presentation software, keep the following additional guidelines in mind when designing the slides for your speech:

- *Avoid relying on text or numbers.* The most effective use of presentation software is for visual, not textual or numerical, representation. The visuals may be still or moving images. (See **Figure 11.1**.)
- *Limit the number of bullet points for each slide.* If you decide to use text, don't bore your audience with lengthy, wordy slides. Use a maximum of four to six bullet points per slide. (See **Figure 11.2**.)
- *Limit the number of words for each bullet point.* Use just a few words or a brief phrase for each bullet point. (See **Figure 11.3**.)
- *Make the type font large and clean.* Keep the font size large (40-point and above for titles; 20-point and above for text), and stay away from script or overly abstract lettering styles. Use sans-serif fonts, such as Arial, Verdana, and Geneva, for maximum readability. (See **Figure 11.4**.)
- *Choose transitions that fit the tone of your topic and visual material.* Presentation software gives you many ways to transition from one slide to the next. Good choices include "fade through black" and "dissolve." Keynote also includes three-dimensional transitions, such as "page flip" and "revolving

Definitions of Patriotism

Merriam Webster Dictionary: love for or devotion to one's country

Wiktionary: Love of country; devotion to the welfare of one's country; the virtues and actions of a patriot; the passion which inspires one to serve one's country.

Ultralingua Online Dictionary: Love of country and willingness to sacrifice for it.

Cambridge International Dictionary of English: when you love your country and are proud of it

Infoplease Dictionary: devoted love, support, and defense of one's country; national loyalty

The Wordsmyth English Dictionary: love for, and devotion and loyalty to, one's nation

▲ **FIGURE 11.1**
Too Much Text

TYPES OF PERFORMING ARTS

- *Juggling*
- *Dance*
- *Circuses*
- *Magic*
- *Opera*
- *Musicals*

- *Storytelling*
- *Art Festivals*
- *Fire Arts*
- *Variety Entertainment*
- *Comedy*

▲ **FIGURE 11.2**
Too Many Bullet Points

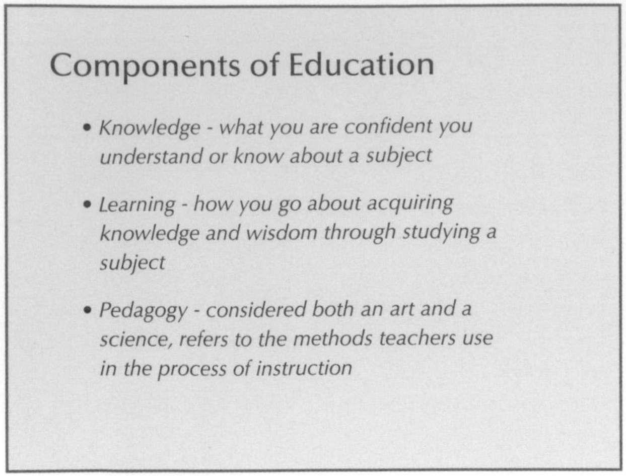

▲ **FIGURE 11.3**
Wordy Bullet Points

▲ **FIGURE 11.4**
Large, Clean Type Font

door." Within a speech, use the same type of transition for all your slides to give the audience a sense of consistency.

- *Avoid special effects.* Special effects allow you to manipulate the visual field of a digital slide in order to put portions of the field in motion. For instance, you can have an image "fly" in from top or bottom, left or right. Audiences usually find these effects annoying and distracting. Any special effect you use should serve a purpose directly related to your speech purpose.

· · · · · · · · · · **THE EVOLVING ART**

Using Color

When deciding which colors to use for your digital slides, choose colors that produce high contrast or the greatest difference between the background and the type. The higher the contrast, the easier it is for audiences to see the type against the background, which in turn makes it easier to read. For example, designing digital slides using a dark background color like dark blue, and a much lighter color for the type, like pale yellow, provides a strong contrast. Some- times it makes sense to match the colors of your slides to the event or organization, such as your school's colors for a presentation that concerns your campus.

HARDWARE SET-UP TIPS

The hardware you use for your presentation software depends mainly on the equipment your school and instructor can make available. Fortunately, many schools and businesses are well equipped to handle PowerPoint, Keynote, and similar software. Your institution may provide a computer and an LCD projector in the room where you'll present your speech. In that case, you'll probably only have to save your digital slides on a flash drive and bring it with you. Familiarize yourself with the equipment in the room well before the day of your speech.

When equipment is not readily available, you may decide to use your own laptop and connect it to a projector supplied by your school. Many speakers find this to be the best solution because they feel most comfortable using their own computers. Any setup you use will require careful planning. Even if you bring your own equipment, know how to make it function properly in the room where you'll be speaking.

If you'd like greater freedom to move around the room during your speech, use a remote control device when you present your digital slides. With a remote, you can advance the slides whenever you want from any place in the room.

REAL-TIME WEB ACCESS

Today more and more classrooms and meeting rooms have internet access, which gives you the option of displaying a website during your speech, a dynamic resource that can be very useful for certain kinds of presentations. When applied to speechmaking, this functionality is termed **real-time web access** (RWA). With RWA you navigate in real time through web pages associated with your topic. You can use RWA to demonstrate how to do something special on the web, such as researching an idea, checking the current status of any topic, or displaying articles found on websites that support your purpose or argument. This web evidence, or **webidence,** gives your presentation an in-the-moment feeling not possible with static digital slides.[11] Because the audience understands that you are functioning in real time, you can also encourage audience participation in your navigations or searches.

The spontaneous nature of RWA and webidence can be used to the speaker's advantage. Still, if you plan to display a web page in real time during your speech, check

▲ Vice President Al Gore won an Academy Award for his documentary, *An Inconvenient Truth.* The film depicts him talking about global warming to a variety of audiences, using powerful images in digital slides to dramatize his points. How could you use digital slides in a creative way to enhance the message of a speech?

Employing a live internet feed as a visual media or information resource during a public speech.

Web sources displayed as evidence during a speech, found by using real-time web access or webpage capture software.

Using Digital Slides

◀◀ ❚❚ ▶▶

Erin introduces sample digital slides and highlights design successes and failures.

PowerPoint Makeover

WATCH It
Watch your
Speech Buddy
video.

USE It
Complete
your
USE It
activity . . .

. . . and apply what
you've learned
to your speech.

This activity gives you a chance to evaluate several digital slides and suggest ways to improve them.

immediately beforehand to make sure access is possible and that the site you intend to show is available.

Tips for Using Presentation Media

▼ Presentation media can enhance your effectiveness as a speaker but can also detract from your message if not used correctly. The following tips will help you integrate presentation media into your speech successfully.

CONSIDER YOUR ROOM AND THE AUDIENCE

To get the maximum effect from your presentation media, be sure you have easy access to the equipment while you speak. Project your images at a height and distance that will make them easily visible for everyone in the audience. In some cases, this may require moving a table to a better position.

When using digital slides or any other media that requires a screen, avoid turning toward the screen where the images are projected. Remain facing your audience while they look at the screen. One advantage of digital slides and real-time web access is that the same images appear on your computer screen. You will always know exactly what's on the big screen simply by observing what's on your computer screen.

PRACTICE WITH YOUR MEDIA

When you practice your speech, incorporate your digital slides, document camera images, and other presentation media so you learn to integrate them smoothly into your speech. Sometimes speakers forget about their media as they give their speeches, so include reminders on your note cards indicating when to use your presentation media.

Arriving early and checking on the technical equipment for your speech helps you manage nervousness and avoid technology mishaps. If possible, check the sharpness and placement of projected images before audience members enter the room. Put your transparencies in order. Check the sound quality of your speakers.

Although presentation media greatly enhance the public speaking experience, you must be prepared for those technologies to fail. Sometimes quick repairs are possible; at other times you just have to continue your speech without the technology you'd planned to use. In these cases, you must improvise. Use the chalkboard or white board. Ask for volunteers from the audience to demonstrate a point. Bring backup visual materials, such as overhead transparencies with key images or graphics.

Effectively managing your technology requires planning and practice. Design digital slides, overhead transparencies, audio clips, and other technological components of your presentation well before the day you must give your speech. Practice using the technology so it becomes a natural part of your presentation.

SPEAK TO YOUR AUDIENCE, NOT YOUR MEDIA

Whatever presentation media you use, always keep your focus on the audience. You may be tempted to look at the screen when using projection media. But when you look at the screen, you turn your back on the audience. Listeners will feel ignored, and their attention will wane. Instead, glance at the actual image on the media equipment, such as the computer screen. As you practice with your presentation media, make a conscious effort to face your practice audience or where the audience would be sitting.

Integrating Presentation Media

◄◄ ▌▌ ►►

Anthony introduces examples of speakers who have integrated presentation media into their speeches effectively.

Exhibit A

This activity gives you practice in evaluating the effectiveness of different kinds of presentation media.

SUMMARY

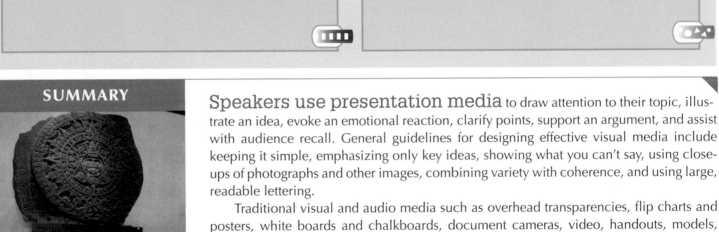

Speakers use presentation media to draw attention to their topic, illustrate an idea, evoke an emotional reaction, clarify points, support an argument, and assist with audience recall. General guidelines for designing effective visual media include keeping it simple, emphasizing only key ideas, showing what you can't say, using close-ups of photographs and other images, combining variety with coherence, and using large, readable lettering.

Traditional visual and audio media such as overhead transparencies, flip charts and posters, white boards and chalkboards, document cameras, video, handouts, models, and sound recordings allow you to enrich your speech. Digital slides have become a frequently used form of presentation media. Although some speakers rely too much on digital slides, the versatility of software programs such as Keynote and PowerPoint offer tremendous flexibility in creating dynamic visual and audio materials.

In the Book

Summary
Key Terms
Critical Challenges

More Study Resources

Speech Studio
Quizzes
WebLinks

Student Workbook

11.1: Brainstorming Images
11.2: Presentation Media Effects
11.3: Slides or a Handout?
11.4: Is It Worth It?
11.5: Edit Your Slides

Speech Buddy Videos

 Video Links

Using Digital Slides
Integrating Presentation Media

Activity Links

PowerPoint Makeover
Exhibit A

▶ Sample Speech Videos

Amanda, "Domestic Violence," problem-cause-solution speech

Cindy, "U.S. Flag Etiquette," informative speech

Speech Builder Express

Visual aids

InfoTrac

Recommended search terms

Presentation tips
Visual aids and public speaking
Visual aid design tips

Audio Study Tools

"Domestic Violence" by Amanda

Critical thinking questions

Learning objectives

Chapter summary

By treating your presentation media as essential components of your speech that require careful preparation and delivery, you can maximize their impact and avoid common problems associated with their use. The key to success in using presentation media is balance: Give media the proper support role in your speech. With all the resources available to you today, remember that *you* are the best delivery system for communicating ideas to your audience.

Guide to Your Online Resources

Your Online Resources for *Public Speaking: The Evolving Art* give you access to the Speech Buddy video and activity featured in this chapter, additional sample speech videos, Speech Builder Express, InfoTrac College Edition, and study aids such as glossary flashcards, review quizzes, and the Critical Challenge questions for this chapter, which you can respond to via e-mail if your instructor requests. In addition, your Online Resources feature live WebLinks relevant to this chapter, including The Gettysburg PowerPoint Presentation, which includes background on how the presentation's slides were developed and statistics on its viewership. Links are regularly maintained, and new ones are added periodically.

Key Terms

document camera 282

flip chart 281

handout 283

model 284

presentation media 277

presentation software 285

real-time web access
 (RWA) 289

transparency 280

webidence 289

white board 282

Critical Challenges

Questions for Reflection and Discussion

1. Although this chapter focuses on how to use presentation media, when should you *not* use them? Why might you not want to use presentation media?

2. Reflect on a public speaking event you've attended recently, or one that you recall particularly well, in which the speaker used presentation media. How effective was the speaker's use of presentation media? How did the media add to the speech? Were there ways in which the presentation media detracted from the speech? How might the speaker have improved his or her use of presentation media?

3. With digital visual and audio files, it's easy to alter an original photograph, video, song, or taped conversation. What are a speaker's ethical responsibilities when developing presentation media for a speech?

12 DELIVERING YOUR SPEECH

AP/W de World Photos

Delivery refers to presenting a speech in public. When you deliver a speech, you merge its verbal and visual components into a presentation before an audience. Scholars have long recognized the importance of delivery for the effective public speaker.[1] All the planning, researching, and organizing you've done for your speech will fall by the wayside if you haven't also developed your delivery skills. The volume of your voice, your posture, how you manage your time during a speech—all of these and more are aspects of delivery.

Your instructor will not expect perfection from your first speech—or any speech, as there is always room for improvement. However, you want to make the best impression you can and achieve your goals for the speech. In this chapter we'll discuss several aspects of effective delivery: selecting an appropriate delivery method; understanding factors that influence a speaker's delivery; managing your voice, body, and audience during your speech; preparing your presentation outline; and practicing your speech.

delivery
The public presentation
of a speech.

Selecting a Delivery Method

▼ **READ it** There are four types of delivery methods: impromptu, extemporaneous, manuscript, and memorized. **Table 12.1** provides an overview of these four methods and the best situations in which to use them. A good rule of thumb is to adopt a style of delivery that enhances the content of your speech and doesn't distract your audience.

IMPROMPTU SPEAKING

Human beings are natural and spontaneous communicators. In your everyday conversations at home, at work, and everywhere else, you constantly communicate random thoughts that spring up in the moment. You do so with no preparation or practice whatsoever.

A type of public speaking in which the speaker has little or no time to prepare a speech.

In public speaking, delivery with little or no preparation is called **impromptu speaking**. Speaking in an impromptu fashion can help you learn how to think and speak on your feet.

TABLE 12.1 ▶ Delivery Methods

METHOD	BRIEF DEFINITION	ADVANTAGES	DISADVANTAGES	TYPICAL SITUATIONS
Impromptu	Speaking without preparation	Flexibility; complete spontaneity	Not researched; can be disorganized; speaker has little, if any, time to practice	Responding to audience questions
Extemporaneous	Giving a speech that has been planned, researched, organized, and practiced	Allows speaker to develop expertise on a topic; allows structured spontaneity; allows speaker to adjust to audience feedback	Researching, organizing, and practicing a speech is time-consuming	Most classroom, professional, and community presentations
Manuscript	Giving a speech that has been written out word for word	Allows speaker to choose each word precisely and time the speech exactly	Speaker uses written rather than spoken language; difficult to modify based on audience feedback	Political speeches
Memorized	Giving a speech that has been committed to memory	Allows speaker to present speech without notes; same speech can be presented many times	Can seem artificial; requires intensive practice	Short ceremonial speeches

Learning how to express yourself on the spot without relying on research, extensive preparation, or notes will help you do well in your public speaking class and in less structured speaking situations beyond the classroom.

An impromptu speaker is given a topic on the spot and often has a minute or two to think about what to say. The idea of impromptu speaking terrifies many people, but if you think about it, life itself is impromptu. For example, when you answer a question in class or speak up during a meeting of a campus organization, you're using impromptu speaking. In this respect, impromptu speaking is simply another way to use the basic communication skills you already have and use regularly.

What should you do in an impromptu speaking situation? **Figure 12.1** provides questions you can ask yourself to quickly develop and organize your thoughts. When you present your speech, do your best to speak coherently. Keep your general purpose in mind—are you informing, persuading, or entertaining your audience about your topic? Don't worry about making mistakes—no one expects an impromptu speech to be perfect.

EXTEMPORANEOUS SPEAKING

For **extemporaneous speaking**, you carefully research, organize, and rehearse your speech before you deliver it. This approach to speaking captures much of the freshness of impromptu speaking, but an extemporaneous speaker has plenty of time to plan and practice. Because of its balance of these characteristics, extemporaneous speaking is sometimes called "structured spontaneity." When you appear spontaneous, your speech comes across as a natural form of communication, not as a rigid or premeditated message. Speaking extemporaneously helps you deliver your message in a fresh and engaged way, greatly maximizing your chances of connecting with your audience and having your speech achieve its purpose. Although the impromptu, manuscript, and memorized delivery methods have their time and place, the extemporaneous method is the most common and the most desirable because its structured spontaneity usually makes it the most effective.

MANUSCRIPT SPEAKING

When politicians and world leaders give speeches, they often appear to be speaking from just a few notes as they look directly at the audience and the camera. However, they're often reading from a teleprompter that displays a manuscript speech—a speech written out word for word. One advantage of **manuscript speaking** is that you can compose the exact language you want to use for your speech. In situations in which a misspoken word

▼ FIGURE 12.1

Developing and Organizing Your Impromptu Speeches

- What is my topic?
- What are my thoughts and feelings about the topic? (Use keywords and phrases to capture your ideas.)
- How do I want to organize my ideas on the topic? (Identify an order for your thoughts.)
- What is a good way to begin my speech? (Write down a few sentences or phrases that will help you begin.)
- What is a good way to end my speech? (Write down a few sentences or phrases that will give your speech closure.)

A type of public speaking in which the speaker researches, organizes, rehearses, and delivers a speech in a way that combines structure and spontaneity.

A type of public speaking in which the speaker reads a written script word for word.

might lead to a tragic misunderstanding—such as when negotiating a peace treaty—manuscript speaking is necessary to maintain absolute precision. However, most of us will never have to speak in such sensitive situations.

You might think it's easier to give your speech from a manuscript—you just write it out and read it to your audience. But reading from a manuscript greatly reduces your ability to make eye contact with your listeners, leaving your audience members feeling ignored and you unable to adapt to their feedback. In addition, when speakers write out their entire speech word for word, they tend to use written rather than spoken language. Because written language is more complex and less personal than spoken language, audience members tend to tune out a speaker who is using language that's meant for reading rather than listening. Audiences tend to favor an extemporaneous style, so avoid reading a speech from a manuscript unless the situation calls for it.

MEMORIZED SPEAKING

A type of public speaking in which the speaker commits a speech to memory.

When delivering a memorized speech, the speaker commits the entire speech to memory and then presents it to an audience. **Memorized speaking** may seem like a perfect solution if you're worried about forgetting what you want to say during your speech. However, memorization can cause several problems. First, if you forget a line, or even a word, you may find it difficult to recover and continue your speech. Second, you can't adapt to audience responses during your speech. Third, memorized speeches often seem artificial and lack spontaneity.

On the other hand, memorized speaking can be useful and appropriate in certain situations. For short speeches, such as a wedding toast or acceptance of an award, knowing exactly what you're going to say reduces the chances that you'll sound unprepared or make off-the-cuff comments you'll regret later. And memorizing *small sections* of your speech, such as your introduction, key transitions, and conclusion, helps reduce anxiety and can increase your self-confidence.

Understanding Factors That Influence Delivery

The speaking situation and speech type are external factors that help determine how you will deliver your speech. This section addresses four important factors unique to each speaker that influence delivery: culture, gender, language fluency and dialect, and physical disabilities.

CULTURE

When you give a speech, your listeners want you to perform well. They expect you to speak more loudly and briskly than usual, to move dynamically, to use gestures, and to emphasize key ideas with flair. Some students find this type of speech difficult to master because it is so different from the way they speak in most social situations.

Cultural factors can also influence how a speaker behaves in front of an audience. For example, the Chinese often say that "only fools shoot off their mouths." In fact, people from China, Japan, Korea, Vietnam, and other East Asian countries often consider it unthinkable to consciously draw attention to themselves. This doesn't mean that in Asian cultures people are passive. Rather, it means that authority, power, strength, and intelligence are to be demonstrated in other ways, such as by showing responsibility to loved ones. Culture also influences how audiences perceive speakers. For example, what American audiences perceive as nervousness in a speaker may be viewed as modesty by Asian audiences.[2] If, based on your cultural, social, or family background, you're used to asserting yourself in more subtle ways, you might have to develop new skills to adapt to the expectations of American audiences.

GENDER

In the past, audiences evaluated female and male speakers differently. For example, men were granted higher status and greater credibility, while women were typically judged based on their clothing and physical attractiveness.[3] Much has changed over the years, and some of the most powerful and eloquent speakers today, such as Maureen Dowd, Condoleezza Rice, Madeleine Albright, and Oprah Winfrey, are well-respected women. Yet research shows that audiences still tend to evaluate speakers based on their sex.

Research in college public speaking classrooms shows that a speaker's gender has little impact on *overall* evaluations of competence: Male and female speakers are viewed as equally capable. However, male speakers are often viewed as more influential and persuasive, even when female and male speakers display similar behaviors. In addition, audiences seem to judge men's and women's credibility differently. Female speakers' credibility tends to rest primarily on their use of trustworthy information sources. In contrast, male speakers' credibility enjoys a broader base, including not only believable sources but also eye contact, organization of ideas, and vocal variety.[4] Of course, as we've discussed, many factors contribute to a speaker's credibility, regardless of gender. A woman who avoids making eye contact, speaks in a monotone, and organizes her points poorly risks making a negative impression on the audience. By the same token, a man who relies only on his voice, eye contact, and speech structure to win over listeners likely will earn low marks as a speaker.

The most challenging delivery issue women face is making themselves heard. Women generally speak at a higher pitch and a lower volume than men, making women's voices more difficult to hear. **Pitch** is the highness or lowness of the speaker's voice, and **volume** is the loudness of the speaker's voice. This difference stems partly from biology—women have shorter vocal cords than men—and partly from culture—girls are expected to talk more quietly than boys.[5] Whatever the reason, female speakers usually must work harder than male speakers to project their voices. Speaking more loudly and at a slightly lower pitch while delivering a speech may feel odd at first because we're used to hearing our voices sound a certain way. But good vocal volume is essential to public speaking—you want your audience to hear your message.

The use of vocal pitch also affects how audiences judge a woman's confidence as a speaker. One way you indicate you're asking a question is to raise the pitch of your voice. Read the following aloud: "How are gender and delivery related in public speaking?" Notice how your voice went up naturally when you said the word *speaking*. Now read this aloud: "Gender affects vocal characteristics in public speaking." This time, notice how your pitch went down with the word *speaking*. When a speaker's voice goes up at the end of a statement, audience members view the speaker as less confident and unsure of the information presented. Research suggests that women tend to do this more than men,[6] so women speakers should watch for this problem, and correct it if necessary, as they practice their speeches.

LANGUAGE FLUENCY AND DIALECT

Stuttering is one of the more common speech impairments that affect public speakers. Researchers estimate that more than 3 million Americans stutter, although most children who stutter cease to do so as they grow older.[7] People who stutter are often characterized as nervous, shy, introverted, and fearful. Research shows these attributes are completely unfounded, yet fluent speakers continue to view people who stutter negatively. However, people who stutter can employ two strategies to change those negative perceptions: acknowledgment and eye contact. Research has found that simply acknowledging you stutter improves your fluency and causes the audience to view you more favorably. Similarly, making eye contact with your audience may not reduce your stuttering, but it will help others view you more positively and respond in more supportive ways. In addition, making eye contact with your audience encourages you to focus on them rather than on yourself, reducing your speech anxiety. Moreover, you're better able to monitor your audience's feedback and respond to it appropriately.[8]

The highness or lowness of a speaker's voice.

The loudness of a speaker's voice.

AP Images/Tiffany Michalka

▲ Because women's voices are often harder to hear than men's voices, women speakers must use strategies to make sure their audiences hear them. Even when women use a microphone, speaking at a higher volume and with a slightly lower pitch will help their audiences understand them.

Dialect is another factor that influences delivery. A **dialect** is the vocabulary, grammar, and pronunciation used by a group of people. Everyone speaks in some dialect, even if they don't recognize it. Although dialects are often associated with specific regions of the United States, such as the South and New England, dialects can also be ethnically based, as with African-American English and Cajun or Creole English.[9] A speaker's dialect is detected in the words used and how they are pronounced. For example, Cajun English replaces the "th" sound with "t" or "d." The phrase "make a bill" means "buy groceries," while "making groceries" means "go grocery shopping."[10]

Dialects can reveal rich cultural traditions and help bind a group together. No dialect is inferior to any other way of speaking, although historically public speaking students have been encouraged to speak in the mainstream American English dialect that most newscasters use.[11] The importance of examining dialect rests in how well your audience can understand you. When you're talking with others in your own dialect group, you don't notice how you use language. But when you speak in front of an audience, you must be more aware of how you use language so that you can ensure your audience understands your message. Does this mean you must learn to speak like a newscaster? No. If you articulate your words clearly, pronounce them correctly, and define terms that might be unfamiliar to your audience, you will be able to bridge most of the differences between your dialect and your audience's.

> The vocabulary, grammar, and pronunciation used by a specific group of people, such as an ethnic or regional group.

PHYSICAL IMPAIRMENTS

Speakers with physical impairments encounter certain issues when they make public presentations. The followng sections offer strategies for speakers using mobility aids and speakers with visual or hearing impairments.

Speakers Using Mobility Aids

Speakers who use crutches or a walker must consider several issues before presenting a speech. First, identify your plan for approaching and leaving the speaker's area to make the minutes before and after your speech as stress-free as possible. Be sure your path to and from the area is unobstructed and easy to reach. Second, determine whether you'll be comfortable standing for your entire presentation. Third, find the best way to manage your note cards. As you practice your speech, you may find that you become uncomfortable or needlessly tired if you stand throughout your speech, or that standing interferes with handling your cards. In either case, you may want to consider sitting for your presentation.

Speakers who use a wheelchair may need to pay special attention to visibility and voice projection. You can increase your visibility by not having a large object, such as a table, between you and your audience. This will allow you to get physically closer to your

© Bob Daemmrich/The Image Works

▲ If you use a mobility aid, reduce stress when you give a speech by planning ahead. For example, consider how you'll approach and leave the speaker's area.

listeners and will keep the focus on you. You'll also be free to move if that's practical and helps emphasize an idea.

Practice speaking so that you attain the best possible voice projection. Sit up as straight as possible, take a deep breath, and breathe out as you speak. To check your volume, practice with a friend in a room that is similar in size to the one where you'll be speaking. Have your friend sit at the back of the room and tell you when your voice can be easily heard. If voice projection is still a problem, use a microphone.

Speakers with Visual Impairments

About 10 million Americans are visually impaired.[12] For public speakers with visual impairments, the key issue is how to recall everything you want to say. Memorization is a safe strategy for short speeches, but committing long speeches to memory is a challenge. Notes in braille are a good solution. If you don't read braille but are able to read large print, try using big note cards with clearly written keywords.

If your visual impairment is such that written notes are not feasible, you might consider three alternatives. First, develop your speech by capturing your ideas on an MP3 player (such as an iPod) or other digital audio recording device, revising until you are satisfied with the speech. Using an earbud, present the speech as you listen to it on an MP3 player. Second, if you write in braille, write out your speech, have a sighted person record it in a digital format, and use the MP3 player as in the first strategy. Keep in mind that listening to and saying your speech at the same time is quite difficult to do and takes considerable practice. The third alternative is to write out your speech and have a sighted person present it for you. You should then be prepared to answer questions after the speech.

Speakers with Hearing Impairments

The Gallaudet Research Institute estimates that nearly 20.3 million people in the United States are deaf or hard of hearing.[13] As a public speaker with a hearing impairment, consider your ability to hear and your comfort with using your voice. If you usually communicate using American Sign Language (ASL), signing and using a sign-to-voice interpreter is a logical choice. If you're confident about your vocal abilities, present your speech aloud. During the question-and-answer session, ask listeners to state questions loudly and clearly, or request a microphone for audience members to use.

People with impairments should adapt the preceding techniques to suit their own physical, cognitive, and sensory requirements. There's no need to tell your audience why you are doing things your way.[14] If you have an impairment that affects your speech delivery, you may want to discuss the matter with your instructor so you'll get the most out of your public speaking class and your audience will get the most out of your speeches.

Managing Your Voice during Your Speech

▼   Your voice is a key tool for getting your audience's attention, emphasizing points, stirring emotions, and conveying the content of your message. Good voice volume, variations in vocal qualities, minimal pauses, and clear articulation and pronunciation are essential for effective public speaking.

SPEAK LOUDLY ENOUGH

Right from the beginning of your speech, speak so that everyone in your audience can hear you. This may take some practice if you feel uncomfortable raising your voice volume above a normal speaking level. However, sufficient volume is crucial; audience members shouldn't have to strain to hear you. If you're not sure what "loud enough" sounds like, practice with a friend in the room where you'll present the speech, or in a similar space. Have your friend sit in the farthest corner of the room, and raise your voice volume until she or he can easily hear you.

VARY YOUR RATE, PITCH, AND VOLUME

Differences stand out to us; sameness does not. Not every point or statement included in a speech carries the same weight or tone. Some parts of your speech may be on the lighter side, others more serious. A faster **rate** (the speed at which a speaker speaks), higher pitch, and louder volume suggest energy and excitement. A slower rate, lower pitch, and softer volume indicate a more solemn and contemplative tone. Speaking in a **monotone**, or without altering pitch, signals that the speaker is petrified or is unexcited about his or her topic. Use **vocal variety** to fit your topic and evoke emotion in the audience.

The speed at which a speaker speaks.

A way of speaking in which the speaker does not alter his or her pitch.

Changes in the volume, rate, and pitch of a speaker's voice that affect the meaning of the words delivered.

AVOID VOCALIZED PAUSES

Some speakers talk more rapidly in front of an audience; others speak more slowly. When giving your speech, observe the time it takes to present the introduction. Is it

Banishing Vocalized Pauses

In everyday conversations, you know it's your turn to speak when the other person pauses. But sometimes you pause even when you're not finished speaking—you're trying to formulate the next point you want to make, or you can't quite think of the word you want. You don't want the other person to jump in and start talking, so you say "ah" or "um" to tell the other person, "I'm not done talking yet." This habit carries over to public speaking. What happens when you pause while presenting your speech? Will audience members start talking? Of course not. But old habits are hard to break. When you hear yourself using a vocalized pause, concentrate on just pausing—your audience will wait for you. Also, as you practice your speech you'll become more sure of what you want to say, reducing those "ahs" and "ums."

"Ah," "um," "you know," and other verbal fillers that speakers use when they're trying to think of what they want to say.

The physical process of producing specific speech sounds to make language intelligible.

The act of saying words correctly according to the accepted standards of the speaker's language.

about the same as when you practiced? Less? More? If you used less time, assess your speaking rate. Are you zooming through your speech, anxious to get it over with? Are you running words together, so audience members can't understand you? Are you out of breath because you're not pausing between sentences and phrases? On the flip side, if you used more time for your introduction than when you practiced, perhaps you're speaking too slowly. Are you using a lot of **vocalized pauses** such as "ah," "umm," and "you know"? These verbal fillers use up time without providing any information. And they hurt your credibility because they make you sound unsure of yourself.[15]

ARTICULATE YOUR WORDS CLEARLY AND PRONOUNCE THEM CORRECTLY

Everyday speech is usually casual and often sloppy. Most speakers give in to poor **articulation**, leaving off the endings of words ("I'm leavin' soon"), skipping sounds entirely ("I'm gonna leave in twenny minutes"), and running words together ("Waddaya think?"). Poor articulation isn't necessarily a problem in casual conversation, but articulating poorly during a speech may cause your audience to strain to understand you and may hurt your credibility. Incorrect **pronunciation** can also damage your credibility. Some common mispronunciations are "git" for *get,* "excape" for *escape,* "pitcher" for *picture,* and "reckanize" for *recognize.* If you're unsure of a word's correct pronunciation, check a dictionary—many online dictionaries include audio files so you can listen to how a word is pronounced. And when you practice your speech in front of a small audience, ask them to point out words you pronounce incorrectly, then practice saying the words aloud correctly until you're comfortable saying them. (See the last section of this chapter for more about practicing your speech.)

Reviewing Vocal Delivery

◀◀ ❚❚ ▶▶

In this video, Janine and Anthony demonstrate effective and ineffective vocal delivery.

Speak Up

This activity asks you first to evaluate various speakers' vocal delivery and then to apply what you're learning about vocal delivery by considering what your own vocal challenges might be.

Managing Your Body during Your Speech

▼ Knowing what to do with your body can significantly reduce speech anxiety. This section outlines specific ways to use facial expressions and body movement effectively when giving your speech.

DRESS FOR THE OCCASION

You may like to think that appearances don't count, but they do, especially in public speaking. Your clothing should enhance your speech and contribute to listeners' perceptions of your dynamism and overall credibility. Dressing appropriately for your speeches demonstrates respect for your audience—you care enough about them and your speech to look your best. Likewise, your physical appearance should not draw unwanted attention. Some instructors require that students dress in corporate business attire for their speeches in order to emphasize the differences between social conversation and public speaking. Your instructor's dress code may not be that formal, but you should dress at least one step up from what you usually wear to school. This advice also applies to audiences outside of school—try to dress about a step up from what you think your audience will be wearing. If you look the part, it will be easier to play the part and manage your nervousness.[16]

FACE YOUR AUDIENCE AND MAKE EYE CONTACT WITH THEM

Your listeners want to know that you're talking to them, not the floor, your notes, a tree outside the window, or a spot on the wall at the back of the room. Really look at all your listeners, from those in the front row to those in the back corners. Avoid simply scanning the room from one side to the other, or looking only at your friends or at classmates who happen to be sitting in the middle of the room, or at your instructor. When you don't look at audience members, they become invisible to you and you become invisible to them.[17] Avoid addressing your audience from a sideways angle or from one side of the room, and *never* speak with your back to the audience. Even when you write something on a chalkboard or white board, turn around and speak to your audience after you've finished writing. Talk to your audience—not to the screen—when using digital slides or an overhead projector. And glance quickly and infrequently at your notes, using them simply to trigger your memory. Good eye contact says you are competent, trustworthy, dynamic, and sociable.

DISPLAY APPROPRIATE FACIAL EXPRESSIONS

You communicate much of how you feel through your face. A smile, frown, or puzzled look can underscore a point. Adjust your facial expression according to the content of your speech and the message you're trying to send. For example, if you smile nervously when talking about a serious topic, such as whether the United States should intervene in the conflict in Darfur, you'll send a mixed message and your audience may misunderstand your intent. However, smiling as you greet your audience before you start your speech lets them know you're pleased to be there.

MAINTAIN GOOD POSTURE

The way a speaker positions and carries her or his body.

Your **posture** is the way you position and carry your body. Shoulders back, head up, hands loosely at your sides, knees slightly bent (don't lock your knees!), feet slightly apart and flat on the floor, with your weight evenly distributed—that's the preferred posture when giving a speech. From this position, you can easily move and gesture. Standing up straight demonstrates your self-assurance; keeping your feet flat on the floor prevents you from shifting your weight from foot to foot or crossing and uncrossing your feet.

MOVE WITH PURPOSE AND SPONTANEITY

The trick to using body movements effectively is to plan them ahead of time but make them appear spontaneous during your speech. When planning your speech, consider what body movements can help you communicate your message in a dynamic way. Will movement help you underscore a point? Demonstrate your confidence? Capture your audience's attention? Now, think about what you can do physically to achieve the effect you want. For example, you might step closer to your listeners to make them feel included, especially when discussing how a point affects them personally. Or you might take a few steps to the left or right to signal a transition from one main point to the next.

Whatever movement you use, make it appear to have a purpose. For example, don't walk around randomly just to release nervous tension—your audience will wonder why you're pacing and may miss what you're saying. In addition, avoid movements that appear staged or overly dramatic. In historic speeches, you sometimes see speakers using stock gestures that were clearly meant to signal specific information, such as holding up three fingers with the statement, "I'll cover three main points in this speech." Today, however, audiences prefer a more natural, conversational style.

AVOID PHYSICAL BARRIERS

In most public speaking contexts, you won't need a podium. In fact, you may be better off not using one. Why? Because a podium puts a physical barrier between you and your audience. In addition, you won't be able to use your entire body to convey your message—most of your body will be hidden behind the podium. You might think, "That's great! The less my audience sees me, the more they'll focus on what I'm saying and the less nervous I'll be." Unfortunately, that's not the case. Instead, your audience will think you look trapped. If you need to use a podium or table to support your visual materials or laptop, stand to the side, not behind the furniture.

RADIATE POSITIVITY

The most fundamental strategy in effectively presenting your speeches is to *radiate positivity*. Facial expressions, posture, gestures, eye contact, dress, tone of voice—everything about you should tell your audience that you're poised, confident, and enthusiastic. Even before you've finished the first sentence of the introduction, your audience should sense that you're delighted to be there and pleased to have the opportunity to talk with them. Avoid self-disparaging comments or attempts at humor that highlight your shortcomings—these will seriously damage your credibility. And remember that you'll think you're more nervous than your audience will, so show you're confident even if you're not feeling that way.[18]

Applying the delivery strategies outlined in these discussions of voice and body will help you give dynamic, engaging, extemporaneous presentations. **Figure 12.2** provides a quick summary of these strategies. After a while most of this will come quite naturally. You'll develop your own style as you become more confident in your public speaking abilities.

WATCH it SPEECH BUDDY VIDEO LINK

Reviewing Physical Delivery

◀◀ ❙❙ ▶▶

In this video, all the Speech Buddies describe and demonstrate different aspects of physical delivery.

USE it ACTIVITY LINK

Stand Tall

This activity gives you a chance to evaluate various speakers' physical delivery and then apply what you're learning in this chapter by considering what your own physical delivery challenges might be.

Managing Your Audience during Your Speech

▼

Managing your audience begins with researching your listeners and designing your message to achieve their goals as well as your own (Chapter 6). If you have developed a speech that your audience finds useful and interesting, and if you present the speech in an enthusiastic, engaging manner, listeners will more likely respond the way you expect them to. You can also help influence an audience's response to you by adjusting your speaking space, involving your audience, respecting your audience's time, accommodating audience members with impairments, responding calmly to rude or hostile audiences, and being prepared for question-and-answer sessions.

ADJUST YOUR SPEAKING SPACE AS NEEDED

Set up the speaking space in a way that's comfortable for you and your audience. Even small modifications can influence how the audience listens to you. For example, if you're in a small conference room with a large table, suggest that audience members turn their chairs so it's easier for them to see you and your digital slides or other presentation aids. This also reduces the likelihood that audience members will talk among themselves. If lighting is harsh or glaring, dim or turn off a few lights so audience members will feel more relaxed. Close doors to hallways and other rooms so you're not interrupted. And in large auditoriums don't be afraid to grab the microphone and get out from behind the podium. Audience members will view you as more confident and personable and will pay more attention to your speech.

INVOLVE YOUR AUDIENCE

When you present your speech, you create a dialogue with your audience. Unlike a monologue, in which one person speaks without any response from others, a dialogue involves reciprocal communication between you and your audience. Of course, the speaker does most of the talking, but audience members communicate too. Managing your audience requires careful attention to your listeners' feedback (Chapter 3).

Make the audience part of your speech by

- Referring to what others have said in their speeches ("As Tasha mentioned in her speech last week . . .").
- Calling on specific audience members ("Hector, what's your reaction to the video clip we just saw?").
- Asking for volunteers ("I need two people to help me demonstrate this process").

▼ FIGURE 12.2

Strategies for Effective Delivery

- Speak loudly enough.
- Vary your voice's rate, pitch, and volume.
- Avoid vocalized pauses.
- Articulate your words clearly and pronounce them correctly.
- Dress for the occasion.
- Face your audience and make eye contact with everyone.
- Display appropriate facial expressions.
- Maintain good posture.
- Move with purpose and spontaneity.
- Avoid physical barriers.
- Radiate positivity.

As you're speaking, observe the audience. Do they seem interested? Bored? Confused? Supportive? Hostile? Enthusiastic? Puzzled? **Nonverbal messages,** such as facial expressions and tone of voice, can be ambiguous. So when managing your audience you may want to check your interpretations. If someone seems confused about a point, you could say, "Anya, you look puzzled. Are you? Other people might be as well, so I can explain that last point in more detail." Some nonverbal behaviors are pretty clear, such as listeners shaking their heads in disagreement or nodding in agreement. Commenting on the behaviors you observe lets your audience know you are interested in their feedback. When you see those shaking heads, you might say, "I see that some of you disagree with me. Let me tell you something that might change your mind." If listeners are nodding, you might say, "I can tell by your reactions that some of you have had the same experience." Again, these strategies allow you to integrate audience members into your speech.

Information that is communicated without words, but rather, through movement, gesture, facial expression, vocal quality, use of time, use of space, and touch.

RESPECT THE AUDIENCE'S TIME

You may be familiar with time-oriented phrases such as "Don't waste my time," "I like to spend my time wisely," and "Time is money." Your listeners will expect you to manage your time effectively. Remember, it's *their* time as well. Make the most of your speaking time so that you achieve your goals and your listeners feel satisfied with the information you've provided.

When you practice your speech, keep your eye on the clock or practice with a watch or stopwatch so that you stay within your time limit. Have a general idea of how much time you spend on each part of your speech. This information will help you pace yourself when presenting your speech to your audience.

As you progress through your speech, monitor your time so that each part of your speech receives adequate attention. For example, if you have three main points and spend half of your speaking time on the first point, you won't be able to fully develop the other two points. On the other hand, as you adjust to your audience's feedback, you may find it necessary to devote more time

▼ Asking an audience member to volunteer for a demonstration is a great way to involve your audience in your speech.

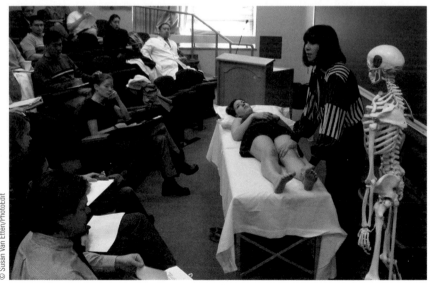

© Susan Van Etten/PhotoEdit

to a particular point and leave out other parts of your speech. For example, you might omit an example or shorten a story in your conclusion. That's part of extemporaneous speaking—adjusting your speech during the presentation.

How can you monitor your time when so many other aspects of delivery demand your attention? Many public speaking instructors use time cards for student speeches. For example, if you have five minutes for your speech, the instructor or a designated student will show you cards that tell you how many minutes you have left. (This is often also true of speeches given at professional conferences and other structured speaking events.) If your instructor doesn't use a timing method, use a watch or stopwatch to keep track of your speaking time.

ACCOMMODATE AUDIENCE MEMBERS WITH IMPAIRMENTS

When presenting a speech to audience members with cognitive, sensory, or physical impairments, accommodate their needs so they can participate fully in the speaking event. Your goal as a speaker is to include everyone and ensure that no one is left out. First, check that audience members who require accommodations have them. For example, an audience member with a hearing impairment may need an interpreter. Second, face the audience so everyone can easily see and hear you. Make sure nothing interferes with your voice projection. Third, be sure to speak loudly, clearly, and not too rapidly. This is especially important for interpreters, who need a moment or two to translate what you're saying. Fourth, describe the content of any visual materials you use, such as digital slides or overhead transparencies, explaining images as well as text. Finally, if you're not sure what you need to do to accommodate audience members, privately ask them before you start your speech.

RESPOND CALMLY TO RUDE OR HOSTILE AUDIENCE MEMBERS

Sometimes audience members express hostility during or after the speech, although this seldom happens in public speaking classes. Some topics can trigger deep emotions. If you're speaking on a controversial topic such as capital punishment or gun control laws, be prepared for negative reactions from audience members who disagree with you. In handling these responses, you must remain calm. Engaging in a shouting match with audience members will damage your credibility. Let hostile audience members know you understand that they disagree with you. If they don't calm down, suggest that you continue the discussion after you've finished your speech.

BE PREPARED FOR A QUESTION-AND-ANSWER PERIOD

Once you've finished your speech, you may be tempted to breathe a sigh of relief and rush off to sit down. However, in many cases audience members will have an opportunity to ask you questions. Researching your audience helps you anticipate those questions; researching your topic helps you answer them. Apply the following guidelines in the question-and-answer session:

- Listen carefully to the question, giving the audience member time to complete it.
- Repeat the question if other audience members couldn't hear it.
- Answer questions as completely as possible.
- If you don't know the answer to a question, admit it and offer to look up the necessary information.

Some speakers dread question-and-answer sessions because they're afraid they won't know an answer and will look foolish. But keep in mind that when audience members ask questions, they're not testing or judging you—they're simply looking for clarification or more information. If you treat the question-and-answer session as a friendly conversation and answer questions as best you can, you'll do fine.

Preparing Your Presentation Outline

In the beginning stages of speech development, you use a working outline (Chapter 4). The complete-sentence outline, described in Chapter 8, elaborates on the working outline by including full sentences detailing all the parts of your speech. The **presentation outline** distills your complete-sentence outline by listing just words and phrases to guide you through the main parts of your speech and the transitions between them. Like the working outline, the presentation outline is brief. Although it may initially be created on-screen or on full sheets of paper, the presentation outline is commonly transferred to note cards for use during practice and the final presentation. **Table 12.2** summarizes the three types of outlines.

> An outline that distills a complete-sentence outline, listing only the words and phrases that will guide the speaker through the main parts of the speech and the transitions between them.

Knowing how to create and use a presentation outline is a fundamental skill for extemporaneous public speaking. The presentation outline allows you to

- Refer comfortably and precisely to the information you have gathered.
- Present that information in a clear and organized way.
- Engage your audience personally and professionally during the speech.

Some students find it difficult to develop the confidence to rely on a relatively small number of words in front of an audience. However, a presentation outline makes it possible for a well-prepared speaker to deliver an abundance of ideas effectively.

TABLE 12.2 ► Types of Outlines

TYPE OF OUTLINE	FUNCTIONS	KEY FEATURES	CHAPTER
Working	Assists in initial topic development; guides research	Includes main points and possible subpoints; revised during research process	4: Developing Your Purpose and Topic
Complete-sentence	Clearly identifies all pieces of information for the speech; puts ideas in order; forms basis for developing the presentation outline	Uses complete sentences; lists all sections of speech and all references; revised during preparation process	8: Organizing and Outlining Your Speech
Presentation	Assists in practicing and giving your speech	Uses keywords; revised as you practice your speech; often transferred to note cards for use during practice and the final presentation	12: Delivering Your Speech ◄ **YOU ARE HERE**

IDENTIFY KEYWORDS

The keywords in a presentation outline are very similar to the keywords or search terms you use online: They identify subjects or points of primary interest or concern. Keywords represent the most important points you want to talk about in your speech, and because they're listed in the same order as the sentences in your complete-sentence outline, they indicate the order in which you want to present those points.

A word that identifies a subject or a point of primary interest or concern.

Although presentation outlines are usually quite short, they can be created only after you've fully researched and developed your speech. However, as you use your presentation outline or note cards to practice your speech, you'll find that you need to move back and forth between your complete-sentence outline and your presentation outline, revising the former and then the latter several times. Each time, you'll be challenged to condense your ideas and information into keywords that will trigger your memory as you present your speech. **Figure 12.3** shows an example of a presentation outline.

Sample Presentation Outline

Title: Feng Shui

Attention getter: (Show four striking visuals revealing *feng shui* principles.)

Thesis: People can have more positive energy if they understand the principles and history of *feng shui* and then apply what they've learned to their everyday lives.

Preview: Today I'll explain the principles, history, and applications of *feng shui* design.

I. Principles
   A. Energy/*chi*
      1. Good *feng shui*
         a. Healthy, positive life
         b. Fortune
      2. Bad *feng shui*
         a. Difficulty
         b. Misfortune
   B. Flow
      1. Harmony
      2. Balance
   C. Design
      1. External principles
         a. Colors
         b. Forms
      2. Internal principles
         a. Colors
         b. Forms

II. History
   A. Origins in ancient China
      1. Culture 5,000 to 6,000 years ago
      2. "Bagua" map
   B. Origins of principles
      1. Space concept
      2. Placement concept

3. Colors concept
　　　　a. Wealth colors
　　　　b. Love colors
　C. Current history
　　　1. Spread of idea in U.S.
　　　2. Spread of idea in other countries
III. Applications
　A. Living spaces
　　　1. House
　　　2. Apartment
　　　3. Dorm room
　B. Using space
　　　1. Room suggestions
　　　2. Placement of objects
　　　3. Connections between elements
　C. Using shapes and colors
　　　1. Round
　　　2. Curves
　　　3. Colors
　　　4. Light

Review: I have described *feng shui* by explaining its basic principles, history, and applications.

Reinforce purpose: *Feng shui* has persisted for centuries in Chinese culture. There must be a reason why.

Closing: *Feng shui* is all about creating positive energy in our lives—who couldn't use a little more of that! Thank you.

TRANSFER INFORMATION FROM YOUR PRESENTATION OUTLINE TO NOTE CARDS

Once you've completed your presentation outline, you're ready to transfer the information from your outline to the five-by-eight-inch note cards you'll use during your speech. Write your keywords on the note cards to remind you of the points you want to cover

Visualizing the Long Quote

You've found a great—though lengthy—quote you want to include in your speech. We've already given you reasons not to write out the quote on your note cards—you'll lose your audience's attention by droning on and on, and you'll look at your notes instead of at your listeners. What should you do? If you're convinced that the quote is essential to your presentation, incorporate it into a presentation aid. To enhance audience members' recall of the quote, you might ask one of them to read it aloud.

in your speech, and organize the cards in the order in which you want to present those points. It's helpful to number your note cards sequentially so that you can easily reorganize them if they get out of order. Stick to your keywords and don't write out a lot of sentences, quotations, or other lengthy bits of information. And make sure the print is large enough for you to read easily as you're giving your speech.

During your presentation, hold your note cards in one hand. The only time you should have both hands on your note cards is when you move from one card to the next. The audience expects you to consult your notes during the speech—it shows you are not just talking off the top of your head or, worse, reciting a memorized speech. Glance at your notes very briefly and infrequently. It's better to lose your place for a second than to hide your face for most of the speech. A good rule of thumb is to *look* at your audience and *glance* at your notes.

CREATE A PERSONAL CUEING SYSTEM

During the speech itself, the note cards serve as a personal *cueing system*: They're always there to cue you, or remind you, of what to say next. Using this technique well requires that you know the subject matter of your speech inside and out. Remember that the note cards aren't a substitute for what you are going to say; they simply remind you of it. At the delivery stage, you should know your subject so well that you need only short prompts to move from one point to the next.

The presentation outline and note cards are your dependable assistants. When developed and used properly, the presentation outline is an excellent tool that allows you to express your ideas with style. And the note cards help you stay on track while allowing you to develop a good rapport with your listeners by appearing informed, organized, and spontaneous.

Practicing the Delivery of Your Speech

▼ Effective practicing does not mean simply putting in time. You need not—indeed, should not—invest hours and hours in practice, because too much practice can rob you of spontaneity. In fact, practicing your speech over and over will not ensure a successful presentation on speech day.[19] What you want is *quality* practice time.

Practice is not a singular activity. As you prepare your speech, you will practice in different ways and at different stages until you are completely ready. Of course, you want to feel absolutely prepared before you stand in front of your audience. But being fully prepared does not mean that the speech you give to your audience will be exactly the same as the speech you practice. You want to appear sharp and well organized, not programmed and predictable.

GIVE A VERSION OF YOUR SPEECH

Think of every speech you give as just one of many possible speeches you could have given with exactly the same information and preparation. You don't have to give a "perfect" speech—you must simply give an excellent *version* of your speech. If you were to give the same speech tomorrow, and again the next day, you would not deliver those speeches in exactly the same way. The speechmaking method you are learning will prepare you to give excellent versions of your speeches—presentations that will look and sound both natural and fresh.

Remember that you should not commit your whole speech or even large sections of it to memory. With excellent preparation and sufficient practice, you'll know what you want to say well enough to say it effectively when you deliver your speech. For example, you will recall certain words and phrases that sounded good when you practiced. You may not say things exactly the same way as you did when you practiced, but you'll feel confident that you know how to make your ideas clear.

PRACTICE YOUR SPEECH IN STAGES

Practicing well is an art in itself and permeates the entire speech preparation process. Flexibility and adaptability are extremely important for speakers, because putting a speech together requires constant rethinking and revision as you research your topic, organize your ideas, identify the language you'll use in your speech, and incorporate presentation media. Review your complete-sentence outline (Chapter 8) as you go along, trying out different parts of your speech to find out how they work or don't work. Practice in stages—section by section. Don't wait until you think you have a finished product.

SPEAKING OF...

Paper versus Cards

Why use note *cards* rather than paper when you deliver a speech? Try this: Hold a piece of paper in your hand while you're standing up. It bends, it crinkles, it's hard to see, and it's noisy. Now write a few notes on the paper and try to use them to cue you as you talk for a few minutes. Lose your place? Miss some key points? Paper is too cumbersome and difficult to handle, even when you cut it into note card–sized pieces. Note cards, in contrast, are made from card stock, which is much heavier than regular copy, printer, or notebook paper. Because it's heavier, it's more durable and it doesn't bend as easily.

Practicing Parts of Your Speech

During this stage of practice, your goals are to check to make sure your speech makes sense, identify keywords that will best trigger your memory, and try out your presentation aids. During this stage, say the words of your speech out loud to determine whether your ideas make sense and your language and delivery techniques seem to be working. By speaking out loud when you practice, you hear the sense of your ideas, or the lack of it. How might you say something more clearly, precisely, humorously, seriously, or persuasively? Practicing out loud allows you to become your own audience member, ready to give instant, productive feedback. Whether you are sitting at a desk, lying on a sofa, or sprawling on the floor, try giving small portions of your speech out loud as if you were facing an audience. Listen for the sense, make adjustments, and keep tinkering with the individual segments of your speech.

Practicing your speech during this stage includes practicing with your presentation aids (Chapter 11). No matter how small the aid or how briefly you'll be using it, include it in your practice sessions so you can be sure that it accomplishes what you want it to and that you can integrate it as smoothly as possible.

Practicing Your Whole Speech

After practicing the various parts of your speech, you will need to practice the entire speech. At this point it is best to practice while standing up, holding your note cards, and integrating your presentation aids. Practicing the whole speech with any media you plan to use allows you to time the performance and observe how your main points flow. You'll also be able to perfect your introduction and conclusion (Chapter 9).

In this stage of practicing, invite friends, family members, coworkers, and others to provide constructive feedback. If you want them to focus on a particular aspect of your presentation, such as transitions or gestures, tell them before you begin your speech. Then

• • • • • • • • • • THE EVOLVING ART

Storyboarding Digital Slides

Filmmakers use storyboards to plan the scenes of a film: Each panel represents a crucial point in the film's narrative. If you think of your speech as a story, you can identify the key scenes. Those scenes then become your digital slides. Storyboarding helps you consider the important ideas you want your audience to grasp and how those ideas fit together. So forget those endless bullet point lists. Use digital slides to visualize your ideas for your audience.

be ready to listen to their comments without becoming defensive, knowing they want you to do your best. Research shows that practicing your speech in front of four or more people improves your presentation on speech day.[20] Videotaping yourself a few times as you practice can also prove helpful because you'll get an idea of how you look and sound.

TIME YOUR SPEECH

Practicing the entire speech also gives you an opportunity to time it. Don't overlook the importance of managing your time well! When you give your speech, you don't want to run out of time before you've presented all your main points and had a chance to wrap up. During practice sessions, you might focus adequately on the speech's content but misjudge how long it will take to present the information. Content must be your first priority, but it has to fit within the time frame indicated by your instructor. Knowing how long your speech will last also gives you confidence and control during the presentation.

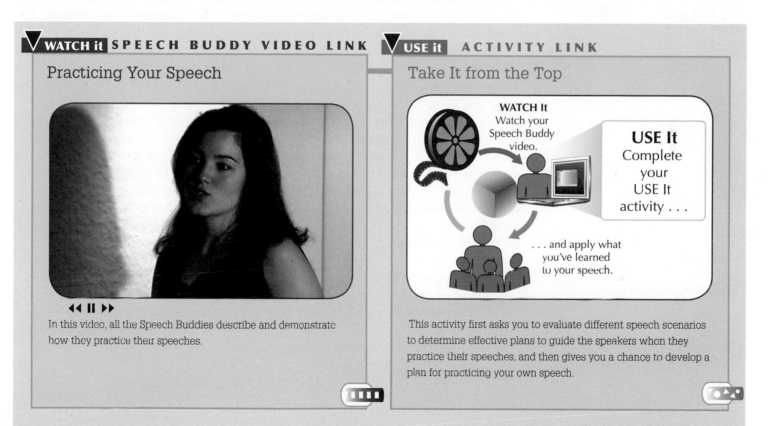

WATCH it SPEECH BUDDY VIDEO LINK

Practicing Your Speech

◀◀ ▐▐ ▶▶

In this video, all the Speech Buddies describe and demonstrate how they practice their speeches.

USE it ACTIVITY LINK

Take It from the Top

WATCH It
Watch your Speech Buddy video.

USE It
Complete your USE It activity . . .

. . . and apply what you've learned to your speech.

This activity first asks you to evaluate different speech scenarios to determine effective plans to guide the speakers when they practice their speeches, and then gives you a chance to develop a plan for practicing your own speech.

SUMMARY

Speakers use four delivery methods: impromptu, extemporaneous, manuscript, and memorized. For most speeches, you'll want to speak extemporaneously, balancing careful planning with flexibility.

Several factors influence a public speaker's delivery, including culture and gender. Cultural norms that differ from those of the United States might require a public speaking student to develop new and adaptive skills. Similarly, women speakers often have to adapt to the fact that audiences evaluate women and men differently in some aspects of speech delivery. For example, audiences evaluate a female speaker's credibility primarily on her use of trustworthy sources, while they evaluate a male speaker's credibility on a broader range of factors. In addition, women often have trouble being heard because they tend to speak in a lower volume and at a higher pitch. A well-prepared speaker can overcome negative audience perceptions, regardless of gender.

Other factors that influence delivery are language fluency, dialect, and physical impairments. Regarding fluency, stuttering and dialect are common issues. Research has found that speakers who stutter may best manage the problem through acknowledgement and eye contact with the audience. And all speakers should examine their dialect and make any adjustments necessary for audience comprehension. Speakers with physical impairments may need to adjust their delivery in ways that work best for them and the audience.

Delivering your speech well means effectively managing your voice, your body, and your audience. In managing your voice and body, apply strategies such as using good vocal variety, clearly articulating your words, dressing for the occasion, making eye contact with your entire audience, and radiating positivity. To manage your audience effectively, adjust your speaking space as needed, involve the audience in your speech, respect the audience's time, accommodate audience members with impairments, handle hostile or rude audience members calmly, and be prepared for questions, answering as completely as you can.

Careful research, planning, organizing, and preparation provide a solid base for presenting your speech. The presentation outline helps you achieve an organized, engaging, and professional presentation. This outline and your note cards serve as your personal cueing system when you give your speech. Practice your speech in stages, distilling your complete-sentence outline into a brief presentation outline. Incorporate any presentation materials into the speech as you practice, making modifications as necessary. Put in quality practice time so that when speech day arrives you're prepared to give an excellent version of your speech. Closely manage your time, adjusting your speech as needed.

Delivering your speech brings together all your planning and preparation. This is your opportunity to shine—do it with flair and style!

▼ REVIEW it DIRECTORY OF STUDY AND REVIEW RESOURCES

In the Book

Summary
Key Terms
Critical Challenges

More Study Resources

Speech Studio
Quizzes
WebLinks

Student Workbook

12.1: Model Speakers
12.2: Deliver a Full Thought to one Person
12.3: Rotating Audiences
12.4: Listening for Delivery Styles
12.5: Filling the Space with Sound

Speech Buddy Videos

  Video Links

Reviewing Vocal Delivery
Reviewing Physical Delivery
Practicing Your Speech

Activity Links

Speak Up
Stand Tall
Take It from the Top

▶ Sample Speech Videos

Katherine, "Is That Kosher?" informative speech

Tiffany, self-introduction speech

Speech Builder Express

Goal/purpose
Thesis statement
Organization
Outline
Supporting material
Transitions
Introduction
Conclusion
Title
Works cited
Completing the speech outline

InfoTrac

Recommended search terms

Speech delivery
Physical speech delivery
Vocal speech delivery
Speech practice
Anxiety and speech delivery

Audio Study Tools

"Turn Off Your TV" by Lisa

Critical thinking questions

Learning objectives

Chapter summary

Guide to Your Online Resources

Your Online Resources for *Public Speaking: The Evolving Art* give you access to the Speech Buddy videos and activities featured in this chapter, additional sample speech videos, Speech Builder Express, InfoTrac College Edition, and study aids such as glossary flashcards, review quizzes, and the Critical Challenge questions for this chapter, which you can respond to via e-mail if your instructor requests. In addition, your Online Resources feature live WebLinks relevant to this chapter, including the American Rhetoric website, classic speeches on the History Channel site, and a site about taming speech anxiety hosted by the University of Hawai'i Maui Community College Speech Department. Links are regularly maintained, and new ones are added periodically.

Key Terms

articulation 306	memorized speaking 300	rate 305
delivery 297	monotone 305	vocalized pauses 306
dialect 303	nonverbal message 312	vocal variety 305
extemporaneous speaking 299	pitch 302	volume 302
impromptu speaking 298	posture 308	
keyword 315	presentation outline 314	
manuscript speaking 299	pronunciation 306	

Critical Challenges

Questions for Reflection and Discussion

1. Public speaking classes usually focus on extemporaneous speaking. What are some situations in which you'll likely give extemporaneous speeches in the future? You encounter impromptu speaking situations almost daily, especially in a college classroom. Give an example of a recent experience you had with impromptu speaking. While you're in school, you usually don't do much manuscript and memorized speaking. When might you use these methods in the future?

2. How have you practiced for speaking situations in the past? How effective were those practice strategies? How do you plan to practice for speeches in the future?

3. One aspect of adapting to your audience is accommodating individuals with disabilities. How might you do this in classroom speeches? In speeches outside the classroom?

4. During and after your speech, you may find that audience members challenge your ideas and conclusions. How might you avoid becoming defensive—a natural reaction—and encourage reasoned discussion?

13 INFORMATIVE SPEAKING

READ it

WATCH it

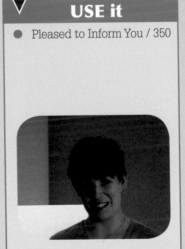

USE it

REVIEW it

SPEECH BUILDER EXPRESS

SPEECH Studio

Informative speeches rely

on information, or knowledge derived from experience, study, or instruction. Today, public speakers giving informative speeches have an advantage that speakers in earlier times lacked: Information from all over the world is easily available online. From the seemingly unlimited access to information sources, to the incredible ease with which you can send information to people almost anywhere on the planet, digital communication technologies give you new ways to interact and share information. You find jobs, take classes, research health issues, learn about other cultures, market products and services, and conduct a host of other information exchanges online.[1] As a public speaker, you can take advantage of today's vastly expanded information environment to research your speech topics, find support for your main points, and refer audiences to additional information and insights about your ideas.

Characteristics of an Informative Speech

Presenting a speech in which the speaker seeks to deepen understanding, raise awareness, or increase knowledge about a topic.

▼ **READ it** In **informative speaking** situations, the speaker seeks to deepen understanding, raise awareness, or increase knowledge about a topic. When you speak to inform, you want audience members to learn something from your speech. To do this, you share information with them.

At the root of all human communication is the connection people make when they share information. When you speak informatively, you make this important connection with your listeners. For this to happen, your listeners must find the speech meaningful, the information accurate, and the message clear. These three qualities, shown in **Figure 13.1**, form the basis of your competence as an informative speaker.

AN INFORMATIVE SPEECH IS MEANINGFUL

Monitoring news sources to analyze and assess the information they produce.

Relating the topic to the audience allows speakers to create a sense of personal meaning with their speeches. For example, speakers often tell stories as a way to personalize a message. Even the creators of today's digital media try to make the experience of long-distance interaction as personal as possible. Instant messages and e-mail, camera phones, and file sharing, for example, give you personal control over the way you share information with others. Public speakers today can use many of the same digital resources and personalization strategies in their speeches.

▼ **FIGURE 13.1**
Characteristics of Competent Informative Speaking

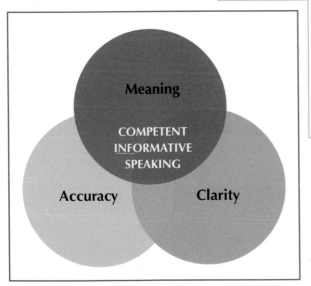

AN INFORMATIVE SPEECH IS ACCURATE

Today's robust information environment has heightened the expectations audiences have about the accuracy of the information they receive from any source. For example, the traditional news media have always sought to gain the public's trust by hiring internal fact checkers to investigate the accuracy of their stories. But now online independent news outlets, bloggers, newsgroups, and other gatewatchers also evaluate the information generated by traditional media. **Gatewatching** involves monitoring news sources to analyze and assess the information those sources produce.[2] This increased vigilance has led news organizations to check their work even more carefully. This principle of gatewatching also applies to informative speaking. Informing your audience effectively requires that you present accurate information. Listeners act as gatewatchers, expecting accuracy in every aspect of your speech: topic choice, supporting materials, organization, language, delivery, and presentation media.

AN INFORMATIVE SPEECH IS CLEAR

Audiences understand information best when it is clearly presented and easy to follow. Clarity unravels confusing and complex ideas, making them unambiguous and coherent. Often, however, clarity presents the greatest challenge to informative speakers.[3] Analyzing your audience and selecting supporting materials appropriate to your topic and listeners provide the foundation for achieving clarity in your informative speech.

Types of Informative Speeches

There are five common types of informative speeches:

1. Speeches about objects and places.
2. Speeches about people and other living creatures.
3. Speeches about processes.
4. Speeches about events.
5. Speeches about ideas and concepts.

These categories suggest general topic areas and are not mutually exclusive. For instance, a speech about a famous person, such as an inventor, would probably include information about the person's best-known ideas. A speech about a place might also be about an event that occurs there. Still, an informative speech generally has one primary focus you'll highlight in your speech.

SPEECHES ABOUT OBJECTS AND PLACES

An **object** is any nonliving, material thing that the human senses can perceive. **Places** are geographic locations. Here are several speech topics and titles addressing objects and places:

Topic	Sample Speech Titles
IMAX cinema	"Beyond Cinerama: The IMAX Film"
	"The Top Three IMAX Films Ever"
Tijuana	"Tijuana: The Challenges of a Mexican Border Town"
	"The Delights of Tijuana"
snowboarding equipment	"Early Innovators of Snowboarding Equipment"
	"Snowboarding Equipment Under $500"

Any nonliving, material thing that can be perceived by the senses.

Geographic locations.

silver mines	"The Great Silver Mines of Colorado"
	"How Silver Is Mined Today"
extraterrestrials	"Ancient Beliefs in Extraterrestrials"
	"Humorous Films about Extraterrestrials"
laser medical technology	"The Latest Advances in Laser Medical Technology"
	"Common Types of Medical Lasers"
Thai food	"The Secret Spices of Thai Food"
	"Thai Food and Drink as Healthy Alternatives"
blogs	"What Makes a Successful Blog"
	"The Daily Read: My Favorite Blogs"
active volcanoes	"The Active Volcanoes of Latin America"
	"The Causes of Volcanic Eruptions"
folk art	"Folk Art in Our Community"
	"Famous American Folk Art"

Your own interests and knowledge can often generate excellent speech topics. Sometimes students believe that the things they know about would not interest an audience. However, with skillful research and delivery, almost anything that is important or interesting to you can be made important or interesting to an audience. Think of the town you grew up in. What would visitors consider its main attractions? Could you show presentation media that would make those attractions come alive for listeners? If the town doesn't have a lot of attractions that might interest tourists, what interesting people live there? What interesting or enlightening experiences occurred there? Don't discount a topic just because you think it wouldn't interest anyone other than you. Consider how you could *make* it interesting.

SPEECHES ABOUT PEOPLE AND OTHER LIVING CREATURES

When choosing a topic for an informative speech about people or other living creatures, reflect on the people who fascinate you or the creatures you think your audience would like to learn more about. Who or what would your audience find meaningful? A well-known celebrity or a lesser-known individual? An international figure or someone much closer to home? Would they be interested in an exotic creature, such as the scimitar-horned oryx or the banded bamboo shark? Or something more common they know little about, such as the bald eagle or the bottlenose dolphin? Here are some sample topics and titles for this type of speech:

Topic	Sample Speech Titles
Michelle Wie	"The Asian Wave in Women's Golf" "Michelle Wie: Professional Golf's New Superstar"
Koko, the "talking gorilla"	"If Gorillas Talk, What Do They Say?" "Learning about Human Speech from Koko, the Talking Gorilla"
Stephen Colbert	"The Real World of Comedian Stephen Colbert" "The Many Roles of Stephen Colbert"
dinosaurs	"When Dinosaurs Ruled the World" "Dinosaurs and the Great Extinction Debate"
Gloria L. Velásquez	"The Poetry of Gloria L. Velásquez" "How Gloria L. Velásquez Became Superwoman Chicana"
The Dalai Lama	"A Brief Biography of the Dalai Lama" "Pathways to Peace According to the Dalai Lama"
Prince William of England	"Prince William and England's Succession to the Throne" "Who Is Prince William of England?"
a local artist	"Insight into the Art of Rolando Diaz" "The Struggles and Successes of Local Artist Rolando Diaz"
tarantulas	"The Truth about Tarantulas" "Tarantulas: Evolution of the World's Scariest Spider"
Kathryn D. Sullivan	"Kathryn D. Sullivan: The First American Woman to Walk in Space" "You Can Become an Astronaut Like Kathryn D. Sullivan"

Biographies Online

Audiences often find speeches about famous people fascinating. Fortunately, the internet offers many resources for researching the famous and not-so-famous, both past and present. The Internet Public Library (ipl.org), developed by the University of Michigan School of Information, provides an excellent starting point for such a search. Its Biographies section includes an index to general biographies as well as biographies in specific categories, such as artists and architects, authors, entertainers, musicians and composers, politicians and rulers, and scientists and inventors.

For the most part, audiences are highly interested in other people and living creatures—that's why the Biography and Discovery Channels are so popular. With careful audience analysis and solid research, informative speeches about these topics can captivate your audience.

SPEECHES ABOUT PROCESSES

How something is done, how it works, or how it has developed.

A speech about a **process**—how something is done, how it works, or how it has developed—facilitates an audience's understanding of the process or explains how audience members can engage in the process themselves. Here are some examples of topics and titles for informative speeches about processes:

Topic	Sample Speech Titles
matching DNA samples	"How DNA Affects Criminal Prosecutions" "DNA and Genetics: Our Genes Tell Our Stories"
selling an item on eBay	"How to Sell Your Stuff on eBay" "The Do's and Don'ts of Selling on eBay"
testing new cars for safety	"Standards for Testing New Cars for Safety" "Test Results on the Safety of New Cars"
dancing the Brazilian samba	"Dancing the Brazilian Samba with Ease" "Fusing Culture with Movement in the Brazilian Samba"

removing computer spyware	"Basic Steps for Removing Computer Spyware" "Avoiding Common Mistakes in Removing Computer Spyware"
fighting wildfires	"Tactics and Techniques Used for Fighting Wildfires" "What I Learned Fighting Wildfires"
buying camping equipment	"Buying Good Camping Equipment at a Low Price" "Choosing Camping Equipment to Fit Your Budget"
producing a TV newscast	"How TV Newscasts Are Produced" "The Latest Digital Techniques in Television News"
tracking global climate change	"The Main Indicators of Global Climate Change" "Tracking Global Climate Change over the Centuries"
podcasting	"Basic Steps in Making Your First Podcast" "Getting People to Listen to Your Podcasts"

Analyze your audience thoroughly before deciding whether you want them to simply understand a process or to enact it themselves. For example, a newscaster speaking to broadcasting students could expect them to participate in producing a TV newscast. In contrast, the listeners in your public speaking class aren't likely to go out and produce a TV newscast, so simply learning more about the process would be sufficient for them. Further, if your listeners already know how to perform a process, they likely won't be very interested in your speech. For instance, many students have iPods or other MP3 players. A speech on how to use an iPod probably isn't appropriate for a group of college students. Many of those students, however, probably don't know how to produce a podcast. So a speech explaining how to go through that process may be of great interest to such an audience.

SPEECHES ABOUT EVENTS

An **event** is a significant occurrence you experience personally or otherwise know about. An event can take place in the past, present, or future. An event does not necessarily need to take place in public—important personal activities and occurrences can be events. Some events, such as concert tours, holiday rituals, fairs, and athletic contests, take place repeatedly. To call something an event gives it a special status and makes this category of informative speeches appealing to public speakers and their audiences. Here are some suggested topics and titles for informative speeches about events:

A significant occurrence that an individual personally experiences or otherwise knows about.

Topic	Sample Speech Titles
college graduation day	"Graduation Day: A Great American Ritual" "The Changing Nature of Graduation Day"
birthday parties	"Ten Essential Ingredients for a Perfect Birthday Party" "Birthday Celebrations in Different Cultures"
Chinese New Year	"The Ancient Tradition of Chinese New Year" "The Best Chinese New Year's Parades in America"
assassination of President Kennedy	"Why We Remain Fascinated by the Assassination of President John F. Kennedy" "How the Assassination of President Kennedy Changed Presidential Security Forever"
World Cup football	"World Cup Football: Who Gets to Play?" "The Cultural Significance of World Cup Football"
Career Day on campus	"Successfully Meeting Employers on Career Day" "The Basics of Career Day at Our School"
the Grammy Awards	"The Grammy Awards as a Pop Culture Ceremony" "The Grammy Awards Yesterday and Today"
the AIDS Walk	"The AIDS Walk: A Response to a Global Crisis" "The AIDS Walk in Our Community"
the birth of a baby	"Giving Birth: What to Expect Before and During Delivery" "The Role of Midwives in Childbirth through the Ages"
Ramadan	"Ramadan: The History of Islam's Holy Ninth Month" "The Importance of Fasting during Ramadan"

For example, consider a celebratory event for the recipient of a Habitat for Humanity house. You can talk about what it takes to plan and promote the event, who attends the event and why, or the social significance of the event. When developing an informative speech about an event, consider its many different aspects and then choose those you think will most interest your audience.

SPEECHES ABOUT IDEAS AND CONCEPTS

Mental activity produces **ideas and concepts**, which include thoughts, understandings, beliefs, notions, or principles. Ideas and concepts tend to be abstract rather than concrete. But over time an idea or concept may be actualized in the physical world and thus become more concrete. For example, a fundraising event usually starts with someone thinking, "We should raise some money so the community center can buy a new computer." Similarly, a concept car displayed at an auto show begins its life as an automobile designer's idea. Initially, however, all ideas and concepts start out as abstractions, and many remain abstract.

When delivering an informative speech about an idea or a concept, the speaker usually explains the origin and main elements of the idea or concept. These aspects of a topic can prove quite extensive and complex, so select a topic that is manageable within your time frame. Here are some sample topics and titles for informative speeches about ideas and concepts.

© David Young-Wolff/PhotoEdit

▲ Events are naturally appealing to audiences because they suggest an unfolding action, such as the actions that led to this celebratory event for the recipient of a Habitat for Humanity house.

Mental activity, including thoughts, understandings, beliefs, notions, and principles.

Topic	Sample Speech Titles
liberty	"Looking Back on Liberty in 1776" "Defining Liberty after 9/11"
religious fundamentalism	"The Roots of Religious Fundamentalism" "What Does It Mean to Be a Religious Fundamentalist?"
the electoral college	"The American Electoral College: How Does It Function?" "Tracing the History of the Electoral College"
marriage	"Views of Marriage across Cultures" "How Marriage Has Changed with the Times"
chaos theory	"Taking the Chaos out of Chaos Theory" "Applying Chaos Theory to Everyday Life"

individual human rights	"What Are Your Individual Human Rights?" "Individual Human Rights: A Guarantee from the United Nations"
dance therapy	"Dance Therapy as a Psychological Technique" "Effective Dance Therapy Techniques"
Chicanismo	"Who Are the *Chicanos*?" "The Cultural Meanings of *Chicanismo* Yesterday and Today"
niche marketing	"How Niche Marketing Developed" "Niche Marketing in a Multicultural Society"
distance learning	"The Beginning of Distance Learning" "Future Directions in Distance Learning"

This list reveals that subjects for speeches about ideas and concepts can be complex and controversial. That's no reason to avoid such a topic. To the contrary, audiences generally like to learn more about intriguing and provocative topics.

Specific Purposes and Thesis Statements for Informative Speeches

The specific purpose you develop for an informative speech should reflect your general purpose: to deepen understanding, raise awareness, or increase knowledge about a topic. For informative speaking, your general purpose is *to inform*, so your specific purpose should begin with a phrase such as "to help my audience learn" or "to make my audience understand."

As you phrase your specific purpose, ask yourself, What do I want my audience to learn? Then, as you phrase your thesis, ask yourself, What do they need to know? Keep in mind that your specific purpose and thesis should clarify your topic for your audience, make it meaningful, express the main ideas accurately, and pique the audience's interest. **Table 13.1** presents several examples of specific purposes and thesis statements for different types of informative speeches.

TABLE 13.1 ▶ Specific Purposes and Thesis Statements for Informative Speeches

INFORMATIVE SPEECH ABOUT...	TOPIC	SPECIFIC PURPOSE	THESIS STATEMENT
Objects and place	The Secret Spices of Thai Food	To help my audience learn about the secret spices of Thai food	Three secret spices give Thai food its unique flavor: lemongrass, galangal, and coriander.
	Beyond Cinerama: The IMAX Film	To make my audience understand how an IMAX film is different from a traditional film	An IMAX film differs from a traditional film in its technical makeup and viewing specifications.
People and other living creatures	How Gloria L. Velásquez Became Superwoman Chicana	To help my audience learn about how Gloria L. Velásquez became Superwoman Chicana	Gloria L. Velásquez became Superwoman Chicana through her poetry, fiction, and music.
	The Truth about Tarantulas	To make my audience understand the truth about tarantulas	True tarantulas are not deadly to humans, usually live a long life, and make great pets.
Processes	How a Dog Show Is Run	To educate my audience about how a professional dog show is run	A professional dog show involves grouping dogs into categories, judging the dogs according to standard criteria, and choosing winners by breed and for the overall show.
	Create Your Own Podcast	To help my audience understand how to create their own podcasts	Creating your own podcast requires creating the content, recording the content, and publishing your podcast.
Events	Career Day	To help my audience understand the features of Career Day on our campus	Career Day on our campus involves meeting with prospective employers, finding out about internships, and enrolling in career-building workshops.
	The Grammy Awards	To make my audience aware of major milestones in the history of the Grammy Awards ceremony	The major milestones in the history of the Grammy Awards ceremony include the first ceremony in 1959, the first live TV broadcast of the ceremony in 1971, Michael Jackson's sweep of eight Grammy awards in 1984, and the canceled ceremony in 2008.

Continued

TABLE 13.1 ▶ Continued

INFORMATIVE SPEECH ABOUT . . .	TOPIC	SPECIFIC PURPOSE	THESIS STATEMENT
Ideas and concepts	Chaos Theory	To help my audience understand the applications of chaos theory to everyday life	Chaos theory helps us understand how organizations, small groups, and individuals function every day.
	Individual Human Rights	To educate my audience about the individual human rights guaranteed by the United Nations	Passed in 1948, the United Nations' Universal Declaration of Human Rights promotes equal rights, worth, and dignity for all individuals.

Organizational Patterns for Informative Speeches

▼ Nearly all the patterns of organization discussed in Chapter 8 work well for informative speeches, including the chronological, spatial, topical, narrative, and cause-and-effect patterns. When choosing a pattern for your informative speech, pick one that complements your topic and promotes your specific purpose.

THE CHRONOLOGICAL PATTERN

The chronological pattern allows you to explain how someone or something has developed over a period of time. With this pattern, you highlight the importance of each step in that development. This pattern works well with informative speeches about objects and places, people and other living creatures, and processes. In the following example the chronological pattern is used to describe the stages in the life cycle of a living creature.

Topic: The Life Cycle of Butterflies

General purpose: To inform

Specific purpose: To help my audience understand the life cycle of butterflies

Thesis: Butterflies go through four stages in their life cycle: egg, larva, pupa, and metamorphosis.

Main points:

    I. The first stage in the life cycle is the butterfly egg.

    II. The second stage is the larva, known as the caterpillar.

    III. The third state is the pupa, also referred to as the chrysalis.

    IV. In the fourth stage, the organism becomes an adult butterfly through metamorphosis.

For informative speeches that demonstrate how to do something, the best approach is a chronological pattern that leads the audience through the process step by step.

Topic: Packing for a trip by air

General purpose: To inform

Specific purpose: To help my audience learn how to pack a carry-on suitcase for a trip by air

Thesis: Packing a carry-on for an airplane trip involves making a list, checking for banned items, taking only what you need, using the "roll up" technique, and putting breakables in plastic containers.

Main points:

    I. First, make a list of everything you think you'll need for the trip

    II. Second, check the Transportation Security Administration's website for a list of banned items.

    III. Third, check the banned item list against your packing list and cross off any disallowed items.

    IV. Fourth, reduce your list by bringing only what you absolutely need.

    V. Fifth, pack using the "roll up" technique to conserve space and prevent wrinkling.

    VI. Sixth, place breakable items in airtight plastic containers.

    VII. Last, double-check your list of items to be sure you didn't forget anything.

THE SPATIAL PATTERN

The spatial pattern allows you to describe the physical or directional relationship between objects or places. This pattern works well with informative speeches about objects, places, people, or other living creatures. For example, if your specific purpose is to highlight certain locations, areas, or spaces in a particular place, use a spatial pattern of organization, as in the following example.

Topic: Zuni Indian Reservations

General purpose: To inform

Specific purpose: To familiarize my audience with the places in North America where the Zuni Indians live

Thesis: The Zuni Indian Reservation includes land in western New Mexico; Catron County, New Mexico; and Apache County, Arizona.

Main points:

    I. The tribal government is based in the main Zuni reservation in western New Mexico, near the Arizona border.

    II. Members of the Zuni tribe also live in Catron County, New Mexico, south of the main reservation in the western part of the state.

    III. The Zuni tribe has land holdings and residences in Apache County, Arizona, in the eastern part of the state, where it shares space with Navajo tribes.

The spatial pattern also can be appropriate for informative speeches about people and other living creatures, as in this speech about a person.

Topic: Gudridur Thorbjarnardottir: World Traveler in the Middle Ages

General purpose: To inform

Specific purpose: To educate my audience about the travels of Gudridur Thorbjarnardottir, who lived during the Middle Ages

---

Main points:

    I. Gudridur Thorbjarnardottir was a native of Iceland.

    II. She also lived in Greenland.

    III. She explored Vinland, or what is now America.

    IV. She went to Rome to tell the Pope about her travels.

THE TOPICAL PATTERN

When using the topical pattern, you divide your topic into subtopics that address the components, elements, or aspects of the topic. Almost any informative speech topic can be organized using this pattern—the subtopics become the main points of the speech. For example, when you simply want your audience to understand a process, use the topical pattern to describe the main features of the process.

Topic: Dog shows

General purpose: To inform

Specific purpose: To make my audience aware of how a professional dog show is run

Thesis: A professional dog show involves grouping dogs into categories, judging the dogs according to standard criteria, and choosing winners by breed, group, and best in show.

Main points:

    I. In large professional dog shows, dogs are divided into breeds, and breeds are classified into groups such as sporting or working dogs.

    II. Dogs are judged according to conformity with the breed standard, as well as personality, age, and sex within breeds.

    III. The winner of each breed then competes within the appropriate group.

    IV. The winners of the groups then compete for best in show.

In speeches about concepts and ideas, when you want to explain rather than simply describe important elements of the topic, the topical pattern can help make your explanation clear.

Topic: Globalization

General purpose: To inform

Specific purpose: To help my audience understand the main differences among the major forms of globalization

Thesis: The five forms of globalization are economic, religious, political, cultural, and media globalization.

Main points:

I. Trade and commerce between cultural groups represents economic globalization.

II. The spread of religious ideas and conversions represents religious globalization.

III. The flow of international political influence represents political globalization.

IV. The movement of cultural goods from one part of the world to another represents cultural globalization.

V. Connecting the world with new communication technologies represents media globalization.

THE NARRATIVE PATTERN

The narrative pattern allows you to retell events as a story or a series of short stories. This pattern works best with informative speeches about objects, places, people, or other living creatures. The narrative pattern has much in common with the chronological pattern, but more strongly emphasizes the dramatic unfolding of events, as in this speech about an object.

> **Topic:** Pluto, a Dwarf Planet
>
> **Specific purpose:** To help my audience understand why Pluto is a dwarf planet
>
> **Thesis:** The story of Pluto began with the discovery of Neptune, reached its peak with naming Pluto a planet in the early 1900s, and ended recently with Pluto's demotion to dwarf planet.
>
> **Main points:**
>
> I. The story of Pluto began with the discovery of Neptune in the 1840s.
>
> II. By the late nineteenth century, scientists believed a mysterious planet was affecting Neptune's orbital plane.
>
> III. In the early twentieth century, the planet Pluto was discovered and named.
>
> IV. The International Astronomical Union began to doubt that Pluto should have the same status as the other celestial bodies circling the sun.
>
> V. In 2006 the International Astronomical Union reduced Pluto to a secondary status, dwarf planet.

The narrative pattern works well for turning the chronology of a person's life events into an absorbing story, adding suspense and dramatic flair to the topic.

> **Topic:** Oprah Winfrey
>
> **General purpose:** To inform
>
> **Specific purpose:** To make my audience aware of major turning points in Oprah Winfrey's life
>
> **Thesis:** Oprah Winfrey was born to poor parents, was a motivated elementary-school student, went on to high school and college, became a highly successful TV talk show host, and came full circle when she opened a school for disadvantaged girls in South Africa.

Main points:

    I. Oprah was born in 1954 in Mississippi to poor, unwed teenage parents.

    II. She moved to Milwaukee, where she became a highly motivated and successful student in elementary and middle school.

    III. Oprah's love of education became the central part of her life as she advanced through high school and college.

    IV. She developed a highly successful career as a television talk show host.

    V. Oprah opened a school for black girls from disadvantaged families in South Africa, saying that doing so was her true calling in life—she had come full circle.

THE CAUSE-AND-EFFECT PATTERN

The cause-and-effect pattern shows how an action produces a particular outcome. This pattern works well with informative speeches about events—after all, events happen for a reason. This example explains how an alternative holiday now celebrated by the Maoris, the indigenous people of New Zealand, came into being.

Topic: Matariki: The Maori New Year

General purpose: To inform

Specific purpose: To raise my audience's awareness of the Maori New Year celebration

Thesis: Matariki, the Maori New Year, is now an official celebration in New Zealand, part of an effort to reclaim and celebrate the Maori's cultural heritage.

Main points:

    I. The Maoris inhabited New Zealand when it was conquered by the English in the eighteenth century.

    II. Maoris lost much of their cultural heritage in the transition to British rule.

    III. In 2004, the Maori New Year became an official day of celebration, resulting in the Maoris reclaiming some of their cultural heritage.

IV. The Maori New Year, Matariki, refers to the appearance of a star cluster that traditionally signals the beginning of the new year.

V. Matariki is now widely celebrated among the Maori of New Zealand.

Guidelines for Effective Informative Speeches

The success of your speech depends greatly on your planning and preparation. The following guidelines will help you prepare an excellent informative speech and add to your repertoire of public speaking skills.

KEEP YOUR SPEECH INFORMATIVE

Whenever you speak about any topic, you may be tempted to evaluate the subject matter, give opinions, or make suggestions—particularly if you hold strong feelings about the subject. In an informative speech, however, you should avoid expressing your personal views. Keep your speech at the level of information sharing. Describe, explain, or demonstrate something, but don't tell the audience what to think or do about it.

Choose a topic that interests you while at the same time determining what you might realistically expect your audience to get out of your speech. Let's say, for instance, you want to speak on the subject of rainforests. What would be an appropriate specific purpose and thesis for an informative speech about rainforests? What do you want your audience to think or do after listening to you? Given the complexities of the topic and the limited time you have to give your speech, you might reasonably expect only to raise the audience's level of awareness about rainforests generally, focusing on their characteristics.

▼ What other organizational patterns could you use to give an informative speech about the Matariki celebration? How would changing the pattern change the focus of your speech?

© travelstock44_x amy

Topic: Rainforests

General purpose: To inform

Specific purpose: To educate my audience about the characteristics of a rainforest

Thesis: Rainforests are characterized by high levels of rainfall, specific types of trees, and four forest layers.

> **Main points:**
>
> I. Rainforests receive high levels of rain.
>
> II. Only certain types of trees live in rainforests.
>
> III. Four layers of vegetation exist in a rainforest.

Notice that the main points focus on informing the audience and avoid taking a position on the topic. In this case, the difference between informing and persuading lies in explaining what rainforests are without advocating an environmental policy.

If you believe you can focus on your informative purpose, and not stray into a persuasive purpose, you will be able to give an acceptable informative speech.

MAKE YOUR SPEECH TOPIC COME ALIVE

Informative speeches come alive when speakers demonstrate a positive attitude and connect the topic to the audience in meaningful ways. You can accomplish this by establishing a context for your topic that excites the audience's imagination and using vivid language to describe the main points. For example, Queen Rania of Jordan opened an exhibit on the ancient Middle Eastern city of Petra at the New York Museum of Natural History with an informative speech on the city's history.[4] Here is part of what she said:

> The magical rose-red city of Petra—whose wonders will enchant you tonight— is like nothing else on earth. It is a remarkable testimony to the human spirit, etched for all time in sandstone and shale. . . .
>
> But Petra is more than just an archeological treasure. Petra, I believe, offers an enduring message to all mankind. In Petra, human beings—ordinary mortals like you and me—saw potential beauty and grandeur in walls of sheer stone. They imagined the possibility of elegance and splendor where others would see only a barren and desolate wilderness.
>
> Most importantly, they had the vision and courage to attempt the impossible. . . . Petra teaches us that nothing is impossible and that even the bleakest and most barren situation contains the promise of hope.
>
> It takes a dream, a plan and a supreme effort—but anything is possible. This is the true wonder of Petra, magical and constant through the centuries. In Jordan, we are proud to be the trustees of this heritage of hope. . . . and bear with pride our responsibility to share it with our region and to the entire world.

Notice how in just a few words Queen Rania makes the "Lost City of Stone" come alive and provides a context for appreciating the exhibit's art and artifacts. She links the story of Petra to recent world events and then suggests that her nation, Jordan, serves as a bridge between the Islamic Middle East and the more diverse West. The exhibit can be seen as a set of presentation materials accompanying her speech, further enhancing the appeal of her message.

CONNECT YOUR TOPIC TO YOUR AUDIENCE

By using techniques that reduce the distance between themselves and their audiences, good speakers encourage audience members to pay attention and focus more intently on the topic. For audiences unfamiliar with your topic, you'll have to connect it to their general life experiences. For audiences familiar with your topic, you can attract and maintain attention by reinforcing commonalities between you and the audience. Help the audience understand how learning about your topic benefits them, and how they can perhaps even incorporate the short lesson into their own lives. Raph Koster, chief creative officer of Sony Online Entertainment, connected his speech topic, "Theory of Fun for Games," to his audience at a Game Developers Conference with language, examples, and humor.[5]

Hi, my name is Raph, and I am a gamer. [audience laughs] Why do we recognize that reference? Why are we ashamed about "Hi, my name is Raph, and I am a gamer"? Why do we see that connection? Why do we have to defend gaming to people? Why do we have to explain to someone or justify why we do what we do?

A Theory of Fun came out of this: a back to basic process of why and how games work. . . . .

People are *really good* at pattern-matching. I'm going to offer the vast oversimplification that what we think of as "thinking" or consciousness is really just a big memory game. Matching things into sets. Moving things into the right place, and then moving on. . . . A really good example of this is faces. The amount of data in a face is enormous. Just enormous. We've only just started to figure things about it in the past few decades; when a bird-watcher spots a bird, the face recognition part of the brain goes off. We see faces everywhere. . . .

So when we see a pattern that we get, we do it over and over again. We build neural connections. Now this is what I call *fun*.

Building those patterns is necessary for our survival. . . . *Fun is the feedback the brain gives while successfully absorbing a pattern.* We need to absorb patterns, otherwise we die. So the brain *HAS* to

▼ A hallmark of memorable speakers is their ability to make their speeches come alive and connect topics to audiences. Civil rights leader Martin Luther King, Jr., President Bill Clinton, and former Texas governor Ann Richards are classic examples. How could you make your next speech come alive for your audience?

give positive feedback to you for learning stuff. We tend to think of fun as being frivolous. The stuff that doesn't matter. And this is the serious games cheer line: I'm here to tell you that fun is not only *not* frivolous but *fundamental to human nature and required for survival*. Therefore what we do is saving the human race from extinction. [laughs]

Right from the beginning, Koster emphasized the powerful natural relationship he has with his listeners. "Hi, my name is Raph, and I'm a gamer." The audience laughed at this clever introduction because, first, they all knew who he was. Raph Koster is a legendary figure in the world of online gaming, and the audience was there specifically to hear what he had to say. Second, by stating the obvious, "I'm a gamer," he made fun of his own superstar status by suggesting that the audience might not know he plays online games. And, because most audience members were online gamers, he was able to establish and reinforce a sense of community with them.

Throughout the presentation, the speaker used language that reaffirms the experiences online gamers share. He used the informal language common in gaming culture and constantly referred to online game players as "we." His tone was upbeat and fresh. He hit on a key word—*fun*—as a featured idea. Then he tied gamers' shared appreciation of fun to his thesis: "Fun is the feedback the brain gives while successfully absorbing a pattern."

INFORM TO EDUCATE

Informative speaking involves more than simply imparting information. A successful informative speaker informs the audience in a way that educates them. After hearing the speech, they should understand the nature and importance of the topic.

Educating your audiences requires demonstrating the relevance of the speech topic to their lives or values. By nature, people respond better to information that promises to enhance their lives in some way. As an informative speaker, you must give your audience a reason to listen. In the following example, Jean-Michel Cousteau addressed a U.S. Congressional Committee in 2001 about progress in researching and preserving the world's oceans. Notice how he skillfully connects his topic to the tragedy of 9/11 and his use of audience-centered language to educate this audience.[6]

Particularly in light of recent events, many of you may wonder why we've chosen to go ahead with Oceans Day. In times of tragedy and trial, the human spirit seeks constancy. What does constancy mean? On a personal level, it might be the constancy of our families, and the love we have for each other. On a professional level, it might be the constancy of our work and the sense of purpose we derive from it. I'd like to suggest even another level of constancy—one we take for granted every day. It's the constancy of the physical environment that surrounds us—the earth, the sky, and of course the water. . . .

We are, in fact, a water planet. Two-thirds of the earth is covered in water, the vast majority being the salt water of the ocean. As you know so well, the ocean is vital to life on earth . . . whether it be as a driver of the climate that provides life-giving rains, as a source of protein, or as a source of life-saving medicines. Yet, we take this precious resource for granted, polluting it, extracting from it—without regard to its now very noticeable limits to handle such activities. Last year alone, 92 stocks in the United States were determined to be over-fished. Coastal wetlands are disappearing at an alarming rate. And polluted waters result in everything from coral reef die-offs to beach closures. As an example of how pollution is affecting the St. Lawrence waterway—beluga whales in that area have shown such high levels of contaminants that they would qualify as toxic waste!

Cousteau's challenge was to educate his audience about the importance of preserving the world's water resources, especially the endangered oceans. To connect his message to the audience, he appealed to their sense of "constancy." People want stability and reliability in their family and professional lives, he said. They need predictability in their physical environments too—in this case, their water supplies. Cousteau encouraged his listeners to become educated about the subject by tying his message to their most basic personal interest—the instinct for survival.

He also employed a variety of relevant supporting materials to illustrate the seriousness of the threat to the world's water supply without trying to overwhelm the audience with too much technical information. Cousteau believes that the way to assure a more favorable water environment in the future is to educate people about the perilous situation of the oceans. In his speech, he helped his audience develop knowledge and understanding about the subject, not just receive information.

USE PRESENTATION MEDIA TO INFORM

Informative speeches frequently include some form of presentation media. Because you often have only a few minutes to give an informative speech, keep your presentation media limited and basic. A few well-placed images to introduce your topic or audio or visual references in support of your main points can prove effective. When you limit and carefully select your presentation media, you direct more attention to the images you do use and increase their potential impact.

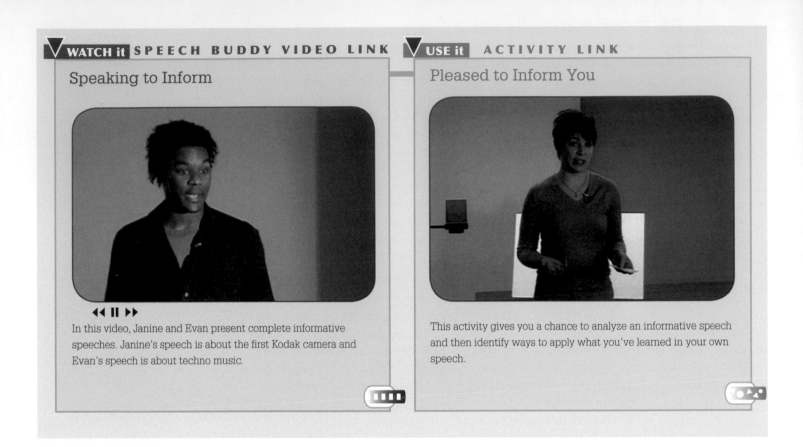

Speaking to Inform

◀◀ ❙❙ ▶▶

In this video, Janine and Evan present complete informative speeches. Janine's speech is about the first Kodak camera and Evan's speech is about techno music.

Pleased to Inform You

This activity gives you a chance to analyze an informative speech and then identify ways to apply what you've learned in your own speech.

Developing an engaging delivery rhythm that moves smoothly and confidently between you, the speaker, and your presentation media is crucial to becoming an excellent speaker. For example, change your slides at just the right time to illustrate and reinforce the specific points you want to make. When used well, presentation media can help make your informative speech a positive experience for you and your audience.

SUMMARY

When you give an informative speech, you seek to deepen understanding, raise awareness, or increase knowledge about a topic. To effectively connect with an audience in order to share information, you must ensure that your speech is meaningful, accurate, and clear.

Most informative speeches are about objects and places, people and other living creatures, processes, events, or ideas and concepts. The general and specific purposes you develop for an informative speech should reflect your overall goal—to foster understanding about a subject or to explain to your audience how to perform a process. Several patterns of organization work well for informative speeches, including the chronological, spatial, topical, narrative, and cause-and-effect patterns. The pattern you choose for an informative speech should complement your general and specific purposes for that speech.

Five strategies for delivering an effective informative speech are to keep your speech informative rather than persuasive, make your speech come alive with colorful language and a topic that sparks your audience's imagination, connect your topic to your audience in meaningful ways, inform to educate, and use presentation media to inform.

In the Book

Summary
Key Terms
Critical Challenges

More Study Resources

Speech Studio
Quizzes
WebLinks

Student Workbook

13.1: Short Informative
Speeches
13.2: Audience Outcomes
13.3: Grading a Teacher
13.4: Audience Attention
13.5: Try a Change Up

Speech Buddy Videos

 Video Links

Speaking to Inform

 Activity Links

Pleased to Inform You

▶ Sample Speech Videos

Curt, "The Illongot Head-
hunters," informative speech

Jeff, "History of Fort Collins, Colorado," informative
speech

Speech Builder Express

Goal/purpose
Thesis statement
Organization
Outline
Supporting material
Transitions
Introduction
Conclusion
Title
Works cited
Visual aids
Completing the speech
outline

InfoTrac

Recommended search terms

Informative speaking
Informative speech topics
Biography
How things work
Community events
Organizational patterns for
speeches

Audio Study Tools

"The Illongot Headhunters"
by Curt

Critical thinking questions

Learning objectives

Chapter summary

Guide to Your Online Resources

Your Online Resources for *Public Speaking: The Evolving Art* give you access to the Speech Buddy video and activity featured in this chapter, additional sample speech videos, Speech Builder Express, InfoTrac College Edition, and study aids such as glossary flashcards, review quizzes, and the Critical Challenge questions for this chapter, which you can respond to via e-mail if your instructor requests. In addition, your Online Resources feature live WebLinks relevant to this chapter, including sites that provide examples of excellent informative speeches. Links are regularly maintained, and new ones are added periodically.

Key Terms

event 333

gatewatching 328

informative speaking 328

ideas and concepts 335

object 329

places 329

process 332

Critical Challenges

Questions for Reflection and Discussion

1. Is clarity just a matter of making an idea understandable, or does it raise ethical questions, too? Why might professional public speakers, especially some politicians, purposefully avoid being clear about their messages?

2. It is often a good idea to choose a topic you already know something about for an informative speech. If you choose such a topic, how might you develop your specific purpose to make the experience as interesting as possible for you and your audience?

3. The difference between an informative and persuasive speech can sometimes be difficult for speakers to grasp. Consider the topics you might choose for an informative speech. How would you keep those topics inside the boundaries of speaking to inform?

14 PERSUASIVE SPEAKING

When Antonio Villaraigosa was elected mayor of Los Angeles, he represented great hope for the millions of Mexican Americans who live in the City of Angels. Villaraigosa grew up in East L.A., a poor Latino part of the city. Before he turned 17, Villaraigosa had dropped out of high school—twice. But soon he straightened himself out, started working hard, and learned to appreciate education. In addition, Villaraigosa developed outstanding persuasive speaking skills. In a **persuasive speech**, the speaker attempts to reinforce, modify, or change audience members' beliefs, attitudes, opinions, values, and behaviors. Through many inspirational public speeches, Los Angeles's first elected Latino mayor in modern history convinced many of the city's residents to envision a brighter future, even in times of declining budgets and economic instability. In his first state of the city address, Villaraigosa said:

> This day isn't about addressing the state of things as they are: It's about the state of our city as it *should* be. Over nine months ago, I stood before you

355

persuasive speech
A speech in which the speaker attempts to reinforce, modify, or change audience members' beliefs, attitudes, opinions, values, and behaviors.

on the south steps of City Hall, and I asked you to dream with me about a different kind of future for Los Angeles. A future where LA is taking the lead as the great global city of the twenty-first century. A future where people in communities around our city are drawn closer together by a world-class transit system. A future where we are growing greener as we grow. Where children can walk to school in safety. And where no kid in any neighborhood in any part of Los Angeles is ever robbed of his or her childhood.

And I asked you to imagine a future where it doesn't matter who you are or where you come from. . . . Whether you're African American, Latino, Caucasian, or Asian. . . . Whether you're gay or straight, rich or poor. . . . Where every Angeleno has a chance to show their talent.[1]

Antonio Villaraigosa has become a major figure in American politics because he understands how to connect with people, stir their hopes and dreams, and move them to act. In short, he speaks persuasively.

This chapter covers the basics of persuasive public speaking, and Chapter 15 explains how you can apply the elements of argument in persuasive situations. The two chapters work together to provide specific strategies for giving an effective and ethical persuasive speech.

Defining Persuasion

Using language, images, and other means of communication to influence people's attitudes, beliefs, values, or actions.

READ it **Persuasion** relies on language, images, and other means of communication to influence people's attitudes, beliefs, values, or actions.[2] You are continually immersed in a sea of persuasive messages. Your doctor tries to get you to adopt a more nutritious diet. A coworker instant-messages you a request for help with a project. Online advertisers use podcasts and interactive games to sell you products and services.

Although you may be informed by persuasive messages like these, informative and persuasive speeches differ in a key way. Informative speakers fulfill the role of *expert* on a topic and seek to facilitate audience understanding about it. In contrast, persuasive speakers take on the role of *promoter* or *proponent*, advocating a particular view on a topic they want the audience to adopt. As a persuasive speaker, you'll become an expert on your topic, but you'll go beyond your expertise to argue for a specific viewpoint you want the audience to accept. Persuasive speakers voice a clear position on a topic, whereas informative speakers remain neutral. For example, for an informative speech on the digital camera, the speaker would make the audience more aware of the topic, say, by describing the camera's history. In contrast, a persuasive speaker would advocate a particular view of the topic, perhaps arguing that traditional cameras are superior to digital ones.

Persuasive speeches address three types of questions: fact, value, and policy. While each of these types of speeches has the general purpose of persuading an audience, they differ in the kind of outcome the speaker seeks. The type of persuasive speech you give influences how you develop your specific purpose and thesis, select main points, and organize your ideas.

Speeches on Questions of Fact

A **question of fact** asks whether something is true or false. In speeches addressing questions of fact, the speaker tries to persuade an audience that something did or did not occur, or that one event caused another. For example, in a criminal court the prosecution attempts to persuade the jury the defendant did engage in illegal activity, while the defense argues the defendant did not.

Chapter 7 defined *facts* as observations you make from your own and others' experiences, and *inferences* as conclusions you draw based on facts. In speeches addressing questions of fact, speakers and listeners must carefully distinguish between facts and inferences. An example of a speech that blurred the line between facts and inferences is former Secretary of State Colin Powell's address to the United Nations on February 5, 2003.[3] In his speech, Powell argued that Iraq's leader, Saddam Hussein, possessed weapons of mass destruction and would use them against other countries, including the United States. Using satellite images, artists' drawings, intelligence findings, audiotapes, and other information, Powell argued an attack was imminent. But much of what Powell presented as fact turned out to be inferences based on facts.[4] The satellite photos, for instance, did show some trucks, but they were water or fire trucks, not decontamination units for people working with biochemicals as Powell implied. Several years later,

> A question that asks whether something is true or false.

and after weapons of mass destruction had not been found in Iraq, Powell admitted he regretted giving the speech and presenting as fact information he later found out was unreliable.[5]

Speeches on questions of fact typically address three issues: what is observed or known, how the observations were made, and whether new observations have changed what people once thought of as fact. Generally, individuals agree on facts because they're verifiable—they can be proven true or false. But sometimes people disagree about what they observe or on how the observations were made. For example, a recent study found on average Americans talk regularly about their personal troubles with two people, down from three in 1985. However, the questions asked implied face-to-face communication only, leaving out other ways to interact, such as text messaging and online chat. You might agree with the study's results but might disagree with how the questions were worded. Because facts can be contested, the speaker must persuade the audience that the version of the facts she or he presents is correct.

People also revise facts based on new observations. Old cigarette ads showed doctors telling people to smoke. Now tobacco products include the U.S. Surgeon General's warning that smoking causes many severe health problems, including lung cancer, strokes, and coronary heart disease.[6] As more research is done on the effects of smoking, the facts about smoking change.

The persuasiveness of a speech addressing a question of fact rests on the speaker's ability to present sound, credible evidence. Facts and statistics typically provide the foundational evidence for speeches on questions of fact. But speakers may also use examples, testimony, definitions, and narratives as supporting evidence. For example, in a persuasive speech arguing that mandatory seatbelt laws save lives, the speaker might include quotes from an interview with a highway patrol officer or a personal narrative about how wearing a seatbelt saved the speaker's life in a car crash.

▲ Speeches on questions of fact often address topics about contested facts, such as effective training methods for athletes and the techniques used to construct the Egyptian pyramids. What questions of fact do you think would make interesting speech topics?

SPECIFIC PURPOSES, THESIS STATEMENTS, AND MAIN POINTS FOR SPEECHES ON QUESTIONS OF FACT

For persuasive speaking, your general purpose is *to persuade,* so your specific purpose should begin with something like "To persuade my audience to [take some sort of action]" or "To convince my audience [to think a certain way]."

When you give a speech on a question of fact, you want the audience to believe or agree with you that something is true or false. Your focus is on reinforcing or changing how people think, but not how they behave as with this example.

> **Topic:** The Peak in Worldwide Oil Production
>
> **General purpose:** To persuade
>
> **Specific purpose:** To convince my audience that oil production in the world has peaked
>
> **Thesis:** Historical evidence shows that worldwide oil production has peaked and can no longer increase.

This example demonstrates how the topic, general purpose, specific purpose, and thesis work together to answer the question of fact you're asking. In this speech you're asking, "Has oil production in the world reached its peak?" Your specific purpose and thesis provide the answer you want your audience to agree with: Yes, "historical evidence shows that worldwide oil production has peaked and can no longer increase."

When creating your main points for a speech on a question of fact, ask yourself, "What would make someone think this claim is true (or false)?" For example, in a speech about the causes of autism, the thesis suggests that the speaker will address theories associated with autism's causes:

> **Topic:** Causes of Autism
>
> **General purpose:** To persuade
>
> **Specific purpose:** To convince my audience that the causes of autism are unknown
>
> **Thesis:** Although there are theories about the causes of autism, the true cause is still unknown.
>
> **Main points:**
>
> I. Genetic theories of autism suggest the disease is caused by an anomaly in the ways certain genes interact with each other, but the research is inconclusive.
>
> II. Viral theories suggest that autism is caused by a virus or infection, although research findings are inconsistent.
>
> III. Some theories, such as the notions that childhood vaccines and poor parenting cause autism, have not been supported.

ORGANIZATIONAL PATTERNS FOR SPEECHES ON QUESTIONS OF FACT

As with an informative speech, choose a pattern of organization for a persuasive speech consistent with your specific purpose and thesis. All the organizational patterns discussed in Chapter 8 can be used for persuasive speeches. For speeches that address questions of fact, speakers usually arrange their main points in a chronological, spatial, topical, or cause-and-effect pattern. The thesis often provides guidance about how best to organize a speech. For example, the thesis for the oil production speech, shown again below, suggests a chronological pattern, which allows the speaker to trace production trends from the past to the present.

Organizational pattern: Chronological

Topic: Worldwide Oil Production

General purpose: To persuade

Specific purpose: To convince my audience that oil production in the world has peaked

Thesis: Historical evidence shows that worldwide oil production has peaked and can no longer increase.

Main points:

    I. The rate of new oil discoveries worldwide has declined since the 1960s.

    II. In 1970, U.S. oil production peaked.

    III. In 1976, the last major oil reserve was found in the Middle East.

    IV. Oil production has not increased in the past ten years.

    V. Demand for oil has quadrupled in the past five years.

The next two examples show how speeches on questions of fact can be organized according to the spatial and topical patterns. Notice how the thesis statements suggest the appropriate pattern to use.

Organizational pattern: Spatial

Topic: Health Risks in International Travel

General purpose: To persuade

Specific purpose: To convince my audience they will encounter health risks when visiting foreign countries

Main points:

    I. When visiting South America, you must consider certain health concerns.

    II. When visiting East Asia, you should be aware of other health risks.

    III. U.S. visitors to South Asia encounter important health risks as well.

    IV. Americans traveling to Africa face several health risks.

Organizational pattern: Topical

Topic: Effectiveness of Vitamin Pills

General purpose: To persuade

Specific purpose: To convince my audience that vitamin pills don't improve health

Main points:

    I. Vitamin intake is necessary for good health.

    II. Sufficient vitamin intake occurs through proper eating habits.

    III. Vitamin pills add nothing to natural vitamin intake.

    IV. Vitamin pills can create health risks.

Speakers use the cause-and-effect pattern of organization for speeches on questions of fact when attempting to prove or disprove one behavior or event causes another. Consider this example about smoke-free restaurants and bars.

> **Topic:** Smoking Bans in Restaurants and Bars
>
> **General purpose:** To persuade
>
> **Specific purpose:** To convince my audience that smoking bans in restaurants and bars increase business
>
> **Thesis:** Banning smoking in restaurants and bars increases business in those establishments.
>
> **Main points:**
>
>   I. Many states and cities have banned smoking in restaurants and bars.
>
>   II. As measured by number of patrons and profits, business increased after smoking bans were enacted in restaurants and bars.

In applying the cause-and-effect pattern of organization to speeches on questions of fact, the speaker must clearly demonstrate causation—that action A led to action B. The smoking ban example does that, with statistics showing increased sales and patronage after the ban was enacted. Still, the speaker must not confuse *correlation* with *causation*. Two actions may appear linked, but may not be related at all. You might observe, for instance, that on the mornings you use your alarm clock to wake you, you're more tired than on the days you don't use your alarm. Does that mean the alarm clock makes you tired? Of course not. The likely explanation is that on the days you don't use your alarm you get more sleep than on the days you do use it. In addition, there may be multiple causes for a single effect, particularly with complex issues. For example, seatbelts do save lives, but decreases in highway death rates over the past twenty years aren't due just to seatbelts. Improved safety technology in cars, more sophisticated road engineering, and crackdowns on drunk driving have also contributed to lowering the number of deaths on U.S. highways.

Speeches on Questions of Value

A **question of value** asks for a subjective evaluation of something's worth, significance, quality, or condition. Questions of value ask if something is good or bad, right or wrong, beautiful or ugly, boring or engaging, funny or serious—all qualitative judgments about something's significance. A question of value, therefore, addresses individual opinions and cultural beliefs rather than proving something true or false. Like speeches on ques-

A question that asks for a subjective evaluation of something's worth, significance, quality, or condition.

tions of fact, speeches on questions of value focus on persuading the audience to believe a certain way, but they don't ask the audience to take action or change their behavior.

Speeches on questions of value address timeless issues such as the morality of war as well as recent concerns such as the ethical uses of social networking websites like Facebook. Topics may be serious, as with the best way to address global warming, or more lighthearted, as with a critique of a city's worst architecture. Still, any discussion based on applying subjective standards will result in some level of disagreement. Because questions of value can prove contentious, they often make for stimulating persuasive speeches, especially if you and your audience view the topic differently.

SPECIFIC PURPOSES, THESIS STATEMENTS, AND MAIN POINTS FOR SPEECHES ON QUESTIONS OF VALUE

In a speech on a question of value, your specific purpose reveals your evaluation of the topic's quality. Do you think something is good or bad, right or wrong, moral or immoral, the best or the worst? Make your position clear so your audience will know exactly what you think after listening to your speech. Then develop a thesis supporting your position.

Topic: Public Art

General purpose: To persuade

Specific purpose: To convince my audience that public art is good for everyone

Thesis: Public art is good for everyone because it rejuvenates commercial areas, gives residents a better quality of life, encourages tourism, and energizes local artist communities.

The main points for a speech on a question of value must clearly represent and strongly support your position. Some speeches addressing questions of value focus on fairly noncontroversial topics, such as recycling is good and littering is bad. But because this type of speech reflects individual judgments, speeches on questions of value more often touch on controversial and sensitive topics such as capital punishment, abortion, the right to die, and animal rights. Your challenge is to make your position on the topic seem reasonable to an audience, especially a negative audience.

As you prepare your main points, ask yourself questions such as, What kinds of supporting materials will best convince my audience to accept my position or change their views? What ideas support my position and how should I organize them? What can I reasonably expect my audience to think after listening to my speech about this topic? The value of school vouchers provides a useful example. This topic has caused much debate among parents, teachers, administrators, church groups, and others concerned with public education. One way to address this controversy is to examine education reforms in a wide range of locations.

Topic: School Vouchers

General purpose: To persuade

Specific purpose: To convince my audience that school vouchers are the best way to solve education problems in K–12 schools

Thesis: School reform movements in the United States and other countries show that school vouchers are the best way to solve current problems in K–12 schools.

Main points:

    I. Elementary- and secondary-school reform movements in Australia provide support for the superiority of a school voucher program over other choices.

    II. Education reform movements in Japan also provide support for school vouchers.

    III. Recent changes in Canada's public school system indicate how a school voucher program would work in the United States.

    IV. Trial programs in U.S. schools show that school vouchers solve current problems.

ORGANIZATIONAL PATTERNS FOR SPEECHES ON QUESTIONS OF VALUE

For speeches that address questions of value, speakers usually arrange their main points in a chronological, spatial, or topical pattern. As with all persuasive speeches, choosing the appropriate organizational pattern for a speech on a question of value influences your ability to convince the audience. For example, in a speech about the use of computer-generated imagery (CGI) in films, a chronological pattern allows you to begin by discussing highly-acclaimed movies made before CGI, strengthening your argument that CGI-based movies are inferior.

Organizational pattern: Chronological

Topic: Computer-generated Imagery (CGI) in Movies

General purpose: To persuade

Specific purpose: To convince my audience that movies using CGI are inferior to movies that don't use CGI

Thesis: Movies using CGI are inferior to movies without CGI because movies with CGI focus more on the CGI technology than on telling a good story.

Main points:

    I. Before computer-generated imagery (CGI), Hollywood produced rich narratives such as *Citizen Kane, Sunset Boulevard,* and *One Flew Over the Cuckoo's Nest.*

    II. CGI was introduced in the early 1970s with the movie *Westworld* and attention turned to CGI and away from writing good stories.

    III. Today the emphasis is on CGI and telling a good story is forgotten, as with *Jumper* and *Pirates of the Caribbean: At World's End.*

A topical pattern of organization works well for a question of value speech when the main points are of about equal importance. In the following example, all three points contribute in different but equally important ways to the thesis.

Organizational pattern: Topical

Topic: Skin-lightening Products

General purpose: To persuade

Specific purpose: To convince my audience that skin-lightening products are unethical

Thesis: Skin-lightening products are unethical because they can cause physical and psychological harm to users and imply that light skin is better than dark skin.

> ***Main points:***
>
> I. Cosmetic products used to lighten the skin can cause physical harm to the users.
>
> II. Cosmetic products used to lighten the skin can cause psychological harm to the users.
>
> III. Cosmetic products used to lighten the skin create a racist impression that light skin is preferable to dark skin.

For an example of a speech on a question of value organized using the spatial pattern, review the speech on school vouchers earlier in the section.

Speeches on Questions of Policy

A **question of policy** asks what course of action should be taken or how a problem should be solved. Note the word *should*—that's your clue that a speech addresses a question of policy rather than a question of fact or value.

Questions of policy may reflect current controversies, such as U.S. immigration policies, or less contentious topics, such as getting more exercise. These questions also range from the general, such as promoting democracy around the world, to the specific, such as academic integrity policies on your campus. Examples of questions of policy include the following:

- Should consumers buy products made in the United States?
- Should we eliminate remedial courses in U.S. higher education?
- How should people protect themselves from identity theft?

Speeches on questions of policy ask the audience to personally take (or not take) a particular action or support (or not support) a particular position.[7] Speakers might request immediate involvement, general support for a social or political movement of some kind, disapproval of an idea, or a change in behavior. For example, a speaker might propose that

- College students should circulate a petition to ban junk food on campuses.
- People should support the animal rights movement.

A question that asks what course of action should be taken or how a problem should be solved.

- Local residents should not approve of changes in the zoning law.
- Everyone should exercise more.

In a general sense, policies are formal doctrines for institutions like governments, organizations, schools, teams, and clubs. These policies often take the form of rules, laws, plans, or codes of behavior that institutions create and enforce. A speech that calls for making noisy leaf blowers illegal, for instance, or a proposal for constructing more affordable housing units in your community, falls into this category. But as the above examples demonstrate, questions of policy address a wide range of issues at the personal, group, institutional, societal, and cultural levels. Moreover, many questions of policy call for individualized responses, such as recommending consumers carefully monitor their purchases of clothing or protect themselves against identity theft.

When choosing a topic for a question of policy speech, you need not stick with traditional public policy controversies like gun control, capital punishment, and the right to die. Unless there's current discussion surrounding the issue, you may want to avoid these topics. Original, thought-provoking topics or unique positions on well-known subjects are more likely to interest your audience than material they've heard many times before. Most important, choose something you truly care about that will resonate with your audience. You might consider, for instance, policy questions involving universal human rights, social justice, or the environment. You may want to present your views on one of the many controversies springing from various interpretations of the U.S. Constitution or government policy, such as flag burning, separation of church and state, or limits on the Patriot Act. Decisions about developing regional public transportation, raising teachers' salaries, or banning negative political campaign ads are examples of other kinds of debatable issues that spring from government policy. Or you may want to choose a more specific, local issue arising from your campus, your workplace, or your community.

UPI Photo/Michael Kleinfeld/Landov

▲ Speeches on questions of policy often ask an audience to take a course of action addressing a need or solving a problem in their community. What problem in your community do you think would make a good topic for a persuasive speech?

Online Resources for Hot Topics

Online resources such as Quintura's topic cloud and Google's Society > Issues page can trigger topic ideas for any type of speech. In addition to those more general sites, the ones below focus more specifically on policy and controversial issues. Use both the general and more specific websites to help you select and research a topic.

Almanac of Policy Issues
policyalmanac.org

An independent, nonpartisan service organization providing background information about public policy issues in the United States, such as civil rights, global warming, and campaign finance

reform. Browse by category and topic or search the site.

ProCon.org: Pros and Cons of Controversial Issues
procon.org

This nonprofit, nonpartisan website identifies controversial topics such as electronic voting machines, medical marijuana, and the Iraq war. The site outlines the pros and cons of each topic and provides links to resources.

IDEA: International Debate Education Association
idebate.org

Although the site's target audience is student debaters, anyone can use it. In addition to an extensive

database detailing the pros and cons associated with many current issues, the organization sponsors Debatepedia, a searchable wiki with hundreds of argument pages on a broad range of topics.

Many college libraries also have online directories of current issues. Some examples are the Palo Alto College in San Antonio (accd.edu/PAC/LRC/issues.htm), St. Ambrose University in Davenport, Iowa (library.sau.edu/bestinfo/Hot/hotindex.htm), and San Diego State University (infodome.sdsu.edu/research/guides/hot/supersites.shtml). If you can't find a hot topics directory on your library's website, contact the reference librarian.

SPECIFIC PURPOSES, THESIS STATEMENTS, AND MAIN POINTS FOR SPEECHES ON QUESTIONS OF POLICY

Unlike speeches on questions of fact and value, speeches on questions of policy often include a call to action, urging the audience to engage in a specific behavior. You may ask your audience to take an immediate action, such as signing a petition, or an action in the future, such as carefully reading the fine print when they sign an employment contract. Sometimes you ask your listeners simply to lend their passive support, as with favoring a campus regulation on skateboards or opposing new zoning laws.

Phrase your specific purpose to clearly indicate what you want your audience to do or agree with. Then develop your thesis so it outlines how you'll support your position.

When you create your main points, choose ones that clearly represent why a change to an existing policy or situation is necessary, what the benefits of a change are, and what you want the audience to take away from your message. As you're preparing your speech, ask yourself these questions:

- What support can I show for my position?
- How close is my audience to my position—positive, negative, divided, uninformed, or apathetic?
- How does what I suggest solve the problem or move the cause forward in some way?

The following examples, one calling on audience members to take action and the other asking for their support of a position, demonstrate how the main points flow from the thesis.

Topic: Personal Emergency Preparedness

General purpose: To persuade

Specific purpose: To persuade my audience to better prepare themselves for natural disasters that may occur in our area

Thesis: Individuals increase their chances of surviving a natural disaster by practicing personal emergency preparedness.

Main points:

I. Hurricane Katrina and other recent natural disasters demonstrate what happens when we fail to prepare for such calamities.

II. Responses to recent natural disasters in our area show that most people are not prepared for them.

III. Personal emergency preparedness is essential to responding appropriately to natural disasters.

IV. Personal emergency preparedness increases your likelihood of surviving a natural disaster.

V. Personal emergency preparedness involves developing an emergency plan, assembling a disaster supplies kit, and identifying local disaster shelters.

> **Topic:** Year-round Education in K–12
>
> **General purpose:** To persuade
>
> **Specific purpose:** To persuade my audience to support the institution of year-round education nationwide
>
> **Thesis:** Year-round K–12 education should be instituted nationwide because of its educational, social, and economic benefits.
>
> **Main points:**
>
> I. The current nine-month school calendar shortchanges students, the taxpayers, and society.
>
> II. Having K–12 students attend school year-round provides educational, economic, and societal benefits.

In the first example, the speaker indicates why a change is necessary, explains what change should occur, and then tells listeners the specific actions they need to take. In this way, the main points support the response the speaker seeks from the audience: to prepare for natural disasters. In the second example, the speaker asks the audience to simply support the position, first demonstrating why a change is necessary and then describing the benefits of the change.

ORGANIZATIONAL PATTERNS FOR SPEECHES ON QUESTIONS OF POLICY

Because speeches on questions of policy ask for some sort of change, speakers must clearly articulate why the change must occur and what should be done. Although the organizational patterns previously described can be applied to this type of speech, three other patterns generally are more effective: problem-solution, problem-cause-solution, and the motivated sequence.

The Problem-Solution Pattern of Organization

The problem-solution pattern presents a need or problem and then shows how to solve it, as the following example demonstrates:

> *Topic:* Corporal Punishment by Parents
>
> *General purpose:* To persuade
>
> *Specific purpose:* To persuade my audience that parents never should physically strike their children
>
> *Main points:*
>
> I. Children suffer serious physical and psychological consequences as a result of corporal punishment.
>
> II. Parents should never physically strike their children.

Using this pattern successfully requires clearly establishing the problem's existence. If listeners aren't convinced the problem exists, the solution becomes irrelevant. Once they think there's a problem, the solution must seem reasonable. In the corporal punishment speech, the solution flows naturally from the problem—hitting children harms them, so parents shouldn't do it. However, if you called for installing video cameras in homes to monitor parents and punish those caught striking their children, the audience likely would consider your solution too extreme.

The Problem-Cause-Solution Pattern of Organization

The problem-cause-solution pattern of organization extends the problem-solution pattern by adding an additional step: the cause of the problem. Consider this example of a speech about junk food on campuses.

> *Topic:* Junk Food on Our Campus
>
> *General purpose:* To persuade
>
> *Specific purpose:* To encourage my audience to sign a petition banning the sale of junk food on our campus
>
> *Thesis:* Junk food should be banned on campus because it contributes to obesity, poor nutrition, and immune system problems.
>
> *Main points:*
>
> I. Many college students are overweight, eat poorly, and have weak immune systems.

II. Junk food is a major contributing factor to these problems.

III. We must work to ban the sale of junk food on our campus.

The first main point explains the problem: Many college students are overweight, eat poorly, and have weak immune systems. The second point identifies the cause of this problem—junk food. The third point provides a solution: Get rid of junk food, at least on campus. Here's another example of a question of policy speech that applies the problem-cause-solution pattern.

Topic: Border Security

General purpose: To persuade

Specific purpose: To convince my audience to support increased border patrols between the United States and Canada

Thesis: We must have better security to prevent illegal immigrants from crossing the U.S.–Canada border.

Main points:

I. Every year, thousands of people cross into the United States illegally from our neighbor to the north, Canada.

II. Security on the U.S.–Canada border is lax, making it easy for people to enter our country illegally.

III. We must increase border patrols between the United States and Canada.

▼ In a persuasive speech on reducing credit card use, you could use the problem-cause-solution pattern to argue people are in debt and spend more money than their budget allows (problem); easy credit causes people to spend money they don't have on purchases they don't need (cause); and refraining from using credit cards is the only way to get spending under control (solution). How would the focus of this speech change if you organized it using another pattern?

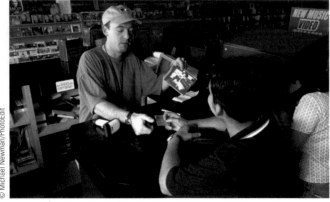

© Michael Newman/PhotoEdit

As with the problem-solution pattern of organization, getting the audience to believe a problem exists provides the foundation for the remainder of a speech using the problem-cause-solution pattern. The speaker must then link the problem with the cause and show that the solution represents a reasonable answer to the problem.

Monroe's Motivated Sequence

Monroe's motivated sequence encourages speakers to focus on audience outcomes when organizing ideas. Composed of five steps summarized in **Table 14.1**, this pattern of organization requires speakers to identify and respond to what will motivate the audience to pay attention.[8]

TABLE 14.1 ► Monroe's Motivated Sequence

STEP	SPEAKER'S ACTION	AUDIENCE'S RESPONSE
Attention	Relate topic to audience to gain attention	I will listen because this is relevant to me.
Need	Establish the problem/current harm	There's a problem that needs my attention.
Satisfaction	Describe the solution to the problem	Here's the solution to the problem.
Visualization	Show benefits of proposed solution and/or costs of not implementing it	I can visualize the benefits of this solution and/or the costs of not implementing it.
Action	Explain how audience can implement proposed solution	I will do this.

1. In the first step, *gaining the audience's attention*, the speaker relates the topic to the listeners, linking it to their lives and providing them with a reason to listen.

2. In the second step, *establishing the need for something or the existence of a problem,* the speaker shows listeners that they lack important information or that there's an issue requiring their attention.

3. In the third step, *satisfying the problem,* the speaker provides audience members with the information they lack or the solution to the problem.

4. In the fourth step, the speaker *helps audience members visualize an outcome* by describing for them what will happen if they apply or don't apply the solution.

5. In the final step, *moving the audience to action*, the speaker details how audience members can implement the solution.

For the motivated sequence to work, each step must build on the previous one. If earlier steps don't elicit the desired audience response, later steps will fall short as well. If you're giving a persuasive speech in which you ask your audience to take some sort of action, all five steps of the motivated sequence apply, as in the following example:

Topic: Simplify Your Life

General purpose: To persuade

Specific purpose: To persuade my audience to take steps to simplify their lives

Thesis: Our consumer culture makes our lives needlessly complex, so we should take concrete steps to simplify our lives.

Steps: **Attention.** We work more hours, spend more time commuting, take fewer vacations, and wade through more e-mail and voicemail than at any time in the past.

Need. We buy things we don't need, waste time watching television and surfing the web, and drive miles out of our way to save a few pennies on gasoline.

Satisfaction. Simplifying your life means figuring out what you value most and focusing on activities that help you fulfill those values.

Visualization. Think about all the time you'd have to do what you like by cutting out all the things you do that aren't really necessary.

Action. There are specific steps you can take to simplify your life, such as concentrating on a few goals and doing them well, setting aside time for yourself, and getting rid of clutter by donating to charity or throwing away the things you don't really use.

If you simply want the audience's agreement or support, you can drop the fifth step of the motivated sequence, the action step, as with the following example:

Topic: Cooperation in Video Games

General purpose: To persuade

Specific purpose: To persuade my audience to support video games that contribute to society by promoting more cooperation and less competition

Thesis: Video games that encourage players to cooperate with each other rather than compete against each other would benefit our society.

> **Steps:** **Attention.** The stereotypical video game player is a teenaged male, but did you know that women account for over 40 percent of interactive game players and the average age of a player is 28?
>
> **Need.** Violent video games make the headlines, but the real problem is the lack of games that help players develop teamwork skills, so essential in today's world.
>
> **Satisfaction.** Video games based on cooperation rather than competition provide a logical way to facilitate the development of teamwork skills.
>
> **Visualization.** Even if you don't play video games, facilitating the ability to cooperate with others contributes more generally to society, as you've probably experienced yourself when working with a team.

In this example, you're not asking the audience to play or develop cooperation-based video games. Instead, you're asking them to agree with you that such games contribute positively to society.

Persuasive speeches address questions of fact, value, and policy. The question you ask influences your specific purpose, thesis, main points, and organization of ideas. Speakers may discuss the same topic in all three types of persuasive speeches. **Table 14.2** on page 376 demonstrates how the type of persuasive speech you choose to give influences how you develop your topic.

Persuading Different Types of Audiences

Just as advertisers must know their audiences well and understand how to reach them effectively, you should know where your audience stands on your topic so you can design a message that will encourage them to listen and consider your views. Chapter 5 explains how to analyze an audience for any type of speech. This section provides specific strategies persuasive speakers use to address the attitudes, values, and beliefs of five common audience positions: negative or hostile, positive or sympathetic, divided, uninformed, and apathetic. These audience positions and strategies are summarized in **Table 14.3** on page 377.

TABLE 14.2 ▶ **Types of Persuasive Speeches on a Single Topic: The U.S. Prison System**

TYPE OF SPEECH	SPECIFIC PURPOSE	THESIS	MAIN POINTS
Question of fact	To convince my audience that U.S. prisons cost more than they did 25 years ago	U.S. prisons cost more to build, maintain, and staff than they did 25 years ago.	I. Prisons cost more to build than they did 25 years ago. II. Prisons cost more to maintain than they did 25 years ago. III. Prisons cost more to staff than they did 25 years ago.
Question of value	To convince my audience that the U.S. prison system is failing	Our prison system is failing because prisons are overcrowded, prison violence is on the rise, and recidivism rates have increased.	I. U.S. prisons are dangerously overcrowded. II. Prison violence is at an all-time high. III. More ex-convicts are ending up back in prison.
Question of policy	To persuade my audience to support U.S. prison system reform	U.S. prisons must be reformed because they're unsafe for both the public and prisoners.	I. Prisons don't protect the public from crime. II. Prisons are dangerous for the health and welfare of prisoners. III. Prison reform that focuses on rehabilitation will help solve the problem. IV. Rehabilitation reduces crime and improves prisoners' health and welfare.

TABLE 14.3 ▶ Types of Audiences and Persuasive Strategies

TYPE OF AUDIENCE AND VIEW OF TOPIC	PERSUASIVE STRATEGIES
Negative (informed → unfavorable or highly unfavorable)	• Establish credibility • Take common-ground approach • Visualize topic in positive ways • Anticipate and address objections
Positive (informed → favorable or highly favorable)	• Incorporate narratives • Rely on engaging evidence to reinforce commitment • Use vivid language and images • Suggest action
Divided (informed → split: half favorable, half unfavorable)	• Integrate strategies for negative and positive audiences
Uninformed (uninformed → no opinion)	• Motivate audience to learn more about topic • Demonstrate expertise and fairness • Use repetition and redundancy • Keep persuasion subtle
Apathetic (informed → not important)	• Gain attention and interest • Show how topic affects audience • Display energy and dynamism • Take a one-sided approach

THE NEGATIVE AUDIENCE

A negative audience, also called a hostile audience, is informed about your topic and holds an unfavorable view of it. A negative audience may seem intimidating, but simple exposure to differing points of view is where effective persuasion starts for many audience members. Suppose, for instance, you want your audience to support an initiative on your campus to abolish all general education requirements. That goal may be unattainable, so you might want to argue for a more moderate step, such as reducing the required number of general education units.

An audience that is informed about a speaker's topic and holds an unfavorable view of the speaker's position.

When you know you'll likely encounter a high degree of resistance to your position on a topic, several strategies will help you achieve your goal.[9]

- *Establish your credibility with the audience.* Developing a positive relationship with the audience, showing an interest in them, and demonstrating your expertise on the topic all contribute to making a good impression.
- *Take a common-ground approach to the topic.* Identify areas of agreement with the audience, then move to areas of disagreement. If listeners perceive they share similar viewpoints with you, they'll be more open to your message.[10] In a speech on same-sex marriage, you might draw parallels between the right of gays and lesbians to marry and other struggles over civil rights—abolishing slavery, passing laws against child labor, or giving women the right to vote, for instance. You could demonstrate how much resistance there was to each of these changes and then point out these rights are now considered ordinary.
- *Help your audience visualize your topic in positive ways.* Often just helping the audience get used to a new idea is the first step in effective persuasion. In a speech advocating increased funding for space exploration, you might show a few compelling digital slides of Mars or distant galaxies to spark the audience's imagination and give them a more favorable impression of the topic.
- *Finally, prepare for your audience's negative reaction to your position.* Consider all the reasons your audience may not agree with you. Then determine how you will confront and overcome those objections in your speech. For example, in a speech on raising the minimum wage in the United States, you could address your listeners' concerns about job loss by pointing to research that shows no such effect. When you acknowledge the audience's concerns in your speech, you demonstrate an understanding of their perspective, which increases your likelihood of winning them over.

THE POSITIVE AUDIENCE

An audience that is informed about a speaker's topic and has a favorable view of the speaker's position.

A **positive audience**, also called a **sympathetic audience**, is informed about your topic and has a favorable view of your position. These audience members want to have their views confirmed and reinforced, take part in a social event that attracts other like-minded people, learn something more about the topic, and in some cases, find out what they can do to advance the cause. Political campaign speeches and religious rallies are common examples of speakers addressing this kind of positive or sympathetic audience. Several strategies will help you focus on reinforcing thoughts and behaviors.[11]

- *Rely on narratives to elaborate on your points.* Stories work especially well to reinforce the position audience members already hold. For example, if you know that your audience believes in the value of environmental responsibility, a speech promoting environmental activism might begin with an exciting story about how you got involved in the topic.

- *Incorporate engaging evidence that further reinforces the audience's commitment to the topic.* Use testimony and examples your audience will find captivating; stay away from long lists of facts, endless statistics, and dull definitions. For example, you might explain how various successful political initiatives—saving forests, rivers, wetlands, and lakes from pollution and urban sprawl, for example—have preserved valuable natural resources and improved the quality of life for all the planet's inhabitants.

- *Use vivid language and images to heighten your audience's enthusiasm for the topic.* Refer to "flourishing, green forests; icy cold, raging rivers; wetlands teeming with wildlife; and cool, inviting lakes" rather than "forests, rivers, wetlands, and lakes." Incorporating a short series of colorful slides displaying the beauty of land and water saved from destruction through political action can also deepen your audience's appreciation for the topic.

- *When audience members already agree with your view, rally them to take action.* For example, you might encourage your audience to join an environmental group in the community or on campus, participate actively in Earth Day this year, support impending environmental legislation, recycle plastic materials, stop junk mail, or boycott products that degrade the environment.

AP Photo/Christophe Ena

▲ Ishmael Beah is an example of a highly credible speaker. Forced to be a "boy soldier" in his native Sierra Leone, Africa, Beah, now 26, advocates for the rights of children exploited in war-torn countries. His personal experiences, sociable speaking style, and well-supported arguments lead audiences to view him sympathetically, despite the views they hold on the topics he speaks about.

THE DIVIDED AUDIENCE

A **divided audience** is informed about your topic but split in its views: half have a favorable view and half have an unfavorable one. Speakers are often faced with divided audiences, especially when addressing diverse audiences or speaking about controversial issues. With a divided audience, the main challenge is persuading those audience members who disagree with you, so you can employ the same basic approach used for a

An audience that is informed about a speaker's topic but equally split between those who favor the speaker's position and those who oppose it.

negative audience. This means that you'll want to clearly establish your credibility and connection with the audience, take a common-ground approach, visualize the topic in positive ways for the audience, and confront possible objections. Still, you want to acknowledge those who agree with you as well. Relevant narratives, appealing testimony and examples, and engaging images will help you target sympathetic audience members and may appeal to hostile listeners as well.

Suppose you're speaking to a community group in an urban neighborhood that has experienced a high rate of street crime in recent years. The specific purpose of your speech is to convince your audience that surveillance video cameras should be installed throughout the area. Some members of your audience favor the idea as a practical way to reduce crime. Other members oppose the idea, viewing it as an intrusion on their right to privacy. Here are a few strategies that will help you address the entire audience effectively:

- *Demonstrate that you recognize the legitimacy of the arguments for and against the issue.* Street crime is a problem that must be solved, yet the right to privacy is a fundamental principle of democracy and should be upheld.
- *Establish your credibility* by citing statistics showing video surveillance does reduce street crime significantly.
- *Establish common ground among all audience members* by saying you are certain everyone in the room agrees with the right to privacy.
- *Address the objection,* that surveillance cameras intrude on the community's right to privacy, by saying that the point is not to take away anyone's rights but rather to restore privacy rights that have been taken away.
- *Reinforce the position of those who agree with you* with testimony and examples from places where surveillance cameras are used.

In the end, you encourage the resisters to rethink their position not only by the strength of your argument and supporting evidence but also because you, the speaker, understand what's at stake in terms of privacy.

THE UNINFORMED AUDIENCE

An audience that is unfamiliar with a speaker's topic and has no opinion about it.

Uninformed audiences are unfamiliar with your topic and have no opinion about it. Audience members potentially could be interested in a topic you care about, but they simply lack exposure to it. For example, military families would want to be informed about a change in benefits for veterans the government was quietly considering. Several strategies will help you provide the information listeners need to facilitate their agreement with you.[12]

- *Motivate your audience to want to learn more about the topic*. You must link the audience with the topic and help them reach the conclusion, "I don't know much about this, but I should." For example, you'd show how the audience would be affected by changing benefits for veterans. Sometimes the relationship isn't readily apparent. Changing benefits for veterans may not seem to affect nonveterans, but increased benefits might mean higher costs for all taxpayers, and decreased benefits might result in a greater burden on local social services.
- *Demonstrate your expertise on the topic and fairness in addressing all perspectives*. As a persuasive speaker, you will argue one side of the issue or the other. What changes in benefits for military families do you support? Without turning your persuasive speech into an informative one, you must describe the issue. Show you've done your research on the topic and can provide listeners with what they need to know to formulate an opinion. Audience members will be much more likely to agree with your position if they believe they have acquired a fair and comprehensive sense of the issue.
- *Use repetition and redundancy to reinforce your points*. Your audience is new to this topic, so provide them with similar information about the topic in several forms. For the speech about veterans benefits, you could define the purpose of these benefits, present facts about the services the government currently offers veterans, show statistics comparing those services with the proposed services, offer testimony from a scholar who studies veterans benefits, and tell a story about a veteran who used those benefits to achieve an important goal, such as completing college. These different types of supporting materials all focus on the veterans benefits, building redundancy into the speech.
- *Keep your persuasion subtle*. Let the audience know your position, but avoid emphatic, inflammatory, or passionate statements. Instead, take a matter-of-fact approach. In the speech about veterans benefits, you might say, "I support the changes to veterans benefits currently under consideration. Let me tell you about it." If you wait to let audience members know your view on the topic, they'll feel deceived and will dismiss the information you've presented. But if you've motivated your listeners to learn more about the topic and have established yourself as an expert, they'll trust you to treat the topic fairly, whatever position you take.

THE APATHETIC AUDIENCE

Apathetic audiences are informed about your topic but are not interested in it. They know about the topic but think it doesn't apply to them. This type of audience challenges a

> An audience that is informed about a speaker's topic but not interested in it.

Using Presentation Media to Energize an Apathetic Audience

Gaining the attention of an apathetic audience often requires more than words alone. Carefully chosen images and sounds relevant to your topic provide an excellent strategy to focus your audience's attention on your ideas. Incorporating appropriate presentation media visualizes your topic for the audience, stirs their emotions, and is often more persuasive than words alone.[15] For example, in the case of encouraging people to support U.S. economic aid to developing countries, several photographs demonstrating the positive effects of such aid, a brief segment from a National Public Radio show on the topic, and a 15-second clip from a documentary on life in the developing world provide examples of images and sounds that could grab the audience's attention right from the start.

speaker to forge a positive link between topic and audience, which can be achieved in the following ways:

- *Gain their attention and pique their interest.* You have to show audience members *why* they should care about the topic. For instance, let's say that you want to argue that the United States should provide economic support to developing countries. To do this, you propose that America should provide start-up loans for small businesses in those countries. Your audience analysis indicates that your listeners believe the topic has no relevance to their lives. But your audience research also indicates that they tend to give to charity and support strengthening local communities overall. You think that with the right appeal you will be able to connect your topic to their sense of social responsibility. Using strong supporting evidence, you might demonstrate the positive impact that economic aid can have on the lives of people who live in the developing world.

- *Show how the topic impacts them.* When listeners identify with a topic and feel it's relevant to them, they're more likely to be persuaded.[13] You might be able to convince your audience to care about this seemingly distant topic by explaining how the health of the U.S. economy depends on the presence of a stable global economic system. You tell them that so long as developing countries struggle economically, the stability of the global economic system is threatened. That situation negatively affects the American economy, the value of the dollar overseas, even national security. So not economically supporting developing countries directly affects the audience's pocketbook and its safety.

- *Show your audience how much you care about the topic through your energy and dynamism.* In promoting U.S. economic support for developing countries, you must demonstrate your deep commitment to and interest in the topic. So you speak rapidly but clearly, raise your vocal volume a bit, take only short pauses, and gesture and move with energy and purpose. These types of nonverbal behaviors signal your passion for the subject.[14]
- *Take a one-sided approach to the topic.* Last, although you must present a balanced treatment of the topic, you need not address all perspectives on it, as you would when facing a negative audience. When audience members are generally apathetic, taking a one-sided approach to the topic is both reasonable and ethical. In persuading the audience, you will want to advocate a viewpoint on the topic that corresponds with the reasons they should care.

The Ethics of Persuasive Speaking

Ethical public speakers must meet the National Communication Association's standards of ethical communication (Chapter 3). Persuasive speakers must adhere to this principle in particular: "We condemn communication that degrades individuals and humanity through distortion, intimidation, coercion, and violence, and through the expression of intolerance and hatred." Ethical persuasive speakers do not attempt to deceive or manipulate the audience. Instead, they present their information and arguments truthfully, accurately, and honestly. In addition, they "endorse freedom of expression, diversity of perspective, and tolerance of dissent."[16]

To demonstrate differences between a persuasive speech that meets ethical standards and one that doesn't, consider the subject of DNA testing to determine a person's genetic ancestry. DNA testing has become an indispensable tool for criminologists—in many cases the key to helping them identify who did or did not commit a crime. And DNA makes it possible for scientists to determine the age of fossil remains. But the science of DNA has also become available for another purpose: to trace personal genetic history.[17]

Encouraging an audience to subscribe to one of the services that analyzes personal DNA certainly could be developed into an interesting persuasive speech. But what ethical considerations are associated with this topic? An ethical speaker would carefully research how DNA tests are done and properly used to show the audience how they can benefit from the testing process, as well as the risks involved. For example, the speaker

SPEAKING OF...

Persuasion or Manipulation?

Persuasion involves using language, images, and other means of communication to influence people's attitudes, beliefs, values, or actions. How does this differ from manipulation? What is the line someone must cross to go from persuader to manipulator? There are two key differences between the two. First, manipulation involves using dishonest means to influence others. Omitting crucial evidence, presenting inaccurate or false information, or intentionally misrepresenting research to influence others to your advantage are examples of manipulation. Second, manipulation often involves abuse of social power by those in a dominant group.[20] For example, a boss who threatens to fire or punish an employee who doesn't agree with the boss's position or a physician who overstates dire health consequences for an uncooperative patient are examples of abusing power to manipulate others. As an ethical speaker, *persuade* rather than manipulate your audiences.

might discuss how DNA tests can help diagnose a genetic disorder like Huntington's disease, warn of predispositions to addictions, or estimate the risk of passing on a genetic disease to a child. The speaker might try to motivate the audience by explaining how DNA tests can help people find unknown parents, siblings, or other relatives. In addition, the speaker could mention that DNA tests can reveal where every audience member's ancestors come from.

Two categories of ethical violations can be identified on this topic: (1) suggesting that DNA tests can deliver something they cannot and (2) failing to mention the drawbacks of DNA testing, which can be serious. For instance, while the tests can indicate a person's genetic makeup (European, African, Asian, Native American), it cannot reveal a person's race.[18] Race is an unreliable way of categorizing people by appearance; it is not a scientific category based on genetics. An ethical speaker would not try to convince an audience that DNA testing can help people identify their race.

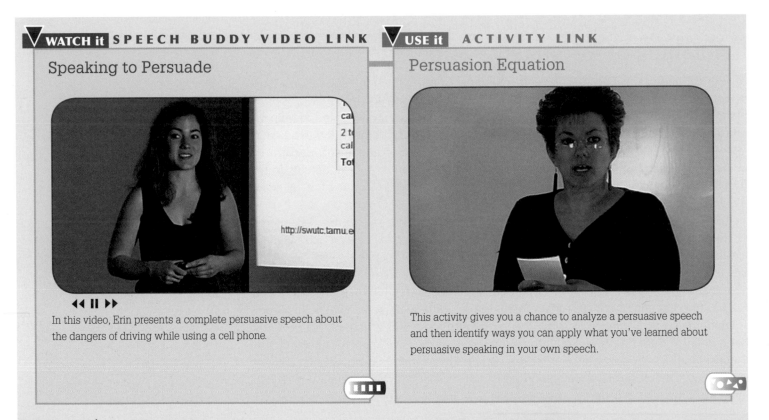

WATCH it SPEECH BUDDY VIDEO LINK

Speaking to Persuade

◄◄ ❚❚ ►►

In this video, Erin presents a complete persuasive speech about the dangers of driving while using a cell phone.

USE it ACTIVITY LINK

Persuasion Equation

This activity gives you a chance to analyze a persuasive speech and then identify ways you can apply what you've learned about persuasive speaking in your own speech.

Perhaps most important, the speaker must warn the audience about the biggest danger associated with DNA testing: the shock many people receive when their DNA results don't match up with their long-held sense of ethnic identity—who they imagined themselves to be. For example, the head of Harvard's African-American Studies Department, Henry Louis Gates, Jr., discovered that his genetic ancestry is as much European as African, completely altering the way he imagined how he descended from his ancestors.[19] Companies that conduct DNA tests warn clients about these risks, especially the possible threat to their ethnic identity. Thus, when persuading others, ethical speakers must consider and address the possible harms their audience may encounter.

SUMMARY

When you persuade others, you use language, images, and other means of communication to influence their attitudes, beliefs, values, or actions. Persuasive speeches may address questions of fact, value, or policy. Speeches on questions of fact ask whether something is true or not true. Speeches on questions of value take a position on the worth of something. Speeches on questions of policy are concerned with what should or should not be done. Speeches on questions of fact or value are typically organized using topical, chronological, spatial, or cause-and-effect patterns. Because speeches on questions of policy ask for action or passive agreement on the part of the audience, the problem-solution, problem-cause-solution, or motivated sequence are the best patterns of organization for such speeches.

In general, persuasive speakers face five types of audiences: negative, positive, divided, uninformed, and apathetic. Each type calls for different persuasive strategies. For example, negative audiences require persuasive speakers to thoroughly demonstrate their credibility, take a common-ground approach, visualize the topic in positive ways, and address audience objections. And for apathetic audiences, speakers must gain and maintain audience attention, relate the topic to the audience, display dynamism, and take a one-sided approach to the topic.

Ethical public speakers must meet the National Communication Association's standards of ethical communication. Ethical persuasive speakers present their information and arguments truthfully, accurately, and honestly, and never deceive or manipulate the audience.

In the Book

Summary
Key Terms
Critical Challenges

More Study Resources

Speech Studio
Quizzes
WebLinks

Student Workbook

14.1: Debate
14.2: RFK in Indy
14.3: Fact, Value, and Policy in Supporting Materials
14.4: Watch Commercials until You Can Define the Ethical Line
14.5: Watch Commercials in Order to Determine Good Visuals

Speech Buddy Videos

▐▐▐▌ **Video Links**

Speaking to Persuade

▐▐▌ **Activity Links**

Persuasion Equation

▶ **Sample Speech Videos**

Carol, "Fat Discrimination," persuasive speech

Lisa, "Breast Cancer Awareness," persuasive speech

 Speech Builder Express

Goal/purpose
Thesis statement
Organization
Outline
Supporting material
Transitions
Introduction
Conclusion
Title
Works cited
Visual aids
Completing the speech outline

 InfoTrac

Recommended search terms

Persuasive speech
Question of fact
Question of value
Question of policy
Ethical communication
Ethical speaking
Audience adaptation
Hostile audience
Sympathetic audience

Audio Study Tools

"Breast Cancer Awareness" by Lisa

Critical thinking questions

Learning objectives

Chapter summary

Guide to Your Online Resources

Your Online Resources for *Public Speaking: The Evolving Art* give you access to the Speech Buddy video and activity featured in this chapter, additional sample speech videos, Speech Builder Express, InfoTrac College Edition, and study aids such as glossary flashcards, review quizzes, and the Critical Challenge questions for this chapter, which you can respond to via e-mail if your instructor requests. In addition, your Online Resources feature live WebLinks relevant to this chapter, including sites where you can find topics for interesting and timely persuasive speeches. Links are regularly maintained, and new ones are added periodically.

Key Terms

apathetic audience 381

divided audience 379

negative (hostile)
   audience 377

persuasion 356

persuasive speech 355

positive (sympathetic)
   audience 378

question of fact 357

question of policy 366

question of value 362

uninformed audience 380

Critical Challenges

Questions for Reflection and Discussion

1. How are you immersed in a sea of persuasion? Give some examples of persuasive messages you've received in interpersonal, public speaking, and mass media contexts. What can you do to become a more critical consumer of persuasive messages?

2. As a persuasive speaker, what steps must you take to avoid manipulating your audience? As an audience member, how can you make sure speakers don't manipulate you?

3. Adapting to the audience is especially important for the persuasive speaker. Consider the other side of the podium—when you're in the audience. What are your responsibilities as a listener in a persuasive speaking situation? What can you do to contribute to the productive communication climate discussed in Chapter 3? For example, how can you disagree with the speaker yet still maintain a climate that encourages dialogue?

4. What unique ethical considerations face persuasive speakers when they're addressing questions of fact? What are the ethical considerations associated with questions of value? What ethical issues must a persuasive speaker addressing a question of policy confront?

15 UNDERSTANDING ARGUMENT

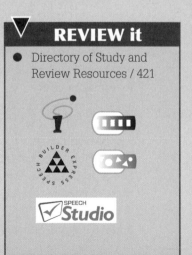

AP Photo/Ted S. Warren

As part of its Google Book Search project, the company set out to digitize all 7 million books in the University of Michigan's library to create an easily searchable electronic database. Publishers quickly voiced concern, asserting that Google's project infringed on copyright laws.[1] In her speech "Google, the Khmer Rouge, and the Public Good," presented to the Professional/Scholarly Publishing Division of the Association of American Publishers, University of Michigan President Dr. Mary Sue Coleman said:

> New technologies and new ideas can generate some pretty scary reactions, and Google Book Search has not been immune. The project, for all that it promises, has been challenged: on the editorial page, across the airwaves, and, with your organization's endorsement, in the court system. It is this criticism of the project that prompted me to accept your invitation to speak—and explain why we believe this is a legal, ethical, and noble endeavor that will transform our society. Legal because we believe

copyright law allows us the fair use of millions of books that are being digitized. Ethical because the preservation and protection of knowledge is critically important to the betterment of humankind. And noble because this enterprise is right for the time, right for the future, right for the world of publishing, right for all of us.[2]

Coleman clearly states her thesis: The Google Book Project is legal, ethical, and noble. But how does she support her thesis and secure the response she seeks from her audience? Through the use of argument.

What Is an Argument?

▼ **READ it** In common usage, the term *argument* refers to a disagreement or a conflict. In public speaking, arguments provide support for persuasive speakers' positions on questions of fact, value, or policy (Chapter 14). Argument forms the foundation of persuasion. Successful speakers formulate arguments effectively and present them well.

An **argument** makes a claim and supports it with evidence and reasoning.[3] In public speaking, a **claim** is the position or assertion a speaker wants the audience to accept, and **evidence** refers to the supporting materials—narratives, examples, definitions, testimony, facts, and statistics—the speaker presents to reinforce the claim. **Reasoning** is the method or process used to represent the claim and arrive at the argument's conclusion.[4] **Figure 15.1** illustrates these elements of an argument.

This chapter discusses the elements of argument in detail and how they work together to create the foundation of a persuasive speech. You'll also learn how speakers use argument in persuasive speaking.

Presenting claims and supporting them with evidence and reasoning.

A position or assertion that a speaker wants an audience to accept.

Supporting materials—narratives, examples, definitions, testimony, facts, and statistics—that a speaker presents to reinforce a claim.

The method or process used to link claims to evidence.

Using Claims Effectively

▼ Claims go beyond facts and other supporting materials to propose conclusions based on the evidence presented. For example, a speaker might say, "Humans cause global warming." That is a claim, or a position the speaker is taking. The speaker might then present scientific studies to support that claim. But the claim "Humans cause global warming" is still an inference based on the results of those studies. So claims require that listeners make a leap from what is known—the evidence—to some conclusion.[5]

Claims lay the groundwork for your thesis. They respond to basic questions about your topic and the position you take. Claims answer the question "What is the speaker asserting?" As you develop your speech, consider the questions your topic raises and how you might respond to them. How you answer those questions will help you identify the claims you'll make in your speech and reveal your position on the topic. Table 15.1 provides an example of the questions a speaker might ask about a speech on banning handguns in the United States and the claims that correspond with those questions.

TYPES OF CLAIMS

Arguments include two types of claims: premises and conclusions. The conclusion is the primary claim or assertion a speaker makes. A premise gives a reason to support a conclusion. Both conclusions and premises are claims; premises are smaller claims that lead up to a conclusion—the central claim or position the speaker promotes.[6] In the speech opening this chapter, Coleman offered one conclusion and three premises as support:

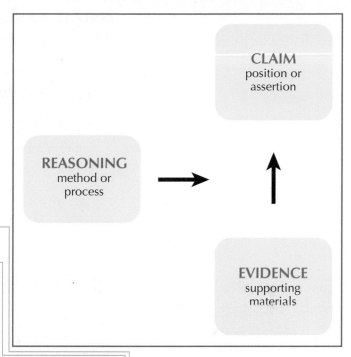

▲ FIGURE 15.1
Elements of an Argument
Source: Adapted from Toulmin (2003).

A primary claim or assertion.

A claim that provides reasons to support a conclusion.

Premise 1: Digitizing all the books in the University of Michigan Library is legal.

Premise 2: Digitizing all the books in the University of Michigan Library is ethical.

Premise 3: Digitizing all the books in the University of Michigan Library is noble.

Conclusion: Digitizing all the books in the University of Michigan Library is right to do.

For audience members to agree with the conclusion, they must agree with all the premises leading up to it. If they find fault with one premise, they're highly unlikely to support the conclusion. In Coleman's case, not everyone in the audience was entirely convinced—some questioned the project's legality and ethical grounding. Still, others agreed the project had merit.[7]

Specific words, either implied or stated, often identify premises and conclusions. Words indicating a premise include *because, whereas, since, on account of,* and *due to.*

TABLE 15.1 ▶ Questions and Claims for Speech on Banning Handguns

TOPIC QUESTION	CLAIM
Why ban handguns and not other types of weapons?	Handguns pose a specific problem that can be addressed by legislation.
To what extent are handguns responsible for violent crime?	Handguns contribute more than other weapons to violent crime.
Wouldn't banning handguns violate the Second Amendment of the Constitution, which guarantees the right for Americans to bear arms?	The Second Amendment needs to be reconsidered in today's context.
How can we be sure that banning handguns will have a positive effect?	Violent crime decreases in places where handguns are illegal.

Words indicating a conclusion include *therefore, consequently, and so, thus,* and *accordingly.* Think of the relationship between premises and conclusions in this way:

Because *(premise 1),* because *(premise 2),* and because *(premise 3),* therefore *(conclusion).*

Coleman asserted that *because* digitizing the books is legal, *because* it is ethical, and *because* it is noble, it is *therefore* right to do. Although *because* and *therefore* were unstated, Coleman made the relationship between her premises and conclusion clear. **Table 15.2** presents additional examples of premises and conclusions.

Sometimes an argument's premises or conclusion are implied rather than explicitly stated. Such arguments, called **enthymemes,** assume the audience will figure out the premise or conclusion on their own. Enthymemes depend on the audience's social information or knowledge to complete the argument.[8] For example, in a speech on a question of policy about making copies of DVD movies, the speaker might argue:

An argument in which a premise or conclusion is unstated.

Premise: Burning DVDs of copyrighted movies is against the law.

Conclusion: Don't burn DVDs of copyrighted movies.

TABLE 15.2 ▶ Examples of Premises and Conclusions

TOPIC	VISUAL ERGONOMICS	GLOBALIZATION AND LABOR	ONLINE DATING SERVICES
Premises	**1:** Poor visual ergonomics when using a computer cause eye strain. **2:** Poor visual ergonomics when using a computer lead to neck and shoulder problems.	**1:** Globalization allows for the free movement of goods between countries. **2:** Globalization allows for the free movement of services between countries. **3:** Globalization allows organizations to freely locate to other countries.	**1:** In today's world, single people are too busy to join clubs and organizations to meet other singles. **2:** Today, people have fewer friends to introduce them to potential romantic partners.
Conclusion	Improving visual ergonomics is essential for the health and safety of computer users.	Globalization should also allow for the free movement of individual workers between countries.	Online dating services are a practical way to meet romantic partners in today's world.

This basic argument leaves out one premise: If you're caught burning DVD copies of movies, you could go to jail, pay a fine, or both. But there's no need for the speaker to say that because the audience already knows it.

Speeches on questions of fact or value often leave the conclusion unstated. In a speech on traffic congestion, for example, the speaker might include these premises:

Premise 1: Traffic congestion in our city wastes time.

Premise 2: Traffic congestion in our city wastes resources.

Premise 3: Traffic congestion in our city increases pollution.

The unstated conclusion is that something should be done about traffic congestion. But as this is a speech addressing a question of fact, the speaker is concerned only with whether or not something is true (or false), not with taking some kind of action.

An enthymeme invites audience participation as they mentally fill in the missing parts of the argument, facilitating a dialogue between the speaker and audience.[9] Encouraging these kinds of thought processes can give the audience a better understanding and a more favorable view of the speaker's argument.[10] Dr. Martin Luther King, Jr., was well known for his persuasive oratory. In a speech at the Dexter Avenue Baptist Church in Montgomery, Alabama, during the early days of the civil rights movement[11] he made these claims:

> **Premise 1:** Love is the best way to respond to enemies.
>
> **Premise 2:** Mass nonviolent resistance to oppression is based on the principle of loving one's enemies.

But King left one premise and the conclusion unstated. First, he omitted the premise that audience members were oppressed. Although he did refer to people of color around the world as oppressed, he did not say, "We are oppressed" or "You are oppressed." He didn't need to—his audience knew it. Second, he left out the conclusion that audience members should join in mass nonviolent demonstrations. This gave his audience something to consider: Should they join in the protests or not? Leaving out part of his argument was one of many strategies King used to engage his audience more deeply in the speech and his position on the topic.

Advertisers also often omit an argument's conclusion, although there's rarely any doubt about what they want the audience to conclude. In an Apple ad campaign, PCs are compared with Macs, but the ads never tell the audience what to do. Instead, the ads present premises such as these:

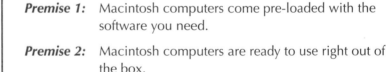

> **Premise 1:** Macintosh computers come pre-loaded with the software you need.
>
> **Premise 2:** Macintosh computers are ready to use right out of the box.

The logical conclusion is that you should buy a Macintosh computer. But the ad never explicitly states that—it's left up to the audience to put together the two premises and conclude they should purchase a Mac.

GUIDELINES FOR PHRASING CLAIMS

To accept a claim, an audience must view it as reasonable. Because claims are assertions, they can always be challenged. Some claims, such as "smoking causes cancer" and "a college education leads to a better job," are easily supported. But others, such as "U.S. employers don't give

▼ Advertisers often rely on visual enthymemes. This ad is trying to persuade the consumer to buy Coke, essentially claiming that if you drink Coke you'll be the super-cool person that the women in the ad are excited to see. The ad assumes your social conditioning will persuade you to come to the conclusion that, yes, you would be cool if you drank Coke.

employees enough vacation time" and "Hunting whales does not impact their survival rates," are not so widely accepted. Even topics that seem completely uncontroversial today haven't always been that way. For example, in earlier eras people strongly questioned the claim "The earth revolves around the sun." Today no one disputes it.

Qualifiers provide a way to make your claims more reasonable to an audience. A **qualifier** indicates the scope of the claim with words such as *probably*, *likely*, *often*, and *usually*. These words help you stay away from indefensible assertions or claims that must hold up in every case. Qualifiers answer the question "How strong is the claim?" For example, instead of claiming "Major airline outsourcing of plane maintenance increases the number of plane accidents," you might say, "Major airline outsourcing of plane maintenance *likely* increases the number of plane accidents." Here you acknowledge that outsourcing probably increases accidents, but you're not definitely sure. There may be other factors leading to an increase in accidents, or it may be that accidents haven't increased at all. **Figure 15.2** shows how a qualifier fits in with the elements of argument.

> A word or phrase that clarifies, modifies, or limits the meaning of another word or phrase.

▼ FIGURE 15.2

Elements of an Argument with Qualifier *Source: Adapted from Toulmin (2003).*

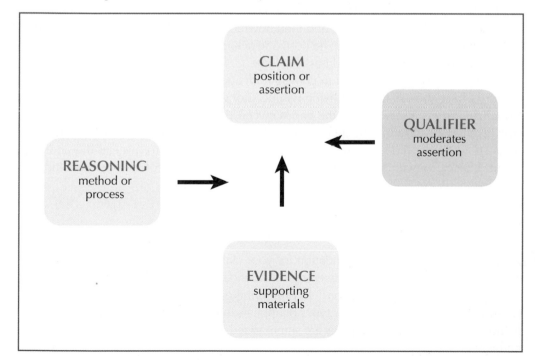

SPEAKING OF...

Images and the Naturalistic Enthymeme

Not all claims are expressed with words; some claims involve images. For example, advertisers often use images to advance their claims that you should buy their products or services. Soft drink ads, for instance, typically show individuals or groups laughing and enjoying themselves. The claims are

Premise 1: Everyone likes to have fun.

Premise 2: Drinking this soft drink is part of having fun.

Premise 3: If you drink this soft drink, you'll have fun.

Conclusion: You should buy this soft drink.

Yet no one has to say anything in the ad—you know how to interpret those visual claims based on your social and cultural experiences. One key reason that visual claims work so well is the *naturalistic enthymeme*—audiences assume that unless there's evidence to the contrary, a camera captures a realistic and natural view of what they would see.[12] Of course, when an image is clearly altered, as with computer-generated imagery in films, the naturalistic enthymeme does not hold true. But even when viewers know images have been staged, as with the soft drink commercials, they still tend to assume that the images represent something real—the first step in visual persuasion.

As a persuasive speaker, you want to anticipate alternative assertions or claims related to your topic by acknowledging, and carefully refuting, objections or different points of view in your speech. Considering other claims lets audience members know you understand their perspective, even if you don't agree with it. This helps you establish a connection with your listeners.[13] Coleman used this strategy in her speech on the Google Book Project. In addressing her claim of legality based on copyright law, she said:

> We know there are limits on access to works covered by copyright. If, and when, we pursue those uses, we will be conservative and we will follow the law. And we will protect all copyrighted materials . . . in that archive.
>
> Let me repeat that: I guarantee we will protect all copyrighted materials. I assure you we understand that providing public access to materials in copyright, particularly those still in print, would be unlawful. Merely because our library possesses a digital copy of a work does not mean we are entitled to, nor will we, ignore the law and distribute it to people to use in ways not authorized by copyright.
>
> Believe me, students will not be reading digital copies of *Harry Potter* in their dorm rooms.[14]

In this example, Coleman addressed her audience's fears that books will be scanned, uploaded to the library's website, and then downloaded in full by hundreds, thousands, or even millions of library users at no cost. She acknowledged the limits of copyright and explained how the library will address the issue.

Similarly, a speech designed to convince an audience that globalization helps poor countries raise their standard of living will be stronger if the speaker acknowledges that globalization has also widened the gap between rich and poor in many countries. By voicing alternative claims, the speaker gains the trust of the audience for being fair. When speakers ignore or hide information they disagree with, or try to mislead the audience about differing viewpoints, they behave unethically and undercut their own position on the topic.

Using Evidence Effectively

Evidence provides the foundation for your claims. Recall that a claim answers the question "What is the speaker asserting?" Evidence answers the question "What is the speaker's support for the assertion?" In presenting evidence to support a claim, the persuasive speaker relies on the four types of appeals introduced in Chapter 1: logos, ethos, pathos, and mythos. These appeals are summarized in **Table 15.3** and discussed in depth in this section.

TABLE 15.3 ▶ Types of Appeals

APPEAL	BRIEF DEFINITION	EXAMPLE
logos	logical proof	facts and statistics
ethos	speaker's credibility	references to own expertise on topic
pathos	emotional proof	a humorous quote or story
mythos	cultural beliefs and values	a well-known fable

LOGOS: APPEALS TO LOGIC

Logical appeals, or logos, can be the most persuasive type of appeal when presented well. In addition, audiences expect experts on a topic to use logical appeals in their speeches.[15] Although logical appeals typically are associated with facts and statistics, definitions and testimony may also fit this category of evidence. **Logical appeals** rely on appearing reasonable and rational to influence an audience. Generally, logical evidence is verifiable. For example, listeners can research the facts a speaker presents or look up a definition the speaker offers.

> Use of rational appeals based on logic, facts, and analysis to influence an audience.

When using logical appeals, effective speakers gather current statistical data, facts, definitions, or expert opinions. For example, a just-released poll of Americans' attitudes toward congressional reform would add considerable weight to an argument favoring changes in political lobbying laws. By demonstrating the currency of your research, you'll earn your audience's respect and keep them listening to you.

In addition, your audience must comprehend the logical evidence you present. Long lists of facts and statistics can overwhelm your listeners and cause them to lose interest. Logical appeals need not be dry and boring. Successful persuasive speakers make evidence clear through their use of language and presentation media.

Dr. Nora D. Volkow, director of the National Institute on Drug Abuse, included logical appeals in her speech "Drug Addiction: Free Will, Brain Disease, or Both?"[16] She presented her speech to Town Hall Los Angeles, an audience of city residents. In this part of her speech, she focused on her claim that drug addiction is a brain disease:

> Drug addiction is a developmental disease. What do we mean by that? What we've learned from many years of epidemiological studies is drug addiction develops during these periods of our lives, during adolescence and early adulthood. This

© A. Ramey/PhotoEdit

▲ Presenting verifiable evidence in a thought-provoking and easily understandable way increases the power of your logical appeals.

Use of the audience's perception of the speaker as competent, trustworthy, dynamic, and likeable to influence an audience.

is a graph [on a digital slide] that actually describes at what age individuals develop, at first, a dependence on marijuana. Similar graphs occur for cocaine, nicotine, and alcohol. You can see the peak at this case is around age 18. By age 25, if you have not become addicted to marijuana the likelihood that you will do so is very minimal. It's not zero but it's very minimal.[17]

Volkow presented data from a large number of studies to support her claim. She used a digital slide to show the statistics, and then explained what the graph meant to the audience.

ETHOS: APPEALS TO SPEAKER CREDIBILITY

The effectiveness of **appeals to speaker credibility** rests in the degree to which the audience perceives the speaker as competent, trustworthy, dynamic, and likeable—the speaker's ethos. Competence or expertise in particular has a direct positive impact on a speaker's persuasiveness. If your audience believes you're an expert on your topic, you're more likely to convince them.

Speaker credibility also depends on the degree to which listeners feel connected to you. Research shows that if you haven't established a good relationship with your audience, expertise alone will not convince them.[18] Your credibility as a speaker, then, relies on more than just doing your research. The audience must also perceive you as likeable or sociable. Open gestures, a slightly faster rate of speech, a somewhat raised voice volume, eye contact, smiling, and other nonverbal behaviors that suggest friendliness, energy, and enthusiasm all contribute to listeners' perceptions of a speaker's sociability.[19]

The degree to which an audience finds a topic personally relevant also influences the effects of speaker credibility.[20] When audience members view the source of a message as highly credible but find the subject uninteresting, they judge the speaker as not very persuasive. Similarly, if audience members don't think the topic applies to them, they don't pay much attention to it.

Dr. Carl J. Schramm's speech on entrepreneurship at a European Union Finance Ministers meeting provides a useful example of appeals to speaker credibility.[21] As president and chief executive officer of the Ewing Marion Kauffman Foundation and a member of the business school faculty at the University of Virginia, Schramm brought much training and experience, or fixed qualifications, to the event. Yet he began his speech by establishing a connection with his listeners, gaining their interest with a bold statement, and indicating the topic's relevance to them:

I am deeply honored to have been asked by Minister Crasser to speak with you about the new economy that awaits us. Simply, we are in the midst of a transformation of capitalism. What is emerging might be called Entrepreneurial Capitalism. This evolution continues to evade description for various reasons, not the least being that economists and officials charged with the management of economic affairs have understandably deep loyalties to our inherited wisdom. We are comfortable with a changing economic landscape that presents a steady stream of challenges requiring different policy approaches. We are not at ease, however, with changing economic theory. Nonetheless, the new economic order overtaking the U.S., Ireland, the U.K., and, to a remarkable degree, transforming China and India, must be recognized for what it is.[22]

Beginning with a humble statement directed to the audience provided a way for Schramm to appear more likeable and friendly. He then got their attention with the statement, "We are in the midst of a transformation of capitalism." He showed the topic's relevance to the audience, referring to "economists and officials charged with the management of economic affairs" and using the pronoun *we*. In these ways, Schramm laid a foundation for his primary appeal to speaker credibility, which he included at a later point in his speech:

> Elsewhere I have proposed part of a conceptual framework for entrepreneurial capitalism and here offer only a précis. The economic model that prevailed through the last century envisioned economic activity as dependent on three central players. Big labor, business, and government coexisted and engaged in a balance of power as a means of achieving two predominant goals—equilibrium and predictability. John Kenneth Galbraith described the balanced duopolies amongst any two players as "countervailing" power relationships.[23]

Schramm went on to explain his conceptual framework, using technical language appropriate to the audience. Note how he referred to his own work, yet also cited the work of others. He used both his research on the topic and an authoritative reference in his appeal to speaker credibility. And by including several charts and figures to help the audience visualize his points, he further demonstrated his competence and produced a more dynamic presentation, enhancing his credibility as a speaker.

PATHOS: APPEALS TO EMOTION

Emotional appeals, or pathos, rely on emotional evidence and stimulation of feelings to influence an audience. Speakers typically use stories, examples, definitions, and testimony in appealing to our emotions. When appeals to emotion work well, they tap into the audience's beliefs and needs, call up personal associations with the topic, and help listeners recall the speaker's message.[24] Emotion can reinforce or change an audience's

Use of emotional evidence and stimulation of feelings to influence an audience.

position on a topic or stir people to action. Emotional appeals alone seldom work to convince an audience, yet in conjunction with other types of appeals they can win over even skeptical listeners.[25]

According to social psychologist Abraham Maslow, humans are motivated by five types of needs: physiological, safety, love/belonging, esteem, and self-actualization.[26]

- *Physiological needs* are those necessary for our body to function, including food, water, and sleep.
- *Safety needs* are associated with the desire to feel free from harm.
- *Love/belonging needs* include wanting to feel part of a group and loved by others.
- *Esteem needs* focus on our status and having others recognize our accomplishments.
- *Self-actualization needs* are concerned with personal growth and self-fulfillment.

You're motivated to fulfill your needs in a hierarchical order, satisfying more basic needs before progressing to higher-order ones (**Figure 15.3**). You interact emotionally and connect with others to satisfy your needs. For example, you depend on others to help you feel safe and loved. Even basic needs such as food and water require the help of others.[27]

Understanding these needs can help you develop appropriate emotional appeals for your audience. Appealing to a positive emotion such as happiness usually proves more persuasive than appealing to a negative emotion such as fear. Yet persuaders commonly use fear appeals to scare audiences into doing or not doing something based on the horrible consequences that might result. These appeals often target the most basic needs—physiological and safety needs. Fear appeals can work, but they don't work very well if the appeal is so threatening that people feel overwhelmed by fear. When that happens, audience members resist the persuasive attempt, deny that the appeal applies to them, and reject any proposed change in thought or behavior. However, if the fear appeal produces a milder emotional response and leads the audience to believe they

▶ **FIGURE 15.3**
Maslow's Hierarchy of Needs[28]

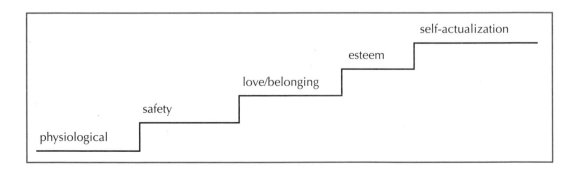

Speaking Situations

can do something to control the danger, they're much more likely to be persuaded.[29] In her speech at the first meeting of the President's Identity Theft Task Force, Deborah Platt Majoras, chair of the Federal Trade Commission, said:

> Personal information is the currency of our new information economy. It permits the global marketplace to be brought digitally to our doorsteps, indeed our fingertips. But like cash currency, it also attracts thieves. These identity thieves are cheats and cowards. Unlike their victims, identity thieves do not work to earn their resources and to establish good names and good credit. Instead, they steal from others in a most insidious manner—by taking their identities.[30]

In defining identify thieves and their victims, Majoras highlighted the fear many people share that someone will steal their personal information and use it to run up bills that the thief never intends to pay. Here she appealed to the audience's safety needs—safety from the theft of private personal information rather than the more traditional sense of safety from physical harm. She went on to list the actions the new task force would take to address this fast-growing problem. When audience members believe they can take action to counteract a threat, a fear appeal is more successful.

Personal narratives are probably the most common way persuasive speakers appeal to audiences' emotions. In a speech given at the University of Richmond, author Lois Lowry recounted several narratives to support her claim that people often avoid or turn away from things that may seem too painful, difficult, or challenging.[31] Near the end of the speech, she told this story:

> In 1994, when *The Giver* was awarded the Newbery Medal, a picture book called *Grandfather's Journey* was awarded the Caldecott. Its author/illustrator was Allen Say. Allen is Japanese, though he has lived in the USA since he was a young man.
>
> He gave me a copy of *Grandfather's Journey* and inscribed it to me. In return, I signed *The Giver* to him, writing my name in Japanese below my usual signature. He chuckled, looking at it, and asked me how I happened to be able to do that.
>
> You can picture the ensuing conversation.
>
> "I lived in Japan when I was eleven, twelve, thirteen," I explain.
>
> "What years?" asks Allen Say.
>
> "1948, 49, 50. I was born in 1937."
>
> "Me too. We're the same age. Where did you live?"
>
> "Tokyo," I tell him.

"Me too," he says. "What part?"

"Shibuya."

"So did I! Where do you go to school?" Allen asks me.

"Meguro. I went by bus each day."

"I went to school in Shibuya."

"I remember a school there," I tell him. "I used to ride my bike past it."

Silence. Then: *Were you the girl on the green bike?*

Allen and I are close friends now. But we had lost 57 years of friendship because we had both turned away. To do otherwise—in that place and that time—would have been *too hard*.[32]

Lowry's story evokes both happiness and sadness—she won a prestigious award and met a new friend, yet also missed out on that friendship for nearly sixty years. She appealed to listeners' esteem and belonging needs, suggesting that satisfying these needs means that individuals must bear some pain along the way.

Persuasive speakers also use presentation media as evidence to elicit emotion. For example, to support the claim that your community needs a new theater, you might show a short clip of an especially powerful performance by the local theater group, presented in its current dilapidated venue. Digital slides of unwanted pets waiting for adoption at the Humane Society can stir feelings of sympathy and buttress the claim that all pets should be spayed or neutered.

Emotional appeals must do more than stimulate an emotional response. Such appeals must serve as evidence—direct support for your claim. When you tell a story, define a term, recite a quote, or show a photograph, you appeal to your audience's emotions in ways that advance your claim. As with any evidence you include in your persuasive speech, an emotional appeal must be relevant to your topic and appropriate to your audience.

MYTHOS: APPEALS TO CULTURAL BELIEFS

Use of values and beliefs embedded in cultural narratives or stories to influence an audience.

Appeals to cultural beliefs, or mythos, rely on the values and beliefs embedded in cultural narratives or stories to influence an audience. Speakers use traditional songs, tall tales, rhymes, proverbs, familiar stories, and the like to suggest a common bond with the audience. For example, the myth of the American hero, who does good deeds, works hard, and triumphs over misfortune, is deeply engrained in our culture.[33] Stories related to this mythic figure tap into our cultural beliefs in helping others, industriousness, and persevering in the face of adversity. Dr. J. Edward Hill, president of the American Medical Association (AMA), said this during a speech at the association's annual meeting:

As many of you know and have heard before, I spent twenty-seven years in Hollandale, Mississippi, a little town in the Delta that is home, not just to the blues, but to some of the poorest patients in America. . . . Worst of all—at least in the eyes of my partner, Dr. John Estes, and myself—shamefully high rates of maternal and fetal mortality. It all came home to me one day, when I drove off to care for a woman who had just given birth, unassisted, at home. She had lost so much blood, she couldn't raise her head without losing consciousness. I can still remember driving her to the town clinic after giving her an emergency transfusion. The woman recovered from her ordeal. But I did not. That night, on television, I watched Neil Armstrong take his famous walk on the moon's surface. I asked myself how a nation as great as ours could put a man on the moon but still couldn't provide basic, obstetrical care to a poor, rural woman in the Mississippi Delta.[34]

Hill's reference to Armstrong's historic feat calls up the image of the American hero, in this case conquering space to set foot on the moon. When faced with a stubborn societal problem, it's common to hear the statement "We can put someone on the moon, but we can't [solve this problem]." Hill's appeal to cultural beliefs frames his story within a significant American event and forecasts that he and his partner do overcome the odds to provide better health care for their patients. The heroic image of Neil Armstrong also serves to support Hill's claim that physicians must be the leaders in changing America's health care system.

Presenting a cultural icon in a novel way provides another strategy that uses mythos. Author Michael Crichton did this in a speech titled "Fear, Complexity, and Environmental Management in the 21st Century" by beginning with an upside-down map of the United States—Texas at the top, North Dakota at the bottom. Crichton used the map to advance his claim that individuals hold "assumptions so deeply embedded in our consciousness that we don't even realize they are there."[35] Showing a well-recognized cultural image from a unique perspective helps the audience examine beliefs they take for granted.

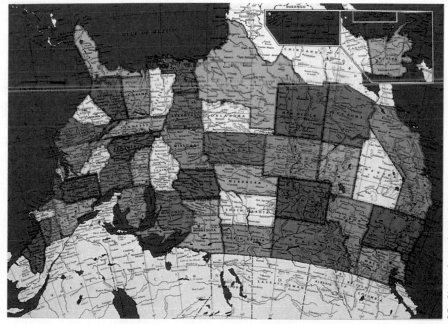

▼ Michael Crichton's use of a recognized cultural image presented from a unique perspective, an inverted map of the United States, prepared the audience for an unconventional view of environmental management.

© Tom Friedman, Courtesy Gagosian Gallery, New York.

Learning about Folk Life and Folklore

The internet provides numerous resources for learning more about myths, legends, folktales, and symbols associated with American and other cultures. The American Folklore Society (afsnet.org) provides definitions of folklore as well as resources on the topic. The Library of Congress's American Folklife Center (loc.gov/folklife) contains an archive of folk culture, the Veterans History Project, StoryCorps, and a host of resources on folk life in the United States—including information on folk life in your state. For a more international view of folklore, visit Professor D. L. Ashliman's Folktexts site (pitt .edu/~dash/folktexts.html), which includes myths and folktales from around the globe. You'll find many of these international stories familiar, as they've made their way into American culture.

GUIDELINES FOR USING EVIDENCE IN ARGUMENT

Follow these guidelines for using evidence effectively in your persuasive speech:

- *Keep your evidence relevant to your topic.* Your audience must be able to quickly and clearly grasp how the evidence you present supports your claim. For example, if you wanted your audience to support returning cultural artifacts to their countries of origin, you would cite statistics concerning the scope of the problem. You might also provide examples of artifacts that have been returned. But you would not mention current artwork and other artifacts not involved in the controversy. Every piece of evidence you include must directly support your argument.
- *Draw your evidence from highly credible sources.* Credible evidence comes from identifiable, respected sources. If you want to demonstrate the unfairness of teachers' salaries, for example, provide data about what they earn from the government agencies that pay them. When conducting interviews, choose individuals who are truly experts on your topic.
- *Select evidence from diverse sources.* Integrating evidence from a variety of sources provides a stronger foundation for your claims, shows you've done your research, and enhances your credibility. For example, in a speech advocating a ban on personal fireworks, you could cite state and local statistics on fireworks-related injuries and property damage, interview the fire chief, and present facts from areas where such a ban is in place.

- *Incorporate evidence addressing all types of appeals.* Effective speakers rely on logos, ethos, pathos, and mythos to advance their claims. Speeches that include only one type of evidence seldom succeed in persuading the audience. Employing logical appeals, appeals to the speaker's credibility, emotional appeals, and appeals to cultural beliefs provides a broad foundation of evidence to support your claims.

Using Reasoning Effectively

Reasoning is the method or process speakers use to link their evidence and claims. Claims answer the question "What is the speaker asserting?" and evidence answers the question "What is the speaker's support for the assertion?" Reasoning answers the question "How are the support and assertion connected?" Reasoning provides the bridge between the claim and the evidence, indicating to the audience why the evidence presented should be accepted as support for the claim. Although there are many types of reasoning, this section discusses only those most relevant to persuasive speaking: deductive, inductive, causal, and analogical. **Table 15.4** summarizes those types of reasoning.

TABLE 15.4 ▶ Types of Reasoning

TYPE	BRIEF DEFINITION	STRENGTHS	WEAKNESSES
Deductive	From general principle to specific case	Relies on established formal logic	Invalid premises leading to false conclusions
Inductive	From specific examples to general principle	Visualize and personalize argument	Lack of representation, sufficiency, relevance
Causal	One event causes another	Useful for explanation and prediction	Incorrect cause-effect link
Analogical	Draw similarities between two distinct cases	Links the unfamiliar with the familiar	Key differences ignored

DEDUCTIVE REASONING

Reasoning from a general condition to a specific case.

In **deductive reasoning**, the speaker argues from a general principle to a specific instance or case. Persuasive speakers apply deductive reasoning to categories of people, objects, processes, and events, claiming that what applies to the group also applies to the individual: "Granny Smith apples are tart. The apple I have is a Granny Smith apple, so it is tart." With deductive reasoning, if the general principle is true, the specific instance must be true as well. You use deductive reasoning in everyday life. You might read a favorable report on job prospects for college students in your major and reach the conclusion that your own job prospects will be good as well. Here you're reasoning from the general—all college students in your major—to the specific—yourself.

Deductive reasoning relies on formal logic and most commonly follows this pattern: major premise (general condition), minor premise (specific instance), and conclusion. With this form of reasoning, also called a **syllogism**, both premises must hold true for the conclusion to be true. Here are some examples:

A form of deductive reasoning consisting of a major premise, minor premise, and conclusion.

Major premise: All triathletes are in excellent physical condition.

Minor premise: Taylor is a triathlete.

Conclusion: Taylor is in excellent physical condition.

Major premise: All accredited colleges and universities must go through a rigorous assessment process for certification.

Minor premise: My college is accredited.

Conclusion: My college went through a rigorous assessment process.

Major premise: No one in our family missed the reunion.

Minor premise: Afarin is part of our family.

Conclusion: Afarin did not miss the reunion.

Major premise: Citizens may rightfully overthrow a tyrannical government.

Minor premise: The King of Great Britain's rule in the American colonies is a tyrannical government.

Conclusion: The citizens of the American colonies may rightfully overthrow the King of Great Britain's government in the colonies.

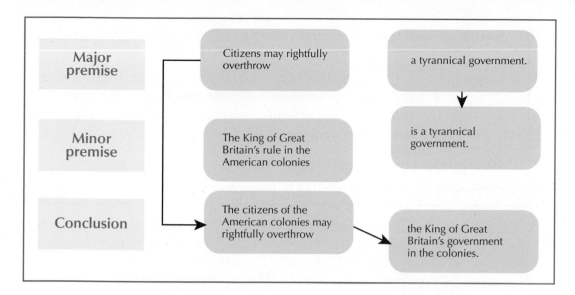

Major premise | Citizens may rightfully overthrow | a tyrannical government.

Minor premise | The King of Great Britain's rule in the American colonies | is a tyrannical government.

Conclusion | The citizens of the American colonies may rightfully overthrow | the King of Great Britain's government in the colonies.

This last syllogism may sound familiar, as it outlines the essential argument set forth in the U.S. Declaration of Independence.[36] Reviewing the words used in each claim—the major premise, the minor premise, and the conclusion—helps you visualize the connections among the three parts of a syllogism. **Figure 15.4** outlines the syllogism underlying the Declaration of Independence.

The major premise makes clear the general condition on which the Declaration of Independence is based: *Overthrowing a tyrannical government is right and moral.* The minor premise establishes the current system governing the American colonies as a tyrannical one. So the obvious conclusion is that the colonies are justified in ending their ties with Great Britain's rule. That's the power of deductive reasoning—the conclusion cannot be questioned because it's determined by the major and minor premises.[37]

For an argument based on deductive reasoning, persuasive speakers must demonstrate the validity of their major and minor premises with supporting evidence, then work their way toward the conclusion. If speakers do this well, listeners cannot easily refute the argument. Consider the following example from a student speech to ban smoking in public places:

Topic: Smoking Ban in Public Places

General purpose: To persuade

Specific purpose:	To convince my audience that smoking should be banned in all public areas in our state
Thesis:	Smoking should be banned in all public areas throughout our state because secondhand smoke harms nonsmokers.
Major premise:	One obligation of the state is to keep individuals safe from harm in public places.
Minor premise:	Smoking in public causes harm to nearby nonsmokers.
Conclusion:	Smoking should be banned in all public places in our state.

For the audience to accept the conclusion that smoking should be banned in public places, the speaker musts first show that (1) the state is responsible for protecting people from harm when they're out in public and (2) secondhand smoke harms nonsmokers. Supporting the major premise may pose a challenge, because the state government cannot protect individuals from all forms of harm. For example, driving, cycling, or walking on a road can prove dangerous. Should the state ban all roads? That's not practical. Instead, states develop laws and regulations to make roads safer, though not completely safe. For the minor premise, the speaker must demonstrate the magnitude of the harm. New research does suggest a link between secondhand smoke and several diseases.[38] Still, the speaker's evidence must convince the audience that the minor premise is true. Once the audience accepts both premises, the conclusion becomes logically apparent.

Deductive reasoning may be *valid* or *invalid*. For deductive reasoning to be valid, the premises and conclusion must be true, as in the previous examples. Sometimes, however, premises do not guarantee a true conclusion. In those cases, the argument is invalid.[39] Consider the following syllogism:

Major premise:	Reducing stress helps students get good grades.
Minor premise:	Playing video games reduces stress.
Conclusion:	Playing video games helps students get good grades.

The speaker may be able to find evidence supporting the major and minor premises. And for some audience members the conclusion may hold true. But for others, playing video games wastes time that could be spent preparing for tests, writing papers, or doing other things that help assure good grades. The conclusion that playing video games will help students get good grades therefore is not proven. It may be true for some people, but other factors limit the conclusion's more general truth. In this case, the conclusion does not necessarily follow from the premises, so the argument is invalid.

In persuasive speaking, there are two keys to applying deductive reasoning when linking claims to evidence. First, the speaker must have sufficient supporting evidence to convince the audience that the general condition (major premise) and specific instance (minor premise) are true or correct. Second, the speaker must have sufficient supporting evidence to show that the conclusion is the correct one based on the premises.

INDUCTIVE REASONING

Speakers use **inductive reasoning** when they support a claim with specific instances or examples. Also called *reasoning by example*, inductive reasoning asks the audience to accept a general claim based on a few cases or even just one case. People naturally think inductively, using their own experiences to draw conclusions about the world.[40] Suppose you practice a speech for your public speaking class in front of friends and do much better than when you only practiced by yourself. Based on that single experience, you decide that practicing with an audience is always better than practicing alone. In this case, you're applying inductive reasoning.

> Supporting a claim with specific cases or instances; also called *reasoning by example*.

When speakers use inductive reasoning to make their arguments, they rely on the principle of probability—that the evidence they present in their argument leads to a conclusion that is *probably* correct. Inductive reasoning depends on the quality of the evidence presented and the way speakers make sense of it. Princell Hair, a journalist and former general manager of CNN/U.S., used inductive reasoning in a portion of his speech to the Radio-Television News Directors Association & Foundation:

> Journalism, be it CNN/U.S. television, CNN.com or any of the other hundreds of news outlets available in this country, provides a sort of "national campfire" around which people gather. . . . Our role as journalists in helping to frame a larger dialogue—to tend that national campfire I just mentioned—has never been more important, or more complicated. The good news for me, and for anyone in this room who wants to be a journalist or who already is a journalist, is that Americans seem to want to listen to—and even join—in the conversation. Simply put, news brands are reaching more people than ever before.
>
> For example, my network CNN alone reaches almost 107 million people in the United States each month. And this 107 million includes only the viewers in homes and using the Web—this doesn't include restaurants, gyms, airports and all those many other places where CNN is available. Worldwide, in a single day, CNN has the power to aggregate 1.7 billion audience impressions.[41]

How Many Examples Are Enough?

How do you know when you have enough evidence when reasoning inductively? You can never know for sure. Unlike deductive reasoning or formal logic, where you're certain of your conclusion, inductive reasoning relies on probability—the idea that the conclusion is likely true. So that's your task as a persuasive speaker: to present enough evidence to show that your position has a high probability of being correct. But it's more than a numbers game. Three diverse and representative examples make a much stronger case than fifty similar examples. If you were arguing, for instance, that all students on your campus support building a new student center and you interviewed only students you know, you wouldn't have an appropriate sample. But if you interviewed a cross-section of students based on demographics such as age, major, class standing, and where they lived, you would have greater confidence in reasoning from those specific cases to the general student population.

Linking two events or actions to claim that one resulted in the other.

Hair begins with his conclusion that news outlets produce a "national campfire" where people gather to talk with each other. He then presents the premise that large numbers of people watch or listen to the news. To support his claims, he uses CNN's viewership as an example. His reasoning follows an inductive pattern—from the specific (CNN) to the general (all news outlets are experiencing increased audience numbers).

Inductive reasoning can be persuasive because it provides specific, concrete evidence that makes the claim more real or understandable. In addition, humans naturally think inductively, so using such reasoning to connect claims and evidence fits well with the audience's thought processes. One example alone, however, seldom convinces an audience of a claim's legitimacy. Inductive reasoning works best when speakers use multiple, diverse, and relevant examples.[42] Later in his speech Hair referred to statistics on website news traffic, broadening the range of his supporting evidence. In addition, examples must clearly represent the general conclusion they support. As a network dedicated to broadcasting news, CNN provides a reasonable example for the claim that more people are watching the news.

CAUSAL REASONING

Persuasive speakers use causal reasoning in four ways: to *explain* why something happened, to identify who's *responsible* for something, to determine whether people can *control* an event, and to *predict* what might occur in the future. In each of these cases, the speaker wants to show the cause of something. In **causal reasoning**, the speaker argues that one action or event resulted in another.[43] People frequently use causal reasoning to make sense of their everyday experiences. You take on an extra project at work, for instance, and after you complete it you get a raise. To explain the increase in salary, you point to your efforts on the project as the cause. Causal reasoning also plays an important role in your attempts to predict the future. If you can determine a causal relationship between two events that occurs consistently, you can expect it will continue to occur. You might observe, for instance, that if you take a brief nap during the day you feel more alert in the evening than on the days you skip a nap. You'd predict, then, that in the future taking a nap will help you feel refreshed later in the day.

U.S. Department of Education Deputy Secretary Raymond Simon used causal reasoning in his testimony about the No Child Left Behind Act before the House Committee on Education and the Workforce. As you probably know, No Child Left Behind is a federal law designed to improve elementary- and secondary-school education. The legislation has both supporters and detractors. Deputy Secretary Simon testified in support of the law:

> You deserve to know whether the No Child Left Behind Act is working as intended. I am here to report that it is. Across the country, test scores in reading and math

in the early grades are rising, and the "achievement gap" is finally beginning to close. Students once left behind, I am pleased to say, are now leading the way, making some of the fastest progress.

We know this because No Child Left Behind measures the academic performance of all students through testing. And we know it because the law breaks down these results by student subgroup—African American, Hispanic, students with disabilities, the economically disadvantaged, limited English proficient, and more.

This disaggregation of data, as it's known, is at the heart of the law. It shines a bright light of accountability on our schools for all parents and taxpayers to see. And it allows teachers to catch students before they fall behind.[44]

In his remarks, Simon elaborated on the effects—better test scores, reduced achievement gap, and identifying students before they fall behind—and attributed them to the No Child Left Behind Act. Later in his comments, he provided more technical information to support his reasoning and described education problems the new law solved. His causal reasoning answered two questions: (1) What is responsible for improvements in K-12 education? and (2) How does the No Child Left Behind Act improve K-12 education?

Causal reasoning can prove quite persuasive because humans are naturally inquisitive—they like to know why and how things happen. People also like a sense of stability and prediction, which causal reasoning can provide. As a persuasive speaker, however, you must be sure that the two events are indeed related and that one truly causes the other. You must consider, for example, other factors that might lead to a particular result. Deputy Secretary Simon credited No Child Left Behind with many academic improvements. But additional variables may be at work as well, such as changes in local and state education practices completely unrelated to No Child Left Behind.

ANALOGICAL REASONING

An *analogy* is a comparison between two things. Analogies work well when the two things compared share clear points of relevance. For example, most people would probably understand the analogy "The internet is an information highway" because both the internet and highways involve networks, points of access, and tools for navigation. But the analogy "The internet is an eggplant" likely wouldn't resonate with an audience because the two objects don't have obvious points of comparison.

▼ When you use causal reasoning, think carefully about what the true causes of an event or action are. For example, does violence in movies cause people to want to commit violence? If so, should violent movies be censored? Or do movies include violence simply because people find this type of simulated violence entertaining? Considering an event or action's true causes—and using supporting evidence to back up your claim—will help you present a stronger argument.

PARAMOUNT PICTURES/THE KOBAL COLLECTION/VAUGHAN, STEPHEN

When persuasive speakers use **analogical reasoning,** they compare two similar objects, processes, concepts, or events and suggest that what holds true for one also holds true for the other. The similarities between the two provide the rationale for the conclusion the speaker offers. In a speech on diversity, McGill University professor Fahri Karakas[45] used analogical reasoning to compare North America and a sweet dessert called Noah's pudding:

> We have today with us a very special, unique, authentic dessert. Let me introduce to you this marvelous dessert, called "Ashura" or "Noah's pudding." Noah's pudding is a sweet dessert prepared of mixed nuts and fruits in a pudding texture in the Middle East in remembrance of the event of the Noah's ark, and the pudding is distributed to friends, family, and neighbors. . . .
>
> Ashura symbolizes diversity and tolerance. Each of the forty ingredients is cooked and prepared in a different fashion. This symbolizes a genuine respect for the differences. Ashura is essentially a celebration of diversity. . . .
>
> North America is like a cup of Noah's pudding as it embodies and contains the diversity and richness of almost all human civilizations. Canada and the United States have become post-national and multicultural societies, containing the globe within their borders, and we know that our diversity is a comparative advantage and a source of continuing creativity and innovation. We grow socially, economically, culturally, and spiritually by valuing our diversity and contributing to the world.[46]

Karakas went on to detail more explicitly the ways in which Ashura and diversity in North America are similar. He used this line of analogical reasoning as a platform to argue that diversity lies at the center of effectively solving global problems such as hunger, illiteracy, and war. The analogy works well—in large part because Karakas provides rich detail in describing the dessert and clearly linking different aspects of it to diversity.

For an analogy to be an argument and not simply a comparison, the speaker must state or imply a premise and a conclusion. Let's examine Karakas's speech:

> *Premise:* Ashura shows that different ingredients can work together harmoniously to produce something extraordinary.
>
> *Premise:* The people of North American are like a cup of Ashura.
>
> *Conclusion:* North Americans can work together to produce something extraordinary.

Comparing two similar objects, processes, concepts, or events and suggesting that what holds true for one also holds true for the other.

As with all arguments, analogical reasoning must include some conclusion.[47] In this case, Karakas applied the analogy to make the assertion that diverse people can jointly address global issues. But just saying, "North Americans are like Ashura" would not have been sufficient—it's only a comparison.

When speakers reason by analogy, the two things compared must have enough similarities to make the comparison believable. For example, a persuasive speaker might argue that alcohol and marijuana are similar, so the latter should be legalized. But the audience must be convinced that the two are truly similar. In addition, the speaker must recognize differences between the things compared. If the differences are larger or more important than the similarities, the analogy won't work. For example, solutions to environmental problems in one city may not translate to another city due to differences in climate and geography, even if the two locations share similar environmental problems.

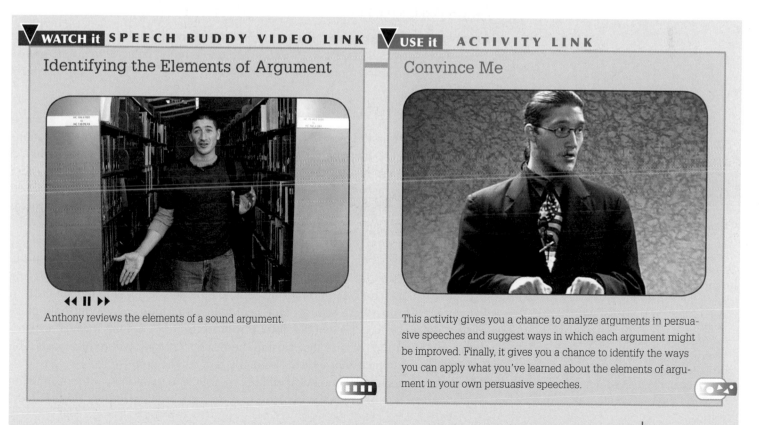

▼ **WATCH it** SPEECH BUDDY VIDEO LINK

Identifying the Elements of Argument

◀◀ ❚❚ ▶▶

Anthony reviews the elements of a sound argument.

▼ **USE it** ACTIVITY LINK

Convince Me

This activity gives you a chance to analyze arguments in persuasive speeches and suggest ways in which each argument might be improved. Finally, it gives you a chance to identify the ways you can apply what you've learned about the elements of argument in your own persuasive speeches.

Avoiding Fallacies in Argument

▼ A **fallacy** is an error in making an argument. The error may be in the claims offered, the evidence presented, or the reasoning process. Whatever the mistake, a fallacy results in an erroneous argument.[48] The challenge for speakers and listeners rests in identifying fallacies. Fallacies often appear valid and reasonable, but upon closer inspection they do not hold up. Fallacies may even persuade the uncritical listener.[49] Yet including fallacies in a persuasive speech—even if unintentionally—reflects poorly on the speaker and ultimately constitutes unethical behavior.

Fallacies fall into four main categories:

1. Faulty assertions
2. Flawed evidence
3. Defective reasoning
4. Erroneous responses

Effective speakers recognize fallacies in their arguments and eliminate them before they make their presentations. **Table 15.5** summarizes common fallacies in public speaking, which are discussed in more detail in this section.

FALLACIES IN CLAIMS

Fallacies stemming from the claims a speaker makes refer to errors in basic assumptions or assertions. The **false dilemma fallacy**, also called *either-or thinking*, occurs when a speaker tries to reduce the choices an audience can make to two even though other alternatives exist. For instance, to say that "We must completely fund this program or it is doomed" fails to acknowledge other options, such as supporting parts of the program and eliminating other parts.

Begging the question, or *circular reasoning*, is another fallacy rooted in a speaker's claims. When speakers beg the question, they imply the truth of the conclusion in the premise or simply assert that the validity of the conclusion is self-evident. In attempting to persuade an audience to support closing some elementary schools to reduce costs, a speaker states, "Closing these schools will save the district money. We will only close schools that will financially benefit the district by closing them." But the speaker has provided no support for the premise that closing these schools really will reduce costs. The premise implies the conclusion, which essentially restates the premise.

When a speaker says that one event will necessarily lead to another without showing any logical connection between the two, the speaker has used the **slippery slope fallacy**.

An error in making an argument.

Argument in which a speaker reduces available choices to only two even though other alternatives exist; also called the *either-or fallacy*.

Argument in which a speaker uses a premise to imply the truth of the conclusion or asserts that the validity of the conclusion is self-evident; also called *circular reasoning*.

Argument in which a speaker asserts that one event will necessarily lead to another without showing any logical connection between the two events.

TABLE 15.5 ▶ Common Fallacies in Public Speaking

FALLACY	BRIEF DEFINITION	EXAMPLE
FALLACIES IN CLAIMS		
False dilemma	Reduce choices to just two	We either raise student tuition or lay off teachers.
Begging the question	Something is true because it is	Our program is the best one because we rate it highly.
Slippery slope	One event leading to another without a logical connection	If we improve this highway, it will lead to urban sprawl.
Ad ignorantiam	True because it hasn't been disproved	Elves must exist because we have no proof that they don't.
FALLACIES IN EVIDENCE		
Red herring	Distract with irrelevant point or example	Spend less time online. Our community is losing its unity, so people should get more involved in it.
Ad populum	Appeal to popular attitude or emotion	If you're a true patriot, you'll support our petition for a new city hall.
Appeal to tradition	Support the status quo	In-person college classes are better than online classes because City College has always taught classes face to face.
Comparative evidence	Inappropriate use of statistics	Violent crime in our city doubled from last year. [Speaker omits previous year's number, which was very low.]
FALLACIES IN REASONING		
Division	Parts of a whole share the same properties	The red states voted Republican. Pat lives in a red state and therefore must have voted Republican.
Hasty generalization	Insufficient examples or inadequate sample	Two local restaurants have seen an increase in business since the stadium was built, so all restaurants have benefited.
Post hoc	Misrepresent causal relationship	The year after the department hired a new manager, sales increased.
Weak analogy	Key dissimilarities make the comparison misleading	Buying stocks is like gambling because both involve money and risk.

Continued

TABLE 15.5 ▶ Continued

FALLACY	BRIEF DEFINITION	EXAMPLE
FALLACIES IN RESPONDING		
Ad hominem	Personal attack	That administrator is an idiot and of course came to a wrong conclusion.
Guilt by association	Claim linked to objectionable person	Osama bin Laden would support this idea.
Caricature	Misrepresenting a claim	My opponent's position is that the police force should be abolished. [In reality, the speaker's opponent is calling for minor budget cuts.]
Loaded words	Emotionally laden, misleading language	Hunting is the senseless murder of innocent creatures.

Although the conclusion might possibly follow from the premise, the speaker skips the steps between them. The speaker argues, for example, "If the government passes a law requiring all citizens to carry a national identification card, it will be a lot easier for politicians to invade our private lives in other ways, too." So a national identity card will lead to the dismantling of all privacy rights. This type of argument is fallacious because one small event will not necessarily lead to a much larger and more significant event.

The ***ad ignorantiam* fallacy**, or *appeal to ignorance,* suggests that because a claim hasn't been shown false, it must be true. Also called the burden of proof fallacy, Senator Joseph R. McCarthy used this tactic in the 1950s to accuse people of being communists. He argued that if people couldn't disprove his allegations, they must be communists. Claims of UFOs, alien abductions, and paranormal activities usually rely on the *ad ignorantiam* fallacy: Scientists have no proof that UFOs don't exist. Therefore, there are UFOs.[50]

> Argument in which a speaker suggests that because a claim hasn't been shown to be false, it must be true; also called an *appeal to ignorance.*

FALLACIES IN EVIDENCE

Even if a speaker presents valid claims, the evidence used to support those assertions may be irrelevant, inaccurate, or insufficient. Sometimes speakers present evidence that has nothing to do with the claim. In these cases, the speaker creates a **red herring**, distracting the audience with irrelevant evidence. To urge the audience to support abolishing

> Argument that introduces irrelevant evidence to distract an audience from the real issue.

all competitive sports on campus, a speaker might argue, "We need to end competitive sports here at our college. The state is in a budget crisis, and tuition is going up." The state's budget crisis and rising tuition are not directly related to the idea of abolishing competitive sports, but mentioning those points does sensationalize the topic—and take the audience's mind off the real issue.

The comparative evidence fallacy occurs when speakers use statistics or compare numbers in ways that mislead the audience and misrepresent the evidence included to support the argument. This may happen unintentionally when a speaker simply misinterprets statistical data. In other cases, the speaker may manipulate the numbers or omit some information and purposefully deceive the audience. For example, some urban universities highlight their low rates of crime by reporting only crimes that occur on the campus itself, leaving out any that are reported even within a block or two of the campus's borders. While the statistics may be accurate, omitting nearby crime incidents may give students, faculty, and staff a false sense of security.

> **comparative evidence fallacy** Argument in which a speaker uses statistics or compares numbers in ways that misrepresent the evidence and mislead the audience.

In addition, speakers may favor statistical evidence too heavily, privileging numbers over other forms of evidence such as testimony, narrative, and examples. Although statistics can provide powerful evidence, they are not always the best choice. Statistics often shed little light on how things work, for instance. A speaker may present statistics showing that students who learn math using a new method score higher on tests than do students using an old method. But the reason for the higher scores may be the increased attention that students using the new method received, rather than the method itself. Without additional evidence, the audience can't be sure of the process that led to the results.[51]

The *ad populum* fallacy is commonly found in advertising. Although effective speakers do employ narratives, examples, and other evidence in appealing to an audience's emotions, the *ad populum* fallacy simply plays on popular attitudes without offering any supporting materials. Speakers may appeal to audience members' prejudices or their desire to be part of the group. If you want to be with the crowd, for instance, you should drive a certain car or use a particular toothpaste. Diet fads fall into this category, too. Remember the "no carbs" craze? Trying to persuade an audience to go on a reduced-carbohydrate diet because everyone's doing it is an example of the *ad populum* fallacy.

> **ad populum fallacy** Argument in which a speaker appeals to popular attitudes and emotions without offering evidence to support claims.

When speakers use the appeal to tradition fallacy, they argue that the status quo or current state of things is better than any new idea or approach. Audience members often find this fallacy persuasive because it argues against change and for the familiar and known. Although the appeal to tradition fallacy seems like an appropriate use of mythos, or an appeal to cultural beliefs, this fallacy asserts the superiority of the status quo simply based on tradition. The appeal to tradition fallacy has been used to argue against allowing women in all-male colleges and in favor of forcing African American children to attend

> **appeal to tradition fallacy** Argument in which a speaker asserts that the status quo is better than any new idea or approach.

segregated schools. Sometimes traditional ways of doing things are indeed the best course of action. But the speaker must present sufficient evidence to support that stance.

FALLACIES IN REASONING

Fallacies in reasoning involve errors in how the speaker links the evidence and the claims. One error in deductive reasoning is the **division fallacy,** in which speakers assume that what's true of the whole is also true of the parts making up the whole. A survey might find, for instance, that students at your college hold a favorable view of current general-education policies. Does this mean all students feel that way? Possibly, but you can't be sure that's the case.

When speakers draw a conclusion based on too few examples or an inadequate sample, they've made a hasty generalization, a flaw in inductive reasoning. The **hasty generalization fallacy** occurs when the speaker makes a claim after offering only one or two examples, or when the examples offered don't represent the larger group. For example, a speaker who argues for improving the quality of national teacher training by using data drawn only from a few schools would not be able to convincingly establish the need for reform at the national level.

The ***post hoc* fallacy,** or *false cause fallacy,* involves concluding that a causal relationship exists simply because one event follows another in time. Say, for instance, that the police chief in your city was fired and shortly thereafter the crime rate increased. Did the firing necessarily lead to the higher crime rate? Maybe, but many other factors could be involved as well, such as the time of year, decreased patrols in an area, better reporting of crimes, or a sudden downturn in the economy. When a speaker argues that one event necessarily caused another, always consider additional possible explanations for why something occurred.

The **weak analogy fallacy** results when two things have important dissimilarities that make the comparison inaccurate and the analogy faulty. Although it's possible to identify similarities between just about any two things you might want to compare, the similarities must contribute to the argument and the dissimilarities must not detract from it. A speaker argues, for example, "Graffiti is like any other form of public art and should be supported." But the process for displaying public art is quite different from that for displaying graffiti. With public art, members of the community decide on the type of art and where it should be placed. With graffiti, the person applying the paint is making those choices.

FALLACIES IN RESPONDING

Listeners may make errors in argument when critiquing a speaker's arguments. Probably the most common fallacy in responding is the ***ad hominem* fallacy,** or the *against*

Argument in which a speaker assumes that what is true of the whole is also true of the parts that make up the whole.

Argument in which a speaker draws a conclusion based on too few or inadequate examples.

Argument in which a speaker concludes a causal relationship exists simply because one event follows another in time; also called the *false cause fallacy.*

Argument in which a speaker compares two things that are dissimilar, making the comparison inaccurate.

Argument in which a speaker rejects another speaker's claim based on that speaker's character rather than the evidence the speaker presents; also called the *against the person fallacy.*

the person fallacy. This fallacy occurs when a claim is rejected based on the speaker's character rather than the evidence. The *ad hominem* fallacy typically follows this pattern: "You think we should adopt the group's plan. Everyone knows you're a mean person. Your position is wrong." The person's character is irrelevant to the initial claim. Although you can certainly examine a speaker's credibility, you must critique an argument based on the evidence presented rather than something about the person that has nothing to do with the topic. Personally attacking the speaker or the source of the evidence takes attention away from the true merits of a claim.

Like the *ad hominem* fallacy, the **guilt by association fallacy** suggests something wrong with the speaker's character—in this case, others who support the speaker's claim. Also known as the *bad company fallacy*, this fallacy links the speaker with someone the audience finds objectionable, deplorable, repulsive, or even evil. Responding to a speaker arguing for national health care, an audience member says, "Fidel Castro set up a national health care system in Cuba. I certainly wouldn't want something in the United States that was designed by a dictator." Of course, other democratic countries, such as Canada and Great Britain, have national health care, but by associating the speaker's claim with someone the audience probably dislikes, the person responding commits a guilt by association fallacy.

The **caricature fallacy**, or *straw man fallacy*, involves misrepresenting a speaker's argument so that just a weak shell of the original claim remains. Then the argument is easily refuted because it appears so implausible or simplistic,[52] much like the ease of pushing over the straw Scarecrow in *The Wizard of Oz*. These fallacies often occur in political campaigns when candidates present distorted and exaggerated views of their opponents' positions. A candidate for mayor who favors education reform may be accused of seeking to abolish the public school system. A candidate for president of the student government who advocates revising the grading system used to assess student performance might be denounced as calling for an end to grades. In both cases, the original claim is misrepresented so that the argument against it becomes obvious.

The **loaded word fallacy** uses emotionally laden words to distract from the speaker's argument and evaluate claims based on a misleading

Argument in which a speaker suggests that something is wrong with another speaker's claims by associating those claims with someone the audience finds objectionable; also called the *bad company fallacy*.

Argument in which a speaker misrepresents another speaker's argument so that only a weak shell of the original argument remains; also called the *straw man fallacy*.

Argument in which a speaker uses emotionally laden words to evaluate claims based on a misleading emotional response rather than the evidence presented.

▼ Speakers who use the caricature, or straw man, fallacy misrepresent an argument to the extent that it seems the argument is as easy to topple as the *Wizard of Oz*'s Scarecrow.

MGM/THE KOBAL COLLECTION

emotional response rather than the evidence presented.[53] The intent in using such language is to refute a speaker's claims without offering any substantial evidence. Responding to a speaker's claim that online gambling should be legalized by saying, "Condoning the corrupt operations of the rapacious online gaming interests will only serve to allow more innocent victims to fall prey to this deplorable vice" may play on emotions but does nothing to refute the original argument.

SUMMARY

The well-constructed argument forms the foundation of persuasive speaking. An argument consists of three elements: claims, evidence, and reasoning. Claims lay the groundwork for the thesis of your speech, answering the question "What am I asserting?" Every claim includes at least one premise and a conclusion. When speakers use an enthymeme, they omit part of the claim, leaving the audience to complete the claim. Qualifiers moderate a claim, indicating where there might be exceptions to the speaker's position.

Evidence refers to the supporting materials presented to back up the claim, answering the question "What is the support for my assertion?" Speakers may use logical appeals (logos), appeals to the speaker's credibility (ethos), emotional appeals (pathos), or appeals to cultural beliefs and values (mythos). Generally the strongest arguments are those that effectively integrate all four types of appeals. In addition, evidence should be relevant to the topic, come from highly credible sources, and represent a diversity of sources.

Reasoning is how speakers connect their evidence and claims. Reasoning answers the question "How are my supporting materials and assertions linked together?" and shows the audience how the evidence you've chosen provides justification for your position on the topic. Persuasive speakers rely on four types of reasoning: deductive, inductive, causal, and analogical. Deductive reasoning refers to arguing from a general principle to a specific case. Inductive reasoning involves giving examples in support of a claim. In causal reasoning, the speaker argues that something caused something else. Speakers using analogical reasoning compare two things that share similarities.

A fallacy occurs when an error is made in constructing an argument. Although fallacies may be persuasive, they are nonetheless a deceptive and unethical approach to convincing an audience. Fallacies may stem from errors in claims, evidence, reasoning, or responding. Common fallacies in claims are false dilemma, begging the question, slippery slope, and *ad ignorantiam*. Fallacies in evidence include red herring, *ad populum*, appeal to tradition, and comparative evidence. Division, hasty generalization, *post hoc*, and weak analogy are fallacies in reasoning. Audience members responding to persuasive arguments may also use fallacies, including *ad hominem*, guilt by association, caricature, and loaded words.

In the Book

Summary
Key Terms
Critical Challenges

More Study Resources

Speech Studio
Quizzes
WebLinks

Student Workbook

15.1: Variations on a Claim
15.2: Presidential Premises
15.3: Faulty Letter to the Editor
15.4: Enthymeme Hunt
15.5: I Need That

Speech Buddy Videos

Video Links

Identifying the Elements of Argument

Activity Links

Convince Me

▶ Sample Speech Videos

Dixie, "Home Schooling: Superiority and Success," persuasive speech

Robert, "Home Schooling: Not the Best Choice," persuasive speech

Speech Builder Express

Goal/purpose
Thesis statement
Organization
Outline
Supporting material
Transitions
Introduction
Conclusion
Title
Works cited
Visual aids
Completing the speech
   outline

InfoTrac

Recommended search terms

Public speaking and argument
Argument and claim
Argument and evidence
Reasoning
Argument and appeals
Enthymemes
Syllogisms
Reasoning fallacies

Audio Study Tools

"Home Schooling: Not the Best Choice" by Robert

Critical thinking questions

Learning objectives

Chapter summary

Guide to Your Online Resources

Your Online Resources for *Public Speaking: The Evolving Art* give you access to the Speech Buddy video and activity featured in this chapter, additional sample speech videos, Speech Builder Express, InfoTrac College Edition, and study aids such as glossary flashcards, review quizzes, and the Critical Challenge questions for this chapter, which you can respond to via e-mail if your instructor requests. In addition, your Online Resources feature live WebLinks relevant to this chapter, including sites where you can find interesting folklore and myths to use in appeals to cultural beliefs. Links are regularly maintained, and new ones are added periodically.

Key Terms

ad hominem fallacy 418

ad ignorantiam fallacy 416

ad populum fallacy 417

analogical reasoning 412

appeal to cultural belief (mythos) 402

appeal to speaker credibility (ethos) 398

appeal to tradition fallacy 417

argument 390

begging the question 414

caricature fallacy 419

causal reasoning 410

claim 390

comparative evidence fallacy 417

conclusion 391

deductive reasoning 406

division fallacy 418

emotional appeal (pathos) 399

enthymeme 392

evidence 390

inductive reasoning 409

fallacy 414

false dilemma fallacy 414

guilt by association fallacy 419

hasty generalization fallacy 418

loaded word fallacy 419

logical appeal (logos) 397

post hoc fallacy 418

premise 391

qualifier 395

reasoning 390

red herring fallacy 416

slippery slope fallacy 414

syllogism 406

weak analogy fallacy 418

Critical Challenges

Questions for Reflection and Discussion

1. Choose a controversial topic you're interested in and identify the claims each side presents. What are the premises and the conclusions each side is asking the audience to accept?

2. Review three or four advertisements in magazines or newspapers, on TV, or online. What appeals do the advertisers use? Give specific examples. How effective are those appeals?

3. Reflect on a recent discussion you've had in which you tried to persuade others to accept your point of view. What type or types of reasoning did you use? How well did your reasoning work?

4. Research on instruction in argumentation and persuasion has found that students who learn about the fundamentals of argument are better at detecting fallacies than are students without formal training in argument. How has what you've learned about argument and fallacies in this chapter made you more alert to fallacious arguments? How has it influenced the way you respond to persuasive messages?

16 SPECIAL OCCASION and GROUP SPEAKING

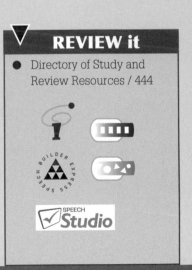

All college students look forward to graduation day. Commencement speeches are a central part of that day. During these speeches, speakers often reflect on their own life experiences. For example, in his recent commencement speech at the College of William & Mary, Jon Stewart, host and executive producer of Comedy Central's *The Daily Show*, reminisced about his undergraduate experiences there. Judy Woodruff's speech to graduates of American University focused on her journalism experiences from college through her current position as CNN senior correspondent. Kermit the Frog, giving a commencement address at Southampton College, reflected back on his time as a tadpole. In 1962, President John F. Kennedy, a Harvard graduate, began his Yale commencement speech by referring to Yale graduates with whom he got along but nonetheless disagreed.

Many of the presentations you'll give outside the classroom will take place on special occasions or involve working in a group. This chapter addresses speeches for special occasions, such as introducing a main speaker or accepting an award. In addition, the chapter provides guidelines for giving various types of small-group presentations and shows how to evaluate them.

Speeches for Special Occasions

▼ **READ it** Special occasion speeches extend the nature of what you do all the time—talk to others about what's going on in your life. When you introduce a friend to someone else, for example, you might say something about your friend as part of the introduction—this is also a common aspect of special occasion speeches. Other kinds of special occasion speeches include speeches of nomination, award presentations, acceptance speeches, after-dinner speeches, and tributes and eulogies. This section also discusses what to do when an occasion calls for speaking on camera.

SPEECHES OF INTRODUCTION

Whenever you attend a public speech given by a well-known person, you'll probably first hear a short speech that introduces that person to the audience. That's a **speech of introduction.** The speech of introduction should prepare the audience for who and what they came to hear: the main speaker and the main speech. A few basic principles apply to speeches of introduction: prepare the audience for the speaker and the occasion, give accurate information, and connect with the audience and the event.

> A short speech that introduces someone to an audience.

Prepare the Audience

In introducing the main speaker, keep your remarks brief yet at the same time prepare the audience for the main speaker and the occasion. The audience expects the introductory speaker to quickly orient them to the main speaker, the topic, and the occasion. For example, when Jonas Gahr Støre, Norway's minister of foreign affairs, introduced Dr. Mohamed ElBaradei, director general of the International Atomic Energy Agency (IAEA), at a luncheon in ElBaradei's honor, he began with:

> At the outset let me congratulate you, Dr. ElBaradei and the IAEA, on receiving the Nobel Peace Prize. It is a prize well deserved. The IAEA is crucial to international peace and security. But people make a difference.
>
> It is thanks to the untiring efforts of Dr. ElBaradei and his collaborators that the agency continues to be an effective and efficient instrument of nuclear disarmament and nonproliferation. May the Prize inspire you to keep up this

crucial work. And may the Prize serve as an inspiration to us all in our endeavours to strengthen the nonproliferation regime.

As a citizen of Norway, I look forward to welcoming you to Oslo on 10 December for the Peace Prize ceremony. Norwegians love Nobel Peace Laureates, and I know this will be no exception.[1]

The speaker indicated the reason for the occasion—ElBaradei's recent receipt of the Nobel Peace Prize for his work in the IAEA—and offered a brief explanation of the Prize's importance.

Be Accurate and Up to Date

When preparing for a speech of introduction, research the speaker as you would any topic. For example, check online for any information the person may have posted, such as a personal website or a page on a social networking site such as Facebook, search for stories in the popular press, and consult encyclopedic entries, such as *Who's Who in America*. If possible, interview the main speaker via e-mail, phone, or webchat, or in person, to get the most accurate and up-to-date information. Once you've composed a draft of your speech, if time permits and the main speaker is agreeable, ask the person to review your remarks for accuracy.

▼ A speech of introduction helps an audience get to know the featured speaker and establishes the speaker's credibility.

Connect with the Audience

Even a speaker the audience knows well needs an introduction that creates a positive response and enthusiasm in the listeners. When the speaker is less well known, the introducer's role in connecting the speaker with the audience becomes all the more important. Making a connection between the main speaker and the audience requires that you know enough about the speaker and what the person intends to say so you can skillfully gain the audience's interest. At a recent Association of Late-Deafened Adults Conference (ALDAcon), Dr. Jane Schlau introduced the keynote speaker in this way:

Our Plenary speaker is Dr. Sanjay Gulati, who has been a very important person in my life. He is a child psychologist and has an impressive history of working with people with hearing loss. But he is about much more than his credentials. We had dinner last weekend and we discussed the presentations we were preparing for this conference. We also did a lot of e-mailing back and forth. He e-mailed me the title he had chosen for his presentation: "Reimagining Deafness." I really like that title, because it says so much about our journey in deafness. It is my great pleasure to introduce to you Dr. Sanjay Gulati.[2]

Schlau personalized the topic and the speaker, making them more accessible to the audience. By mentioning her communication with the speaker and directly linking his topic to the purpose of the conference, the introducer sparked interest and prepared the audience to listen to the keynote speech.

SPEECHES OF NOMINATION

Like speeches of introduction, speeches of nomination focus on the qualifications or accomplishments of a particular person. **Nomination speeches** demonstrate why a particular individual would be successful at something if given the chance.

For nomination speeches, a few simple guidelines apply. First, who does the nominating can be just as important as what is said about the nominee. The person who nominates someone for something—an elected office, position, citation, prize, or award, for example—should be well respected and liked by those who will choose from a field of competing candidates. The nominator should be asked to do the job, or at least be fully supported by the nominee. Especially when the stakes are high, nomination speeches should be arranged well in advance.

The nominator must have accurate, concise, and compelling information about the nominee. Audience members want to know why they should consider a particular candidate favorably. What are the strongest reasons for choosing this person to serve in some capacity or be given recognition for something the nominee has accomplished? The speaker should justify the nomination in a way that creates confidence in the individual as deserving of the job or of formal appreciation.

Most nomination speeches are brief. When making a nomination, accurately identify the nominee, cite the best reasons for selecting the person, personalize the candidate without being too informal, express confidence in how the nominee will perform, ask for the group's support, and thank the group. For instance, if you were nominating someone for treasurer of a school organization, you might say, "I nominate Rhea Salazar for treasurer of our club. Rhea is an excellent person for the position because she has earned top grades in all her accounting classes and has worked part-time as a bookkeeper for a local bakery. I've known Rhea for several years, and I've observed her dedication to the tasks she sets out to do. She's organized, detail-oriented, and a problem-solver. I know she'll serve our organization well. So please give her your support. Thank you."

AWARD PRESENTATIONS

Award presentations celebrate what someone has already done well. To help audience members understand the context for a particular award, the presenter provides back-

Speech that demonstrates why a particular individual would be successful at something if given the chance.

Speech that recognizes an individual to celebrate something the person has done well.

ground information about the award and if necessary, the occasion. As always, speakers should be flexible, responding to the actual situation. The speaker must take into account how much knowledge the audience has about the award and about the occasion for giving it. For some audiences, particularly those who have attended the same ceremony in the past, little needs to be said about the origins and purpose of the award. In this situation, the speaker should briefly but strongly reinforce the nature and importance of the award.

Award presentations have much in common with nominations in that both types of speeches focus on the positive qualities of an individual. When presenting the University of Virginia Engineering School's inaugural Robert A. Bland Award in Engineering and Applied Science to Dr. Cato T. Laurencin, the school's dean, Dr. James H. Aylor, said in part:

> To many of his African-American mentees, Professor Laurencin has provided the first tangible example of achievement in the science and engineering arena by an African American, and this has resulted in a cadre of African-American clinicians, engineers, and researchers who themselves are determined to follow in his example of achievement and success.
>
> Comments like, "He has helped me initiate collaborations"; "He has helped me make valuable connections"; "He has opened doors to funding opportunities"; "He has enabled me to be more efficient in teaching my classes"; "He has helped me in writing successful proposals". . . sprinkle the pages of the many letters we received supporting his nomination for this award.
>
> Clearly it is his constant attention to education that forms his strengths as a leader.[3]

Dr. Aylor underscored the qualities of the nominee that led to his being granted the award, citing specific comments others had made praising the recipient's abilities as a mentor.

When presenting an award, shine a spotlight on the award, the recipient, and the occasion. Audiences appreciate a crisp and useful orientation to the situation and the person, followed by the giving of the award and some words from the recipient.

ACCEPTANCE SPEECHES

Audiences expect individuals who are recognized, honored, or awarded to give an **acceptance speech** after they step up to the podium or move to the front of the room. If you were to find yourself in the position of being publicly recognized, what should you say? Most individuals who receive honors or awards know in advance that they have won, so you'll have plenty of time to prepare.

acceptance speech Speech given by an individual who is being recognized, honored, or given an award.

When accepting an award, some general rules apply. Most important, award recipients should thank the presenter, organization, and audience; demonstrate humility; and keep their remarks succinct. In addition, some acceptance speakers may contextualize the award by discussing the work or activity that won them the award or providing a personal narrative that is relevant to the occasion.

Be Thankful and Humble

You've seen enough award ceremonies to know the audience expects certain responses from award winners. Everyone thanks the people who helped them succeed. For example, when Powderburn won Best Metal Band at the 2007 Austin Music Awards, the group thanked "everyone who has ever helped us or made it easier in this town for us to do what we love and appreciate us for being good song writers and not just for our genre. Thank you, everyone." The group members went on to thank "our fans on YouTube and MySpace . . . and everyone who voted."[4]

Award winners also tend to minimize their accomplishments, demonstrating a sense of perspective, even humility. Accepting an award for her children's nonfiction book, *Gorilla Doctors: Saving Endangered Great Apes*, author Pamela S. Turner ended her speech by saying:

> I am so very grateful that the Bank Street College of Education has found *Gorilla Doctors* worthy of an award given for inspiring young readers. I certainly can't take credit for making children interested in animals; they already are interested. I can't take credit for making children empathize with animals, either; children already have empathy. I do hope I've encouraged children to combine scientific knowledge with their interest and empathy. I hope the result will be children better equipped to share this world respectfully, humbly, and lovingly with the rest of the animal kingdom. Thank you.[5]

Closing her speech in this way shifted the audience's focus to the more general goal of raising children's awareness of treating animals ethically. In this way, Turner acknowledged the impact her book might have on children's attitudes toward animals, but noted that many other factors are involved as well.

Be Succinct

When speakers have the stage, they may be tempted to go on and on. But listeners expect comments made when accepting an award to be brief and to the point. The Webby Awards likely hold the record for shortest acceptance speeches—recipients are allowed only five words. For

▼ Showing enthusiasm for an award demonstrates for your audience how thankful you are. Be sure your level of enthusiasm is appropriate for the occasion—some awards presentations are more formal than others.

AP Photo/Gary He

example, the 2006 speeches included "This is poetic justice" by Justice Learning (Law category), "Even better than rocket science," by the National Science Foundation website (Government category), and "Note to self: update resume," by Monster Career Advice (Employment category).[6] Few award ceremonies call for speakers to say only five words, but you still want to keep your remarks brief when accepting an award.

In accepting the Oscar for best documentary feature film, *An Inconvenient Truth,* director Davis Guggenheim and former Vice President Al Gore together uttered just 153 words:

> **Davis Guggenheim:** Wow. I made this movie for my children, and my father taught me to make great movies. My beautiful wife [points to her in audience]. All of us who made this film, Laurie, Lawrence, Scott and Lesley. We did so because we were moved to act by this man [gestures to Al Gore]. Jeff Skoll funded it. John Lesher released it so beautifully, but all of us were inspired by his fight for thirty years to tell this Truth to all of us. Thank you, Al. We are so inspired. We share this with you.

> **Al Gore:** Thank you. I want to thank Tipper and my family, thank the Academy and everyone on this amazing team. My fellow Americans, people all over the world, we need to solve the climate crisis. It's not a political issue, it's a moral issue. We have everything we need to get started, with the possible exception of the will to act, that's a renewable resource. Let's renew it.[7]

In less than a minute the speakers thanked those associated with the film, explained why they had participated in the project, and elaborated on the work yet to be done.

Contextualize the Award

Speakers may provide a context for an award by describing activities they participated in that led to the award or telling a story related to the occasion. These comments personalize the award and help the audience feel more connected with the recipient. In accepting the International Gandhi Award for his work on leprosy, Yohei Sasakawa traced his social activism to his father:

> For more than thirty years, I have worked to eliminate leprosy from the world. My father, Ryoichi Sasakawa, was the main reason I became involved in this mission.
>
> He died in 1995 at the age of 96. As a young man, he had seen the misery and anguish that leprosy caused individuals and families, and his life's ambition was to alleviate their suffering. But more than just offering comfort and encouragement, he wanted to ensure that every single person who required treatment had access to it.
>
> As his son, I am carrying on his work, and doing my utmost to finish what he began.[8]

Explaining the motivation for his work gave the audience a better understanding of Sasakawa's interests in eradicating both the physical disease and social stigma of leprosy. In addition, he provided a context for his work with which many people likely could identify.

AFTER-DINNER SPEECHES

After-dinner speeches usually serve as a featured part of an organizational event. These events were originally scheduled as dinner gatherings, but today they are just as likely to be scheduled for breakfast or lunch. Whatever the time of day, the goal of an after-dinner speech is to contribute something pleasurable to the event. After-dinner speeches amplify and extend the good feelings the event sponsors want to create for everyone in attendance. Speakers accomplish this by being entertaining and lighthearted while staying focused on a central theme.

Be Entertaining and Lighthearted

Most after-dinner presentations are lighthearted speeches to entertain, although the topic can be serious for some occasions.

Humor is a cornerstone of after-dinner speeches, but it isn't the only way to entertain and enlighten an audience. Being humorous comes more easily to some speakers than it does to others, so don't force the issue if you don't feel comfortable in that role. After-dinner speeches often include jokes or funny anecdotes, but not every occasion for an after-dinner speech calls for humor. Sharing thoughtful reflections, making insightful comments about a topic of interest to the group, and using language creatively can please the audience too.

Focus on a Theme

Although most after-dinner speeches have an upbeat, enjoyable quality, they should also develop a thesis and have a point. The audience should feel not only entertained but also enriched in some way.

Imagine, for example, that you've been asked to give an after-dinner speech to your former classmates at a high school reunion. You might good-naturedly tell a few stories about some of your old friends and teachers, but you'd also want to develop a theme. For instance, you might want to speak about how important those high school days were for everyone and how much you've all benefited from knowing each other. For an after-dinner speech at an annual sales convention, you might make fun of how difficult it was to introduce a new product line during the year. But ultimately you'd want to say something about how successful the product and company have become during the past year.

Avoid Presentation Media for After-Dinner Speeches

Audiences for after-dinner speeches don't want to be lectured to, be challenged too seriously, feel offended, or think they should be taking notes. Except for very special and limited purposes, speakers in these situations should avoid using presentation media.

An audio or video segment might be appropriate for a speech that focuses on sports, media, music, or fashion, for instance, but even then speakers must be careful. All the rules that apply to the use of presentation media in general pertain to the after-dinner speech in

even greater measure, especially concerning the technical aspects. Unless the room is equipped precisely for the use of presentation media, speakers should avoid using them.

TRIBUTES AND EULOGIES

Sometimes people are honored for something they've done, for who they are, for where they've been in life, or for where they're headed. **Speeches of tribute** give credit, respect, admiration, gratitude, or inspiration to a person or group who has accomplished something significant, lives in a way that deserves to be praised, or is about to embark on an adventure. **Eulogies** are a special kind of speech of tribute presented as retrospectives about individuals who have died.

> Speech that gives credit, respect, admiration, gratitude, or inspiration to someone who has accomplished something significant, lives in a way that deserves to be praised, or is about to embark on an adventure.

You may very well have occasion to give one or more of these speeches. Perhaps you've already done so. Weddings, anniversaries, retirements, school reunions, even family birthday parties or welcome home gatherings frequently call for speeches of tribute. The best man or maid of honor, or both, may be asked to give a brief tribute to a newly married couple. A returning veteran from a war zone might be praised by his best friend at a party in his honor. A successful classmate from high school might be recognized at a school reunion. The daughter of a couple celebrating their golden anniversary might toast her parents' marriage.

> Speech of tribute presented as a retrospective about an individual who has died.

You sometimes see and hear impassioned praise of famous people—past Presidents, civil rights leaders, sports heroes, or entertainers, for instance—in eulogies that are shown on television and the web. But most eulogies take place much closer to home. Family members and friends often find it appropriate to eulogize deceased loved ones at funeral ceremonies. Eulogies not only praise or shed light on the person who has passed away, but they also help surviving family members and friends cope with the loss.

Emphasize Emotion Appropriately

Tributes and eulogies often are quite emotional. The mood of the tribute depends on the occasion, but speeches of tribute are generally warm, friendly, and positive. For example, in a speech of tribute for the state's law librarians, Connecticut Chief Justice Chase T. Rogers said in part:

> In 2007, we honor our law librarians with this year's Law Day Award. . . . Our law librarians . . . have one finger on the pulse of a keyboard and another on the pulse of how human beings assist, encourage, and educate others to learn and push ahead. An editorial in the *Denver Post* several years ago put it this way: "Librarians are very special people. They are the caregivers of the world of the mind, the nurturers of dreams and the defenders of truth. Perhaps no other profession is so marked by the singular generosity of its practitioners."
>
> On behalf of the entire Judicial Branch, I couldn't agree more. We are indeed fortunate that you have chosen to devote yourselves to the law libraries of the Judicial Branch, and most important, to the members of the public they serve. Thank you and congratulations.[9]

The chief justice identified the qualities of law librarians that led to the decision to honor them on the state's Law Day. She praised their work and contributions not only to the law but also to society in general.

Provide Inspiration

Speeches of tribute often inspire the audience as well as praise the person being honored. In this eulogy for her father, "Crocodile Hunter" Steve Irwin, eight-year-old Bindi Irwin stressed the importance of continuing his work:

> My daddy was my hero. He was always there for me when I needed him. He listened to me and taught me so many things. But most of all he was fun.
>
> I know that Daddy had an important job. He was working to change the world so everyone would love wildlife like he did. He built a hospital to help animals and he bought lots of land to give animals a safe place to live. He took me and my brother and my mum with him all the time. We filmed together, caught crocodiles together, and loved being in the bush together.
>
> I don't want Daddy's passion to ever end. I want to help endangered wildlife just like he did. I had the best daddy in the whole world. And I will miss him every day. When I see a crocodile I will always think of him, and I know that Daddy made this zoo so everyone could come and learn to love all the animals. Daddy made this place his whole life. Now it's our turn to help Daddy. Thank you.[10]

Speaking to thousands of people gathered at Australia Zoo for the memorial service, Bindi Irwin revealed her personal feelings about her father and at the same time encouraged others to carry on his mission of wildlife conservation.

The rules for giving an effective speech of tribute are flexible. Some speeches are written in manuscript form and read to the audience, while others are presented extemporaneously. In either case, the speaker must be exceptionally well prepared. Responsibly accepting and executing the challenge of giving a speech of tribute or eulogy is often greatly appreciated by the audience and particularly rewarding for the speaker.

MEDIATED SPEAKING

Access to the mass media opens up new ways to extend your ventures into public speaking. But traditional media make up only a part of the field of public speaking possibilities. Information and communication technologies offer a constantly expanding world of opportunities. For instance, you might want to set up a website for yourself or for an organization, where you deliver an introduction or other message by video streaming. Or you could prepare, deliver, and record a talk about any topic that interests you and post it on YouTube or a similar video-sharing website.

When presenting a speech in front of a camera, keep the following general guidelines in mind:

- If you'll be speaking at a media event, such as an interview at a local TV station, try to learn as much as possible about the structure and format of the event *before* your appearance. Ask about the event's format, how long your part will last, and whether an audience will be present
- Dress appropriately. With the exception of black, dark colors work better than light colors overall, and solid colors should be worn rather than prints or patterns. Pay the greatest attention to your shirt, jacket, blouse, or tie because in most situations you won't be shown below the waist.
- Write a brief presentation outline with keywords and phrases that you can quickly review shortly before the camera rolls. This will prompt you to stress the most important points you want to make.
- Limit your physical movement but try not to look stiff or uncomfortable.
- Be assertive, confident, and to the point, but present yourself as thoughtful, reasonable, comfortable, and friendly.
- Speak clearly, with good volume, and not too fast.
- Avoid jargon or acronyms that only specialists or others who are knowledgeable about your topic would understand.
- If you're speaking to an in-person audience, focus on them and not the camera.

There is no standard media appearance. Some appearances are initiated by a group or media spokesperson; others take the form of responses to inquiries from the media. Some appearances are planned well in advance; others occur without much notice at all. Media appearances can last an hour or more, or they can last a minute or less. You might talk one-to-one with an interviewer or be part of a group or panel. Media appearances may occur in a studio or at another location. But the guidelines listed above apply to all of these situations.

Presenting in Small Groups

With the popularity of teams and groups in organizations on the rise, you'll encounter many situations that require you to work with others and then present information to an audience.[11] Group presentations usually involve both interacting within the group and speaking to those outside the group. A **small group** is a collection of individuals who interact and depend on one another to solve a problem, make a decision, and achieve a common goal or objective. In your public speaking class, you may have worked in groups to develop various skills associated with public speaking, such as brainstorming for topics or analyzing your audience. Your instructor might also assign a group presentation. Working in groups in a classroom setting and giving group presentations prepare you for participating in team-based organizations and other professional contexts.[12] This section explains how to give and evaluate five types of group presentations: oral reports, panel discussions, round table discussions, symposiums, and forums.

A collection of individuals who interact and depend on one another to solve a problem, make a decision, or achieve a common goal or objective.

ORAL REPORT

A report in which one member of a group presents the group's findings.

When a group presents an **oral report**, one representative from the group gives the entire report. This often happens with work teams in organizations. Various members of the organization develop the report, and then one of the group members presents the findings to management or upper administration. Effective oral reports clearly recognize the contributions of all group members. The speaker should use pronouns such as *we* and *us* to indicate that the group, rather than the individual, produced the report. In addition, specific references to group members or units in the organization that wrote the report acknowledge everyone's contributions. The speaker must be fully versed in all aspects of the report, asking group members for clarification where needed.

The oral report format provides consistency and smooth transitions between the sections of a presentation. Oral reports avoid the inherent disruptions associated with each team member taking her or his speaking turn. Audience members need only adjust to one person's speaking style. An oral report's strengths can lead to its weaknesses, however. The team relies on one spokesperson, who may or may not accurately represent the perspectives of all group members. Also, the speaker might not be familiar with all aspects of the report and therefore may have difficulty answering questions after the formal presentation. In this situation, all group members should be encouraged to participate.

PANEL DISCUSSION

You've likely viewed **panel discussions** on weekend TV talk shows. A moderator or facilitator asks questions to direct the group's interaction, which occurs in front of an audience. Group members are experts on the subject under discussion and know beforehand the general topic that will be covered. The moderator usually provides an introduction, giving an overview of the topic and the discussion's purpose. Then the moderator may state each person's credentials or ask panelists to introduce themselves.

A discussion in which a moderator asks questions of experts on a topic in front of an audience.

A discussion in which expert participants discuss a topic in an impromptu format without an audience present.

Although panel discussions are not rehearsed, they are not entirely impromptu either. Discussants often have notes and may refer to them during the discussion. Some questions may be unexpected and the responses spontaneous. Still, participants prepare carefully and don't simply "wing it" when the discussion starts. One example of a panel discussion occurs during the Career Day sponsored each semester by the Communication Studies Department at San José State University. To give students firsthand information about what they can do with a degree in communication, the department invites several alumni to talk about their careers in communication-related professions. A faculty member serves as the discussion facilitator. After the formal presentation, audience members—mostly communication majors and minors—ask the panelists questions.

▼ Although only one group member delivers an oral report, it's a good idea for members to work together to prepare the report. This ensures that the entire group contributes to the speech and can help answer questions after the formal presentation.

ROUND TABLE DISCUSSION

Unlike panel discussions, **round table discussions** do not have audiences—only the group members are present. All group members participate in a round table discussion, which may or may not have a leader or facilitator. Because speakers are experts on the topic under discussion, responses are impromptu. Nevertheless, speakers arrive prepared, knowing the discussion topic and often the other participants, too.

The setting for a round table discussion is generally informal, with speakers sitting in a circle to facilitate dialogue and engaged participation. Either the facilitator or the person who organized the discussion provides an overview or introduction

AP /Image Source

Exchanging Ideas around the Table

Participating in a round table discussion may seem intimidating at first because you don't have a rehearsed speech to present. But this format provides an excellent way to exchange ideas with others and learn about perspectives and topics you may not know much about. Consider organizing round table discussions on your campus that focus on local, regional, national, and global topics of interest to you and other students. Getting people together for discussions helps improve speaking skills and allows for the free flow of new ideas and information.

A presentation format in which each member of a group presents a speech about a part of a larger topic.

The question-and-answer session following a group's formal presentation.

that includes the discussion's purpose, procedures for conducting the discussion, and a time limit. Similarly, the facilitator or organizer presents a brief closing, summarizing the main themes to come out of the discussion and what will be done with the information. In addition, either the discussion is recorded or someone is assigned to take notes so the information participants generate can be used at a later date.

Round table discussions provide a venue for individuals to exchange information and ideas about a topic. All discussants are encouraged to participate, maximizing the opportunity to consider different points of view on the same subject. Often round-table discussions are convened to generate new ideas and innovative approaches to a problem. For example, in an effort to develop strategies for stimulating the local economy, the *Akron Beacon Journal* brought together local experts to discuss promoting entrepreneurship, small-business growth, and startups in northeastern Ohio. The product of that discussion was a list of recommendations distributed to local community leaders.[13]

SYMPOSIUM

If you're giving a group presentation in your public speaking class, you're probably using a symposium format. In a **symposium,** the group chooses a topic and divides it into different areas. Each group member then presents a speech on her or his subtopic. For example, your group might choose music and identify jazz, hip-hop, country, classical, and rock as the subtopics. Speakers usually follow the same organizational pattern in order to provide continuity among the speeches. In the music example, each speaker might discuss the music genre's history, identify two or three key artists or groups, and provide a few examples.

Most group interaction occurs in the early stages of the symposium's development. Thoroughly planning the format in advance is essential. For example, group members must discuss whether or not to use a podium, the formality of their attire, the presentation media they will use, and how they will structure their speeches.

Once the groundwork for the symposium is complete, group members work independently to prepare their individual speeches. In the later stages of speech preparation, group members come together to practice and make any necessary adjustments.

FORUM

After presenting an oral report, panel discussion, or symposium, audience members often want to ask questions. The question-and-answer session following the formal group presentation is a **forum.** As with individual speeches, group members must practice effective listening skills and answer audience members' questions as thoroughly and honestly as possible.

Coordinating group members' responses can prove challenging in forums. Before the presentation, decide which group members will handle which question areas. Group members should choose someone to facilitate the forum. The obvious choice after a panel discussion is the moderator. For oral reports, the group may choose the presenter or ask another member of the group to serve as facilitator. In symposiums, any member of the group may lead the question-and-answer session.

VIDEOCONFERENCING

With webcams becoming standard on new computers, web chat and other forms of online video communication are becoming more commonplace for group presentations. In **videoconferencing,** people at multiple physical locations use video to communicate orally and visually in real time. Videoconferencing used to require expensive equipment, but now can be done using a personal computer, webcam, and interactive software and hence has become inexpensive and more commonplace.[14] Nevertheless, videoconferencing still requires careful planning and preparation.

A small group presentation in which individuals at multiple physical locations interact in real time orally and visually, using video and high-speed computer technology.

PREPARATION AND PRACTICE

Good presenters in any situation prepare note cards based on a presentation outline. Before the videoconference, they practice what they're going to say when they display the visuals. Not surprisingly, research shows that individuals who are better prepared for their videoconference session have a more positive and productive experience.[15]

Videoconference presenters prepare their digital slides well in advance. In addition, before the presentation they check that all equipment in all locations functions properly. For example, microphones are tested for audibility and cameras for visibility.

During the Presentation

On the day of the conference, arrive or set up early and complete a final check of the equipment. Dress appropriately—don't wear bright or white clothing or jewelry that will glare in the camera's eye. Have all your notes and your visual and audio materials ready.

Once the presentation begins, be mindful of what you are doing and saying at all times. Video is unforgiving, picking up sounds and movements not ordinarily noticed. Avoid extraneous noises such as tapping a pencil or unzipping a backpack. When you are not speaking, devote all your attention to whoever is speaking and appear genuinely interested in that person. For a videoconference, use the mute button on your microphone to keep background noises to a minimum, particularly when the videoconference involves many people or several sites.

When it's your turn to talk, speak clearly and crisply. Although you might think audience members focus most on the video aspect of videoconferencing, research shows that audio—your voice—receives the most attention.[16] Balance a dynamic delivery with the constraints of video. Excessive movement clutters the screen and distracts from your ideas. Too much moving about can also detract from the picture's technical quality. Monitoring your body movement is especially important when using a webcam because the camera doesn't follow you around. In addition, slow connection speeds often cause video problems. If necessary, switching to audio-only mode will at least allow you to continue speaking and complete your presentation.

Watch your time limit and stick to it so that everyone has a chance to speak. If the presentation includes a question-and-answer session, assign a facilitator beforehand. Explain the session's format as you begin, and announce how much time the group will allot to questions.

After the Presentation

Once the presentation has ended, thank the speakers and audience members for their participation. Note what went well and what you would do differently the next time you speak in videoconference.

Evaluating Small Group Presentations

In evaluating group presentations, focus on their "groupness," or the way they fit together into a cohesive whole. Group presentations emphasize group rather than individual effort. So in addition to what is usually expected in an excellent oral presentation—well researched, audience centered, engaging language, appropriate presentation media, and the like—evaluation focuses on signs that the presentation truly reflects a group endeavor.[17] Assess the coherence of a group presentation in five primary areas: preparation as a group, coordination of the presentation, effective listening, clear references to the group, and achievement of the group's goal.

PREPARATION AS A GROUP

Preparation as a group provides the foundation for a coherent group presentation. Even in a panel discussion, in which presenters do not practice together, group members keep the others in mind as they prepare for the presentation. Similarly, participants in a round table discussion typically develop notes for their presentations within the context of what other presenters will say.

Symposiums require the most preparation as a group. Although group members talk about their own subtopics, those subtopics must come together and form a coherent whole in the presentation. For example, suppose a group chooses the topic of unusual team sports, with kabaddi, badminton, canoe polo, curling, and korfball as the subtopics. Before beginning in-depth research, group members must agree on the main points they'll cover in their speeches. They might, for instance, all talk about the sport's general description, history, and what makes it especially unique or interesting. The group would want to avoid having one person discussing only history, another covering only how the game is played, and a third focusing on why the audience should learn how to the play the game. This advanced preparation as a group becomes evident in the group's presentation, with speakers following a similar format, smooth transitions between speakers, and no repetition of identical material.

COORDINATED PRESENTATIONS

How well group members coordinate their presentations is a second area of assessment. For example, in a forum, group members should decide in advance who is responsible for questions in specific topic areas. This avoids the problem of either several group members responding to a question at the same time, or blank looks and no one responding. With panel discussions, the moderator or facilitator assumes primary responsibility for the smooth flow of discussion. Still, listeners expect group members to avoid interrupting or talking over each other. Symposiums provide multiple points for evaluating how well the group members coordinate the presentation. For example, each speaker should provide a smooth transition to the next. And although presentation media need not be identical, some standardization gives the audience an impression of continuity and prior planning.[18] Finally, regardless of the type of group presentation, an effective opening overview and closing summary give the presentation a sense of cohesion.[19]

EFFECTIVE LISTENING

Effective listening plays a key role in the success of any group presentation. No matter what the setting, group members should display active listening skills, such as giving the speaker their complete attention, nodding, looking at the speaker, taking brief notes, and showing interest in what the speaker has to say. Group members should not work on their own presentations, talk or whisper with each other, or engage in any other activities that detract from the group's presentation.

Careful listening is especially important in round table and panel discussions because participants likely do not know exactly what others will say. Appropriately responding to other speakers requires close attention to the discussion. In addition, round table and panel discussions typically include speakers with different—and opposing—viewpoints, making critical listening essential. In these types of group presentations, audience members expect participants to carefully examine other speakers' ideas and supporting evidence.

CLEAR REFERENCES TO THE GROUP

Listening to group members as they present helps speakers refer to what their co-presenters have said. These clear references to the group are a fourth important area for evaluation and provide another mechanism for linking together the parts of a group presentation. In a symposium, a speaker might say, "As Sheila remarked in her presentation . . ." or, "Similar to what Drew found . . ." These comments help demonstrate how the different pieces of

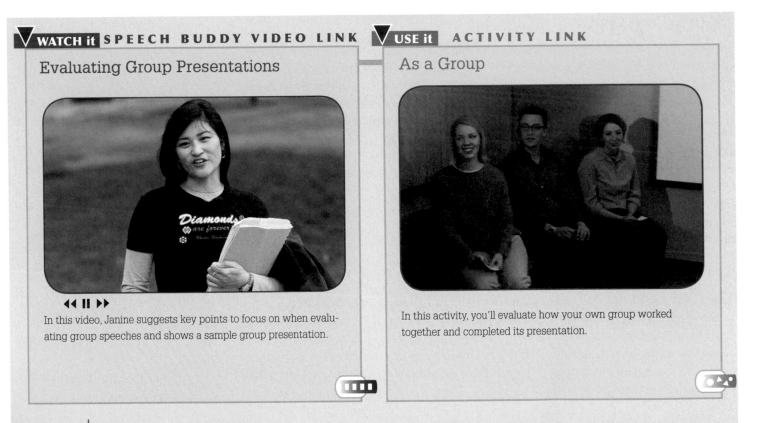

▼ **WATCH it** SPEECH BUDDY VIDEO LINK

Evaluating Group Presentations

◄◄ ❚❚ ►►

In this video, Janine suggests key points to focus on when evaluating group speeches and shows a sample group presentation.

▼ **USE it** ACTIVITY LINK

As a Group

In this activity, you'll evaluate how your own group worked together and completed its presentation.

the presentation fit together. In an oral report, the speaker might refer to specific aspects of the project that individual group members worked on. These brief acknowledgments personalize the report and indicate how different members of the group contributed to the project. Using the pronouns *we, our,* and *us* also reflects a sense of groupness. Responding to a question during a forum, the speaker might say, "In our research, we found . . ." or, "It surprised us when . . ." In making clear references to the group, audiences should learn about both individual contributions and group efforts in the presentation.

GOAL ACHIEVEMENT

The final area for evaluating group presentations concerns the degree to which the group achieved its goal. For an oral report, the speaker must give a balanced view of all the members' perspectives and adequately cover the report's sections. All participants in a panel discussion should have an equal opportunity to speak and respond appropriately to the moderator's questions. Round table discussions rely on a free flow of information among speakers that produces possible solutions to problems. Symposiums are designed to either inform or persuade audience members. Forums should allow for full audience participation. Evaluation of the group's goal attainment determines the group's ultimate success: Did the group achieve what it set out to do?

SUMMARY

Many special occasions call for some type of speech. Speeches of introduction prepare the audience to listen to the main speaker. Speeches of nomination focus on the qualities that make the nominee the best person for the position or award. Award presentations provide background information about the award and the recipient. Speakers accepting awards should be thankful and humble in their brief comments. After-dinner speeches are meant to entertain. Tributes and eulogies typically provide inspiration. Some occasions call for mediated speaking.

Groups may give several types of presentations, including oral report, panel discussion, roundtable discussion, symposium, and forum. For an oral report, one member of the group presents the entire report. Panel discussions involve a moderator asking questions of experts on a topic in front of an audience. Round table discussions also include expert speakers, but the focus is on the exchange of ideas among participants, so an audience is not present. Symposiums are the most common form of classroom group presentations. Speakers each choose a subtopic of the group's topic and present individual speeches to an audience. Forums are question-and-answer sessions. They may stand alone, but more often they occur directly after an oral report, panel discussion, or

In the Book

Summary
Key Terms
Critical Challenges

More Study Resources

Speech Studio
Quizzes
WebLinks

Student Workbook

16.1: Introducing . . .
16.2: Television Appearance
16.3: Watch and Critique an
       Award Show
16.4: Group Experiences
16.5: Failed Media Appearances

Speech Buddy Videos

 Video Links

Evaluating Group
Presentations

Activity Links

As a Group

▶ Sample Speech Videos

Jennifer, Megan, Stephanie, and Daniel, "The Dirty Truth about Antibacterial Products," persuasive group presentation

Lawrence Small, Dedication address at the opening of National Museum of the American Indian, special occasion speech

Speech Builder Express

Goal/purpose
Thesis statement
Organization
Outline
Supporting material
Transitions
Introduction
Conclusion
Title
Works cited
Visual aids
Completing the speech
   outline

InfoTrac

Recommended search terms

Commencement speech
Speech of introduction
Nomination speech
Award acceptance
After-dinner speech
Speech of tribute
Eulogy
Keynote address
Mediated public speaking
Small group presentation
Effective small groups
Symposium
Videoconferencing

Audio Study Tools

"The Dirty Truth about Antibacterial Products" by Jennifer, Megan, Stephanie, and Daniel

Critical thinking questions

Learning objectives

Chapter summary

symposium. Groups often use videoconferencing to connect people in geographically dispersed locations.

In addition to all the qualities that go into effective public speaking, group presentations must form a unified whole. A group presentation's cohesiveness is evaluated in five areas: preparation as a group, coordination of the presentation, active listening, clear references to the group, and achievement of the group's goal.

Guide to Your Online Resources

Your Online Resources for *Public Speaking: The Evolving Art* give you access to the Speech Buddy video and activity featured in this chapter, additional sample speech videos, Speech Builder Express, InfoTrac College Edition, and study aids such as glossary flashcards, review quizzes, and the Critical Challenge questions for this chapter, which you can respond to via e-mail if your instructor requests. In addition, your Online Resources feature live WebLinks relevant to this chapter, such as the Center for Digital Storytelling and Video Conference Etiquette Tips. Links are regularly maintained, and new ones are added periodically.

Key Terms

acceptance speech 429	oral report 436	speech of tribute 433
award presentation 428	panel discussion 437	symposium 438
eulogy 433	round table discussion 437	videoconferencing 439
forum 438	small group 436	
nomination speech 428	speech of introduction 426	

Critical Challenges

Questions for Reflection and Discussion

1. Which types of speeches for special occasions can you imagine yourself giving? Why?

2. *Forum* in Latin means "marketplace" and "a place of public discussion." As a speaker, how can you encourage audience members to offer differing views during your group's question-and-answer session? What do you need to avoid that might deter the audience from speaking out?

APPENDIX
SPEECHES FOR ANALYSIS

Speeches by Public Figures

U.S. SENATOR BARACK OBAMA

Speech to Commemorate the Groundbreaking of the Dr. Martin Luther King Jr. Monument

On November 13, 2006, U.S. Senator Barack Obama delivered this speech to celebrate the groundbreaking of a monument on the National Mall in Washington, DC, in honor of Dr. Martin Luther King Jr. Obama used the occasion to commemorate Dr. King's legacy and to inspire the audience to continue Dr. King's work. As you read his speech, notice how Obama related his many references to King's accomplishments and speeches to the present-day audience.

I want to thank first of all the King family; we would not be here without them. I want to thank Mr. Johnson and the foundation for allowing me to share this day with all of you. I wish to recognize as well my colleagues in the United States Senate who have helped make today possible: Senators Paul Sarbanes and John Warner, who wrote the bill for this memorial, Senators Thad Cochran and Robert Byrd, who appropriated the money to help build it. Thank you all.

I have two daughters, ages five and eight. And when I see the plans for this memorial, I think about what it will be like when I first bring them here upon the memorial's completion. I imagine us walking down to this tidal basin, between one memorial dedicated to the man who helped give birth to a nation, and another dedicated to the man who preserved it. I picture us walking beneath the shadows cast by the Mountain of Despair, and gazing up at the Stone of Hope, and reading the quotes on the wall together as the water falls like rain.

And at some point I know that one of my daughters will ask, perhaps my youngest, will ask, "Daddy, why is this monument here? What did this man do?"

How might I answer them? Unlike the others commemorated in this place, Dr. Martin Luther King Jr. was not a president of the United States—at no time in his life did he hold public office. He was not a hero of foreign wars. He never had much money, and while he lived he was reviled at least as much as he was celebrated. By his own accounts he was a man frequently racked with doubt, a man not without flaws, a man who, like Moses before him, more than once questioned why he had been chosen for so arduous a task—the task of leading a people to freedom, the task of healing the festering wounds of a nation's original sin.

And yet lead a nation he did. Through words he gave voice to the voiceless. Through deeds he gave courage to the faint of heart. By dint of vision, and determination, and most of all faith in the redeeming power of love, he endured the humiliation of arrest, the loneliness of a prison cell, the constant threats to his life, until he finally inspired a nation to transform itself and begin to live up to the meaning of its creed.

Like Moses before him, he would never live to see the Promised Land. But from the mountain top, he pointed the way for us—a land no longer torn asunder with racial hatred and ethnic strife, a land that measured itself by how it treats the least of these, a land in which strength is defined not simply by the capacity to wage war but by the determination to forge peace, a land in which all of God's children might come together in a spirit of brotherhood.

We have not yet arrived at this longed-for place. For all the progress we have made, there are times when the land of our dreams recedes from us—when we are lost, wandering spirits, content with our suspicions and our angers, our long-held grudges and petty disputes, our frantic diversions and tribal allegiances.

And yet, by erecting this monument we are reminded that this different, better place beckons us, and that we will find it not across distant hills or within some hidden valley, but rather we will find it somewhere in our hearts.

In the Book of Micah, Chapter 6, verse 8, the prophet says that God has already told us what is good: "What doth the Lord require of thee," the verse tells us, "but to do justly, and to love mercy, and to walk humbly with thy God?"

The man we honor today did what God required. In the end, that is what I will tell my daughters—I will leave it to their teachers and their history books to tell them the rest. As Dr. King asked to be remembered, I will tell them that this man gave his life serving others. I will tell them that this man tried to love somebody. I will tell them that because he did these things, they live today with the freedom God intended, their citizenship unquestioned, their dreams unbounded. And I will tell them that they too can love. That they too can serve. And that each generation is beckoned anew, to fight for what is right, and strive for what is just, and to find within itself the spirit, the sense of purpose, that can remake a nation and transform a world. Thank you very much.

Source: http://obama.senate.gov/speech/061113-dr_martin_luthe/

QUESTIONS FOR DISCUSSION AND ANALYSIS

1. Identify Obama's general purpose, specific purpose, and thesis. How did the speaker reinforce his general purpose, specific purpose, and thesis in the introduction and conclusion to his speech?

2. What strategies did Obama use to connect Dr. King's life and work to his audience? For example, how did he use supporting materials that would resonate with his 2006 audience? What did he say to inspire his audience to carry on Dr. King's work?

3. How did Obama use audience-centered language to engage his audience? Give at least three examples.

To read, watch, and analyze more speeches by public figures, access your online resources for *Public Speaking: The Evolving Art*. These resources include the following speeches:

Informative

- "The Other E in e-Learning," Marcela Perez de Alonso

Persuasive

- "A Whisper of AIDS," address at the 1992 Republican National Convention, Mary Fisher
- Speech in London's Trafalgar Square for the campaign to end poverty in the developing world, Nelson Mandela

Special occasion

- Eulogy for Rosa Parks, Michigan governor Jennifer Granholm
- Dedication address at the opening of National Museum of the American Indian, Lawrence Small

Speeches by Students

LISA TAYLOR

"Turn Off Your TV"

Lisa Taylor gave this persuasive speech in an introductory public speaking class at San José State University. Her assignment was to give a six- to eight-minute persuasive speech that incorporated presentation media and at least three sources. As you read the outline of Lisa's speech, consider how effective she is at remaining audience-centered, how well she supports her ideas, and how reasonable her proposed solution is.

Specific purpose: To persuade my audience to spend their leisure time doing more productive and fulfilling things than watching TV.

Thesis statement: We Americans waste much of our valuable leisure time watching TV, when we should be spending that time on more productive and fulfilling activities.

Introduction

I. "Dost thou love life? Then do not squander time, for that's the stuff life is made of." (Benjamin Franklin)

II. If you're like me, you don't have enough hours in the day.
    A. You attend classes.
    B. You work part-time or full-time.
    C. You have family commitments, personal business, and homework.
        1. You have family errands such as grocery shopping, dry cleaning, and doctor's appointments.
        2. You have personal business such as car repair and banking.
        3. You have school commitments such as homework and research for papers.

Body

I. Every day I have a long list of tasks, and often I must add more before I can even complete the tasks already on the list.
    A. There are only twenty-four hours in the day.
    B. If you subtract time for necessities such as sleep and personal care, you probably have fewer than ten hours a day of leisure time.

Transition: There simply aren't enough hours in the day, are there?

II. What if I told you that you could find more time in the day?
    A. Since 1985 Americans have gained four to eight hours a week of leisure time. (Bureau of Labor Statistics, American Time Use Survey, 2006 results)
        1. We've doubled the amount of time we spend in sports and exercise activities.
        2. We spend fewer hours in paid employment than we did previously.
        3. We spend 20 percent less time on our grooming than we did twenty years ago.
        4. We sleep an hour a night more than we did forty years ago.
        5. We spend three hours a day, more than twenty hours a week, watching television.

Transition: So, what does this mean to you?

    B. Almost half of our leisure time is spent watching television.
        1. My goal here is not to talk about the ills of television.
            a. I'm not going to talk about whether the media has too much control over our lives.
            b. I'm not going to talk about whether sex and violence on television is good or bad for society.
            c. And I'm not going to talk about the fact that Americans are overweight because we watch too much television and are too sedentary.
        2. My goal is to talk about how much time we waste in front of the television.

Transition: Some suggest that computers, electronic toys, and the Internet waste even more time than watching television.

    C. Outside of paid work, we spend only about twenty minutes a day on our computers. (ATUS, 2006 results)
        1. The experience of using our computers is much different than the experience of watching TV.
            a. The interaction with electronics is less passive; we make choices and decisions, and we tell the equipment what to do. (Winn, *The Plug-In Drug,* 2002)
            b. "You watch television to turn your brain off, and you work on your computer when you want to turn your brain on." (Steve Jobs, co-founder of Apple Computer)
        2. Much of the time we spend using computers is multitasking.
        3. In addition, computers can save us time.
            a. For example, online search engines enable us to research in much less time than it takes to do research at the library.
            b. The Internet also allows us to spend less time on tasks such as errands and shopping.

Transition: So why am I standing here telling you this? What does this mean to you?

III. Outside of work and sleep, we spend more hours a day watching television than any other activity.
   A. The time we spend watching television is time wasted.
      1. Watching television is passive and doesn't stimulate our minds.
      2. It's time we could be using to do something more productive and fulfilling.
   B. If you think there aren't enough hours in the day, try turning off your TV.
      1. What could you do with three more hours a day?
         a. Spend time with friends, hang out at the quad or the coffee shop, or have a beer.
         b. Read a book, study, learn a new sport or a new hobby, or have more time for your friends.
         c. Spend time with your family.

Transition: As Benjamin Franklin suggested, if you love time, don't waste it.

      2. If you're game, turn off your television for one week.
         a. Depending on your TV habits, you could have twenty to thirty more hours of free time.
         b. To motivate you, make a list of things you'd like to do with that time.

Conclusion

I. Consider turning off your TV for a week as a social experiment or a class assignment.
   A. Do whatever it takes to motivate you.
   B. Try it and see what happens.
II. If you're like me, you'll never turn on the TV again.

Works cited

BrainyQuote.com. Benjamin Franklin Quotes. http://www.brainyquote .com/quotes/authors/b/benjamin_franklin.html (accessed September 6, 2007).

Kaiser Family Foundation. "The Media Family: Electronic Media in the Lives of Infants, Toddlers, Preschoolers and their Parents." May 2006. http://www.kff.org/entmedia/upload/7500.pdf (accessed September 13, 2007).

Snell, Jason. "Steve Jobs on the Mac's 20th Anniversary." *Macworld*, February 2004.

U.S. Census Bureau. "American Time Use Survey, 2006 results." Sponsored by the Bureau of Labor Statistics. June 28, 2007. http://www .bls.gov/news.release/pdf/atus.pdf (accessed September 13, 2007).

Winn, Marie. *The Plug-In Drug: Television, Computers, and Family Life*. New York: Penguin Group, 2002.

Questions for Discussion and Analysis

1. How does Lisa gain her audience's attention at the beginning of the speech? How effective is her attention-getter?

2. Identify the types of supporting materials Lisa uses to persuade her audience. How do they work together to help her achieve her specific purpose? How convinced are you after reading through her outline?

3. Does this speech address a question of fact, value, or policy? How closely does Lisa follow the guidelines for the type of persuasive speech she gave?

To read, watch, and analyze more speeches by students, access your online resources for *Public Speaking: The Evolving Art*. These resources include the following speeches:

Self-introduction

- Speech of self-introduction, Tiffany Brisco
- Speech of self-introduction, Adam Currier
- Speech of self-introduction, Jessica Howard
- "El Equipo Perfecto (The Perfect Team)," Uriel Plascencia, interpreted by Kelly Bilinski
- Handed-down story speech, Dory Schaeffer
- "Study Abroad," Anna
- "Left on a Doorstep," Cara

Informative

- "U.S. Flag Etiquette," Cindy Gardner
- "The Integration of the NBA," Arthur Gray
- "Sikhism," Ramit Kaur
- "How to Become a Successful Business Person," Husam Al-Khirbash

- "Impressionistic Painting," Chris Lucke
- "History of Fort Collins, Colorado," Jeff Malcolm
- "Wrath," David Manson
- "Why Pi?" Katy Mazz
- "Meat-free and Me," Tiffany Mindt
- "Terrestrial Pulmonate Gastropods," Shaura Neil
- "Educational Requirements to Become a Pediatrician," Ganiel Singh
- "The Ilogot Headhunters," Curt
- "Is That Kosher?" Katherine

Invitational

- "Creationism versus the Big Bang Theory," Cara Buckley-Ott

Persuasive

- "Breast Cancer Awareness," Lisa Alagna

- "Drinking and Driving," Peter Bodrog
- "Fat Discrimination," Carol Godart
- "Drinking," Matthew Naso
- "Wear a Ribbon," Loren Rozakos
- "Fair Trade," Kelly Scott
- "Light Pollution," Courtney Stillman
- "Domestic Violence," Amanda
- "Anatomy of a Hate Crime," Chuck
- "Home Schooling: Superiority and Success," Dixie
- "Home Schooling: Not the Best Choice," Robert

Group

- "The Dirty Truth about Antibacterial Products," Jennifer, Megan, Stephanie, and Daniel

GLOSSARY

acceptance speeches Speeches given by individuals who are being recognized, honored, or given an award.

ad hominem **fallacy** Argument in which a speaker rejects another speaker's claim based on that speaker's character rather than the evidence the speaker presents; also called the *against the person fallacy*.

ad ignorantiam **fallacy** Argument in which a speaker appeals to popular attitudes and emotions without offering evidence to support claims.

ad populum **fallacy** Argument in which a speaker suggests that because a claim hasn't been shown to be false, it must be true; also called an *appeal to ignorance*.

alliteration Repetition of a sound in a series of words, usually the first consonant.

analogical reasoning Comparing two similar objects, processes, concepts, or events and suggesting that what holds true for one also holds true for the other.

analogy A type of comparison that describes something by comparing it to something else that it resembles.

anecdote A brief narrative.

antithesis Juxtaposition of two apparently contradictory phrases that are organized in a parallel structure.

apathetic audience An audience that is informed about a speaker's topic but not interested in it.

appeal to cultural belief (mythos) Use of values and beliefs embedded in cultural narratives or stories to influence an audience.

appeal to speaker credibility (ethos) Use of the audience's perception of the speaker as competent, trustworthy, dynamic, and likeable to influence an audience.

appeal to tradition fallacy Argument in which a speaker asserts that the status quo is better than any new idea or approach.

argument Presenting claims and supporting them with evidence and reasoning.

arrangement The way the ideas in a speech are organized.

articulation The physical process of producing specific speech sounds to make language intelligible.

attention getter The first element of an introduction, designed mainly to create interest in a speech.

attitude How an individual feels about something.

audience The intended recipients of a speaker's message.

audience-centered Describes a speaker who acknowledges the audience by considering and listening to the unique, diverse, and common perspectives of its members before, during, and after the speech.

audience-centered communication Adapting a speech to a specific situation and audience.

audience analysis Obtaining and evaluating information about an audience in order to anticipate their needs and interests and design a strategy to respond to them.

audience research questionnaire A questionnaire used by speakers to assess the knowledge and opinions of audience members; can take the form of an e-mail, web-based, or in-class survey.

award presentations Speeches that recognize individuals to celebrate something they have done well.

begging the question Argument in which a speaker uses a premise to imply the truth of the conclusion or asserts that the validity of the conclusion is self-evident; also called *circular reasoning*.

behavior An observable action.

belief Something an individual accepts as true or existing.

bibliographic information A source's complete citation, including author, date of publication, title, place of publication, and publisher.

blog Short for web log, a webpage that a blog writer, or blogger, updates regularly with topical entries.

body The middle and main part of a speech; includes main and subordinate points.

brainstorming The free-form generation of ideas in which individuals think of and record ideas without evaluating them.

call number The number assigned to each book or bound publication in a library to identify that book in the library's classification system.

captive audience Individuals who feel they must attend an event.

caricature fallacy Argument in which a speaker misrepresents another speaker's argument so that only a weak shell of the original argument remains; also called the *straw man fallacy*.

causal reasoning Linking two events or actions to claim that one resulted in the other.

cause-and-effect pattern A pattern that organizes a speech by showing how an action produces a particular outcome.

channel A mode or medium of communication.

chronological pattern A pattern that organizes a speech by how something develops or occurs in a time sequence.

claim A position or assertion that a speaker wants an audience to accept.

cliché An expression so overused it fails to have any important meaning.

closed-ended question A question that limits the possible responses, asking for very specific information.

coherence An obvious and plausible connection among ideas.

communication climate The psychological and emotional tone that develops as communicators interact with one another.

comparative evidence fallacy Argument in which a speaker uses statistics or compares numbers in ways that misrepresent the evidence and mislead the audience.

competence The qualifications a speaker has to talk about a particular topic.

complete-sentence outline A formal outline using full sentences for all points developed after researching the speech and identifying supporting materials; includes a speech's topic, general purpose, specific purpose, thesis, introduction, main points, sub

conclusion The end of a speech, in which the speaker reviews the main points, reinforces the purpose, and provides closure. In reasoning, a primary claim or assertion.

connotative meaning A unique meaning for a word based on an individual's own experiences.

context The situation within which a speech is given.

copyright A type of intellectual property law that protects an author's original work (such as a play, book, song, or movie) from being used by others.

copyright information A statement about the legal rights of others to use an original work, such as a song (lyrics and melody), story, poem, photograph, or image.

credibility An audience's perception of a speaker's competence, trustworthiness, dynamism, and sociability.

cultural diversity Differences in cultural backgrounds and practices around the globe.

cultural norms Prescriptions for how people should interact and what messages should mean in a particular setting.

culture Values, beliefs, and activities shared by a group.

currency How recent information is—the more recent, the more current.

deductive reasoning Reasoning from a general condition to a specific case.

deep web The portion of the World Wide Web composed of specialty databases, such as those housed by the U.S. government, that are not accessible by traditional search engines; also called the invisible or hidden web.

definition A statement that describes the essence, precise meaning, or scope of a word or a phrase.

delivery The public presentation of a speech.

demographics The ways in which populations can be divided into smaller groups according to key characteristics such as sex, ethnicity, age, and social class.

denotative meaning An agreed-upon definition of a word, found in a dictionary.

dialect The vocabulary, grammar, and pronunciation used by a specific group of people, such as an ethnic or regional group.

dialogue Occurs when speakers are sensitive to audience needs and listen to audience members' responses, and listeners pay careful attention to speakers' messages so they can respond appropriately and effectively.

direct quote Comments written in response to an open-ended question in an audience research questionnaire.

discussion list An e-mail–based distribution list that allows members to e-mail everyone who belongs to the list using just one e-mail address; also called a listserv.

divided audience An audience that is informed about a speaker's topic but equally split between those who favor the speaker's position and those who oppose it.

division fallacy Argument in which a speaker assumes that what is true of the whole is also true of the parts that make up the whole.

document camera A projection device that uses a video camera to capture and display images, including 3-D visual materials.

dynamism An audience's perception of a speaker's activity level during a presentation.

emotional appeal (pathos) Use of emotional evidence and stimulation of feelings to influence an audience.

enthymeme An argument in which a premise or conclusion is unstated.

environment The external surroundings that influence a public speaking event.

ethical communication The moral aspects of our interactions with others, including truthfulness, fairness, responsibility, integrity, and respect.

ethnocentrism The belief that one's own worldview, based on one's own cultural background, is correct and best.

ethos Appeals that are linked to the speaker's credibility.

eulogies Speeches of tribute presented as retrospectives about individuals who have died.

euphemism A word used in place of another word that is viewed as more disagreeable or offensive.

event A significant occurrence that an individual personally experiences or otherwise knows about.

evidence Supporting materials—narratives, examples, definitions, testimony, facts, and statistics—that a speaker presents to reinforce a claim.

example An illustration or case that represents a larger group or class of things.

extemporaneous speaking A type of public speaking in which the speaker researches, organizes, rehearses, and delivers a speech in a way that combines structure and spontaneity.

external noise Conditions in the environment that interfere with listening.

fact An observation based on actual experience.

fair use Using someone else's original work in a way that does not infringe on the owner's rights, generally for educational purposes, literary criticism, and news reporting.

fallacy An error in making an argument.

false dilemma fallacy Argument in which a speaker reduces available choices to only two even though other alternatives exist; also called the *either-or fallacy*.

feedback Audience members' responses to a speech.

flip chart A large pad of paper that rests on an easel, allowing a speaker to record text or drawings with markers during a speech.

forum The question-and-answer session following a group's formal presentation.

gatewatching Monitoring news sources to analyze and assess the information they produce.

general purpose The speaker's overall objective: to inform, to persuade, or to entertain.

goodwill An audience's perception that a speaker shows she or he has the audience's true needs, wants, and interests at heart.

guilt by association fallacy Argument in which a speaker suggests that something is wrong with another speaker's claims by associating those claims with someone the audience finds objectionable; also called the *bad company fallacy*.

handout Sheets of paper containing relevant information that are distributed before, during, or after a speech.

hasty generalization fallacy Argument in which a speaker draws a conclusion based on too few or inadequate examples.

hate speech Words that attack groups such as racial, ethnic, religious, and sexual minorities.

hearing The physical response to sounds.

hedge A qualifier, such as *probably*, that makes a statement ambiguous.

ideas and concepts Mental activity, including thoughts, understandings, beliefs, notions, and principles.

idiom An expression that means something other than the literal meaning of the words.

illusion of transparency The tendency of individuals to believe that how they feel is much more apparent to others than is really the case.

impromptu speaking A type of public speaking in which the speaker has little or no time to prepare a speech.

inclusive language Words that don't privilege one group over another.

inductive reasoning Supporting a claim with specific cases or instances; also called *reasoning by example*.

information overload Occurs when individuals receive too much information and are unable to interpret it in a meaningful way.

informative speaking Presenting a speech in which the speaker seeks to deepen understanding, raise awareness, or increase knowledge about a topic.

internal consistency A logical relationship among the ideas that make up any main heading or subheading in a speech.

internal noise Thoughts, emotions, and physical sensations that interfere with listening.

internal summary A review of main points or subpoints, given before going on to the next point in a speech.

interpretation An individual's internal process of assigning meaning to words.

interview guide A list of all the questions and possible probes an interviewer asks in an interview, as well as notes about how the interviewer will begin and end the interview.

introduction The beginning of a speech, including an attention getter, a statement of the thesis and purpose, a reference to the speaker's credibility, and a preview of the main points.

invention Discovering what you want to say in a speech, such as choosing a topic and developing good arguments.

invitation to imagine Asking listeners to create a scene or situation in their minds.

jargon Technical language used by members of a profession or associated with a specific topic.

keyword During research for supporting materials, a term associated with a topic and used to search for information related to that topic. In a presentation outline, a word that identifies a subject or a point of primary interest or concern.

language The system of words people use to communicate with others.

leading question A question that suggests the answer the interviewer seeks.

listening Involves hearing, interpreting, responding to, and recalling verbal and nonverbal messages.

listening anxiety Anxiety produced by the fear of misunderstanding, not fully comprehending, or not being mentally prepared for information you may hear.

loaded word fallacy Argument in which a speaker uses emotionally laden words to evaluate claims based on a misleading emotional response rather than the evidence presented.

logical appeal (logos) Use of rational appeals based on logic, facts, and analysis to influence an audience.

logos Appeals to logic.

manuscript speaking A type of public speaking in which the speaker reads a written script word for word.

media credibility Perceptions of believability or trust that audience members hold toward communications media, including TV, the internet, newspapers, radio, and news magazines.

memorable message A sentence or group of sentences included in the conclusion of a speech, designed to make the speaker's thesis unforgettable.

memorized speaking A type of public speaking in which the speaker commits a speech to memory.

memory Using the ability to recall information to give an effective speech.

message The words and nonverbal cues a speaker uses to convey ideas, feelings, and thoughts.

metaphor A language device that demonstrates the commonalities between two dissimilar things.

metasearch engine A search tool that does not actually search the web for information, but rather compiles the results from other search engines.

model A copy of an object, usually built to scale, that represents the object in detail.

monologue Occurs when speakers and audience members aren't actively engaged in the public speaking process and neither party listens to the other.

monotone A way of speaking in which the speaker does not alter his or her pitch.

mythos Appeals to cultural beliefs and values.

narrative A description of events in a dramatic fashion; also called a story.

narrative pattern A pattern that organizes a speech by a dramatic retelling of events as a story or a series of short stories.

negative (hostile) audience An audience that is informed about a speaker's topic and holds an unfavorable view of the speaker's position.

neutral question An unbiased and impartial question seeking a forthright answer.

newsgroups Online text-based forums in which participants discuss particular topics; also called Usenet.

noise Anything that interferes with the understanding of a message.

nomination speeches Speeches that demonstrate why a particular individual would be successful at something if given the chance.

nonsexist language Words that are not associated with either sex.

nonverbal message Information that is communicated without words, but rather, through movement, gesture, facial expression, vocal quality, use of time, use of space, and touch.

object Any nonliving, material thing that can be perceived by the senses.

open-ended question A broad, general question, often specifying only the topic.

oral citation A source of information that a speaker mentions, or cites, during a speech.

oral report A report in which one member of a group presents the group's findings.

panel discussion A discussion in which a moderator asks questions of experts on a topic in front of an audience.

parallelism Using the same phrase, wording, or clause multiple times to add emphasis.

pathos Appeals to emotion.

pattern of organization A structure for ordering the main points of a speech.

persuasion Using language, images, and other means of communication to influence people's attitudes, beliefs, values, or actions.

persuasive speech A speech in which the speaker attempts to reinforce, modify, or change audience members' beliefs, attitudes, opinions, values, and behaviors.

pervasive communication environment The ability to access and share information in multiple forms from multiple locations in ways that transcend time and space.

pitch The highness or lowness of a speaker's voice.

places Geographic locations.

plagiarism Presenting someone else's ideas and work, such as speeches, papers, and images, as your own.

positive (sympathetic) audience An audience that is informed about a speaker's topic and has a favorable view of the speaker's position.

***post hoc* fallacy** Argument in which a speaker concludes a causal relationship exists simply because one event follows another in time; also called the *false cause fallacy*.

posture The way a speaker positions and carries her or his body.

premise A claim that provides reasons to support a conclusion.

presentation media Technical and material resources ranging from presentation software and real-time web access (RWA) to flip charts and handouts that speakers use to highlight, clarify, and complement the information they present orally.

presentation outline An outline that distills a complete-sentence outline, listing only the words and phrases that will guide the speaker through the main parts of the speech and the transitions between them.

presentation software Computer software that allows users to display information in multimedia slide shows.

preview of main points The final element of the introduction, in which the main points to be presented in the body of the speech are mentioned.

primacy effect An audience is more likely to pay attention to and recall what a speaker presents at the beginning of a speech than what is presented in the speech body.

primary question A question that introduces a new topic or subtopic in an interview.

primary source Information that expresses an author's original ideas or findings from original research.

problem-solution pattern A pattern that organizes a speech by describing a problem and providing possible solutions.

process How something is done, how it works, or how it has developed.

pronunciation The act of saying words correctly according to the accepted standards of the speaker's language.

psychographics Psychological data about an audience, such as standpoints, values, beliefs, and attitudes.

public speaking A situation in which an individual speaks to a group of people, assuming responsibility for speaking for a defined length of time.

qualifier A word or phrase that clarifies, modifies, or limits the meaning of another word or phrase.

question of fact A question that asks whether something is true or false.

question of policy A question that asks what course of action should be taken or how a problem should be solved.

question of value A question that asks for a subjective evaluation of something's worth, significance, quality, or condition.

rate The speed at which a speaker speaks.

real-time web access Employing a live internet feed as a visual medium or information resource during a public speech.

reasoning The method or process used to link claims to evidence.

recency effect An audience is more likely to remember what a speaker presents at the end of a speech than what is presented in the speech body.

red herring fallacy Argument that introduces irrelevant evidence to distract an audience from the real issue.

relabeling Assigning more positive words or phrases to the physical reactions and feelings associated with speech anxiety.

relevance How closely a webpage's content is related to the keywords used in an internet search.

reliability The consistency and credibility of information from a particular source.

review of main points The portion of the conclusion of a speech in which the main points presented in the body of the speech are briefly mentioned again.

rhetoric Aristotle's term for public speaking.

rhyme Using words with similar sounds, usually at the end of the word, to emphasize a point.

round table discussion A discussion in which expert participants discuss a topic in an impromptu format without an audience present.

search engine A sophisticated software program that hunts through documents to find those associated with particular keywords.

secondary question A question that asks the interviewee to elaborate on a response.

secondary source Others' interpretation or adaptation of a primary source.

signpost A transition that indicates a key move in the speech, making its organization clear to the audience.

simile A language device that compares two things that are generally dissimilar but share some common properties, expressed using *like* or *as*.

slang Informal, nonstandard language, often used within a particular group.

slippery slope fallacy Argument in which a speaker asserts that one event will necessarily lead to another without showing any logical connection between the two events.

small group A collection of individuals who interact and depend on one another to solve a problem, make a decision, or achieve a common goal or objective.

sociability The degree to which an audience feels a connection to a speaker.

spatial pattern A pattern that organizes a speech by the physical or directional relationship between objects or places.

speaker The person who assumes the primary responsibility for conveying a message in a public communication context.

specific purpose A concise statement articulating what the speaker will achieve in giving a speech.

speech anxiety Fear of speaking in front of an audience.

speech of introduction A short speech that introduces someone to an audience.

speeches of tribute Speeches that give credit, respect, admiration, gratitude, or inspiration to someone who has accomplished something significant, lives in a way that deserves to be praised, or is about to embark on an adventure.

sponsored link A link whose owner has paid a search engine company such as Google to place the link in the results list of a search.

spotlight effect A phenomenon that leads us to think other people observe us much more carefully than they actually do.

standpoint The psychological location or place from which an individual views, interprets, and evaluates the world.

statistics Numerical data or information.

style The language or words used in a speech.

summary statistics Information in the responses to an audience research questionnaire that reflects trends and comparisons.

supporting materials Evidence used to demonstrate the worth of an idea.

syllogism A form of deductive reasoning consisting of a major premise, minor premise, and conclusion.

symbol Something, such as a word, that stands for something else, such as a person, place, thing, or idea.

symposium A presentation format in which each member of a group presents a speech about a part of a larger topic.

tag question A question added onto the end of a declarative statement that lessens the impact of that statement.

target audience The particular group or subgroup a speaker most wants to inform, persuade, or entertain.

technophobia Fear that others will react negatively if one appears inept at using technological aids.

testimony An individual's opinions or experiences about a particular topic.

thesis A single declarative sentence that captures the essence or central idea of a speech.

tone Use of language to set the mood or atmosphere associated with a speaking situation.

topic The main subject, idea, or theme of a speech.

topical pattern A pattern that organizes a speech by arranging subtopics of equal importance.

transition A word, phrase, sentence, or paragraph used throughout a speech to mark locations in the organization and clearly link the parts of a speech together.

transparency A clear, acetate page displayed by means of an overhead projector.

trustworthiness An audience's perception of a speaker as honest, ethical, sincere, reliable, sensitive, and empathic.

uninformed audience An audience that is unfamiliar with a speaker's topic and has no opinion about it.

validity The soundness of the logic underlying information presented by a source.

value An ideal that serves as a standard of behavior.

videoconferencing A small group presentation in which individuals at multiple physical locations interact in real time orally and visually, using video and high-speed computer technology.

visualization Imagining a successful communication event by thinking through a sequence of events in a positive, concrete, step-by-step way.

vocalized pauses "Ah," "um," "you know," and other verbal fillers that speakers use when they're trying to think of what they want to say.

vocal variety Changes in the volume, rate, and pitch of a speaker's voice that affect the meaning of the words delivered.

volume The loudness of a speaker's voice.

voluntary audience Individuals who can choose to attend or not attend a speaking event.

weak analogy fallacy Argument in which a speaker compares two things that are dissimilar, making the comparison inaccurate.

web directory An online list that organizes webpages and websites hierarchically by category; also called a search index.

webidence Web sources displayed as evidence during a speech, found by using real-time web access or webpage capture software.

white board A smooth white board that can be written or drawn on with markers.

working outline An outline that guides you during the initial stages of topic development, helping to keep you focused on your general purpose and clarify your specific purpose.

REFERENCES

CHAPTER 1

[1] Frobish, T. (2000). Jamieson meets Lucas: Eloquence and pedagogical model(s) in *The Art of Public Speaking*. *Communication Education, 49*, 239–252.

[2] Fox, S. (2005). *Digital divisions: There are clear differences among those with broadband connections, dial-up connections, and no connections at all to the internet.* Pew Internet & American Life Project. Retrieved February 2, 2007, from pewinternet.org.

[3] Ford, W. S. Z., & Wolvin, A. D. (1993). The differential impact of a basic communication course on perceived communication competencies in class, work, and social contexts. *Communication Education, 42,* 215–223.

[4] Ford & Wolvin (1993).

[5] Fox, S. (2006). *Online health search 2006*. Retrieved February 2, 2007, from pewinternet.org.

[6] Seibold, D. R., Kudsi, S., & Rude, M. (1993). Does communication training make a difference? Evidence for the effectiveness of a presentation skills program. *Journal of Applied Communication Research, 21,* 111–131.

[7] Langer, E. (1998). *The power of mindful learning*. New York: Perseus Publishing.

[8] Fleury, A. (2005). Liberal education and communication against the disciplines. *Communication Education, 54,* 72–79.

[9] Addley, E. (2005, June 5). Office hours: Stand up and be counted: Although we may hate public speaking, it's a vital skill, says Esther Addley. *The Guardian*, p. 2; Krapels, R. H., & Davis, B. D. (2003). Designation of "communication skills" in position listings. *Business Communication Quarterly, 66*(2), 90–96; Maes, J. D., Weldy, T. G., & Icenogle, M. J. (1997). A managerial perspective: Oral communication competency is most important for business students in the workplace. *Journal of Business Communication, 34,* 67–80.

[10] Ford & Wolvin (1993).

[11] Wirtz, C. (2003, April–May). Public speaking: An accounting marketing tool. *The National Public Accountant*. pp. 14–15.

[12] Gittlen, S. (2004, July 26). The public side of you: Be it for budget negotiations, project updates or industry conference panels, great public skills speaking will get you noticed—and promoted. *Network World*, p. 1; Green, M. C., & Brock, T. C. (2005). Organizational membership versus informal interaction: Contributions to skills and perceptions that build social capital. *Political Psychology, 26,* 1–25; Lublin, J. S. (2004, October 5). To win advancement, you need to clean up any bad speech habits. *Wall Street Journal*, p. B1.

[13] Hassam, J. (2002). Learning the lesson—Speaking up for communication as an academic discipline too important to be sidelined. *Journal of Communication Management, 7*(1), 14–20; Murphy, T. A. (2005). Deliberative civic education and civil society: A consideration of ideals and actualities in democracy and communication education. *Communication Education, 53,* 74–91.

[14] McMillian, J. J., & Harriger, K. J. (2002). College students and deliberation: A benchmark study. *Communication Education, 51,* 237-253; West, M., & Gastil, J. (2004). Deliberation at the margins: Participant accounts of face-to-face public deliberation at the 1999-2000 World Trade protests in Seattle and Prague. *Qualitative Research Reports in Communication, 5,* 1–7.

[15] Hufstetter, P. J. (2005, November 13). Teen wins mayor race by 2 votes. Retrieved March 6, 2006, from post-gazette.com.

[16] Fritz, C. A. (1922). A brief review of the chief periods in the history of oratory. *Quarterly Journal of Speech Education, 8*(1), 26–48.

[17] Smith, C. R. (2003). *Rhetoric and human consciousness: A history* (2nd ed.). Prospect Heights, IL: Waveland.

[18] Smith (2003).

[19] Habinek, T. (2005). *Ancient rhetoric and oratory*. Oxford, England: Blackwell; Jasinski, J. (2001). *Sourcebook on rhetoric: Key concepts in contemporary rhetorical studies*. Thousand Oaks, CA: Sage; Smith (2003); Yagcioclu, S., & Cem-Deger, A. (2001). Logos or mythos: (De)legitimation strategies in confrontational discourses of sociocultural ethos. *Discourse & Society, 12,* 817–852.

[20] Jasinski (2001).

[21] Gross, A. G., & Dascal, M. (2001). The conceptual unity of Aristotle's rhetoric. *Philosophy and Rhetoric, 34,* 275–291.

[22] Hoogestraat, W. E. (1960). Memory: The lost canon? *Quarterly Journal of Speech, 46,* 141–147.

[23] Ishii, S. (1992). Buddhist preaching: the persistent main undercurrent of Japanese traditional rhetorical communication. *Communication Quarterly, 40,* 391–397.

[24] Fisher, W. R. (1987). *Human communication as narration: Toward a philosophy of reason, value, and action*. Columbia: University of South Carolina Press; Sprague, A. (2004). *The wisdom of storytelling in an information age*. Lanham, MD: Scarecrow Press.

[25] Coopman, T. M. (2006, September). *Dumping dichotomies: Embracing the pervasive communication environment*. Paper presented at the Association of Internet Researchers conference, Brisbane, Australia.

[26] Johannesen, R. L. (2002). *Ethics in human communication* (5th ed.). Prospect Heights, IL: Waveland; Rosenstand, N. (2006). *The moral of the story: An introduction to ethics* (5th ed.). New York: McGraw-Hill.

[27] Baron, L. (2001). Why information literacy? *Advocate, 18*(8), 5–7.

[28] Elwood, J. (2005). Presence or PowerPoint: Why PowerPoint has become a cliché. *Development and Learning Organizations, 19*(3), 12–14.

CHAPTER 2

[1] Ellis, M. (2003, April 30). Too scared for words: Fear of public speaking can be overcome, experts insist. *The Columbus Dispatch*, p. G1; Zimmerman, J. (2003, May 19). Fear not: Alleviating your anxiety over public speaking takes practice, humor and knowing the audience. *The Press Enterprise*, p. D1.

[2] Addison, P., Ayala, J., Hunter, M., Behnke, R., & Sawyer, C. (2004). Body sensations of higher and lower anxiety sensitive speakers anticipating a public presentation. *Communication Research Reports, 21,* 284–290; Phillips, G. C., Jones, G. E., Rieger, E. J., & Snell, J. B. (1997). Normative data for the personal report of confidence as a speaker. *Journal of Anxiety Disorders, 11,* 215–220.

[3] Addison et al. (2004); Behnke, R. R., & Sawyer, C. R. (2001). Patterns of psychological state anxiety in public speaking as a function of anxiety sensitivity. *Communication Quarterly, 49,* 84–94; Dwyer, K. K.

(2000). The multidimensional model: Teaching students to self-manage high communication apprehension by self-selecting treatments. *Communication Education, 49,* 72–81; Harris, K. B., Sawyer, C. R., & Behnke, R. R. (2006). Predicting speech state anxiety from trait anxiety, reactivity, and situational influences. *Communication Quarterly, 54,* 213–226.

[4] Duff, D. C., Levine, T. R., Beatty, M. J., Woolbright, J., & Sun Park, H. (2007). Testing public anxiety treatments against a credible placebo control. *Communication Education, 56,* 72–88.

[5] Booth-Butterfield, J., & Cottone, R. (1991). Ethical issues in the treatment of communication apprehension and avoidance. *Communication Education, 40,* 173–179.

[6] Witt, P. L., & Behnke, R. R. (2006). Anticipatory speech anxiety as a function of public speaking assignment type. *Communication Education, 55,* 167–177.

[7] McCroskey, J. C. (1970). Measures of communication-bound anxiety. *Speech Monographs, 37,* 269–277.

[8] Feldman, P. J., Cohen, S., Hamrick, N., & Lepore, S. J. Psychological stress, appraisal, emotion and cardiovascular response in a public speaking task. *Psychology and Health, 19,* 353–368.

[9] Hsu, C. (2004). Sources of differences in communication apprehension between Chinese in Taiwan and Americans. *Communication Quarterly, 52,* 370–389; Sawyer, C. R., & Behnke, R. R. (1999). State anxiety patterns for public speaking and the behavior inhibition system. *Communication Reports, 12,* 33–41.

[10] Field, A. P., Hamilton, S. J., Knowles, K. A., & Plews, E. L. (2003). Fear information and social phobic beliefs in children: A prospective paradigm and preliminary results. *Behaviour Research and Therapy, 41,* 113–123.

[11] Kelly, L., & Keaten, J. A. (2000). Treating communication anxiety: Implications of the communibiological paradigm. *Communication Education, 49,* 45–57; Sawyer, C. R., & Behnke, R. R. (2002). Reduction in public speaking anxiety during performance as a function of sensitization processes. *Communication Quarterly, 50,* 110–121.

[12] Edwards, C. C., Myers, S. A., Hensley-Edwards, A., & Wahl, S. (2003). The relationship between student pre-performance concerns and evaluation apprehension. *Communication Research Reports, 20,* 54–61.

[13] Cornwell, B. R., Johnson, L., Berardi, L., & Grillon, C. (2006). Anticipation of public speaking in virtual reality reveals a relationship between trait social anxiety and startle reactivity. *Biological Psychiatry, 59,* 664–666; Edwards et al. (2003); Horvath, N. R., Moss, M. N., Xie, S., Sawyer, C. R., & Behnke, R. R. (2004). Evaluation sensitivity and physical sensations of stress as components of public speaking state anxiety. *Southern Communication Journal, 69,* 173–181; Keaten, J. A., &

Kelly, L. (2004). Disposition versus situation: Neurocommunicology and the influence of trait apprehension versus situational factors on state public speaking anxiety. *Communication Research Reports, 21,* 273–283; Kozasa, E. H., & Leite, J. R. (1998). A brief protocol of cognitive modification and gradual exposure of reduction of fear symptoms of public speaking. *Journal of Behavior Therapy and Experimental Psychiatry, 29,* 317–326.

[14] Gilovich, T., Kruger, J., & Medvec, V. H. (2002). The spotlight effect revisited: Overestimating the manifest variability of our actions and appearance. *Journal of Experimental Social Psychology, 38,* 93–99; Gilovich, T., Medvec, V. H., & Savisky, K. (2000). The spotlight effect in social judgment: An egocentric bias in estimates of the salience of one's own actions and appearance. *Journal of Personality and Social Psychology, 78,* 211–222.

[15] Haigh, J. (1994). Fear, truth and reality in making presentations. *Management Decision, 32(6),* 58–60; Hirsch, C. R., Mathews, A., Clark, D. M., Williams, R., & Morrison, J. A. (2006). The causal role of negative imagery in social anxiety: A test in confident public speakers. *Journal of Behavior Therapy & Experimental Psychiatry, 37,* 159–170; Kopecky, C. C., Sawyer, C. R., & Behnke, R. R. (2004). Sensitivity to punishment and explanatory style as predictors of public speaking state anxiety. *Communication Education, 53,* 281–285; McCullough, S. C., Russell, S. G., Behnke, R. R., Sawyer, C. R., & Witt, P. L. (2006). Anticipatory public speaking state anxiety as a function of body sensations and state of mind. *Communication Quarterly, 54,* 101–109.

[16] Clarkson, M. (2003). *Intelligent fear: How to make fear work for you.* New York: Marlowe & Company.

[17] Ayres, J., & Sonandré, D. M. A. (2003). Performance visualization: Does the nature of the speech model matter? *Communication Research Reports, 20,* 260–268; Beatty, M. J., & Valencic, K. (2000). Context-based apprehension versus planning demands: A communibiological analysis of anticipatory public speaking anxiety. *Communication Education, 24,* 58–71; Peurifoy, R. Z. (2005). *Anxiety, phobias, and panic* (updated and revised). New York: Warner; Vassilopoulos, S. P. (2005). Anticipatory processing plays a role in maintaining social anxiety. *Anxiety, Stress & Coping, 18,* 321–332.

[18] Ayres, J., & Ayres, T. A. (2003). Using images to enhance the impact of visualization. *Communication Reports, 16,* 47–55; Ayres, J., Hsu, C., & Hopf, T. (2000). Does exposure to visualization alter speech preparation processes? *Communication Research Reports, 17,* 366–374.

[19] Patient handout: Relaxation techniques. (2003). *Alternative Medicine Alert, 6(7),* 81–82; Cosnett, G. (2003). Just breathe: Taking in a bit of fresh air isn't as easy as you think. *Training & Development Journal, 56(9),* 17–18.

[20] Donnet, N. (1989) Letting nervousness work for you. *Training & Development Journal, 43(4),* 21–23.

[21] Behnke, R. R., & Sawyer, C. R. (1999). Public speaking procrastination as a correlate of public speaking communication apprehension and self-perceived public speaking competence. *Communication Research Reports, 16,* 40–47.

[22] Ellis (2003).

[23] Ayres, J. (1996). Speech preparation processes and speech apprehension. *Communication Education, 45,* 228–235.

[24] MacIntyre, P. D., & Thivierge, K. A., (1995). The effects of audience pleasantness, audience familiarity, and speaking contexts on public speaking anxiety and willingness to speak. *Communication Quarterly, 43,* 456–466.

[25] Smith, T. E., & Frymier, A. B. (2006). Get "real": Does practicing speeches before an audience improve performance? *Communication Quarterly, 54,* 111–125.

[26] Smith & Frymier (2006).

[27] Ayres, 1996; Behnke, R. R., & Sawyer, C. R. (2001). Patterns of psychological state anxiety in public speaking as a function of anxiety sensitivity. *Communication Quarterly, 49,* 84–94; Behnke, R. R., & Sawyer, C. R. (2004). Public speaking anxiety as a function of sensitization and habituation processes. *Communication Education, 53,* 164–173; Bowers, Jr., D. A., & Bowers, V. M. (1996). Assessing and coping with computer anxiety in the social science classroom. *Social Science Review, 14,* 439–443; Finn, A. N., Sawyer, C. R., & Behnke, R. R. (2003). Audience-perceived anxiety patterns of public speakers. *Communication Quarterly, 51,* 470–481.

[28] Addison, P. (2003). Worry as a function of public speaking state anxiety tips. *Communication Reports, 16,* 125–131.

[29] Clarkson (2003).

[30] Gray, J. A. (1995). A model of the limbic system and basal ganglia: Applications to anxiety and schizophrenia. M. S. Gazzaniga (Ed.), *The cognitive neurosciences* (pp. 1165–1176). Cambridge, MA: Bradford.

[31] Gilovich, T., Savitsky, K., & Medvec, V. H. (1998). The illusion of transparency: Biased assessments of others' ability to read one's emotional states. *Journal of Personality & Social Psychology, 75,* 332–346; Savitsky, K., & Gilovich, T. (2003). The illusion of transparency and the alleviation of speech anxiety. *Journal of Experimental Social Psychology, 39,* 618–625.

[32] MacIntyre, P. D., & MacDonald, J. R. (1998). Public speaking anxiety: Perceived competence and audience congeniality. *Communication Education, 47,* 359–365.

CHAPTER 3

[1] Leslie, L. Z. (2004). *Mass communication ethics: Decision making in a postmodern culture* (2nd ed.). Boston, MA: Houghton Mifflin; Rosenstand, N. (2006). *The moral of the story: An introduction to ethics* (5th ed.). New York: McGraw-Hill; Ruggiero, V. R. (2001). *Thinking critically about ethical issues* (5th ed.). New York: McGraw-Hill.

[2] Hanley, C. J. (2003, August 10). U.S. justification for war: How it stacks up now. *The Seattle Times*, pA4.

[3] Kirtley, J. (2004). Scalia and his speeches. *American Journalism Review, 26*(3), 70.

[4] National Communication Association (1999) NCA credo for ethical communication. Retrieved October 30, 2005, from natcom.org.

[5] Rosenfeld, L. B. (1983). Communication climates and coping mechanisms in the classroom. *Communication Education, 32,* 167–174.

[6] Academy of Management (2005). Code of ethics. Retrieved February 25, 2007, from aomonline.org; Association for Educational Communications and Technology (2005). Code of ethics. Retrieved February 25, 2007, from aect.org; National Speakers Association (2003). Code of professional ethics. Retrieved February 25, 2007, from nsaspeaker.org

[7] National Communication Association.

[8] Associated Press. (2005, November 12). Radio station pulls plug on chef's program. *The Seattle Times,* p. B3; Glassman, M. (2004, April 1). Shaw, D. L. (2005, October 14). CNY principal admitted plagiarism: So. Cayuga administrator loses job after not being recommended for tenure. *The Post-Standard,* p. A1.

[9] Gayle, B. M. (2004). Transformations in a civil discourse public speaking class: Speakers' and listeners' attitude change. *Communication Education, 53,* 174–184.

[10] Leets, L. (2001). Explaining perceptions of racist speech. *Communication Research, 28,* 676–706

[11] Chong, D. (2006) Free speech and multiculturalism in and out of the academy. *Political Psychology, 27*(1), 29–54; Demaske, C. (2004). Modern power and the first amendment: Reassessing hate speech. *Communication Law and Policy, 9*(3), 273–316.

[12] Gates, Jr., H. L. (2004). America behind the color line. Speech presented at the Commonwealth Club, January 28, 2004. Retrieved November 2, 2005, from commonwealthclub.org/archive/04/04-01gates-speech.html.

[13] Fawkner, M., & Keremidchieva, G. (2005). Plagiarism, cheating, and academic dishonesty: Have you been there? *Information & Security, 14,* 113–137.

[14] Olson, S. (2005). Schools face prevalence of online plagiarism: Educators try to thwart growing cheating problem as Web sites make it easy for students to purchase papers. *Indianapolis Business Journal, 26*(13), 17.

[15] Nienhaus, B. (2004). Helping students improve citation performance. *Business Communication Quarterly, 67,* 337–348.

[16] Johannesen, R. L. (2001). Communication ethics: Centrality, trends, and controversies. In W. B. Gudykunst (Ed.), *Communication yearbook 25* (pp. 201–235). Mahwah, NJ: Lawrence Erlbaum.

[17] Agar, M. (1994). Language shock: Understanding the culture of conversation. New York: William Morrow.

[18] Lull, J. (2000). *Media, communication, culture: A global approach.* New York: Cambridge University Press.

[19] Neuliep, J. W., Hintz, S. M., & McCroskey, J. C. (2005). The influence of ethnocentrism in organizational contexts: Perceptions of interviewee and managerial attractiveness, credibility, and effectiveness. *Communication Quarterly, 53,* 41–56.

[20] Lund, D. (2006). Rocking the racism boat: School-based activists speak out on denial and avoidance. *Race, Ethnicity & Education, 9,* 203–221.

[21] Cochran, J. (2002, October 24). A lawyer's life. Speech presented to the Commonwealth Club of California. Retrieved July 23, 2006, from commonwealthclub.org.

[22] Habinek.

[23] Oliver, R. T. (1965). *History of public speaking in America.* Boston: Allyn and Bacon.

[24] Sellnow, D. D., & Treinen, K. P. (2004). The role of gender in perceived speaker competence: An analysis of student peer critiques. *Communication Education, 53,* 286–296.

[25] Blumenstein, L. (2006). ACL listening tour at Louisville. *Library Journal, 131*(5), 17–18; Haskell, M. (2005, September 2). "Listening tour" focus: Health care. *Bangor Daily News*, B1; *PR Newswire* (1999, June 30). Hillary Rodham Clinton listening tour July 7–10, 1999, p. 2769; Winchester, D. (2005, May 8). Parents quiz schools chief on achievement gap. *St. Petersburg Times*, p. 9.

[26] Bostrom, R. N. (1996). Memory, cognitive processing, and the process of "listening." *Human Communication Research, 23,* 298–305.

[27] Halone, K. K., & Pecchioni, L. L. (2001). Relational listening: A grounded theoretical model. *Communication Reports, 14,* 59–71; Krauss, R. M. (1987). The role of the listener: Addressee influences on message formulation. *Journal of Language and Social Psychology, 6*(2), 81–98.

[28] Reisberg, D. (1978). Looking where you listen: Visual cues and auditory attention. *Acta Psychologica, 42,* 331–341.

[29] Clark, A. J. (1989). Communication confidence and listening competence: An investigation of the relationships of willingness to communicate, communication apprehension and receiver apprehension to comprehension of content and emotional meaning in spoken messages. *Communication Education, 38,* 237–248.

[30] Coopman, S. (1997). Personal constructs and communication in interpersonal and organizational contexts. In G. Neimeyer & R. Neimeyer (Eds.), *Advances in personal construct psychology,* Vol. 4 (pp. 101–147). Greenwich, CT: JAI Press.

[31] Bavelas, J. B., Coates, L., & Johnson, T. (2002). Listener responses as a collaborative process: The role of gaze. *Journal of Communication, 52,* 566–580; Thomas, L. T., & Levine. T. R. (1994). Disentangling listening and verbal recall: Related but separate constructs? *Human Communication Research, 21,* 103–127; White, G. (1998). *Listening.* Oxford, England: Oxford University Press.

[32] Nichols, R., & Stevens, L. M. (1957). Listening to people. *Harvard Business Review, 35,* 85–92.

[33] Brownell, J. (2006). *Listening: Attitudes, principles, and skills* (3rd ed). Boston: Allyn and Bacon.

[34] King, P. E., & Behnke, R. R. (2004). Patterns of state anxiety in listening performance. *Southern Communication Journal, 70,* 72–80.

[35] National Communication Association (1999).

[36] Underwood, J. D. M., & Underwood, G. (2005). The selective nature of memory: Some effects of taking a taking a verbal record: A response to A. Plaut. *Journal of Analytical Psychology, 50,* 59–67.

[37] Hammond, S. C., Anderson, R., & Cissna, K. N. (2003). The problematics of dialogue and power. In P. J. Kalbfleisch (Ed.), *Communication yearbook 27* (pp. 125–157). Mahwah, NJ: Lawrence Erlbaum; Johannesen, R. L. (2000). Nel Noddings's uses of Martin Buber's philosophy of dialogue. *Southern Communication Journal, 2 & 3,* 151–160; Levine, L. (1994). Listening with spirit and the art of team dialogue. *Journal of Organizational Change Management, 7*(1), 61–73; Stewart, J., & Zediker, K. (2000). Dialogue as tensional, ethical practice. *Southern Communication Journal, 2 & 3,* 224–242.

[38] Thomas, Z. (2005, March 6). It pays to be a good listener: 100 best companies to work for 2005. *Sunday Times* (London), p. 8.

[39] Pearce, W. B., & Pearce, K. A. (2000). Combining passions and abilities: Toward dialogic virtuosity. *Southern Communication Journal, 2 & 3,* 161–175.

[40] Gibb, J. R. (1961). Defensive communication. *Journal of Communication, 11,* 141–148.

CHAPTER 4

[1] Cronkhite, G. (1986). On the focus, scope, and coherence in the study of human symbolic activity. *Quarterly Journal of Speech, 72,* 231–246; Kellermann, K. (1992). Communication: Inherently strategic and primarily

automatic. *Communication Monographs, 59,* 288–300; Motley, M. T. (1990). On whether one can(not) not communicate: An examination via traditional communication postulates. *Western Journal of Speech Communication, 54,* 1–20.

² Keith, W. (2004). Planning a no-sweat presentation. *Government Finance Review, 20*(4), 55–56.

³ Williams, G. (2002). Looks like rain: If you've thought and thought and still haven't come up with any great ideas, don't sweat. *Entrepreneur, 30*(9), 104–110.

⁴ Osborn, A. F. (1957). *Applied imagination.* New York: Scribner; Prendergast, K. (2003, September 29). The ideal setting for ideas. Brainstorming sessions can be productive if done the correct way. *The Press Enterprise,* p. A7; Wellner, A. S. (2003). A perfect brainstorm. *Inc., 25*(10), 31–35.

⁵ Kupperman, M. A (2003). Perfect brainstorm. *Inc., 25*(10), 31–2, 35.

⁶ Snyder, A., Mitchell, J., Ellwood, S., Yates, A., & Pallier, G. (2004). Nonconscious idea generation. *Psychological Reports, 94,* 1325–1330.

⁷ Kollins, T. K. (1996). Tips for speakers. *Association Management, 48*(8), 175–179.

⁸ Ogden, H. V. S. (1948). On teaching the sentence outline. *College English, 10*(3), 152–158.

⁹ House, J. (1993). The first shall be last: Writing the essay backwards. *The English Journal, 82*(6), 26–28.

¹⁰ Watkins, K. J. (2005) Will they throw eggs? *Journal of Accountancy, 199* (4), 57–61.

CHAPTER 5

¹ Gates, B. (2005, October 12). Remarks by Bill Gates, Chairman and Chief Software Architect, Microsoft Corporation, University of Michigan, Ann Arbor, Michigan. Retrieved December 26, 2005, from microsoft.com/billgates/speeches.asp; Gates, B. (2005, October 13). Remarks by Bill Gates, Chairman and Chief Software Architect, Microsoft Corporation, University of Waterloo, Waterloo, Ontario, Canada. Retrieved December 26, 2005, from microsoft.com/billgates/speeches.asp.

² Morgan, N. (2003). *Working the room.* Cambridge, MA: Harvard Business School Press.

³ Haynes, W. L. (1990). Public speaking pedagogy in the media age. *Communication Education, 38,* 89–102.

⁴ Welch, J. M. (2005). The electronic welcome mat: The academic library web site as a marketing and public relations tool. *The Journal of Academic Librarianship, 31,* 225–228.

⁵ Agrawal, A., Basak, J., Jain, V., Kothari, R., Kumar, M., Mittal, P. A., Modani, N., Ravikumar, K., Sabharwal, Y., & Sureka, R. (2004). Online marketing research. *IBM Journal of Research & Development, 48,* 671–676.

⁶ Park-Fuller, L. M. (2003). Audiencing the audience: Playback Theatre, performative writing, and social activism. *Text and Performance Quarterly, 23,* 288–310.

⁷ Weissman, J. (2003). *Presenting to win: The art of telling your story.* Harlow, Essex, UK: Financial Times Prentice Hall.

⁸ Bennett, S. (1998). *Theatre audiences.* London: Routledge; Jamieson, K. H., & Campbell, K. K. (2000). *The interplay of influence.* Belmont, CA: Wadsworth; McQuail, D. (1997). *Audience analysis.* London: Sage; Tradut, P. (2004). *Media, audience, effects: An introduction to the study of media content and audience analysis.* Boston: Allyn & Bacon; Yopp, J. J., & McAdams, K. C. (2002). *Researching audiences.* Boston: Allyn & Bacon.

⁹ McCarty, H. (1998). *Motivating your audience.* Boston: Allyn & Bacon.

¹⁰ Myers, F. (1999). Argumentation and the composite audience: A case study. *Quarterly Journal of Speech, 85,* 55–71.

¹¹ U.S. Department of Commerce. (1996). *Population projections of the United States by age, sex, race and Hispanic Origin: 1995–2050.* Retrieved March 3, 2007, from census.gov.

¹² National Center for Education Statistics. (2004). *Digest of education statistics, 2004: Chapter 3, postsecondary education.* Retrieved March 3, 2007, from nces.ed.gov

¹³ Brown, L. I. (2004). Diversity: The challenge for higher education. *Race Ethnicity and Education, 7,* 21–34; Bylander, J., & Rose, S. (2007). Border crossings: Engaging students in diversity work and intergroup relations. *Innovative Higher Education, 31,* 251–264; Engberg, M. E. (2007). Educating the workforce for the 21ˢᵗ century: A cross-disciplinary analysis of the impact of the undergraduate experience on students' development of a pluralistic orientation. *Research in Higher Education, 48*(3), 283–317; Mor Barak, M. (2005). *Managing diversity: Towards a globally inclusive workplace.* Thousand Oaks: Sage; van Knippenberg, D., & Schippers, M. D. (2007). Work group diversity. *Annual Review of Psychology, 58,* 515–541.

¹⁴ Myers, F. (1999). Political argumentation and the composite audience: A case study. *Quarterly Journal of Speech, 85,* 55–71.

¹⁵ Atkinson, J. (2005). Conceptualizing global justice audiences of alternative media: The need for power and ideology in performance paradigms of audience research. *The Communication Review, 8,* 137–157; Harding, S. (1991). *Whose science? Whose knowledge? Thinking from women's lives.* Ithaca, NY: Cornell University Press.

¹⁶ Blethen, F. (2003, January 17). *Diversity: The American journey.* Keynote address presented at the third annual Martin Luther King Jr. Holiday Assemblies of the Granite Falls, Washington High School and Middle School. Retrieved March 5, 2007, from seattletimescompany.com

¹⁷ Orbe, M. P., & Warren, K. T. (2000). Different standpoints, different realities: Race, gender, and perceptions of intercultural conflict. *Qualitative Research Reports in Communication, 1*(3), 51–57.

¹⁸ Dietz, T., Kalof, L., & Stern P. C. (2002). Gender, values, and environmentalism. *Social Science Quarterly, 83,* 353–364.

¹⁹ Fowler, G. A., Steinberg, B., & Patrick, A. O. (2007, March 1). Mac and PC's overseas adventures: Globalizing Apple's ads meant tweaking characters, clothing and body language. *The Wall Street Journal,* p. B1.

²⁰ SRI Consulting Business Intelligence. (2001–2007). Welcome to VALS™. Retrieved March 4, 2007, from sric-bi.com/VALS/.

²¹ Miller, N. (2007). Snack attack: Minifesto for a new age. *Wired, 15.03,* 124–135.

²² Johnson, S. (2007). Snacklash. *Wired, 15.03,* 178.

²³ Yook, E. L. (2004). Any questions? Knowing the audience through question types. *Communication Teacher, 18,* 91–93.

²⁴ Parsons, R. D. (2007). A challenge to minority business owners. *Vital Speeches of the Day, 73*(1), 32–33.

²⁵ Black, C. (2007, January 11). *Putting the pieces together.* Remarks given at the Magazine Publishers of American Breakfast with a Leader. Retrieved March 18, 2007, from hearstcorp.com/speeches/speechesarchive2007.html.

²⁶ Myers, S. A. (2004). The relationship between perceived instructor credibility and college student in-class and out-of-class communication. *Communication Reports, 17,* 129–137; Myers, S. A., & Bryant, L. E. (2004). College students' perceptions of how instructors convey credibility. *Qualitative Research Reports in Communication, 5,* 22–27.

²⁷ Miller, A. (2002). An exploration of Kenyan public speaking patterns with implications for the American introductory public speaking course. *Communication Education, 51,* 168–182.

²⁸ Smith, C. R. (2003). *Rhetoric and human consciousness: A history.* Prospect Heights, IL: Waveland.

²⁹ Aune, R. K., & Kikuchi, T. (1993). Effects of language intensity similarity on perceptions of credibility, relational attributions, and persuasion. *Journal of Language and Social Psychology, 12,* 224–237; Myers & Bryant; Pfau, M., & Kang, J. G. (1991). The impact of relational messages on candidate influence in televised political debates. *Communication Studies, 42,* 114–128.

³⁰ Queen Noor (2005, April 11). *Medallion speaker address.* Presented to the Commonwealth of California. Retrieved July 27, 2006, from commonwealthclub.org

CHAPTER 6

[1] Rainie, L., & Horrigan, J. (2005). *A decade of adoption: How the internet has woven itself into American life*. Retrieved February 12, 2005, from pewinternet.org.

[2] Fallows, D. (2005). *Search engine users: Internet searchers are confident, satisfied and trusting—but they are also unaware and naïve*. Retrieved February 12, 2005, from pewinternet.org.

[3] Hansel, S. (2005, January 25). Google and Yahoo are extending search ability to TV programs. *The New York Times*, p. C7.

[4] Campbell, D. G., & Fast, K. V. (2004). Academic libraries and the semantic web: What the future may hold for research-supporting library catalogues. *Journal of Academic Librarianship, 30*, 382–390.

[5] Fitzgerald, M. A. (2004). Making the leap from high school to college: Three new studies about information literacy skills of first-year college students. *Knowledge Quest, 32*(4), 19–24.

[6] Christensen, E. W., & Bailey, J. R. (1998). Task performance using the library and internet to acquire business intelligence. *Internet Research: Electronic Networking Applications and Policy, 8*(4), 290–302.

[7] "Major search engines deliver significantly different results." (2005, May 12). *InformationWeek*. Retrieved May 20, 2005, from informationweek.com.

[8] "Piled high." (2005, May 16). *Seattle Times*, p. C1.

[9] Hamm, S. (2004, July 16). So many pages, such feeble search. *Business Week Online*. Retrieved February 21, 2005, from businessweek.com.

[10] Devine, J., & Egger-Sider, F. (2004). Beyond Google: The invisible web in the academic library. *Journal of Academic Librarianship, 30*, 265–259; Fallows (2005); Fox, S., & Fallows, D. (2003). *Internet health resources: Health searches and email become more commonplace, but there is room for improvement in searches and overall internet access*. Retrieved February 15, 2005, from pewinternet.org.

[11] Palmer, S. (2004, August 8). The blog connection. *The Register-Guard* (Eugene, OR), p. L1; Taylor, C. (2004, December 27). 10 things we learned about blogs. *Time*, p. 110; Witt, H. (2004, September 18). True or false: Blogs always tell it straight. *Chicago Tribune*. Retrieved February 15, 2005, from chicagotribune.com.

[12] Gillmor, D. (2004). *We the media: Grassroots journalism by the people, for the people*. Sebastopol, CA: O'Reilly Media; Johnson, T. J., & Kaye, B. K. (2004). Wag the blog: How reliance on traditional media and the internet influence credibility perceptions of weblogs among blog users. *Journalism and Mass Communication Quarterly, 81*, 622–642.

[13] Redfern, V. (2004). Natural language thesaurus: A survey of student research skills and research tool preferences. *Australian Academic Research Libraries, 35*(2), 137–150.

[14] Fallows (2005).

[15] Bangerter, A. (2000). Self-representation: Conversational implementation of self-presentation goals in research interviews. *Journal of Language and Social Psychology, 19*, 436–462; Johnson, J. C., & Weller, S. C. (2002). Elicitation techniques for interviewing. In J. F. Gubrium & J. A. Holstein (Eds.), *Handbook of interview research: Context & method* (pp. 491–514). Thousand Oaks, CA: Sage.

[16] Stewart, C. J., & Cash, W. B. (2008). *Interviewing: Principles and practices* (12th ed). New York: McGraw-Hill.

[17] Johnson, J. M. (2002). In-depth interviewing. In J. F. Gubrium & J. A. Holstein (Eds.), *Handbook of interview research: Context & method* (pp. 103–119). Thousand Oaks, CA: Sage.

[18] Spano, S., & Zimmermann, S. J. (1995). Interpersonal communication competence in context: Assessing performance in the selection interview. *Communication Reports, 8*, 18–26.

[19] Stax, H. P. (2004). Paths to precision: Probing turn format and turn-taking problems in standardized interviews. *Discourse Studies, 6*(1), 77–94.

[20] Stein, M. L., & Paterno, S. F. (2001). *Talk straight, listen carefully: The art of interviewing*. Ames, IA: Iowa State University Press.

[21] American Psychological Association (2001). *Publication manual of the American Psychological Association* (5th ed.). Washington, DC: American Psychological Association; Gibaldi, J. (2003). *MLA handbook for writers of research papers* (6th ed.). New York: Modern Language Association of America.

CHAPTER 7

[1] Student dissident Shen Tong offers a firsthand account of the violent crackdown in Tiananmen Square, China. (1994). In R. Torricelli & A. Carroll (Eds.), *In our own words: Extraordinary speeches of the American century* (pp. 385–388). New York: Kodansha International.

[2] Smith, C. R. (2003). *Rhetoric and human consciousness: A history*, 2nd ed. Prospect Heights, IL: Waveland.

[3] Muscari, P. G. (2005). A plea for mythos. *Dialogue & Universalism, 15*(3/4), 99–106; Yagcioglu, S., & Cem-Deger, A. (2001). Logos or mythos: (De)legitimation strategies in confrontational discourses of sociocultural ethos. *Discourse & Society, 12*, 817–852.

[4] Fisher, W. R. (1987). *Human communication as narration: Toward a philosophy of reason, value, and action*. Columbia: University of South Carolina; Limon, M. S., & Kazoleas, D. C. (2004). A comparison of exemplar and statistical evidence in reducing counter-arguments and responses to a message. *Communication Research Reports, 21*, 291–298; Roberts, K. G. (2004). Texturing the narrative paradigm: Folklore and communication. *Communication Quarterly, 52*, 129–142.

[5] Bono. (2004, May 17). Because we can, we must. University of Pennsylvania *Almanac* Between Issues, May 19, 2004. Retrieved September 25, 2004, from upenn.edu/almanac/between/2004/commence-b.html.

[6] Kelly, R. (2005, April 26). Through our eyes: A shared community vision for Saint Paul. State of the City Address, 2005, presented at the Dorothy Day Center, St. Paul, MN. Retrieved May 12, 2005, from stpaul.gov/mayor/speeches.

[7] Morrison, T. (2004, December 7). Toni Morrison—Nobel Lecture. Nobel Foundation. Retrieved September 25, 2004 from: nobelprize.org.

[8] Kaminski, J., Call, J., & Fischer, J. (2004). Word learning in a domestic dog: Evidence for "fast mapping". *Science, 304*, 1682–1683.

[9] Annan, K. A. (2004, September 21). Secretary-General's address to the General Assembly. Retrieved September 25, 2004, from un.org.

[10] Amory, L. (2007, August 10). Imagine a world . . . Speech presented at the Rocky Mountain Institute RMI25 Gala. Retrieved December 28, 2007, from rmi.org

[11] Bhatia, P. K. (2002). Introduction to President's speech by Edward Seaton. Retrieved October 11, 2004, from www.asne.org.

[12] Brain, M. (2004). How CDs work. Retrieved December 30, 2007, from www.howstuffworks.com.

[13] Clements, W. M. (2002). *Oratory in Native North America*. Tucson: University of Arizona Press; Dauenhauer, N. M., & R. Dauenhauer, R. (Eds.) (1990). *Haa tuwunáagu yís, for healing our spirit: Tlingit oratory* (Vol. 2). Seattle: University of Washington Press/Juneau: Sealaska Heritage Foundation.

[14] *Compact Oxford English Dictionary* (2004). Grief. Retrieved January 6, 2005, from askoxford.com/concise_oed

[15] David Kadashan (1990). Hoohah, 1968. In N. M. Dauenhauer, & R. Dauenhauer (Eds), *Haa tuwunáagu yís, for healing our spirit: Tlingit oratory* (Vol. 2, pp. 235–239). Seattle: University of Washington Press/Juneau: Sealaska Heritage Foundation.

[16] Associated Press. (2004, September 5). People Mover goes full circle again; Despite construction, a half-million people rode it last year. Operators expect a 60 percent rise. *The Grand Rapids Press*, p. A20; Chinni, D. (2001, March 8). Detroit's gambit to lure people back downtown. *The Christian Science Monitor*, p. 3.

[17] Freemantle, T. (2004, September 21). Eye on CBS; Rather apologizes for Guard story; After the mea culpa, what's left for Rather? Veteran anchor the latest face

in the debate over media credibility. *The Houston Chronicle*, p. 1.

[18] Hoeken, H. (2001). Anecdotal, statistical, and causal evidence: Their perceived and actual persuasiveness. *Argumentation, 15*, 425–437.

[19] Fox, M. J. (2005, July 13). *Senate rally for HR 810.* Retrieved December 27, 2005, from michaeljfox .org/news.

[20] Lipinski, W. O. (2001, November 6). Statement of Congressman William O. Lipinski: Special order speech—greater airline security. Retrieved October 10, 2004 from house.gov.

[21] Pew Research Center for the People and the Press (2007, August 9). *Internet news audience highly critical of news organizations: Views of press values and performance: 1985–2007.* Retrieved December 29, 2007, from people-press.org.

[22] Horrigan, J. B. (2006, March 22). *For many broadband users, the internet is a primary news source.* Pew Internet & American Life Project. Retrieved August 20, 2006, from pewinternet.org; Lenhart, A., Madden, M., & Hitlin, P. (2005). *Teens and technology: Youth are leading the transition to a fully wired and mobile nation.* Pew Internet & American Life Project. Retrieved December 4, 2005, from pewinternet.org; Pew Research Center for the People and the Press (2007, August 9). *Internet news audience highly critical of news organizations.*

[23] Madden, M. (2006, April 26). *Internet penetration and impact.* Pew Internet & American Life Project. Retrieved August 20, 2006, from pewinternet.org.

[24] Horrigan, J. B., & Morris, S. (2005, November). *Relief donations after Hurricanes Katrina and Rita and use of the internet to get disaster news.* Retrieved December 26, 2005, from pewinternet.org.

[25] Loory, S. H. (2005). CNN today: A young giant stumbles. *Critical Studies in Media Communication, 22*, 340–343.

[26] Pew Research Center for the People and the Press (2007, August 9). *Internet news audience highly critical of news organizations.*

[27] Fahmy, S., & Wanta, W. (2005). Testing priming effects: Differences between print and broadcast messages. *Simile, 5*(2); Lanie, L. (2001). *How Americans used the internet after the terror attack.* Pew Internet & American Life Project. Retrieved December 4, 2005, from pewinternet.org; Pew Research Center for the People and the Press (2004). *News audiences;* Pew Research Center for the People and the Press (2007). *Internet news audience highly critical of news organizations;* Project for Excellence in Journalism. (2007). *The state of the news media 2007.* Retrieved December 30, 2007, from stateofthemedia.org/2007.

[28] Fallows, D. (2007, February 6). *Election newshounds speak up: Newspaper, TV and internet fans tell how and why they differ.* Retrieved December 30, 2007, from pewinternet.org; Pew Research Center for the People and the Press (2007). *Internet news audience highly critical of news organizations;* Project for Excellence in Journalism (2007).

[29] Maier, S. R. (2005). Accuracy matters: A cross-market assessment of newspaper error and credibility. *Journalism & Mass Communication Quarterly, 82*, 533–551.

[30] Project for Excellence in Journalism (2007).

[31] Belo Interactive. (2004). *Online credibility survey.* Retrieved December 30, 2007, from dallasnews.com/ sharedcontent/dws/spe/credibility/.

[32] Lee, T. (2005). The liberal media myth revisited: An examination of factors influencing perceptions of media bias. *Journal of Broadcasting & Electronic Media, 49*, 43–64. Pew Research Center for the People and the Press (2007).

CHAPTER 8

[1] Adams, T., & Scollard, S. (2005). *Internet effectively: A beginner's guide to the World Wide Web.* Boston: Pearson.

[2] Lynch, C. (1995). Reaffirmation of God's anointed prophet: The use of chiasm in Martin Luther King's "mountaintop" speech. *Howard Journal of Communications, 6*(1/2), 12–31; Schank, R., & Berman, T. (2006). Living stories: Designing story-based education experiences. *Narrative Inquiry, 16*, 220–228.

[3] Campbell, K. K., & Huxman, S. S. (2003). *The rhetorical act: Thinking, speaking, and writing critically,* 3rd ed. Belmont, CA: Wadsworth.

[4] Awosika, M. (2003, March 18). Legendary Fabergé eggs still popular. *Sarasota Herald-Tribune*, p. E1.

[5] Leech, T. (2004). *How to prepare, stage, and deliver winning presentations.* New York: American Management Association.

[6] Leech (2004).

[7] *Merriam-Webster Online Dictionary.* (2004). Subordinate. Retrieved October 24, 2004.

[8] American Psychological Association. (2001). *Publication manual of the American Psychological Association,* (5th ed.). Washington, DC: American Psychological Association; Gibaldi, J. (2003). *MLA handbook for writers of research papers* (6th ed.). New York: Modern Language Association of America.

CHAPTER 9

[1] Novogratz, J. (2005, July). TEDTalks: Jacqueline Novogratz. Retrieved March 19, 2007, from ted. com/tedtalks.

[2] Dennis, M. J., & Ahn, W-K. (2001). Primacy in causal strength judgments: The effect of initial evidence for generative versus inhibitory relationships. *Memory & Cognition, 29*, 152–164; Miller, J. K., Westerman, D. L., & Lloyd, M. E. (2004). Are first impressions lasting impressions? An exploration of the generality of the primacy effect in memory for repetitions. *Memory & Cognition, 32*, 1305–1315; Richter, L., & Kruglanski, A. Q. (1998). Seizing on the latest: Motivationally driven recency effects in impression formation. *Journal of Experimental Social Psychology, 34*, 313–329.

[3] Winfrey, O. (2002). Oprah Winfrey's acceptance speech. Retrieved December 4, 2005, from oprah.com.

[4] Cosby, B. (2004, May 17). *Pound cake speech.* Presented at the NAACP's Gala to Commemorate the 50th Anniversary of Brown v. Board of Education, Constitution Hall, Washington DC. Retrieved December 4, 2005, from americanrhetoric.com.

[5] Visco, F. (2005, May 22). Speech presented at the 13th Annual Advocacy Training Conference, Washington DC. Retrieved December 4, 2005, from natlbcc.org.

[6] O'Connor, S. D. (2004, June 13). Full text of remarks by Supreme Court Justice Sandra Day O'Connor at the 113th Commencement Ceremony. Retrieved December 3, 2005, from news-service.stanford.edu.

[7] Oppliger, P. A. (2003). Humor and learning. In J. Bryant, D. Roskos-Ewoldsen, & J. Cantor (Eds.), *Communication and emotion: Essays in honor of Dolf Zillmann* (pp. 255–273). Mahwah, NJ: Lawrence Erlbaum; Wanzer, M. B., & Frymier, A. B. (1999). The relationship between student perceptions of instructor humor and student's reports of learning. *Communication Education, 48*, 48–62.

[8] Downs, V. C., Javidi, M., & Nussbaum, J. F. (1988). An analysis of teachers' verbal communication within the college classroom: Use of humor, self-disclosure, and narratives. *Communication Education, 37*, 127–141.

[9] Hackman, M. Z. (1988). Reactions to the use of self-disparaging humor by informative public speakers. *Southern Speech Communication Journal, 53*, 175–183.

[10] Fisher, M. (1992). Mary Fisher: 1992 Republication National Convention address: A whisper of AIDS. Retrieved December 4, 2005, from americanrhetoric .com.

[11] Atkin, N. (2005). Building capacity in Aboriginal communities and non-Aboriginal institutions. *Vital Speeches of the Day, 72*(1), 19–22.

[12] Costabile, K. A., & Klein, S. B. (2005). Finishing strong: Recency effects in juror judgments. *Basic & Applied Social Psychology, 27*, 47–58; Shakarian, D. C. (1995). Beyond lecture: Active learning strategies that work. *JOPERD: The Journal of Physical Education, Recreation & Dance, 66*(5)21–24; Vroomen, B. D. J. (1997). Modality effects in immediate recall of verbal and non-verbal information. *European Journal of Cognitive Psychology, 9*, 97–110.

[13] Crano, W. D. (1977). Primacy versus recency in retention of information and opinion change. *Journal of*

Social Psychology, 101(1), 87–96; Igou, E. R., & Bless, H. (2003). Inferring the importance of arguments: Order effects and conversational rules. *Journal of Experimental Social Psychology, 39,* 91–99.

[14] Eardley, A. F., & Pring, L. (2006). Remembering the past and imagining the future: A role for nonvisual imagery in the everyday cognition of blind and sighted people. *Memory, 14,* 925–936; Page, M. P. A., Cumming, N., Norris, D., Hitch, G. J., & McNeil, A. M. (2006). Repetition learning in the immediate serial recall of visual and auditory materials. *Journal of Experimental Psychology / Learning, Memory & Cognition, 32,* 716–733; Tremblay, S., Parmentier, F. B. R., Guérard, K., Nicholls, A. P., & Jones, D. M. (2006). A spatial modality effect in serial memory. *Journal of Experimental Psychology / Learning, Memory & Cognition, 32,* 1208–1215.

[15] Brown, R. M. (nd). Retrieved March 13, 2006, from quotationspage.com.

CHAPTER 10

[1] Words of wisdom from a young orator (2004, July 29). *The Virginian Pilot,* p. B10.

[2] Obama, B. (2004, July 27). Speech presented at the Democratic National Convention, Boston, MA. Retrieved September 9, 2005, from presidentialrhetoric.com.

[3] SIL International. (2005). A brief history of SIL International. Retrieved January 14, 2005 from sil.org.

[4] Ogden, C. K., & Richards, I. A. (1923). *The meaning of meaning: A study of the influence of language upon thought and of the science of symbolism.* New York: Harcourt, Brace.

[5] Pear, R. (2004, February 24). Education chief calls union "terrorist," then recants. *The New York Times.* Retrieved February 25, 2004, from nytimes.com.

[6] *Compact Oxford English Dictionary* (2004). Car. Retrieved January 14, 2005, from askoxford.com/concise_oed; Investorwords.com (2005). Car. Retrieved January 14, 2005, from investorwords.com; *Webster's Revised Unabridged Dictionary* (1913). Retrieved January 17, 2005, from humanities.uchicago.edu/orgs/ARTFL/forms_unrest/webster.form.html, p. 216; *Dorland's Illustrated Medical Dictionary* (2002). CAR. Retrieved January 14, 2005, from mercksource.com.

[7] Baldwin, T. (2004). Keep the flame alive for rights. In Ridinger, R. B. (Ed.). *Speaking for our lives: Historic speeches and rhetoric for gay and lesbian rights (1892–2000)* (pp. 804–806). Binghamton, NY: Harrington Park Press.

[8] Yim, S. (2003, October 9). Dictionary editor tells Portland, Ore., audience how new words get chosen. *The Oregonian.* Retrieved January 17, 2005, from oregonian.com.

[9] Logue, C. M., & Messina, L. M. (Eds.) (2003). *Representative American speeches 2002–2003.* New York: H. W. Wilson, p. 58.

[10] Manovich, L. (2001). *The language of new media.* Cambridge, MA: MIT Press.

[11] The original draft of President Bill Clinton's apology to the American people for his "improper relationship" with Monica Lewinsky & the speech he ultimately gave (1999). In R. Torricelli & A. Carroll (Eds.), *In our own words: Extraordinary speeches of the American century* (pp. 435–438). New York: Kodansha International.

[12] *Roget's New Millennium Thesaurus* (2005). Available at thesaurus.reference.com.

[13] Noveck, J. (2005, September 7). The use of the word "refugee" touches a nerve. *The Seattle Times,* p. A16.

[14] Eckert, P., & McConnell-Ginet, S. (2003). *Language and gender.* Cambridge, England: Cambridge University Press; Mulac, A., Bradac, J. J., & Gibbons, P. (2001). Empirical support for the gender-as-culture hypothesis: An intercultural analysis of male/female language differences. *Human Communication Research, 27,* 121–152.

[15] Haleta, L. L. (1996). Student perceptions of teachers' use of language: The effects of powerful and powerless language on impression information and uncertainty. *Communication Education, 45,* 16–27; Ruva, C. L., & Bryant, J. B. (2004). The impact of age, speech style, and question form on perceptions of witness credibility and trial outcome. *Journal of Applied Social Psychology, 34,* 1919–1944; Sparks, J. R. & Areni, C. S. (2002). The effects of sales presentation quality and initial perceptions on persuasion: A multiple role perspective. *Journal of Business Research, 55,* 517–528.

[16] Timmerman, L. M. (2002). Comparing the production of power in language on the basis of sex. In M. Allen, R. W. Preiss, B. M. Gayle, & N. A. Burrell (Eds.), *Interpersonal communication research: Advances through meta-analysis* (pp. 73–88). Mahwah, NJ: Lawrence Erlbaum.

[17] Natalle, E. J., & Bodenheimer, F. R. (2004). *The woman's public speaking handbook.* Belmont, CA: Wadsworth.

[18] Women doctors change U.S. medical care (2005, January 12). Retrieved January 30, 2005, from medlineplus.gov.

[19] Billings, A. C., Halone, K. K., & Denham, B. E. (2002). "Man, that was a pretty shot": An analysis of gendered broadcast commentary surrounding the 2000 men's and women's NCAA Final Four Basketball Championships. *Mass Communication and Society, 5,* 295–315; Gidengil, E., & Everitt, J. (2003). Talking tough: Gender and reported speech in campaign news coverage. *Political Communication, 20,* 209–232; Shugart, H. A. (2003). She shoots, she scores: Mediated constructions of contemporary female athletes in coverage of the 1999 U.S. women's soccer team. *Western Journal of Communication, 67,* 1–31; Vavrus, M. D. (2000). From women of the year to "soccer moms": The case of the incredible shrinking women. *Political Communication, 17,* 193–200.

[20] Billings et al. (2002); Shugart (2003).

[21] Kimberlin, J. (2004, May 24). The women of NASCAR: Hot guys, hotter cars putting more female fans in stands. *The Virginian Pilot,* p. E1.

[22] Chao, E. L. (2005, February 3). Remarks prepared for delivery by U. S. Secretary of Labor Elaine L. Chao, *LATINA Style* 50, Washington, DC. Retrieved March 5, 2005, from dol.gov.

[23] Jolie, A. (2005, March 8). Speech at the National Press Club. Retrieved September 9, 2005, from npr.org.

[24] McCormick, S. (2003). Earning one's inheritance: Rhetorical criticism, everyday talk, and the analysis of public discourse. *Quarterly Journal of Speech, 89,* 109–131.

[25] Lennox. A. (2005, March 22). Annie Lennox speech. Retrieved April 3, 2005, from thedevelopmentline.co.uk/46664minisite.

[26] In Gottheimer, J. (Ed.) (2003). *Ripples of hope: Great American civil rights speeches.* New York: Basic Books, p. 459.

[27] Gottheimer (2003), p. 462.

[28] In Logue, C. M., & Messina, L. M. (Eds.) (2002). *Representative American speeches 2001–2002.* New York: H. W. Wilson, p. 87.

[29] Schwarz, T. J. (2003, November 12). Inaugural speech. Retrieved April 8, 2005, from purchase.edu.

[30] Carmona, R. H. (2005, February 7). *The value and promise of every child.* Keynote speech presented at the 2005 National Early Childhood Conference Hosted by U.S. Department of Education, Office of Special Education Programs, Washington, DC. Retrieved January 15, 2006, from surgeongeneral.gov/news/speeches/02072005.html. Emphasis added.

[31] Weiss, E. (2005, March 3). Lessons learned from survivors. Retrieved April 8, 2005, from feminist.com.

[32] Jenkins, S. P. (2005, March 31). Raising the bar on integrity. Retrieved April 10, 2005, from boeing.com.

[33] Nussbaum, M. C. (2003, May 16). Compassion and global responsibility. Commencement address at Georgetown University, Washington, DC. Retrieved May 2, 2005, from humanity.org/commencements.

[34] DeNeal, D. (2004, October 12). Katabasis and Anabasis: A four year journey. *Wabash Magazine,* summer/fall. Retrieved May 2, 2005, from wabash.edu/magazine.

[35] Hackman, M. Z. (1988). Reactions to the use of self-disparaging humor by informative public speakers. *Southern Speech Communication Journal, 53,* 175–183.

[36] Natalle & Bodenheimer (2004).

[37] Hirst, R. (2003). Scientific jargon, good and bad. *Journal of Technical Writing and Communication, 33,* 201–229.

[38] Cole, J. G., & McCroskey, J. C. (2003). The association of perceived communication apprehension, shyness,

and verbal aggression with perceptions of source credibility and affect in organizational and interpersonal contexts. *Communication Quarterly, 51*, 101–110.

CHAPTER 11

[1] White, C., Easton, P., & Anderson, C. (2000). Students' perceived value of video in a multimedia language course. *Educational Media International, 37*, 167–175.

[2] Galbreath, S. C., & Booker, J. (2000). Making multimedia presentations easy. *Public Management, 82*(5), 10–17.

[3] Wormald, K. E. (2004). Pump up your presentations. *OfficeSolutions, 21*(2), 48–49.

[4] Cyphert, D. (2004). The problem of PowerPoint. Visual aid or visual rhetoric? *Business Communication Quarterly, 27*, 80–84.

[5] Mahin, L. (2004). PowerPoint pedagogy. *Business Communication Quarterly, 27*, 219–222.

[6] DuFrene, D. D., & Lehman, C. M. (2004). Concept, content, construction, and contingencies: Getting the horse before the PowerPoint car. *Business Communication Quarterly, 27*, 64–88.

[7] Mahin (2004).

[8] DuFrene & Lehman (2004).

[9] Jones, J. H. (2004). Message first: Using films to power the point. *Business Communication Quarterly, 27*, 88–91.

[10] Blokzijl, W., & Naeff, R. (2004). The instructor as stagehand. Dutch student responses to PowerPoint. *Business Communication Quarterly, 27*, 70–77.

[11] Bell, S. (2004). End PowerPoint dependency now! *American Libraries, 35*(6), 56–59.

CHAPTER 12

[1] Johnstone, C. L. (2001). Communicating in classical contexts: The centrality of delivery. *Quarterly Journal of Speech, 87*, 121–143.

[2] Martini, M., Behnke, R. R., & King, P. E. (1992). The communication of public speaking anxiety: Perceptions of Asian and American speakers. *Communication Quarterly, 40*, 279–288.

[3] Natalle, E. J., & Bodenheimer, F. R. (2004). *The woman's public speaking handbook*. Belmont, CA: Wadsworth.

[4] Sellnow, D. D., & Treinen, K. P. (2004). The role of gender in perceived speaker competence: An analysis of student peer critiques. *Communication Education, 53*, 286–296.

[5] Natalle & Bodenheimer (2004).

[6] Natalle & Bodenheimer (2004).

[7] National Institute on Deafness and Other Communication Disorders (2006, January 13). Statistics on voice, speech, and language. Retrieved July 30, 2006, from nidcd.org.

[8] Whaley, B. B., & Golden, M. A. (2000). Communicating with persons who stutter: Perceptions and strategies. In D. O. Braithwaite & T. L. Thompson (Eds.), *Handbook of communication and people with disabilities: Research and application* (pp. 423–438). Mahwah, NJ: Lawrence Erlbaum.

[9] Connor, C. M., & Craig, H. K. (2006). African American preschoolers' language, emergent literacy skills, and use of African American English: A complex relation. *Journal of Speech, Language & Hearing Research, 49*, 771–792; Oetting, J. B., & Garrity, A. W. (2006). Variation within dialects: A case of Cajun/Creole influence within child SAAE and SWE. *Journal of Speech, Language & Hearing Research, 49*, 16–26.

[10] Melançon, M. E. (2005). Stirring the linguistic gumbo. Retrieved September 3, 2006, from pbs.org.

[11] Greene, D. M., & Walker, F. R. (2004). Recommendations to public speaking instructors for the negotiation of code-switching practices among black English-speaking African American students. *Journal of Negro Education, 73*, 435–442.

[12] American Federation of the Blind. (2006). Blindness statistics. Retrieved July 30, 2006, from afb.org.

[13] Harrington, T. (2004, July). Statistics: Deaf population of the United States. Retrieved July 30, 2006, from library.gallaudet.edu.

[14] Omansky, B. (2006, August 2). Personal communication.

[15] Christenfeld, N. (1995). Does it hurt to say um? *Journal of Nonverbal Behavior, 19*(3), 171–186; Engstrom, E. (1994). Effects of nonfluencies on speakers' credibility in newscast settings. *Perceptual and Motor Skills, 78*, 739–749.

[16] Geonetta, S. C. (1981). Increasing the oral communication competencies of the technological student: The professional speaking method. *Journal of Technical Writing and Communication, 11*(3), pp. 233–244.

[17] Croft, A. C. (1992). Ten ways to ruin a good new business presentation. *Public Relations Quarterly, 37*(3), 25–29.

[18] Hackman, M. Z. (1988). Reactions to the use of self-disparaging humor by informative public speakers. *Southern Communication Journal, 53*, 175–183; Savitsky, K., & Gilovich, T. (2003). The illusion of transparency and the alleviation of speech anxiety. *Journal of Experimental Social Psychology, 39*, 618–625.

[19] Smith, T. E., & Frymier, A. B. (2006). Get "real": Does practicing speeches before an audience improve performance? *Communication Quarterly, 54*, 111–125.

[20] Smith & Frymier (2006).

CHAPTER 13

[1] U.S. Department of Commerce (2004). *Entering the broadband age: A nation online*. Retrieved February 20, 2005, from ntia.doc.gov.

[2] Bruns. A. (2005). *Gatewatching: Collaborative online news production*. New York: Peter Lang.

[3] Rowan, K. E. (1995). A new pedagogy for explanatory public speaking: Why arrangement should not substitute for invention. *Communication Education, 44*, 236–250.

[4] Al-Abdullah, Rania, Queen of Jordan (2003, October 14). Petra: Lost city of stone—excerpts. Speech presented at the New York Museum of Natural History, New York City. Retrieved September 10, 2006, from queenrania.jo.

[5] Koster, R. (2005, March 7). Keynote: A theory of fun for games. Retrieved September 16, 2006, from crystaltips.typepad.com/wonderland/2005/03/raphs_keynote.html.

[6] Cousteau, J. (2001, September 25). Congressional Oceans Day Keynote Address. Retrieved September 16, 2006, from oceanfutures.org.

CHAPTER 14

[1] Villaraigosa, A. R. (2006, April 21). *"Accelerating our ambitions": Mayor Antonio Villaraigosa's first state of the city address*. Retrieved June 21, 2006, from lacity.org/mayor/.

[2] Borchers, T. A. (2005). *Persuasion in the media age* (2nd ed.). New York: McGraw-Hill.

[3] Powell, C. (2003, February 5). Iraq: Denial and deception. Speech presented to the United Nations Security Council. Retrieved June 25, 2006, from whitehouse.gov/news/releases/2003/02/20030205-1.html.

[4] Hanley, C. J. (2003, August 10). U.S. justification for war: How it stacks up now. *Seattle Times*, p. A4.

[5] Weisman, S. R. (2005, September 9). Powell calls his U.S. speech a lasting blot on his record. *The New York Times*, p. A10.

[6] Centers for Disease Control and Prevention (2004). Surgeon General's 2004 Report: The health consequences of smoking on the human body. Retrieved June 25, 2006, from cdc.gov/Tobacco/sgr/sgr_2004/sgranimation/flash/index.html.

[7] Simons, H. W. (2001). *Persuasion in society*. Thousand Oaks, CA: Sage; Tracy, L. (2005). Taming hostile audiences. *Vital Speeches of the Day, 71*(10), 306–312.

[8] McKerrow, R. E., Gronbeck, B. E., Ehninger, D., & Monroe, A. H. (2003). *Principles and types of public speaking*, 15th ed. Allyn & Bacon.

[9] Simons (2001).

[10] Neuman, Y., Bekerman, Z., & Kaplan, A. (2002). Rhetoric as the contextual manipulation of self and

nonself. *Research on Language and Social Interaction, 35*, 93–112.

[11] Simons (2001).

[12] Simons (2001).

[13] Claypool, H. M., Mackie, D. M., Garcia-Marques, T., McIntosh, A., & Udall, A. (2004). The effects of personal relevance and repetition on persuasive processing. *Social Cognition, 22*, 310–335.

[14] Lewis, T. V. (1988). Charisma and media evangelists: An explication and model of communication influence. *Southern Communication Journal, 54*, 93–111.

[15] Goossens, C. (2003). Visual persuasion: Mental imagery processing and emotional experience. In Scott, L. M., & Batra, R. (Eds.), *Persuasive imagery: A consumer response perspective* (pp. 129–138). Mahwah, NJ: Lawrence Erlbaum.

[16] National Communication Association (1999). NCA credo for ethical communication. Retrieved June 23, 2006, from www.natcom.org.

[17]Brown, K. (2002, March 1). Tangled roots? Genetics meets genealogy. *Science,* 1634–1635; Jasanoff, S. (2006). Just evidence: The limits of science in the legal process (DNA fingerprinting and civil liberties). *Journal of Law, Medicine & Ethics, 34*, 328–241; Mulligan, C. J. (2006). Anthropological applications of ancient DNA: Problems and prospects. *American Antiquity, 71*(22), 365–380.

[18] Ossorio, P. N. (2006). About face: Forensic genetic testing for race and visible traits. *Journal of Law, Medicine & Ethics, 34*, 277–292.

[19] Kalb, C. (2006, February 6). In our blood; DNA testing: It is connecting lost cousins and giving families surprising glimpses into their pasts. Now scientists are using it to answer the oldest question of all: Where did we come from? *Newsweek,* p. 46.

[20] O'Brien, A. J., & Golding, C. G. (2003). Coercion in mental healthcare: The principle of least coercive care. *Journal of Psychiatric & Mental Health Nursing, 10*(2), 167–173; Van Dijk, T. A. (2006). Discourse and manipulation. *Discourse & Society, 17*, 359–383.

CHAPTER 15

[1] Walker, L. (2006, May 18). Google's goal: A worldwide web of books. *Washington Post,* p. D1.

[2] Coleman, M S. (2006). Google, the Khmer Rouge and the public good. *Vital Speeches of the Day, 72*(9), 263–269; p. 264.

[3] Munson, R., & Conway, D. A. (2001). *Basics of reasoning.* Belmont, CA: Wadsworth.

[4] Toulmin, S. E. (2003). *The uses of argument* (updated ed.). Cambridge, UK: Cambridge University Press.

[5] Campbell, K. K., & Huxman, S. S. (2003). *The rhetorical act* (2nd ed.). Belmont, CA: Wadsworth.

[6] Munson & Conway (2001).

[7] Foster, A. L. (2006). U. of Michigan president defends library's role in book-scanning project. *Chronicle of Higher Education, 52*(24), 40.

[8] Brugidou, M. (2003). Argumentation and values: An analysis of ordinary political competence via an open-ended question. *International Journal of Public Opinion Research, 15*, 413–430; Dickinson, G.; Anderson, K. V. (2004). Fallen: O. J. Simpson, Hillary Rodham Clinton, and the re-centering of White patriarchy. *Communication and Critical/Cultural Studies, 1*, 271–296; Smith, C. A. (2005). President Bush's enthymeme of evil: The amalgamation of 9/11, Iraq, and moral values. *American Behavioral Scientist, 49*, 32–47.

[9] Bitzer, L. F. (1959). Aristotle's enthymeme revisited. *Quarterly Journal of Speech, 45*, 399–408.

[10] Walker (2006); Williams, M. A. E. (2003). Arguing with style: How persuasion and the enthymeme work together in *On Invention,* Book 3. *Southern Communication Journal, 68*, 136–151.

[11] King, Jr., M. L. (1957, November 17). Loving your enemies. Delivered at the Dexter Avenue Baptist Church in Montgomery, Alabama. Retrieved July 3, 2006, from stanford.edu/group/King/popular_requests/voice_of_king.htm.

[12] Finnegan, C. A. (2001). The naturalistic enthymeme and visual argument: Photographic representation in the "Skull Controversy." *Argumentation and Advocacy, 37*, 133–149.

[13] Simons, H. W. (2001). *Persuasion in society.* Thousand Oaks, CA: Sage; Tracy, L. (2005). Taming hostile audiences. *Vital Speeches of the Day, 71*(10), 306–312.

[14] Coleman (2006), p. 265.

[15] Artz, N., & Tybout, A. M. (1999). The moderating impact of quantitative information on the relationship between source credibility and persuasion: A persuasion knowledge model interpretation. *Marketing Letters, 10*(1), 51–62, Lindsey, L. L. M., & Ah Yun, K. (2003). Examining the persuasive effect of statistical messages: A test of mediating relationships. *Communication Studies, 54*, 306–321.

[16] Volkow, N. D. (2006). Drug addiction: Free will, brain disease, or both? *Vital Speeches of the Day, 72*(16/17), 505–508.

[17] Volkow (2006), p. 506.

[18] Pornpitakpan, C. (2004). The persuasiveness of source credibility: A critical review of five decades' evidence. *Journal of Applied Social Psychology, 34*, 243–281.

[19] Buller, D. B. (1992). Social perceptions as mediators of the effect of speech rate similarity on compliance. *Human Communication Research, 19*, 286–311.

[20] Bordia, P., DiFonzo, N., Haines, R., & Chaseling, E. (2005). Rumors denials as persuasive messages: Effects of personal relevance, source, and message characteristics. *Journal of Applied Social Psychology, 35*, 1301–1331; Eckstein, J. J. (2005). Conversion conundrums: Listener perceptions of affective influence attempts as mediated by personality and individual differences. *Communication Quarterly, 53*, 401–419.

[21] Schramm, C. R. (2006). Making the turn: Entrepreneurial capitalism and its European promise. *Vital Speeches of the Day, 72*(16/17), 480–488.

[22] Schramm (2006), p. 480.

[23] Schramm (2006), p. 481.

[24] Braun-Latour, K. A., & Zaltman, G. (2006). Memory change: An intimate measure of persuasion. *Journal of Advertising Research, 46*(1), 57–72; Page, T. J., Thorson, E., & Heide, M. P. (1990). The memory impact of commercials varying in emotional appeal and product involvement. In Agres, S. J., Edell, J. H., & Dubitsky, T. M. (Eds.), *Emotion in advertising: Theoretical and practical explorations* (pp. 255–268). Westport, CT: Quorum Books

[25] Perse, E. M., Nathanson, A. I., & McLeod, D. M. (1996). Effects of spokesperson sex, public service announcement appeal and involvement on evaluations of safe-sex PSAs. *Health Communication, 8*, 171–189.

[26] Maslow, A. H. (1954). *Motivation and personality.* New York: Harper; Maslow, A. H. (2000). *The Maslow business reader.* New York: Wiley; Maslow, A. H., with Stephens, D. C., & Heil, G. (1971). *Maslow on management.* New York: Wiley; Maslow, A. H. (1999). *Toward a psychology of being* (3rd ed.). New York: Wiley; Rowan, J. (1998). Maslow amended. *Journal of Humanistic Psychology, 38*(1), 81–92.

[27] Hanley, S. J., & Abell, S. C. (2002). Maslow and relatedness: Creating an interpersonal model of self-actualization. *Journal of Humanistic Psychology, 42*(4), 37–57.

[28] Adapted from Maslow (1999).

[29] Moore, D. J., & Harris, W. D. (1996). Affect intensity and the consumer's attitude toward high impact emotional advertising appeals. *Journal of Advertising, 25*(2), 39–50; Roskos-Ewoldsen, D. R., Yu, H. J., & Rhodes, N. (2004). Fear appeal messages affect accessibility of attitudes toward threat and adaptive behaviors. *Communication Monographs, 71*, 49–69; Witte, K. (1992). Putting the fear back into fear appeals: The extended parallel process model. *Communication Monographs, 59*, 329–349; Witte, K. (1994). Fear control and danger control: A test of the extended parallel process model (EPPM). *Communication Monographs, 61*, 113–134.

[30] Majoras, D. P. (2006, May 22). Remarks by FTC chairman Deborah Platt Majoras, Initial meeting of the President's Identity Theft Task Force. Retrieved July 8, 2006, from ftc.gov/speeches/06speech.htm.

[31] Lowry, L. (2005, March). How everything turns away. Speech presented at the University of Richmond

"Quest" series. Retrieved July 9, 2006, from loislowry .com.

[32] Lowry (2005), pp. 23–24.

[33] Dorsey, L. G. (1997). Sailing into the "wondrous now": The myth of the American Navy's world cruise. *Quarterly Journal of Speech, 83,* 447–465; Winfield, B. H., & Hume, J. (1998). The American hero and the evolution of the human interest story. *American Journalism, 15*(2), 79–99.

[34] Hill, J. E. (2006, June 10). The coming revolution will not be viewed on television: Physicians turning trust into action. Presented at the annual meeting of the American Medical Association House of Delegates, Chicago. Retrieved July 10, 2006, from ama-assn.org.

[35] Crichton, M. (2005, November 6). Fear, complexity, & environmental management in the 21st century. Speech presented at the Washington Center for Complexity and Public Policy, Washington, D.C. Retrieved July 11, 2006, from crichton-official.com.

[36] Howell, W. S. (1976). The Declaration of Independence: Some adventures with America's political masterpiece. *Quarterly Journal of Speech, 62,* 221–233.

[37] Trent, J. D. (1968). Toulmin's model of an argument: An examination and extension. *Quarterly Journal of Speech, 54,* 252–259.

[38] Centers for Disease Control and Prevention. (2004). Surgeon General's 2004 Report: The health consequences of smoking on the human body. Retrieved June 25, 2006, from cdc.gov/Tobacco/sgr/sgr_2004/ sgranimation/flash/.

[39] Munson, R. & Conway, D. A. (2001). *Basics of reasoning.* Belmont, CA: Wadsworth.

[40] Lin, T., & McNab, P. (2006). Cognitive trait modeling: The case of inductive reasoning ability. *Innovations in Education & Teaching International, 43*(2), 151–161.

[41] Hair, P. (2004, April 21). Remarks presented at the Radio-Television News Directors Association & Foundation luncheon. Las Vegas. Retrieved July 11, 2006, from rtndf.org.

[42] Heit, E., & Feeney, A. (2005). Relations between premise similarity and inductive strength. *Psychonomic Bulletin & Review, 12,* 340–344.

[43] Epstein, R. L. (2006). *Critical thinking* (3rd ed.). Belmont, CA: Wadsworth; Munson & Conway (2001).

[44] Simon, R. (2006, June 13). Deputy Secretary Raymond Simon's testimony before the House Committee on Education and the Workforce. Retrieved July 14, 2006, from ed.gov/news.

[45] Karakas, F. (2006). Noah's pudding: Reflection on diversity, richness, living in harmony and peace through Ashura. *Vital Speeches of the Day, 72*(12), 369–373.

[46] Karakas (2006), pp. 369–370.

[47] Epstein (2006).

[48] Ikuenobe, P. (2004). On the theoretical unification and nature of fallacies. *Argumentation, 18,* 189–211.

[49] Hansen, H. V. (2002). The straw thing of fallacy theory: The standard definition of "fallacy." *Argumentation, 16,* 133–155; Neuman, Y., Glassner, A., & Weinstock, M. (2004). The effect of a reason's truth-value on the judgment of a fallacious argument. *Acta Psychologica, 116*(2), 173–184.

[50] Walton, D. The appeal to ignorance, or *argumentum ad ignorantiam. Argumentation, 13,* 367–377.

[51] Broadfoot, P. (2004). "Lies, damned lies, and statistics!": Three fallacies of comparative methodology. *Comparative Education, 40,* 3–6.

[52] Munson & Conway (2001), p. 82.

[53] Munson & Conway (2001), p. 83.

CHAPTER 16

[1] Støre, J. G. (2006, February 24). Luncheon in the Honour of Dr. ElBaradei, New York, 31 October 2005. Retrieved December 9, 2007, from norway-geneva.org.

[2] Schlau, J. (2006). Introduction of keynote speaker Dr. Sanjay Gulati. Retrieved December 9, 2007, from hearinglossweb.com.

[3] Aylor, J. H. (2007). Robert A. Bland Award, 2007, Presentation speech. Retrieved December 10, 2007, from seas.virginia.edu/awards.

[4] Powderburn (2007). Powderburn acceptance speech. Retrieved December 9, 2007, from youtube.com.

[5] Turner, P. S. (2006). Acceptance speech for the 2005 Flora Stieglitz Straus Award. Retrieved December 9, 2007, from bankstreet.edu.

[6] Webby Awards (2006). Archived winner speeches. Retrieved December 9, 2007, from webbyawards .com/press/archived-speeches.php.

[7] Guggenheim, D., & Gore, A. (2007, February 25). Acceptance speech. Retrieved December 7, 2007, from oscar.com.

[8] Sasakawa, Y. (2007). International Gandhi Award 2007 acceptance speech. Retrieved December 9, 2007, from nippon-foundation.or.jp/eng/.

[9] Rogers, C. T. (2007, May 1). *Chief Justice Rogers Law Day Ceremony Honoring Law Librarians.* Retrieved March 6, 2008, from jud.ct.gov/external/news/Speech/ rogers_050107.html

[10] Irwin, B. (2006, September 19). Eulogy for Steve Irwin. Retrieved December 13, 2007, from youtube.com.

[11] LaFasto, F., & Larson, C. E. (2001). *When teams work best: 6,000 team members and leaders tell what it takes to succeed.* Thousand Oaks, CA: Sage; Pettigrew, A. M., & Fenton, E. M. (2000). *The innovating organization.* London: Sage.

[12] Chen, G., Donahue, L. M., & Klimoski, R. J. (2004). Training undergraduates to work in organizational teams. *Academy of Management Learning & Education, 3*(1), 27–40; Greenberg, L. W. (1994). The group case presentation: Learning communication and writing skills in a collaborative effort. *Medical Teacher, 16,* 363–367.

[13] Business roundtable discussion transcript (2006, February 5). *Akron Beacon Journal.* Retrieved February 21, 2006, from www.ohio.com/mld/ohio/business/ 13729361.htm.

[14] "Videoconferencing sees record growth" (2007). *Business Communications Review, 37*(8), 6.

[15] Anderson, A. H. (2006). Achieving understanding in face-to-face and video-mediated multiparty interactions. *Discourse Processes, 41,* 251–287.

[16] Adams, T., & Scollard, S. (2006). *Internet effectively: A beginner's guide to the World Wide Web.* Boston: Pearson.

[17] Light, W. H. (2007). Reframing presentation skills development for knowledge teams. *Organization Development Journal, 25,* 99–110.

[18] Hanke, J. (1998). Presenting as a team. *Presentations, 12*(1), 74–78.

[19] Bayless, M. L. (2004). Change the placement, the pace, and the preparation for the oral presentation. *Business Communication Quarterly, 67,* 222–225.

INDEX

ABOUT THE AUTHORS

Stephanie J. Coopman is Professor and Acting Chair of Communication Studies at San José State University, where she regularly teaches public speaking as well as courses in ethics, persuasion, critical thinking, internet communication, organizational communication, and quantitative methods. She has conducted numerous workshops on teaching public speaking and communication pedagogy. Professor Coopman has published her research in a variety of scholarly outlets, including *Communication Education, Western Journal of Communication, Communication Yearbook, American Communication Journal, Journal of Business Communication,* and *Management Communication Quarterly*.

James Lull is Professor Emeritus of Communication Studies at San José State University. Winner of the National Communication Association's Golden Anniversary Monograph Award, he has taught public speaking for more than twenty-five years. An internationally recognized leader in media studies and cultural analysis, Professor Lull is author or editor of twelve books with translations into many languages. Dr. Lull holds an Honorary Doctorate from the University of Helsinki, Finland, and an Honorary Professorship at Aarhus University, Denmark. He regularly gives plenary addresses and seminars at universities in Europe and Latin America.